Paideia: the Ideals of Greek Culture

By WERNER JAEGER

Translated from the German Manuscript
By GILBERT HIGHET

VOLUME III

THE CONFLICT OF CULTURAL IDEALS
IN THE AGE OF PLATO

OXFORD UNIVERSITY PRESS
New York   Oxford

Oxford University Press
Oxford   New York   Toronto
Delhi   Bombay   Calcutta   Madras   Karachi
Petaling Jaya   Singapore   Hong Kong   Tokyo
Nairobi   Dar es Salaam   Cape Town
Melbourne   Auckland

and associated companies in
Beirut   Berlin   Ibadan   Nicosia

Printing (last digit): 9 8
Printed in the United States of America

CONTENTS

PREFACE

THIS, the third volume of *Paideia,* immediately follows Volume II, 'The Search for the Divine Centre'. Readers who wish to learn more about the plan of the entire work and the place of the two new volumes in it are referred to the Preface to the second volume.

Volume II described the birth of 'philosophy' out of the problem of paideia. It traced the growth of this great new power in human life through the classical stage of its early unfolding, from Socrates' stirring question 'Is education (in more than a technical sense) really possible?' up to its natural climax in Plato's *Republic.* The magnificent struggle of philosophy to establish the existence of supreme values which should form the ideal aim of human life and education was described in that volume as the search for 'the divine centre', and was contrasted with the centrifugal tendencies of the sophistic era, which had declared that man was the measure of all things.

The third volume now takes up the general trend of the great reconstructive effort of the Greek spirit which reached its highest momentum after the fall of the Periclean empire, at the end of the Peloponnesian war. This book sets out from the same point as its predecessor, but it pursues a different line of intellectual development. It treats of the logical antithesis to the philosophical forces of the age—namely, those cultural forces which depend upon practical experience and common sense rather than upon first principles. It is this conflict of cultural ideals to which the title refers. In the second part, the book returns to Plato, and discusses the later stage of his career as a philosopher. His prophetic last work, *The Laws,* is a prelude to the tragic finale: the decline and fall of the free city-state, which marks the close of the classical period of Greek culture.

I want to acknowledge on this occasion my deep appreciation of the important part which my wife has taken in preparing my book for publication. With untiring patience and perseverance she has taken upon herself the endless trouble of deciphering the original manuscript of the three volumes and putting it into typewritten form, not to speak of our frequent discussions on its contents. It is a pleasure to me to express my special thankfulness to my friend and colleague, Dr. Herbert Bloch, for his expert help in selecting the decorations on the jackets of the second and third volumes.

WERNER JAEGER

Harvard University
Cambridge, Massachusetts
October 1943

BOOK FOUR

THE CONFLICT OF CULTURAL IDEALS
IN THE AGE OF PLATO

GREEK MEDICINE AS PAIDEIA

PLATO speaks of doctors and medicine in such high terms that, even if the early medical literature of Greece were entirely lost, we should need no further evidence to infer that, during the late fifth and the fourth centuries before Christ, the social and intellectual prestige of the Greek medical profession was very high indeed. Plato thinks of the doctor as the representative of a highly specialized and refined department of knowledge; and also as the embodiment of a professional code which is rigorous enough to be a perfect model of the proper relation between knowledge and its purpose in practical conduct, and which he constantly cites, to make his readers understand how theoretic knowledge can help to transform the structure of human life. It is no exaggeration to say that Socrates' doctrine of ethical knowledge, on which so many of the arguments in Plato's dialogues turn, would be unthinkable without that model, medical science, to which he so often refers. Of all the branches of human knowledge then existing (including mathematics and natural science) medicine is the most closely akin to the ethical science of Socrates.[1] However, we must examine Greek medicine not simply as a preliminary stage in the intellectual development which led to the philosophy of Socrates, Plato, and Aristotle, but also because it was in the form which it then possessed that it grew into something more than a mere craft, into a leading cultural force in the life of the Greek people. From that time, despite some opposition, medicine became more and more a regular part of general culture (ἐγκύκλιος παιδεία). It has not regained that prestige in the culture of our time. The highly developed medical science of to-day, which grew out of the rediscovery of Greco-Roman medical literature during the humanistic era, is too severely specialized[2] to hold the same place as its ancestor.

The complete incorporation of medical science in later Greco-Roman culture can best be seen from the Greek point of view in Galen, and from the Roman, in the 'encyclopaedias' of Cato, Varro, and Celsus, none of whom was a doctor.[3] But that was merely the acknowledgement of the great influence and prestige which it had won in and after the second half of the fifth century. There were several reasons for its holding that position. The first was that, during that period, it had been for the first time represented by men of such broadly universal views as to raise it to a high intellectual level which it maintained for centuries. The second was that by coming into conflict with philosophy, it was fertilized: it reached a clear understanding of its own purpose and methods, and worked out the classical expression of its own particular conception of knowledge. No less important was the final fact that Greek culture had always been the culture of the body as well as of the soul. That truth was embodied in the dual system which made up early Greek education—gymnastics and 'music'. One sign of the new era is that in any description of physical training the doctor is always mentioned along with the trainer [4]—just as in the intellectual sphere the philosopher appears beside the musician and the poet. The unique position of the doctor in classical Greece is mainly due to his relation to paideia. We have been tracing gymnastic education throughout its development from Homer, through the poetry in which its ideals are given form and colour, to Plato, where they are to win their place in the scheme of human life. Unlike gymnastics, medicine very early produced a literature of its own, which reveals its true nature to us, and which is the real reason for its world-wide influence. From it we learn that—although Homer [5] praises the doctor's skill as 'equalling the worth of many other men'—medical science as such was really created by the age of reason.

When it first appears in the history of Greek civilization, it takes more than it gives. The clearest evidence for its dependent position is this: all the medical literature of the fifth and fourth centuries which exists in complete form is in Ionic prose. Some of it was probably written in Ionia; but that does not by any means explain the whole situation. Hippocrates himself lived and taught on the island of Cos, whose inhabitants spoke Doric. The fact that he and his school wrote Ionic, and probably even spoke it in scientific discussions, can be explained only by the influence of the superior Ionic civilization and science. There had always been doctors; but the craft of healing in Greece had not developed into a methodical science sure of its aim until it felt the influence of Ionian natural philosophy. It is essential not to let this fact be obscured by the downright anti-philosophical attitude of the Hippocratic school, in whose works we first meet Greek medicine.[6] Had it not been for the earliest Ionian natural philosophers with their quest after a 'natural' explanation of all events, with their efforts to trace every effect back to its cause and to show how all the chain of causes and effects made up a necessary universal order, and with their firm belief that all the secrets of the world could be penetrated by the unprejudiced observation of things and the power of reason, medicine would never have become a science. We can read the notes made by the doctors of the Pharaohs more than two thousand years before Christ, and admire the astonishing accuracy and subtlety of their observations. They had already gone far on the road towards working out causal conceptions and universally applicable theories.[7] It is impossible not to ask why, after reaching such a high stage of development, Egyptian medicine did not become a science in our sense of the word. Their doctors had little to learn about specialization and empirical observation. But the answer is simple. The Egyptians could not conceive of nature as a universal whole, as the Ionians could and did. They were (as we now know) wise enough, and realistic enough, to conquer the forces of magic and spells which still passed for medicine in the old-fashioned Greek world of Pindar. But it was only Greek medicine, which had learnt from its philosophical predecessors how to look for universal laws, that could create a theoretical system capable of upholding a real scientific movement.

As early as Solon (who was profoundly influenced by Ionia) we find an entirely objective insight into the laws which govern illness, and the unbreakable connexion of part and whole, cause and effect. Such clear and penetrating vision was impossible anywhere but in Ionia at that time. Solon assumes the existence of such universal laws, and on that assumption bases his 'organic' doctrine that political crises are dislocations of the health of the social organism.[8] In another poem, he divides man's life into seven-year periods, which succeed one another in a rhythmical pattern. Although it was written in the sixth century, it has a close kinship to the treatise *On hebdomads* and other 'Hippocratic' works, all much later in date; for, like it, they all tend to trace the laws governing phenomena back to similarities in numerical relationships—as was done by Solon's contemporary Anaximander of Miletus in his cosmology, and later by the Ionian Pythagoras and his school.[9] The idea that every age has something 'suitable' to its powers appears in Solon too, and reappears later as the basis of the medical theory of diet.[10] There was another doctrine coined by natural philosophy: that all natural phenomena were a sort of legal compensation paid by things to one another. This often appears in medical writers, who explain physiological and pathological events as compensations or retributions.[11] Closely allied to this is the idea that the normal healthy state of the organism or of all nature is *isomoiria*—equivalence of all its basic elements. This appears, for example, in the treatise *On airs, waters, and places,* written by a medical scientist, and in various other relevant contexts.[11a] It is doubtful whether other fundamental ideas in Greek medicine—for instance that of mixture (κρᾶσις) and that of harmony—were derived from natural philosophy, or were borrowed by natural philosophy from medical thought.

But there is no doubt about the origin of the dominating conception, Nature (φύσις). In discussing the sophists and their educational theory, we referred to the epochal importance of the idea that human *physis* should be the basis of the whole educational process.[12] We found the same idea given historical application in Thucydides; we saw how his historical thinking is founded on the assumption that there is such a thing as 'human nature', always and everywhere the same.[13] In this, as in much else, both the sophists and Thucydides were influenced by contemporary medicine, which had discovered the idea of human nature (φύσις τοῦ ἀνθρώπου) and based all its work upon it. But in that point medicine itself depended on the concept of the great physis, the Nature of the universe (φύσις τοῦ παντός), which was an idea developed by Ionian philosophy. The introduction to the treatise *On airs, waters, and places* is a splendid expression of the way in which Hippocratean medical thought depends on the philosophical view of nature as a whole. 'Anyone who wishes to study medicine correctly must do as follows. First, he must study the effects of each season of the year—for the seasons are not at all similar, but are very different from one another, both in themselves and in their changes. Then he must study warm and cold winds, chiefly those which affect all mankind, and then those which are particular to any one region. He must also study the effects of different waters; for, just as they differ in taste and weight, so their effects differ widely. Whenever the doctor arrives at a city unknown to him' (here, as usual at that time, he is thought of as a travelling physician) 'he must first examine its position, to see how it lies in relation to the various winds and the sunrise . . . and what kind of water it has . . . and the nature of its soil . . . If he knows how its climate changes with the seasons, and when the stars rise and set . . . he will be able to tell what the year is going to be like . . . If anyone thinks that this is too like natural science, he should understand, on second thoughts, that astronomy can help medicine very greatly indeed. For human diseases change along with the seasons.' The man who faced the problem of illness in this way obviously had a very superior mind. We can see that principally in his sense of the wholeness of things. He does not isolate a disease and examine it as a special problem in itself. He looks steadily and clearly at the man who has the disease, and sees him in all his natural surroundings with their universal laws and their own special characteristics. The spirit of Milesian natural philosophy finds just as clear a voice in the memorable words of the essay *On the divine disease* (i.e. epilepsy). Its author observes that this disease is no more or less divine than any other, and arises from the same natural causes as others do. In fact, they are all divine, and all human.[13a] The conception of physis, on which so much of pre-Socratic philosophy had been based, was most successfully applied and extended in the medical theory of the physical nature of man—the theory which was to be the pattern for all the later applications of the concept to man's spiritual nature.

During the fifth century, the relation between natural philosophy and medicine began to change. Medical discoveries, particularly in the physiological field, were taken over by philosophers like Anaxagoras and Diogenes of Apollonia; and there also appeared philosophers who were themselves doctors, like Alcmaeon, Empedocles, and Hippon, all of whom belonged to the Western Greek school. At the same time this blending of interests influenced medical scientists in their turn, and they began to take over some of the systems worked out by philosophers, as the basis for their own theories; we have already observed this in some of the Hippocratean treatises. Thus, after the first fertilizing contact between these two very different types of thought, there followed a period of uncertainty during which they invaded each other's territory, and all the boundaries between medicine and philosophy were in danger of breaking down. It is in that period —a critical one for the independent existence of medicine—that the earliest extant Greek medical literature begins.

At this point we must make a brief study of the philological problem which this literature presents. The fact that so much of it was preserved, the stylistic form in which it is written, and the peculiar way in which it has come down to posterity, show that it was produced by the practice and teaching of the famous medical school on the little island of Cos. This school attained its highest influence in the latter half of the fifth century under its famous head, Hippocrates—who is the very embodiment of medicine for Plato in the early fourth century (just as Polyclitus and Phidias embody the plastic arts), and who is cited by Aristotle as the perfect example of a great doctor.[14] Even a hundred years later the school still had a brilliant president—Praxagoras, who worked out the theory of the pulse. All the complete medical treatises which have survived from the fifth and fourth centuries bear the name of Hippocrates, and they have all come down to us *en bloc,* as a corpus with a fixed form. Yet modern scholarship has shown that they cannot all be the work of one author, for separate treatises often contradict and even attack one another. This was known to students of the subject in classical times too: for Hippocrates, like Aristotle, had a spiritual rebirth in the Hellenistic age, when schools of Hippocratic and Aristotelian research grew up, which survived as long as Greek culture—and with it medical science—continued to live. Galen's copious and learned commentaries on the Hippocratic writings, and all the Hippocratic lexica and exegeses which have survived, complete or in fragments, from the later Greco-Roman world, show us something of this branch of scholarship. We cannot but respect its skill and knowledge, although we cannot share its confidence that the real Hippocrates can still be extracted from the mass of Hippocratic treatises. Modern critics also have attempted to set aside a certain number of works from the collection, and to ascribe them to Hippocrates himself; but the number has grown smaller and smaller, and varies according to the particular line of medical thought (among the many represented in the corpus) which each scholar holds to be characteristic of Hippocrates himself. And so, after all that industrious and subtle research, it seems that we must resign ourselves and acknowledge our ignorance of the truth.[15]

On the other hand, there are plenty of these 'Hippocratic' treatises: so that during the search for the true Hippocrates scholars have involuntarily worked out a more detailed picture of medical science in the classical age of Greek thought. Although only its outlines are so far clear, it is an extraordinarily interesting spectacle. It does not simply present one system of doctrine, but shows us the very life of a science, with all its ramifications and conflicts. It has become plain that the corpus as we now have it is not Hippocrates' 'Collected Works' as sold in the bookshops of his day, but a complete collection of the old medical writings found in the archives of the medical school at Cos by Alexandrian scholars of the third century, who had set out to preserve Hippocrates' writings (like those of other classical authors) for posterity. Clearly they had not been revised or purged of heterogeneous matter. Some of them were published as literature, or at least written for publication. Others were copious collections of original notes. Others again were commentaries written, not to be read by the public, but for the information of the author's colleagues. And some of the collection was not written in the Coan school at all—naturally enough, for science would soon have come to a standstill if the scientists had paid no attention to the ideas and discoveries of others. These extraneous works were preserved among the archives of the school, and the master's works were mixed up with his pupils', because the school was an impersonal institution. And, besides, every member of it knew what his colleagues' opinions were. We find the same kind of thing in the collected works of men like Plato and Aristotle who headed great philosophical schools,[16] although to a smaller extent than in the case of Hippocrates.

One of the solemn provisions in the Hippocratic oath, to be

taken by everyone admitted to the school, was that he should keep secret what he learnt. Normally, medical knowledge descended from father to son, as son followed father in the profession. Thus, when a stranger was accepted as a student, he became, as it were, the son of his teacher; and therefore pledged himself to teach his art, without a fee, to his master's children.[17] It was probably quite usual for a pupil (like an apprentice) to inherit his master's practice by marrying his daughter. We are expressly told that Hippocrates' son-in-law Polybus was a doctor. As it happens, he is the only member of the Coan school whom Aristotle quotes by name—citing his detailed description of the venous system, still extant in one of the most famous works in the 'Hippocratic' corpus.[18] That one trait casts a bright light on the whole collection. Although, in Hippocrates' time, the dominance of great individual personalities was beginning to make itself felt in medicine (as it had done at a much earlier stage in poetry and in art, and in philosophy from the very beginning), the corporate solidarity of the medical profession was still so strong that it was rare, in professional practice, for ideas and doctrines to be attributed to their originators. Evidently it was in public lectures that medical researchers first spread their personal views abroad under their own names. Several such lectures still exist in the Hippocratic corpus, but the names of even their authors are lost. Works proceeding from other schools—such as the 'Cnidian doctrines', giving the views held in the older and equally eminent medical institute at Cnidus in Asia Minor—are quoted in a Hippocratic treatise,[19] but until now no scholar has been successful in proving that any extant treatise bears the authentic stamp of any particular school outside Cos. At the end of the fifth century the individual had such wide freedom to express his views that we cannot legitimately use every deviation from Coan theory as evidence for the doctrine of other schools. Still, the research of the past hundred years has proved the existence both of an Asiatic school centring in Cnidus and of a Western Greek school centring in Sicily,[20] although our knowledge of the work done there must remain fragmentary, in default of evidence.

Medical literature was a complete novelty in Greek intellectual history, for this reason: although it was intended to teach, and to teach directly, it was little if at all addressed to the average man, as philosophy and poetry were. Its appearance is the main example of a historical trend which we shall now come to notice more and more—the tendency of life to become increasingly specialized and of knowledge to split up into sectional professions which could be entered by only a few specially trained men with high intellectual and moral qualifications. It is significant that the medical authors often speak of 'laymen' and 'professionals'—a distinction which was to have a long and important history, but meets us here for the first time. Our word 'layman', originating in the mediaeval church, first meant a person not in holy orders, and thence a person not initiated into professional secrets; but the Greek word *idiotés* carries a social and political connotation. It means a man who pays no attention to the state and the community, but simply attends to his private affairs. In contrast with him, the doctor is a *demiourgos,* a 'public worker'—as indeed every artisan was called who made shoes or utensils for the public. Often laymen are distinguished from the doctor, viewed in this light, by being called 'the people' (δημόται). The name *demiourgos* vividly brings together the two sides of the doctor's profession—its social and its technical aspects—while the difficult Ionic word χειρῶναξ (which is used as a synonym for it) signifies only the latter aspect.[21] There is no word to distinguish the Greek doctor with his higher skill from what we should consider as an ordinary artisan; and the same holds for the sculptor and the painter. However, there is something in Greek medicine which resembles our use of the word 'layman', with its implication 'uninitiated'. That is the beautiful close [22] of the Hippocratic Law: 'Secret things are revealed only to initiates. It is forbidden to reveal them to profane persons before they are initiated into the mysteries of knowledge.' Here we have mankind divided, as if by a religious rite, into two classes, one of which is severely debarred from an arcane knowledge. This line of thought raises the doctor's importance above that of a mere artisan, both technically and socially; but, more than that, it is an eloquent testimony to the lofty character of the medical calling and its deep consciousness of its duty—written, if not by Hippocrates himself, then certainly by someone who realized what his profession had gained from its increased knowledge of nature. Certainly it shows that a real difficulty was felt about the position of this new type, the physician, isolated but full of high pretensions, within the framework of society.

But in reality the new science of medicine was not so sharply distinguished from the general intellectual life of Greece. It endeavoured to establish a place for itself there. Although it was founded on a special branch of knowledge which set it apart from the general public, it deliberately tried to impart that knowledge to them and to find ways and means of making them understand it. It created a special type of medical literature addressed to non-medical readers. By good fortune, we still possess some of both types—the treatises written for specialists, and others addressed to the public at large. Most of the works we have belong to the first class and cannot be treated here as fully as they deserve. Our interest is naturally concentrated on the second type, not only because its literary quality is higher, but because it is really a part of what the Greeks called paideia.²³ At the time when medical scientists first brought their problems before the public—both in lectures (ἐπιδείξεις) like those of the sophists, and in 'speeches' written in order to be read (λόγοι)—no one actually knew how far an *idiotés* ought to trouble himself about such matters. When the doctors came forward to rival the travelling sophistic lecturers, they were trying to gain public prestige and authority. Their intellectual eminence was great enough not only to awaken passing interest in their subject, but to create something like a medical public. It was made up of 'medically cultured' men who had a particular, though not a professional, interest in the problems of medicine, and were distinguished from the general mass who had no opinion on the subject, by being competent to pass judgment upon such problems. Of course the best opportunity for the doctor to introduce medical ideas to the lay public was when he was actually treating his patients. In *The Laws* Plato gives an amusing description of the difference between the slave-doctor and the scientifically trained physician who treats free men. He says it consists in their attitude to their patients. The slave-doctor hurries from bed to bed, giving out prescriptions and orders without discussion (ἄνευ λόγου)—i.e. without explaining his treatment, simply working on routine and previous experience. He is an absolute tyrant. If he heard a free doctor talking to free patients in a manner very like scientific instruction (τοῦ φιλοσοφεῖν ἐγγύς), and defining the origins of the disease by going back to the nature of all bodies, he would laugh heartily and say what most so-called doctors retort in such cases: 'You fool, you are not *curing* your patient; you are *educating* him, as if you wanted not to make him healthy, but to make him into a doctor.' [23a] But Plato believes that that same medical method which depends on a fundamental education of the patient is the ideal of scientific healing. He takes over that view from contemporary medical science. In the Hippocratic corpus we find several discussions of the best way to acquaint laymen with the physician's problems. 'It is particularly necessary in talking about this art to speak so that laymen can understand' says the author of *On ancient medicine*. One must begin with the diseases from which people have actually suffered. Being laymen, they cannot understand their diseases, with their causes and treatments, but it is easy to explain all that to them simply by getting everyone to remember his own experiences. The author says it proves a physician's skill if his statements agree with the recollections of the patient.[24]

We need not quote all the passages in which this author discusses how to instruct laymen, or directly addresses them. Not all doctors followed his plan of proceeding inductively and helping the patient by information gathered from his own experience. Others, with a different outlook or in different circumstances, did the exact opposite, and elaborated general theories of the nature of disease before a lay audience (like the author of the treatise *On the nature of man*), or even (like the author of *On the art*) invited the public to judge whether medicine was or was not a real art. In Plato's *Symposium,* the doctor Eryximachus delivers a long and witty lecture to laymen after dinner, about the nature of Eros from the standpoint of medicine and natural philosophy.[25] In cultivated society there was a special interest in such topics, which was increased by their connexion with the fashionable natural philosophy. In young Euthydemus, who later became a passionate adherent of Socrates, Xenophon describes this new kind of medical amateur. His only interests are intellectual: he has already bought a whole library, with books on architecture, geometry, astronomy, and, above all, medicine.[26] It is not hard to understand how a terrible experience like the plague during the Peloponnesian war gave rise to an extensive medical literature, eagerly read by the public. Thucydides was a medical amateur himself, and was led by the number of contradictory hypotheses about the cause of the epidemic to write his famous description of the symptoms of the disease, which deliberately eschews any attempt to suggest its origins.[27] Still, it betrays, even in the details of its terminology, his close study of specialist literature on the subject.

Aristotle begins his book *On the parts of animals* with these words:[28] 'About every science, whether it is noble or mean, there are two attitudes possible. One deserves the name of scientific knowledge, and the other is a sort of culture (παιδεία). For the mark of the cultured man is that he can judge correctly whether another man's explanation is right or wrong. That is in fact what we think the generally cultured man is, and culture is the ability to do that. Only, we think the cultured man is able to judge about practically everything by himself, while the other man can do so for only one special field. For in special fields too there must be a cultured man corresponding to the universal type we have described.' And in his *Politics* he expressly makes the same distinction between the professional student of nature and the cultured man who is interested in it as an amateur—for that is the point he is making. There[29] he mentions three different grades of knowledge: that of the practising physician, that of the man engaged in creative medical research, who communicates his discoveries to the physician, and that of the man who is medically cultured. Here too he remembers to add that there are such amateurs in every special field. What he wants to prove by this example is that not only practical politicians but also men who are politically trained have the right to judge political problems; but his choice of medicine as an example proves that the type was comparatively common in the field of medicine.

This distinction between professional students of a subject and those who are interested in it merely as a part of general culture has appeared before. We saw it in the young Athenian nobles who eagerly attended the sophists' lectures but were far from wishing to become professional sophists themselves.[30] In *Protagoras* Plato showed very wittily how even the most enthusiastic of the sophists' audience kept his mental reservations.[31]

The same applies, in the medical sphere, to Xenophon's Euthydemus, who was a keen reader of medical books but was horrified when Socrates asked him if he wanted to become a doctor.[32] The multiplicity of the interests shown in his heterogeneous library is characteristic of the new 'universal culture'. Xenophon records this conversation with Euthydemus under a special heading—'Socrates' attitude to Paideia'.[33] This shows that, in certain circles, the word *paideia* was coming to have the sense of 'universal culture.' Our task here is not to trace the development of any one special branch of culture, but to describe it in all the wealth of its manifestations. One of the most important of these was medical culture. Aristotle's conception of the man who is cultured in medicine or natural science is less vague than Plato's or Xenophon's. When he says that such a person can pass judgment, he means he has some idea of the right way to attack a problem, although that does not imply that he knows the whole truth about it. Only the scientific student knows that. But the cultured man has the ability to judge, and his flair is often more reliable than even that of the productive scholar in his own field. The appearance of this new type between the pure specialist and the pure layman is a characteristic phenomenon in the history of Greek culture after the age of the sophists. Aristotle simply takes it for granted. We can see it most clearly in early medical literature, which is greatly concerned to make converts. The admission of special sciences into the field of general culture is always limited by firm social standards: no more is allowed than it is proper for a gentleman to know. In Aristotle too we meet the ethical maxim, from which he drew conclusions of vast importance for the development of culture, that excessive specialization (ἀκρίβεια) could not go with liberal culture and true gentlemanliness.[34] See how, even in the age when science was triumphant, the old aristocratic culture still reared its proud head!

The time at which we first meet what Greece called 'the physician's art' in the earliest medical literature was indeed critical enough to arouse wide interest in the kind of public we have described. By reasoning from the regular scientific ideas used by the medical scientists of Hippocrates' era, we have tried to reconstruct the influence which natural philosophy exercised on medicine, and to realize how deeply it thereby transformed the science. It needs a fair amount of historical imagination to do so fully and to measure the vast gulf between it and its primitive predecessors. Still, we must make the effort, if we are not to assume that the existence of a highly developed medical science in the fifth century was a perfectly natural thing needing no explanation. We might well think it was, especially since so many of its ideas are current to-day, while during the last century we have so greatly improved on it in details. The history of Greek medicine, as known to us through its literature, begins with its struggle against the domination of the theories of natural philosophy—a struggle which was only a symptom of the great and inevitable revolution which had then, to all intents and purposes, definitely closed. Thenceforward medicine was founded on knowledge of the laws governing the reaction of the organism to the effects of those forces that underlie both the universal process of nature and the physical life of man, in normal and in abnormal conditions. Once this firm point of departure had been established, it was easy to move away from it in many directions: the Greek mind, with its innate purposefulness, acuteness, and logic, set out to explore every path of knowledge as far as the experience at its disposal would allow. It was entirely natural that, when the great concepts of natural philosophy were taken over into medicine, its cosmological ideas should enter along with them and disturb men's minds.

We have already observed that the later natural philosophers, like Empedocles, broke through the barriers and learned how to adapt medical ideas to their own purposes. This is the same kind of synthesis as Empedocles' combination of empirical natural philosophy and religious prophethood. His successes as a practising doctor must have increased the prestige of his medical teaching. His philosophical theory of the four elements lived on in medical science for centuries in the doctrine of the four basic qualities, hot, cold, dry, and wet. It either coalesced very strangely with the dominant medical theory of the fundamental 'humours' of the body, or else drove out all its rivals and became the sole basis of medical theory. This example is enough to show how philosophical ideas pushed their way into medicine, and how various were its reactions to them: how some scientists accepted them all without question, and immediately began to think in terms of hot, cold, dry, and wet; how others endeavoured to graft this theory of qualities on the already existing theory of humours, so as to reach a compromise between the two; while others again rejected it as useless, or of merely subordinate interest for the physician. It casts a bright light on the intellectual alertness of the profession and its awareness of every new advance in the knowledge of nature. The haste with which the physicians of that time applied insufficiently tested theories to explain medical phenomena was only partially a fault characteristic of the Greek mind. Chiefly, it was due to the inadequacy of their experience. In physiology and pathology, theoretical reasoning was still in its infancy. There is less reason, therefore, to be surprised at its excessive daring or schematization than at the speed and sureness with which the Greek physician, whose first aim was to cure the sick and whose eyes were always bent on that mark, guarded against impractical speculation and kept the way open for real advances in knowledge.

Now, with its return to careful empiricism and detailed observation of the needs of each case, medicine was definitely marked off as an art independent of all natural philosophy (by whose aid it had risen to become a science), and at last became its true self. The unknown author of the treatise *On ancient medicine* makes this assertion with the greatest assurance. At that time, of course, he was not alone in his contention; he was the voice of what we might with justice call a school. The school is the school of Hippocrates, whether Hippocrates himself wrote the treatise or not; and it is therefore correct to call the Coan school the founders of medicine as an independent science. The thesis of this writer is that medicine has no need for a new 'hypothesis', since it has long been a real and genuine art. Therefore he refuses to support the doctors who believe that it is essential to a real techné to have one single principle and to refer all separate phenomena to it, as philosophers do in their theories.[35] That belief, he holds, will not free physicians from unscientific indecision in fixing the causes of disease (as people think it will); and still less will it ensure that every patient gets the right treatment. It simply means abandoning the sure foothold of experience on which the art of healing has hitherto stood, in favour of an uncertain theory. That may be the only possible way in the dark realms of the unknown, through which philosophy gropes and stumbles; but in order to enter it, the physician must throw away all that medical experience has gained during its slow, laborious, and sure advance from its primitive beginnings centuries before. He brings that development startlingly home to his readers by starting from the old-fashioned idea that the doctor is the man who tells us what to eat and drink. It was only step by step that, through long experience, men learned to eat foods different from those of animals, and to make distinctions between the various kinds of food. But the doctor's prescription of certain definite foods for the invalid is a higher stage again: for a healthy man's food would be just as dangerous for a sick man as an animal's food for a healthy man.[36]

It was that step forward which allowed medicine to develop into a true techné, for no one would use that word for a skill which everyone understood, like cooking. Yet the principle of nourishment is the same for a sound man and a sick: each must have what is *suitable*.[37] However, suitability does not mean simply that heavy foods are to be distinguished from light foods; it implies also that quantities must be fixed, and they are different for every different constitution. The sick man can be hurt by eating too little, just as he can be hurt by eating too much. The real doctor is recognized by his power to estimate what is appropriate for each individual case.[38] He is the man who has the sure judgment to pick the right quantity for everyone. There is no standard of weight or measure by which one could fix quantities on a general basis. That must be done wholly by feeling (αἴσθησις), which is the only thing that can compensate for the lack of such a rational standard.[39] That is where practising physicians make most of their mistakes, and he who makes only a small one now and then is indeed a master of his calling. Most doctors are like bad pilots. As long as the weather is all right their inexpertness is not noticeable, but in a bad storm everyone sees that they are useless.

The author of the book is against all generalizations. He contests the assertion made by some 'physicians and sophists' that no one can understand medicine without knowing what man is, how he originated, and what stuff he is made on. In theory, these thinkers were perfectly right, of course, and if everyone had been content with this kind of empiricism, modern medical chemistry could never have been discovered. But in view of the primitive knowledge of elements which was all that was available at that time, his scepticism was justified in practice. 'Their theory runs into philosophy, as in the case of Empedocles and others who have written about Nature.' In saying this, he is not attacking Empedocles himself (as his words have usually been taken to mean), but defining *philosophy* (which had not yet acquired the connotations we give it [40]) by adding 'as in the case of Empedocles and such people'. He meets the efforts of his opponents to raise medicine to the supposedly higher rank of natural philosophy with the proud remark: [41] 'I believe that there is no other way of getting exact knowledge of nature than through medicine.' Strange as the words sound to our ears, they were apt and just in his time. Investigators of nature had not yet learnt the duty of exactness. The one science of nature which learned it before all the others was medicine, because in medicine success depends entirely on accurate observation of details, and failure means the life of a human being. Not what man is in himself, but 'what he is in relation to what he eats and drinks and how he lives and how all that affects him'—*that* our author considers to be the central problem.[42] He warns the doctor not to believe he has done enough to solve it by saying, 'Cheese is heavy, for it upsets you if you eat too much.' He wants to know *how* it upsets you, and why, and which part of the human body cannot bear cheese. Anyhow, cheese has different effects on different people, and there are different reasons for the heaviness of heavy food. So it is foolish to talk generally about 'human nature' in medicine.

The seven books called *Epidemiai, Visits,* give the right background for this deliberately reserved empirical attitude, typical as it is of the new trend in medicine. They are mostly composed of case-records from what seems to have been a long practice, centring on the islands and mainland of northern Greece.[43] Separate cases are often distinguished by the name of the patient and his town. In this work we can see directly how the experience of individual practitioners grew into the mighty structure of medical science to which the whole Hippocratic corpus bears witness. The style of these 'memoranda' (ὑπομνήματα) is the best illustration of the rule on which these doctors worked, and which we meet again in Aristotle—that experience grows out of sense-perception aided by memory.

Clearly *Visits* is the work of more than one observer. It is an embodiment of the great sentence with which the Hippocratic *Aphorisms* opens [44]: 'Life is short, the art is long, opportunity fleeting, experiment dangerous, and judgment difficult.' But the true student never stops at details, although he is unwilling to lose sight of them. Truth can never be dissolved into the infinite variety of individual cases; or, if it could, it would have no real meaning for us. That is how medical thinkers of that age arrived at the conception of types (εἴδη) of human nature, of bodily structure, of dispositions, illnesses, and so forth.[45] *Eidos* means, to begin with, 'form'; and then the visible 'signs' differentiating the form of one group of individuals from another group; but it is at once extended to any distinguishable features common to any multiplicity of related phenomena, and (especially in the plural) takes the meaning of 'type' or 'kind'. That kind of generalization is accepted even by the author of *On ancient medicine*.[46] What he rejects is assertions in the manner of the pre-Socratics, such as 'Heat is the principle of nature, and the cause of all health and sickness'. According to him, there are in man salt, bitter, sweet, acid, sour, bland, and innumerable other qualities, each with a different effect, which when mixed, do not appear separately and are not injurious; [47] but as soon as one of these gets separated from the others it is injurious. This is the old doctrine of Alcmaeon of Croton—that the domination (μουναρχίη) of one force in the organism causes its sickness, and the equality (ἰσονομίη) of forces causes its health.[48] But the author of *On ancient medicine* disregards both the doctrine of the four dominant qualities and the famous theory of the four Humours (blood, phlegm, yellow bile, and black bile) which was later, especially after Galen, held to be the basis of Hippocratic medicine.[49] In that he is the direct opposite of the schematizing dogmatist who wrote *On the nature of man,* and who was once held to be Hippocrates himself.

Though the author of *On ancient medicine* is violently opposed to philosophy *as it was then conceived,* though he sometimes strikes a sharp blow at short-sighted empiricists too, and seems to be deliberately trying to give offence, still it is impossible not to be amazed at the great number of new avenues of

philosophical exploration which he opens up. It is difficult to resist the impression that he himself knows that, though he has
no fancy to be called 'sophist'. It is true that modern philologists who study the history of medicine usually follow him in
thinking of a philosophical doctor as the opposite of an empirical scientist like this particular author: a man whose head is full
of big cosmological theories and whose tongue is heavy with
great noble words borrowed from the works of the pre-Socratic
natural philosophers—something like the author of the four
books *On diet,* who sounds now like Heraclitus and now like
Anaxagoras or Empedocles. But it was not because a few physicians found and adopted ready-made theories of nature that
medicine opened up new realms of philosophical thought, but
because its ablest students, on a truly original, a Columbus-like
voyage, set out to discover what 'nature' was—starting from
one realm in it which no other before them had explored so
intimately, so sympathetically, or with such full understanding
of its special laws.

We have already shown that Plato, with his sure instinct, had
from the very beginning been in close touch with medicine. But
we may here explain the connexion in a little more detail: for
there is no better illustration of the new methods and conceptions of medicine than its influence on the philosophy of Plato
and Aristotle. Another excellent reason for studying it here is
that it brings up what is really the central problem of paideia.
It was not an accident that, when Plato was establishing his
science of ethics and politics, he modelled it neither on the
mathematical type of knowledge, nor on speculative natural
philosophy, but (as he says in *Gorgias* and many other works)
on medical science. In *Gorgias* he explains what he holds to be
the essence of a true techné by pointing to medicine, and he
takes its distinguishing characteristics from that example.[50] A
techné is that knowledge of the nature of an object, which aims
at benefiting man, and which is therefore incomplete as knowledge until it is put into practice. According to Plato, the doctor
is the man who recognizes the sickness because of his knowledge
of its opposite, health, and can therefore find ways and means
to bring that which is sick back to its normal condition. That
is his model for the philosopher, who is to do the same for the

soul of man and its health. This comparison between Plato's science, the 'healing of the soul', and the science of the doctor explains and brings to life two features which they have in common. Both kinds of knowledge base their judgments on the objective knowledge of nature herself—the doctor works on his insight into the nature of the body, the philosopher on his understanding of the nature of the psyché. But each explores his special realm of nature not merely by treating it as a series of facts, but by expecting to find in the natural structure of either the body or the soul that guiding principle which prescribes the conduct both of the philosopher and teacher and of the doctor. Health, the doctor calls the norm of physical existence; and it is as health that Plato's ethical and political teaching is to penetrate the soul of man.

In *Gorgias,* Plato's interest in medicine is chiefly directed to discussing the form and essence of a true techné. But what he says of it in another important passage, in *Phaedrus,* is more concerned with the physician's method than with the nature of the art. Here he maintains that medicine should be the model for true rhetoric [51]—meaning (as in *Gorgias*) his own art of political philosophy, which is to lead men to what is best for themselves. But what does he think is the essential point about the method of medicine? I believe that his readers have often been led astray by his earlier remark, made half in fun, that Pericles was such a powerful orator and spiritual leader because he had learnt bombast (ἀδολεσχία) about Nature from the philosopher Anaxagoras. Now, the dialogue goes on to assert, it is impossible to apprehend the soul 'apart from the nature of the whole', and this assertion is illustrated by the example of Hippocrates, who applies the same principle to knowledge of the body. Therefore, scholars have usually concluded that Plato was using Hippocrates as a type-name for physicians with some knowledge of natural philosophy, like the philosophaster attacked by the author of the treatise *On ancient medicine.* But the accurate description of Hippocrates' method which follows really leads to an entirely different conclusion; and Plato's remarks here too are meant simply and solely to furnish a model for rhetoric and its art of treating souls. Hippocrates teaches (says Socrates in the dialogue) that we should first of all ask whether the object about which we wish to acquire genuine skill has a single or complex (πολυειδές) nature. If it is simple, we should then inquire what power it has to affect or be affected by something else; while if it has many forms (εἴδη) we should count them, and study each of them in the same way, by inquiring how it affects or is affected by other things.

This description of the Hippocratic method does not apply to the kind of doctor who begins to treat a cold by defining the universe and its fundamental causes. It is much more like the genuine observer's procedure that is employed all through the best works in the Hippocratic corpus. It is not the 'philosophical physician' attacked in the essay *On ancient medicine* for talking in broad generalizations about the nature of man, that corresponds to Plato's description of Hippocrates, so much as the 'empirical' author of that essay himself, who maintains, against the philosophical point of view, that the natures of men are different in kind, and that the effects of cheese on their stomachs must therefore be just as different. It would be hasty to conclude that the essay was therefore written by Hippocrates himself: Plato's description suits the authors of *On diet in acute illness* and *Visits* quite as well. Scholars have tried again and again to use Plato's description of the Hippocratic method as a touchstone to separate the true works of Hippocrates from the rest of the corpus. But they have failed—not only because they misinterpreted the passage in Plato, but also because of the breadth and vagueness of his description, which uses the name of Hippocrates to exemplify an attitude that was widely prevalent in scientific medicine in the late fifth and the fourth centuries. Possibly it was Hippocrates who originated the method. But it seems that among the medical works which have survived there are a number by other doctors who learnt it from him. The only thing we can be sure of is that the spacious generalizations about natural philosophy characteristic of the author of the work *On the nature of man* (to whom Galen applied Plato's words), or the attitude attacked in the treatise *On ancient medicine* are pretty much the opposite of what Plato describes as the method of Hippocrates—careful analysis of nature (διελέσθαι τὴν φύσιν), enumeration of its types (ἀριθμήσασθαι τὰ εἴδη), and definition of the appropriate treatment for each (προσαρμόττειν ἕκαστον ἑκάστῳ).

It does not need much knowledge of Plato's dialogues to see

that the procedure which he here describes as peculiar to medicine is actually the procedure which he used himself, especially
in his later works. It is really astonishing to read the medical
texts and discover how much they prefigure the method of
'Socrates' as described by Plato. We have already seen how,
under the compulsion of facts, the empirical physicians began
to take individual cases of the same character, which they had
defined by long study, and 'look on them together' (to use
Plato's phrase) as types or forms (εἴδη). When the medical
authors are speaking of a number of these types, they call them
εἴδη; but when they want simply to bring out the unity underlying a complexity of phenomena, they use the concept of 'one
Idea', 'one Form'—i.e. one aspect or appearance (μία ἰδέα).
Study of the expressions *eidos* and *idea* and of the way in which
Plato uses them (without reference to the medical literature)
has led to the same result.[52] These concepts, first used by doctors
in studying the body and its functions, were transferred by Plato
to the particular subject he was investigating—the realm of
ethics—and from there to his entire ontology. Before him, medical science had recognized that the manifold nature and diversity
of diseases (πολυτροπίη, πολυσχιδίη) was a great problem, and had
endeavoured to establish the exact number of types of each
disease [53]—just as Plato does in his dialectical analysis, which
he also calls division and breaking down of general concepts into
their types.[53a]

In comparing medical science to philosophy, Plato is thinking
principally of its normative character. Therefore he mentions
the pilot as another example of the same kind of knowledge,
and Aristotle followed him in doing so. But they both borrowed
the comparison of doctor and pilot from the essay *On ancient
medicine,* where it was first used in this connexion.[53b] But while
Plato is concerned mainly with the fact that pilot and doctor
both learn to recognize the standard of action, Aristotle uses
the suggestive comparison to prove another point. One of the
great problems discussed in his *Ethics* is how to apply a standard, which is universal, to the life of an individual and to separate cases, which at first sight seem to be incapable of being
settled by general rules. The question is particularly important
in the field of education. There Aristotle makes a fundamental

distinction between the education of the individual and the education of the community, and supports it by the example of medicine.[53c] But he also uses medicine to show how the individual man can find the right standard for his own conduct: for medicine shows that correct moral conduct, like healthy physical diet, consists in preserving the mean between excess and deficiency. We can understand this expression better if we recollect that, according to Aristotle, morality is concerned with the regulation of our instincts—desire and aversion. Plato, before him, had used the medical concepts of filling and emptying in discussing the theory of lust, and had concluded that lust was one of the spheres in which there could be 'a More or a Less' needing regulation.[53d] Aristotle says that the standard is the mean—not, however, a rigidly fixed mathematical point between the extremes, not the absolute middle of the scale, but the right mean for the individual concerned. Hence, ethical conduct consists in 'aiming' at the mean between excess and deficiency which is right for us.[53e] In this connexion every word used by Aristotle—*excess, deficiency, the mean* and *the right proportion, aiming,* and *perception* (αἴσθησις)—as well as his denial that an absolute rule exists and his assertion that a standard appropriate to the nature of the individual must be found: all this is borrowed directly from medicine, and his discussion of the matter is actually modelled on the treatise *On ancient medicine*.[54]

We should be convicting ourselves of ignorance of the Greek way of thinking if we tried to qualify that dependence for the sake of guaranteeing to Aristotle what we might make the modern error of calling 'originality'. Such originality is a false criterion and only makes its users misjudge the facts. Plato and Aristotle gain higher authority for their teaching by supporting it on the results gained in a parallel field of thought. In the structure of Greek life every part supports and is supported by the others: stone upholds stone. It is important to realize that this principle in the development of Greek thought, which we have already seen at work in every earlier stage of its growth, is now confirmed in such a decisive point as the central Platonic and Aristotelian doctrine of human areté. And it is not simply a matter of analogy, as it might seem at first glance. The medical doctrine of the correct treatment for the body is, so to speak, raised to a higher power when it is embodied in the Socratic doctrine of the correct care and treatment of the soul. Plato's and Aristotle's concept of the areté of man contains the aretai of the body as well as those of the soul.[55] Thus, medicine is wholly assimilated into Plato's philosophical anthropology, his science of Man. From this point of view an entirely new light is cast on the question how far the special science of medicine belongs to the history of paideia. Medical science does more than give the intelligent public some inkling of medical problems and medical thought. Through its concentration on one realm of human life, that of the body, it makes discoveries of the most vital importance to philosophy in its task of working out a new picture of human nature, and thereby it assists in moulding the individual more closely to the ideal of humanity.

For our purposes it is not necessary to examine the whole of Greek medical thought with the same degree of precision and detail. A great deal of it is concerned simply with the minutiae of medical research and practice, which have no immediate connexion with our subject. But there is one more contribution made by fifth-century and fourth-century medicine to the great spiritual process of forming the Greek ideal—something which has only recently been recognized as important by modern medical science and developed as it deserves to be. This is the doctrine of the preservation of health, and it was the genuinely creative contribution made by Hippocratic medicine to educational science. We can understand it only against the broad background of the concept of universal Nature, which emerges from the medical writings of that period. We have already pointed out that Greek medical thought was dominated by the idea of Nature. But what was its concrete meaning? How did the Hippocratic researcher interpret the power of physis? So far, no one has undertaken to make a systematic study of the idea of Nature in early Greek medical literature, although it would cast much light on the whole intellectual history of that era, as well as on later periods. Throughout it all the true doctor is presented as the man who never thinks of the part without thinking of the whole, who always sees it as it affects and is affected by everything else. We may recall here Plato's description of Hippocrates in *Phaedrus*.[56] What he had in mind was what we call the organic view of nature. He wanted, by the example of medical method, to show that in every subject it is necessary to grasp the function of the part within the whole and thereby to define the appropriate treatment for the part. It is notable that medicine provides the illustration for this method of approaching a problem. In *Phaedo* [57] Plato blames the early natural philosophers for their failure to consider the element of immanent purpose in the universe—a point which is closely connected with the organic view of nature. So what he looked for without success in natural philosophy he found in medical science.

Of course, nineteenth-century science and medicine did not see Greek medicine in this light. Their prejudiced views helped, in turn, to create the assumptions used by more recent students of the history of medicine in dealing with the Greeks. [58] No doubt they knew that the teleological approach to natural phenomena was essential in the work of later Greek doctors, Galen above all. But there, one glance was enough to show them that the evil influence of philosophy had distorted medical thought. And they held Hippocrates to be Galen's antithesis, the perfect empiric—which amounted to saying that he could not possibly have held any teleological theories. He was thought to be one of the chief ancient representatives of the doctrine of purely mechanical causation in nature. [58a] And yet we cannot help suspecting all this to be false when we think of the concept of proportion. As we saw, it dominates the treatise *On ancient medicine,* and it had a profound influence on the practice of Greek doctors in general. At the same time it shows us the correct sense in which to speak of teleology in this connexion. The doctor's duty is to restore the secret proportion when it is disturbed by disease. In health, nature herself produces that proportion, [59] or else she herself *is* the right proportion. Closely connected with the conception of proportion and symmetry is that of mixture, which really means a sort of equal balance between the various forces ruling the organism. [60] Nature strives to attain that intelligible standard (for that is how we must describe it); and from that point of view it is easy to understand how Plato can call strength, health, and beauty the 'virtues' (ἀρεταί) of the body and speak of them as parallel to the ethical virtues of the soul. What he means by areté is that symmetry of parts or forces in which, according to medical ideas, normal health consists. [61] We need not be surprised, therefore, at finding the word areté in

early medical works.[62] It was not first introduced by Plato's influence. That way of looking at nature is typical of ancient Greek
medicine as a whole: the purposefulness underlying her rule
comes out especially clearly in sickness. The doctor does not
treat a sick man by interfering with nature. Symptoms of illness
—particularly fever—are actually the beginning of the process
by which the normal state is restored. That process is initiated
by the body itself, and all that the doctor need do is to watch
for the point where he can step in to help the natural urge to
self-healing. Then nature will help herself.[63] This is the principal
axiom in Hippocrates' doctrine of sickness; at the same time it
is the most precise statement of its teleological basis.

Two generations later, Aristotle defined the relation of art to
nature by saying that art imitated nature, and was invented
to compensate its defects.[64] This view assumes that nature has an
all-pervading purpose, and it sees in nature art's prototype. But
during the age of the sophists some physicians had proved that
the human organism was ruled by purpose, by making compari-
sons and signalizing resemblances between the several parts of
the body and technical tools and inventions. There is a good
example of this kind of teleology in Diogenes of Apollonia.
This man was at once a natural philosopher and a doctor, and
has therefore been thought to be the originator of the theory.[65]
Certainly it started in medical circles. In the Hippocratic corpus
we find it in the essay *On the heart*.[66] The first book of the
treatise *On diet* contains a different, more mystical type of
teleology, according to which all arts are imitations of man's
nature and are to be understood by arcane analogies with it—
and the author adds a number of far-fetched examples as
proof.[67] This has nothing in common with either Aristotle or
Diogenes, but at least it shows how widespread the idea was in
contemporary medical thought, and how many shapes it took.
'The physician's art is to abolish what gives pain and to make
people healthy by taking away the cause of their sufferings.
Nature can do that unaided. If one is in pain from sitting down,
one should stand up; if one is pained by moving about, one
should rest: this, and many other elements of the doctor's art,
already exist in nature.' [68] These are the author's personal speculations. But the Hippocratic school also holds that the physician's duty is merely to serve and supplement nature. Thus, in

Visits, we read: 'The patient's nature is the doctor that cures his illness.' [68a] That means that the individual physis is an entity which works with a purpose in view; but in the following sentence (or rather aphorism) the universal physis is mentioned. Nature finds her own ways and means, without conscious intelligence—e.g. in the blinking of the eyes, the movements of the tongue, and similar phenomena. The later natural philosophers (influenced, as we have pointed out, by medical thought) solved the problem of the purpose of nature by assuming that divine reason, immanent in the whole world, had ordered everything in a purposeful way.[69] The Hippocratics avoided all such metaphysical hypotheses; but still they admired nature for acting with unconscious purpose. The modern theory of vitalism bridges the gap between the conscious and the unconscious by using a physiological concept and asserting that purposive processes in the organism are responses to stimuli. Hippocrates does not have that idea. Ancient science never quite made up its mind *how* such processes began, but it was perfectly certain of the fact that they did take place. It held that purpose in nature was always connected with animate life, and animate life is the sole object of medical science.

In the above-mentioned passage from *Visits* its author brings in the idea of an unconscious paideia which guides nature into doing what is necessary: εὐπαίδευτος ἡ φύσις ἑκοῦσα, οὐ μαθοῦσα, τὰ δέοντα ποιεῖ. In Littré's edition of Hippocrates (a valuable work, considering its date, but, although its text is the best available for most of the corpus, inadequate from the point of view of textual criticism) this remark is reversed, and reads: 'Nature is uneducated and has learnt nothing, but yet does what is correct.' The same kind of negative idea occurs in the later writer who composed *On food,* a little essay abounding in aphorisms: 'The natures of all things had no teacher.' [70] That almost looks as if he had read the variant in our passage of *Visits* and was imitating it. If he did, he was on the wrong track, for his contemporaries would think it a wild paradox to say that anything could be done correctly without paideia. Therefore, since nature herself does what is right without having learnt how, she must possess the genius of self-education (εὐπαίδευτος). She develops her masterly skill by using it directly on the task with which she is concerned. That reading, which appears in the best manu-

scripts, was used by the compiler of the maxims attributed to
Epicharmus; for in exactly the same way he explains the wisdom of nature by suggesting that she educated herself. Nature's
unconscious reasoning is thought of as parallel to man's conscious 'culture' [71]. That idea is more profound than the sophists'
notion which occasionally turns up in medical works—that the
moulding of human nature by paideia is parallel to agriculture
and the domestication of animals.[72] For paideia, looked at in
that way, is no more than training and discipline imposed from
outside; whereas according to the views of the Hippocratics, it
has an unconscious and spontaneous preliminary stage in the
purposive action of nature herself. That view makes nature
more rational, and reason more natural. The same sort of intellectual attitude is responsible for the brilliant use of spiritual
analogies to explain physical events, and vice versa. By this
means the author of *Visits* strikes out vivid sentences like
'Physical exertion nourishes the limbs and the flesh, sleep the
intestines', and 'Thought is the soul's walk abroad'.[73]

When we consider the idea that nature is an unconscious and
spontaneous force acting purposively, we can more easily understand the remark in the essay *On food:* 'Nature is enough for
everyone in everything.' [74] But, just as the doctor with his art
facilitates the restorative activity of nature when her equipoise
has been disturbed, it follows also that his duty is to prevent an
impending disturbance and to keep watch over the preservation
of normal conditions. In classical times, more than at any other
period until a few decades ago, the doctor was more concerned
with healthy people than with invalids. The branch of medicine
treating of health went under the general name of *hygiene*
(τὰ ὑγιεινά), and its main concern was 'diet'—which meant, for
the Greeks, not only the regulation of a sick person's food, but
a man's whole routine of living, especially the rules governing
his food and the exertions demanded of him. Hence it was inevitable for the physician, working on a teleological conception
of the human organism, to undertake a great educational task.
The care of health was in ancient times almost entirely a private
affair. Largely, it depended on the cultural level of the individual
in question, as well as on his practical intelligence, his needs,
and his means. It was of course always connected with gym-

nastics, which occupied an important part of the average man's day. Gymnastic exercise itself was the product of long years of hygienic experience and necessitated constant control of the body and its activities. The gymnastic trainer preceded the doctor as the specialist who advised his patients how to take care of their bodies. And he was not superseded when the new theories of 'diet' were elaborated—he always kept his place beside the physician. Although medicine started by trying to encroach on the realm of gymnastics, the dietetic works which have survived show that the two spheres were quite soon delimited, and in some matters the doctor accepted the authority of the trainer as final.

We still have some remains of what was once a copious medical literature from many periods of Greek culture, discussing the correct diet for daily life; and by reconstructing its development we can throw some valuable light on the changes that took place in Greek social life at various epochs. But here we are concerned only with its beginnings. The earliest works on hygiene are lost. For the period towards the end of the fifth century and the beginning of the fourth, in which that branch of Greek physical culture was first developed, we have a short treatise called *On regimen in health*. And if we could accept the usual chronology, we should have two more pieces of evidence: one work in four books, called *On diet*, very famous in antiquity; and large fragments of a lost book by the distinguished physician Diocles of Carystus, preserved in later authors. However (as we shall show) both of these must be dated later than has usually been done. We can, indeed, study them together as representative of a single epoch, showing as they do certain typical features. But the difference in their methods of treating the subject shows that it was fairly highly developed when they were written, and that their authors were men of pronounced individual character. They must therefore be described separately. Besides, a complete history of the science of diet at that period must bring in those rules for the regime of healthy persons which are scattered here and there throughout the other works in the Hippocratic corpus.

The treatise *On regimen in health* [75] was written to guide laymen in choosing the proper system for their daily 'diet'. So was another little book, the treatise *On affections*, which was therefore often put next to it in manuscripts, even in classical times. The latter begins by discussing the difficulties of educating laymen and by inquiring how much medical knowledge they need in order to look after themselves and prevent their diseases from growing worse; or, if that is impossible, to understand more of the doctor's treatment and assist him in administering it. And it ends with a description of the diet for sick persons, written to be understood by the average reader. It is therefore exactly parallel in construction to the work *On regimen in health* —which shows why the ancients ascribed them both to the same author. The regulations it gives for the healthy man's regime cover the food and exercise appropriate for various seasons, places, constitutions, ages, and sexes; but it is all in very general terms, nevertheless. The author's main idea is to preserve a sort of medical balance of power: in cold seasons he prescribes much solid food and little fluid, with the opposite in hot weather, in order to compensate the effects of winter by increasing warmth and dryness and those of summer by moisture and coolness. Thus, he always tries to emphasize the opposite of any quality which threatens to dominate the body. For he believes (like the author of the work *On the nature of man*) that diseases are caused by the fact that our bodies are made not of one element but several, and that the right proportion between them is easily distorted by the excessive increase of any of the four qualities—heat, cold, moisture, and dryness. The theory is rightly rejected as too systematic by the author of the work *On ancient medicine,* but it is not hard to see that its very schematism made it easy to use. It makes diet a kind of simple diplomacy applied to the body: a skill which has only a few different factors to deal with. It is not yet nearly so highly developed as it was to become about a hundred years later in the work of Diocles. Diocles actually regulated the whole day from morning till night, while this earlier work merely gives some description of the change in diet appropriate for the two extremes, summer and winter, and for the two transition-periods, spring and autumn. The chief difficulty in living by his rules would not be that they were too detailed but that they were too general. Since the relation of the doctor and the trainer was not yet fixed, the author of the work follows out his theory in directing that exercise be increased or diminished according to the season, without asking the trainer for his advice.[76]

The large work in four books *On diet* is a different kind of thing. It is a real encyclopaedia, which the author says was an attempt to collect, and where necessary to supplement, the already rich literature in this particular field.[77] He was a philosopher; he liked systematic theories; but it is not right to call him a compiler. It is doubtful whether the problem has been brought nearer solution by those who have hitherto endeavoured to analyse his work. They have sliced it up into gobbets and labelled them as copied from various originals: this from a sophist imitating Heraclitus, this from a pupil of Anaxagoras, this from the dietician Herodicus, and so on.[78] For instance, they have asserted that certain parts of the book sound like Heraclitus, and that we can set them apart from those which go back to some natural philosopher. But the natural philosopher in his turn is not entirely a follower of Anaxagoras: some of his ideas are quite Empedoclean, others are reminiscent of Diogenes of Apollonia. We should really make up our minds to accept the author's assertion that he has felt many different influences but intends to be no less universal as a philosopher than as a doctor. All this proves that he belongs to a time later than Hippocrates, and thus it is initially improbable that (as generally believed) he is the person attacked as a philosophizing doctor by the man who wrote *On ancient medicine* in the last thirty years of the fifth century. On the contrary, he appears to have been writing after that book had appeared, because he seems to have read it. Certainly he takes pains to obey its directions and not to stop short at generalities; in fact, he expressly points out again and again that in medicine nearly everything depends on the individual factor. He is also exercised by the problem of exactness. It is useless, he declares, to lay down broad universal rules stating what supply of heat and cold is healthy for the body (as the earlier work *On regimen in health* does). Instead, he desiderates an accurate description of the effect of all types of food. His work was famed in antiquity as an inexhaustible mine of detailed information.[79] Galen held that the second book of it was worthy of Hippocrates, despite the variegated philosophy of Book I, and other extraneous material. And even if much of it is not original, but copied by the author from his sources, it is still impossible not to recognize that he has passed beyond the old theoretical dispute between philosophy and empirical medicine and is deliberately attempting to unite both these factors.

The Hippocratic school taught that the doctor must attend to the patient's whole constitution, to his climatic and regional surroundings, and to changes in cosmic phenomena which affected him; and this author holds that that necessarily implies a philosophical interest in universal nature. The author of *On ancient medicine* thought it vitally important to know which part of the organism dominated the rest at any one time. This man also considers that problem vitally important, but he holds that it cannot be solved without knowing what parts compose the human body.[80] Diagnosis is inseparable from gnosis—the understanding of the nature of the universe. That understanding brings knowledge of the details of a correct regime—knowledge mainly of foods and their effect on different constitutions, but also of physical exercise and gymnastics. That is just as important as knowledge of correct nourishment; and yet the author of the work *On ancient medicine,* like many other early physicists, says nothing about it whatever.[81] The writer of *On diet* teaches that the two contrary factors of nourishment and exercise should be carefully and systematically balanced. This is an adaptation of the ideal of symmetry, which earlier writers had applied chiefly to food. It must, he implies, be extended to physical exercise and its relationship to nutrition.[82] Probably he is here following the theories of Herodicus of Selymbria, the first to give exercise a dominant position in the regimen and to work it out systematically. Himself a trainer, he used gymnastics to cure his own illness and made it into a therapeutic system for himself and others. He must have brought it to a certain degree of distinction, because he is widely known. The sarcastic author of the sixth book of *Visits* says he killed his fever-patients by giving them too much sport and too many steam-baths; and Plato says jokingly that he could not cure himself, but artificially postponed his own death by 'torturing' himself for years. Aristotle mentions his remark that many men cannot properly be praised for their good health, since the only way they maintain it is to abstain from every pleasure. According to Plato, that would be most apposite for Herodicus himself.[82a] Perhaps our author takes such care to lay down proper proportion in nutrition and physical exercise because he is answering these criticisms, which were obviously very common in the fourth century. Other doctors had hotly asserted the 'independence' of the art of medicine. But our author has a much broader conception of medicine, to which he does not try to apply that ideal, because, he says, it is impossible to find the exact proportion of nutrition and exercise appropriate for each individual. I think it is impossible not to see in this a polemic against the author of *On ancient medicine,* whose leading ideas are all repeated here and expressly contradicted. This writer holds that the art of medicine is kept from reaching true perfection because it is impossible to solve the problem of the individual and his needs.[83] He is prepared to grant that the physician could approach his ideal more closely if, like the trainer, he had the individuals whom he treated constantly under his eyes. But that is impossible.[84]

He does not wish to do as most physicians do, and start after the disease has taken hold. He therefore writes out a detailed regimen which, if observed, should prevent the onset of disease. This is both prodiagnosis and prophylaxis—his own invention. It arose from his observation that the individual cannot possibly be treated correctly unless he himself can be made to help the doctor in his duty much more than at present, and act as a conscious assistant in his own treatment.[85] After laying down in the first book the theories of natural philosophy which are to be his general assumptions, the author goes on in Book II to describe the effects of various climates and regions on health, and then those of all kinds of vegetable and animal food, down to the most insignificant. This gives us a chance to appreciate the astonishing richness and variety of diet which the civilized Greeks commanded. The doctor's list is even fuller than the long menus which are rattled off in so many Doric and Attic comedies. It is just as systematic as the rest of his treatise. He begins by dividing up the huge variety of possible plant-foods into cereal and vegetable types. Only herbs and fruit are omitted, and they appear after the meats, because (from the dietetic point of view) they are classified as 'delicacies' or 'relish' (ὄψον). Animal foods are divided into mammals (and these subdivided into old and young mammals), birds, fish, and shellfish. Wild and domestic animals are discussed for their various effects as food. After this come animal products and dishes made with them: eggs, milk, cheese; honey is treated along with drinks because it was usually mixed with them.

Even the short chapter on cheese is enough to contradict the prevailing view that the author is the man so violently attacked in the essay *On ancient medicine* for hasty generalizing. That essay actually quotes the case of cheese to prove its point, saying that the physician addicted to generalizations affirmed that *all* cheese was injurious to the health. The writer of this work, on the other hand, says (quite correctly) that cheese is heavy, but adds that it is nourishing too.[86] The accepted dating of the two books should therefore be reversed, since it is clear that this dietician has read and used not only *On ancient medicine,* but others of the older Hippocratic works. For example, he copies word for word the list of climatic factors which are enumerated as important from a medical point of view in the introduction to the essay *On airs, waters, and places,*[87] and he lays down that physical exercise should be determined with relation to these factors. Also, we cannot deny that he knew the views expressed in *Visits,* and that the Coan school possessed a copy of his work. In *Visits* (as we have seen) thought is brilliantly called 'the soul's walk abroad'.[88] This writer took up the idea (from whatever source) and made systematic use of it in his own way: for he classifies not only thinking but also the activity of the senses and speech as 'exercise'. They are, however, put in a special category as 'natural' exertions, which sets them in contrast to the different kinds of walking and gymnastic exercise, classified as artificial or 'violent' exertions.[89] The theory of psychical movement connected with this doctrine sounds very like the author's own creation, for he says that when the soul exerts itself it grows hot and dry, and that the exhaustion of the body's moisture helps to make it thin.

We cannot resist the conclusion that the essay *On diet* takes us not only out of the fifth century but far into the fourth. There are several proofs of this: language, style, and subject-matter. One will suffice. The author recommends that massage be carried on with a mixture of oil and water, which does not heat the body strongly (οὐ δεινῶς).[90] Now, we possess a large fragment of a special study of this question by Diocles of

Carystus, dedicated to the memory of his father, the physician Archidamus, and named after him. Archidamus had condemned the customary massage with oil because it heated the body too much. Diocles confutes the reasons he gives and suggests a compromise—massage with mixed oil and water in summer and with pure oil in winter.[91] The recommendation of massage with oil and water and the reason advanced for it (to avoid heating the body) are so individual that the agreement of Diocles with the author of the treatise *On diet* cannot be mere coincidence. There is no need to argue which of them originated the idea. As I have proved in my book on Diocles, he was still alive after 300, and reached the height of his career not long before that year.[92] We cannot put *On diet* so late as that. Apart from everything else, there is no trace in it of the influence of Aristotle and the Peripatetic school, which is evident throughout the work of Diocles. Therefore, its author knew about the condemnation of oil massage by Diocles' father and considered it to be an exaggeration. He compromised on massage with oil and water mixed, so as not to heat up the body too much. Diocles accepted this compromise for the summer season and kept massage with pure oil for the winter. There are other reasons too for believing that he had read *On diet* and made use of it. If this argument is accepted, the work was written by a contemporary of Diocles' father Archidamus. The strongly eclectic character of the book, its length, and the great number of other books which it quotes [92a] serve also to date it to that period.

There is another point which helps us to place the author in the fourth century. That is his marked inclination to divide up his material into systematic types and classes, for that method flourished in the fourth century. It is true that, even in the fifth, we saw a tendency in all fields of medical experiment to work out types (εἴδη); but here that process has reached a later stage. It is particularly clear in the beautifully systematic arrangement of the animal- and plant-worlds on which the author bases his detailed description of the various possible foods. Some years ago his zoology attracted the attention of certain zoological specialists,[93] who found it hard to believe that a doctor could have elaborated a system so complex and so closely akin to Aristotle's, merely for a dietetic purpose. It seemed to be too painstakingly detailed and too completely dominated by an interest in zoological theory. On the other hand, we never hear of zoology's being treated as an independent science in the fifth century, before Aristotle; and that seemed to be the right date for the essay. In this dilemma, scholars concluded that the Hippocratic school must have made a comprehensive study of zoology for medical purposes (although no ancient author says it did), and from the work *On diet* they reconstructed a 'Coan zoological system'. Yet, even in that form, it is impossible to believe that systematic zoological theories so like those of Aristotle really existed in the fifth century.[94] We can understand the enigma presented by the structure of the work better if we date it to the age of Plato. There is a famous passage by the comedian Epicrates, written at the same time, which speaks of attempts made in the Academy to classify the whole animal and vegetable world, and says that a Sicilian doctor took part in them.[95] It is true that the visitor was bored, and showed it very rudely; but the very fact of his presence indicates that these researches attracted medical visitors from some distance, though they might be disappointed by the lack of empiricism manifested in them. Minds of very different types were drawn to Plato's school from far countries, and no doubt this Sicilian doctor was only one of many such visiting scientists.[95a] Some of the work done by the Academy in this subject was published later by Speusippus and used by Aristotle. The zoological system of the essay *On diet* shows resemblances to the work of them both.[96] Still, it would be safer to analyse its classification of plants and its method of approach to other types before making a final judgment on its relation to Speusippus and Aristotle. All we can do here is to describe, in general, the kind of intellectual milieu to which its author belonged. We need not assume that he must be later than Plato's attempt to classify the animals and plants. Plato himself, in his fullest explanation of his dialectic system of classification (*Phaedrus* 265f.), says that it should be modelled on the method of Hippocrates.[97] True, he does not say that that method was ever applied to organisms other than man, but it is not hard to believe that by Plato's time the medical schools had extended it to plants and animals as well, and that philosophers and doctors had a common interest in that type of investigation.

One remarkable thing is that the essay *On diet* uses the word 'soul' far oftener than any other work in the Hippocratic corpus.

It is rather exceptional to find it in any of the others.[98] This cannot be accidental. It is not enough to account for it by saying that the author copied it from his Heraclitean source, since he speaks of the soul not only in passages dealing with natural philosophy but in those concerning diet too, and devotes the entire fourth book to the psychic reflexes of physical processes, as shown in dreams. His casuistical interpretation of different kinds of dream-pictures has much in common with Indian and Babylonian dream-books, both earlier and later than his work. Scholars have decided that here at least Greek medical science shows direct Oriental influence.[98a] This would have been perfectly possible at an earlier date; but it fits best into the fourth century, for it was then that the Ionian doctor Ctesias and Eudoxus of Cnidus acquired a close personal knowledge of the Orient and Eudoxus imparted some of it to Plato's Academy.[99] The Greeks were really not ready to accept either the wisdom or the superstition of the East about the spirit's dream-life before their thought had come to centre itself on the 'soul'—and that, in this particular scientific and theoretical form, did not happen until the fourth century. Again it was the Academy that gave the most memorable expression to these new ideas. Plato's doctrine of the soul was the source from which the Academy drew its philosophical interest in the soul's dream-life and its real meaning.[100] Early in his career Aristotle discussed the question in several dialogues. The man who wrote *On diet,* although his thoughts are strongly individual, may well have been influenced in considering the question of dreams by the work done in the Academy.

Like Aristotle in his dialogues, he begins with the Orphic conception that the soul is most free when the body sleeps, for then it is collected all together and undivided and entirely by itself.[100a] But he gives this dogma a peculiar medical twist: he says that during sleep the soul also mirrors the physical condition of its owner most clearly, not being confused by external influences. Aristotle's work *On the interpretation of dreams* (still extant) shows that the meaning of dreams was scientifically discussed in the fourth century. He observes that dreams are the effect of experiences in real life, without therefore believing that they actually foretell the future. Similarly, the author of *On diet* does not directly accept oneiromancy: he tries to change it from prophecy into prognostication. But he follows his original authority too far, and ends by giving way to superstition.

The language of the book is more reminiscent of the middle of the fourth century than of its beginning, or of any earlier period. Ionic was still being written all through the fourth century, and these elaborate and sometimes tedious sentences, with their antitheses and balanced clauses, point to the era of Isocratean rhetoric rather than to that of Gorgias. They could not have been written at the same time as the entirely unsophisticated and unrhetorical specialist treatises which we can (with due caution) ascribe to the time of Hippocrates or his immediate successors. And the less specialist, more popular works of the older generations, although they are more strongly influenced by sophistic models, are still very different from the prose of this work. Its style varies greatly from chapter to chapter. Most scholars say that its author is simply copying a number of different works. But since he can write so artistically when he wishes, it is probably just an affectation of versatility: something comparable to the ideal of synthesis which he announces in his introduction. He says that he will probably be despised for his lack of originality, because he is combining the theories of numerous predecessors; but he really seems to be quite proud of it.[101] This is the idea we first meet in Isocrates (although in him it concerns form rather than content)—'mixture of styles' is the highest literary art, and synthesis the aim of the author. Finally, the author of this work, like Isocrates, is very anxious about his reputation for originality; and that anxiety too is characteristic of the fourth century.

Another distinguished doctor is usually placed in the first part of the fourth century: Diocles, from Carystus in Euboea, who worked in Athens and whose fundamental ideas are closely akin to those of both the Hippocratic and the Sicilian schools.[102] Among other books, he wrote a famous one on diet; large fragments of it are preserved in a medical anthology compiled by the Emperor Julian's physician Oribasius. However, it has recently been pointed out that the language of these fragments shows the refinement of Isocratean training, and has many features pointing to the latter half of the fourth century rather than its beginning. This conjecture has been questioned,[103] but other considerations make it perfectly certain. Diocles was a younger contemporary of Aristotle. He was his pupil, and belongs to the generation of the Peripatetics Theophrastus and Strato; they studied along with him, and they provide the first extant evidence for his life and work.[104] Like that of the Hippocratic scientist who wrote *On diet,* his style is highly polished, and, although it is a specialist work, his book aspires to be pure literature—a significant fact for the intellectual status and educational aims of medicine in the fourth century. Still, it is not rhetorical, but deliberately simple. In that, perhaps he is influenced by the new ideal of scientific style which prevailed after Aristotle introduced it.

In the largest extant fragment [105] Diocles expounds his theory of diet by describing a day's routine. He does not, like the author of *On regimen in health,* explain the best way to live by prescribing broadly contrasting diets for the four seasons. Nor does he, like the writer of *On diet,* work out an exhaustive systematic description of types of food and drink and physical exercise. He treats diet as a whole covering all man's life. His little drama gets a natural unity of time by being completed in one day; but he is always careful to distinguish between various ages and to make allowances for the change of seasons. He starts by treating a summer day at length, and then adds directions for spending a day in winter and in other seasons. That was the only possible way to do what he set out to do.

We have seen how early natural philosophy affected Greek medicine, and how the new empirical medicine in its turn worked upon the philosophy of Plato and Aristotle. In Diocles, who is obviously influenced by the great Athenian philosophical schools, medical science once more receives more than it gives, although it does give something in return.[105a] In explaining the proper diet by the method of describing a typical day, he is obviously copying Plato's and Aristotle's way of thinking—they always look at human life *as a whole* and make the ideal of right living into the standard for all men to follow. No doubt other writers on diet set up standards too; but they merely say, 'One must do this or that', or else they describe the effect of a certain type of food on the body and leave it to the reader to draw his own practical conclusion. Diocles does neither one nor the other. Instead, he always states what is suitable and beneficial for men.

Both ethics and art in the fourth century are dominated by the idea of suitability. Human life must be regulated by some standard, and that was the kind of standard which the spirit of the age—over-individualized, no doubt, but still sensitive and tasteful—could best accept. All the details of life were embraced, as if in a fine and hardly perceptible net, by the idea of the Suitable. That which is *suitable* is the behaviour dictated by tact and by a delicate perception of the appropriate in every relationship. Diocles' theory of diet carries this idea over into physical life. It is impossible not to notice how he uses the word 'suitable' (ἁρμόττον) at every new prescription, like a teacher driving home a lesson.[106] And the idea of *proportion* (σύμμετρον, μέτριον) occurs very often too.[107] In that, Diocles is deeply influenced by Aristotelian ethics; and, from another point of view, he is dependent on Aristotle's logic—he blames physicians for always trying to find a cause for conditions, instead of realizing that many general phenomena must simply be taken as existing, without need of proof or derivation.[108] Logical minds cannot help being alarmed by the fact that even mathematics, the most rigorous of all sciences, simply has to assume that numbers and quantities possess certain properties. Aristotle made a careful study of the problem presented by these assumptions—axioms, as they are called in mathematics. He taught that both philosophy and the separate sciences are based on certain immediate suppositions which are incapable of proof. Diocles introduced this idea to medical science, which in the Hellenistic age was to become the chief battleground of the great war of methods between empiricism, dogmatism, and scepticism.

He begins his exposition of diet with the moment of waking up,[109] which he places shortly before sunrise, for the whole life of the Greeks was fitted to the natural course of the day. The chief meal was taken in the evening, shortly before sunset in summer and naturally later in winter. After it, men with weak constitutions are told by Diocles that they should go to bed at once, and stronger persons as soon as they have taken a short, leisurely walk. This being so, there is nothing strange about the early hour of rising, and indeed we know of it from other Greek evidence. Diocles says we should not rise immediately we wake, but wait till the heaviness of sleep leaves our limbs, and then rub our neck and head at the places where they pressed on the pillow. Next (even before emptying the bowels) we should rub the whole body lightly and equally all over with a little oil, mixed with water in summer,[110] and flex all our joints. He does not recommend a bath after this, only that the hands should be washed and the face and eyes bathed in pure cold water. Then he gives detailed directions for care of the teeth, nose, ears, hair, and scalp. (The scalp must, he says, be kept supple and clean so that it can perspire, but must also be hardened.) After this anyone who has work to do should have something to eat, and then begin his duties. Those who have not, should take a walk before or after breakfast—long or short, according to their constitution and state of health. The walk, if taken after breakfast, should not be long or quick. After it is over, they should sit down and attend to business at home, or occupy themselves in some other way till it is time for exercise. Then young men should go to the gymnasium, and old people and invalids to the bath, or to some other sunny place, to be anointed with oil. The amount and difficulty of the exercises taken should be suitable to the age of the person taking it. For elderly men, it is enough to be gently massaged, to move about a little, and then to have a bath. It is better to massage oneself than to be massaged by someone else, because one's own movements are a substitute for gymnastic exercise.

After the morning exercise comes luncheon, which should be light and not filling, so that it can be digested before the gymnastics of the afternoon. Directly after luncheon, there should be a short siesta in a dark and cool, but not draughty, place; and then more business at home, a walk, and finally (after another short rest) the afternoon's exercise. The day ends with dinner. Diocles says nothing about the separate exercises, and all the literature about diet would tell us nothing about this important branch of Greek physical culture if the author of the treatise On diet had not been so systematic—after his classification of all foods and drinks, he enumerates all possible kinds of psychical and physical exertions, among which are included gymnastic exercises. Diocles cuts them out of his regimen, so to speak, and leaves them to the trainer to direct. But the whole scheme of his day is based on two fixed points: exercise in the morning and exercise in the afternoon. His vivid description makes us fully realize how the whole life of the Greeks (unlike that of any other people) revolved around their gymnastics. His dietetic theory could well be described as a recommendation to regulate all that part of the day which is not spent on exercise by accurate medical prescription, and to bring it into complete harmony with one's gymnastic routine.

The aim of all this is to attain the best possible diathesis— the best possible permanent condition for general health and for every kind of physical exertion. Diocles says so several times. But of course he realizes that the world is not run to suit medical theory, and he does not talk as if men simply lived in order to look after their health. The writer of *On diet* also recognizes that a certain social difficulty exists—that some compromise must be found between the doctor's ideals and the actual conditions of the patient's life. He reaches the same conclusion as Diocles. He draws up an ideal régime for the man who has nothing to do but keep fit, and then makes allowances for those who have to work and have little time left for the care of the body.[111] We must not imagine that the Greek doctors wrote only for the rich. Contemporary philosophers did the same thing—they described a *bios* to be lived by the man who was entirely at leisure, and then left individuals to make their own deductions from this ideal.

And yet perhaps the life led by a citizen of a Greek city-state in the fourth century allowed him more time to spend on the culture of his spirit and the care of his body than any other life ever lived by man. The example of the medical system of bodily care shows that, even in its democratic form, the Greek polis was a social aristocracy; and that fact was responsible for the high average level of general culture which it attained. Not one of the main types produced by our own professionalized existence—business man, politician, scholar, labourer, or farmer —would fit into the framework of Greek life. So far as those types had been developed in Greece, they stood out of the pattern even then. Yet it is not hard to understand how the philosophy of Socrates and the dialectic skill of the sophists developed in the gymnastic school. It would be wrong to assume that the *kaloi kagathoi,* the gentlemen, spent all day there, oiling themselves, training, rubbing themselves down, dusting themselves with sand and washing it off again, so earnestly as to turn even the free agôn into an arduous, specialized sport. Plato speaks of the three physical virtues—health, strength, and beauty—as joining to form one chorus with the virtues of the soul—piety, courage, temperance, and justice. They all equally symbolize the symmetry of the world-order, the harmony which is reflected both in the physical and in the psychical life of the individual. Even physical culture, as understood by Greek doctors and trainers, was a spiritual thing. It imposed one supreme standard upon men—the duty of preserving a noble and healthy balance between their physical powers. If, then, equality and harmony are the essence of health and all other physical perfections, then 'health' comes to mean something greater—it grows into a universal standard of value applying to the whole world and to the whole of life. For its foundations, equality and harmony, are the forces which (according to the ideas underlying this doctrine) create that which is good and right, while pleonexia, aggrandizement, disturbs it. Greek medical science was both the root and the fruit of this doctrine, from which it constantly draws strength and sustenance, and which, despite the variations created by individual or racial characteristics, is the universal view of all classical Greeks. The reason why medicine rose to such a representative position in Greek culture was that it revealed, clearly and impressively, in the sphere most accessible by immediate experience, the inalienable significance of this fundamental Greek ideal. In this higher sense, we may say that the Greek ideal of culture was the ideal of Health.

2

THE RHETORIC OF ISOCRATES AND ITS CULTURAL IDEAL

GREEK literature of the fourth century reflects a widespread struggle to determine the character of true paideia; and within it Isocrates, the chief representative of rhetoric, personifies the classical opposition to Plato and his school. From this point on, the rivalry of philosophy and rhetoric, each claiming to be the better form of culture, runs like a leitmotiv throughout the history of ancient civilization. It is impossible to describe every phase of that rivalry: for one thing, it is rather repetitious, and the leaders of its opposing sides are not always very interesting personalities.[1] All the more important, therefore, is the conflict between Plato and Isocrates—the first battle in the centuries of war between philosophy and rhetoric. Later, that war was sometimes to degenerate into a mere academic squabble, in which neither side possessed any genuine vital force; but at its beginning the combatant parties represented the truly moving forces and needs of the Greek people. The field on which it was waged lay in the very centre of the political scene. That is what gives it the vivid colouring of a truly historical event, and the large sweep which keeps our interest in it permanently alive. In retrospect, we realize that in this conflict are symbolized the essential problems of that whole period of Greek history.

Today as of old, Isocrates has, like Plato, his admirers and exponents; and there is no doubt that since the Renaissance he has exercised a far greater influence on the educational methods of humanism than any other Greek or Roman teacher. Historically, it is perfectly correct to describe him (in the phrase used on the title-page of several modern books) as the father of 'humanistic culture'—inasmuch as the sophists cannot really claim that title, and from our own pedagogic methods and ideals a direct line runs back to him, as it does to Quintilian and Plutarch.[2] But that point of view, dictated as it is by modern academic humanism, is vastly different from the attitude of this book—for our task here is to examine the whole development of Greek paideia and to study the complexities and antagonisms inherent in its problems and its meaning.[3] It is important to notice that what is often regarded by contemporary educators as the essence of humanism is mainly a continuation of the rhetorical strain in classical culture; while the history of humanism is a far broader and richer thing than that, for it contains all the manifold survivals of Greek paideia—including the world-wide influence exercised by Greek philosophy and science.[4] From this point of view, it is clear that an understanding of the true Greek paideia at once entails a criticism of modern academic humanism.[5] On the other hand, the position and character of philosophy and science within Greek civilization as a whole cannot be properly estimated until they are seen striving against other types of intellectual activity in order to be accepted as the true form of culture. Ultimately, both the rivals, philosophy and rhetoric, spring from poetry, the oldest Greek paideia; and they cannot be understood without reference to their origin in it.[6] But as the old rivalry for the primacy of culture gradually narrows to a dispute about the relative values of philosophy and rhetoric, it becomes clear enough that the ancient Hellenic partnership between gymnastic training and 'musical' culture has at last sunk to a much lower level.

To one who has just read Plato's *Protagoras* and *Gorgias* it seems obvious that the educational system of the sophists and rhetors was fundamentally an outworn ideal; and, if we compare it with the lofty claims advanced by philosophy—the claim that henceforth *all* education and *all* culture must be based on nothing but the knowledge of the highest values—it really was obsolete. And yet (as we have seen from our first glance over the later centuries of Greek history [7]) the older type of education, the method of the sophists and the rhetoricians, remained unconquerably active and alive beside its rival, and in fact continued to hold a leading place as one of the greatest influences on the spiritual life of Greece. Perhaps the savage scorn with which Plato attacks and persecutes it may be partly explained by the victor's feeling that he is at war with an enemy who is, as long as he remains within his own frontiers, unconquerable. It is difficult for us to understand the violence of his detestation, if we think of his attacks as directed solely against the great sophists of Socrates' generation, considered as embodiments of the type of culture which he loathed: Protagoras, Gorgias, Hippias, Prodicus. When he wrote his dialogues, these men were dead, and, in that rapid century, half forgotten. It needed all Plato's art to call the strong personalities of the famous sophists out of the shadows to life once more. When he made his caricatures of them (caricatures which in their way are quite as immortal as his idealized portrait of Socrates), a new generation had grown up; and he was attacking them, his contemporaries, as well as his predecessors. We need not go so far as to see, in the opponents whom he describes, mere masks for notable men of his own age; and yet, in his presentment of the sophists, there are many contemporary traits. And there is one absolutely certain fact: Plato never argues with dead men, with historical fossils.

Nothing shows how strong and vital sophistry and rhetoric were, at the time when he began his struggle against them, more clearly than the personality of Isocrates, who actually entered on his career after *Protagoras* and *Gorgias* were written.[8] It is particularly interesting that from the very outset he contested the claims of Plato and the Socratic circle, and defended sophistic education against their attacks. This means that he was writing from the firm conviction that such criticisms did not seriously shake his position. He was really a genuine sophist: indeed, it was he who brought the sophistic movement in education to its culminating point. Biographical tradition represents him as the pupil of Protagoras, of Prodicus, and especially of Gorgias; and archaeologists of the Hellenistic age found proof of the third of these connexions in his tombstone, which bore a figure they identified as Gorgias, pointing to a celestial globe.[9] Another tradition asserted that Isocrates had studied with the great rhetor in Thessaly—doubtless during the last phase of the Peloponnesian war.[10] Plato too, in his *Meno,* mentions that some part of Gorgias' career as a teacher was passed in Thessaly[11]: an interesting proof of the fact that the new culture was penetrating even the frontier lands of Greece. Isocrates' first great book, the *Panegyricus,* which brought him fame almost overnight, closely resembles Gorgias' *Olympicus;* and the fact that he deliberately chose to compete with

such a celebrated author in treating the same theme—a call
to the Greeks to achieve national unity—is, according to Greek
usage, a proof that he considered himself Gorgias' pupil. And
the chief evidence for the fact is the dominant position he
assigns to rhetoric—that is, to the most concrete, the least purely
theoretical, type of sophistic culture. Throughout his life he
aimed, like Gorgias, at teaching the art or craft of speaking
(λόγων τέχνη) ; [12] but he preferred to apply the title 'sophist' only
to theorists, whatever their special interests might be. He used
it, among others, for Socrates and his pupils, who had done so
much to discredit the name. His own ideal he called 'philosophy'.
Thus, he completely inverted the meanings given by Plato to the
two words. Today, when Plato's definition of 'philosophy' has
been universally accepted for centuries, Isocrates' procedure appears to have been a mere whim. But really it was not. In his
time, those concepts were still developing, and had not yet finally
hardened into their ultimate shapes. It was not Plato, but Isocrates, who followed the general idiom in calling Socrates and his
pupils 'sophists' quite as much as Protagoras or Hippias; and
in using 'philosophy' to mean intellectual culture in general,[13]
which is the sense it has in Thucydides, for example. He could
well have said (as Pericles says in Thucydides [14]) that the
characteristic mark of the whole Athenian state was its interest in things of the mind, φιλοσοφεῖν, and he does actually say
something of the kind in the *Panegyricus*. Athens, he writes, invented culture (φιλοσοφία)—and he is obviously thinking of the
whole community rather than of the small group of sharp-witted
dialecticians gathered round Plato or Socrates.[15] What he was
aiming at was universal culture, contrasted with one definite
creed or one particular method of attaining knowledge, as
preached by the Platonists. Thus, in the opposing claims made
by both sides to ownership of the title 'philosophy', and in the
widely different meanings given to the word by the opponents,
there is symbolized the rivalry of rhetoric and science for leadership in the realm of education and culture.[16]

Isocrates, then, was the post-war representative of the sophistic and rhetorical culture which had flourished in the Periclean period. But he was much more. To think of him as nothing more than that is to ignore the best and most characteristic
aspects of his personality. The particular way in which he dis-

tributes the emphasis, magnifying the importance of rhetoric and of practical politics, and pushing mere sophistry and theory into the background, shows his fine perception of the Athenian attitude to the new culture. It had, during his boyhood and youth, achieved an astonishing success in his native city of Athens; but it had also been violently opposed. Although he was far from being the first Athenian to declare himself its pupil and its champion, it was not really naturalized in Athens until he gave it a truly Athenian dress. In Plato the rhetors and sophists who argue with Socrates are always at a disadvantage, simply because they are foreigners, and do not understand the real problems of Athens and the Athenians. They always seem to be outsiders, as they enter the close, compact Athenian society, bringing with them their knowledge, 'imported ready-made', as it were.[17] Of course they all speak the same international language, in which they can be understood by every educated man. But it never has the Athenian overtones. They lack the casual grace and the social ease without which they cannot achieve full success in the Athenian world. Their wide culture and their fabulous technical skill are admiringly welcomed, but in a deeper sense they remain ineffectual—at least for the time. Before it could become effective, the new element had to coalesce with the very special way of life which characterized the incomparable state of Athens; and none but an Athenian could bring about the coalition—an Athenian who, like Isocrates, was fully alive to the nature of his city and of the crisis which then confronted it. It was a full generation after its first appearance in Athens that rhetoric was naturalized there, under the influence of the tremendous events of the war and the post-war years—events which wrought a deep change in the very nature of rhetoric. At the same time it was profoundly affected by the moral reformation initiated by Socrates,[18] and by the great social crises which had shaken the Athenian state throughout Isocrates' youth and early manhood. The new generation, heir to the Periclean system, found tasks of enormous difficulty confronting it. It was rhetoric, and not philosophy in the Platonic sense, that seemed to Isocrates to be the intellectual form which could best express the political and ethical ideas of his age, and make them part of the intellectual equipment of all contemporary Athenians. With this new conception of its purposes, Isocrates' rhetorical teaching emerged as part of the great post-war educational movement of Athens, into which all the efforts of his day to reform and rejuvenate the Athenian state were inevitably destined to flow.

The factors which brought this about were very various. Despite his mastery of language and of style, Isocrates was not a born orator. And yet, by its very nature, the Athenian democracy still held that no man could be an effective political force unless he were a master of oratory. He says himself that physically he had a weak constitution. His voice was not nearly powerful enough to reach large audiences; and he had an invincible fear of making a public appearance. Crowds terrified him.[19] In speaking without embarrassment of this agoraphobia, Isocrates was not merely offering an excuse for his complete abstention from all political activity; besides that, he felt that his strange condition was a very personal feature of his character, rooted far in its depths. As with Socrates, his refusal to enter politics was not a sign of lack of interest, but the result of a profound intellectual and spiritual conflict—a conflict which both hampered his activity and at the same time enlarged his understanding of the part he must play in the contemporary political crisis. Like the Platonic Socrates, he was convinced that he must initiate the much-needed reformation in some other way than by entering an active career as an orator in the assemblies and the law courts. Thus, he felt that the personal disabilities which made him unfit for normal political life summoned him to a higher vocation. His weakness was his destiny. But whereas Socrates, with his incessant questioning and examining, became an explorer in the sphere of morality, and found himself at last standing before the closed gates of a new world of knowledge, the more practical Isocrates, although for the time being he was deeply impressed by the personality of his great contemporary, and constantly strove to rival the lofty standard he set, felt nevertheless that his special gifts and his natural dislike for the mob predestined him to become within a small circle the teacher of a new type of political action.[20]

Even the age in which he lived seemed to make this course inevitable. In the calm and concentration of his retirement, he wished to educate statesmen who could give new direction to the efforts of the misguided masses and to the politics of the Greek states, which had long been revolving hopelessly in a closed circle. He set out to inspire every pupil with a passion for the new aims which occupied his own mind. There was within him a political visionary whose thought moved in the same direction as that of the practical statesmen, and was led like them by such aspirations as Power, Glory, Prosperity, Progress. Gradually his experience led him to modify his aims; but from the very beginning he held that they could not be fulfilled by the outworn methods of the Periclean age—competitive diplomacy and exhausting wars between the separate Greek city-states. In that his thought is wholly a product of the weakness of Athens after the Peloponnesian war. Dreamer that he was, in his visions of the future he overleapt that weakness. He believed that Athens could play a leading part in Greek affairs only in peaceful agreement with Sparta and the other Greek states, with entire equality between victors and vanquished; for then the intellectual superiority of Athens to her coarser rivals would assure that she acquired the balance of power.[21] Only such establishment of equality among the Greek states and their devotion to one great national purpose could arrest the dissolution of Greece, and therewith the total annihilation of the small separate states—which hitherto had striven only to destroy one another, although none of them had ever acquired a real superiority over all the rest, with the supreme power which would impose a lasting peace on the entire nation. To save Greece, a common national purpose must be found. And, after the bitter experiences of the Peloponnesian war, Isocrates considered that the essential duty of true statesmanship was to find it. True, there was an urgent preliminary: the political life of the Greek state had to be purged of its deep corruption, and of the cause of that corruption—the poisonous mutual hatreds of the separate states and parties. It was exactly that selfish hatred of each for his neighbour which, according to Thucydides' tragic description, had during the Peloponnesian war served as a justification for every kind of monstrous crime, and had destroyed the foundations of all established moral codes.[22] But Isocrates did not, like the Platonic Socrates, believe that the sorely needed reformation could be achieved by the creation of a new moral world, a state as it were within each man's soul.[23] He held that the *nation,* the idea of Greece, was the point round which the new elements in the spiritual renaissance were to crystallize. Plato had accused rhetoric of being able only to teach men how to convince an audience, without pointing out any ideal to be pursued: and therefore of being only a practical means to provide intellectual instruments by which to achieve immoral ends.[24] That weakness in the pretensions of rhetoric was undeniable; and, at a time when the conscience of the best of the Greeks was constantly becoming more sensitive, it was a real danger for the art. In the adoption of the Panhellenic ideal, Isocrates saw the way to solve this problem also. The essential was to find a mean, as it were, between the moral indifference which had previously characterized rhetorical education, and the Platonic resolution of all politics into morality, which from a practical point of view was certain to lead away from all politics.[25] The new rhetoric had to find an ideal which could be ethically interpreted and which at the same time could be translated into practical political action. This ideal was a new moral code for Greece. It gave rhetoric an inexhaustible theme; in it the ultimate topic of all higher eloquence seemed to have been discovered once and for all. In an age when the old beliefs were losing their binding force and the long-established structure of the city-state was breaking up (the structure in which, till then, the individual had felt his own moral foundations securely embodied), the new dream of national achievement appeared to be a mighty inspiration. It gave life a new meaning.

In that critical time, therefore, Isocrates was, by his own choice of rhetoric as a career, driven to formulate the new ideals which we have described. It is entirely probable that he had been directly impelled towards them by Gorgias, whose *Olympicus* set forth the theme that was to be the centre of Isocrates' life-work. That happens often enough: in his last years a great master formulates an ideal, inspires his pupil with admiration for it, and through it shapes and directs his pupil's entire career. If Isocrates wanted to become a politician without being an orator, if he wished to assert himself as an educator and a rhetorical teacher against the competition of Socratic philosophy and of the earlier type of rhetoric, and to make head against their criticisms, he had found the only possible method of doing so in his concentration on the new ideal. That explains the doggedness with which he followed it to the end. His weak-

nesses make it easy enough to criticize him; but it is hard to
find a man who fulfilled his self-imposed task more completely
than Isocrates, and who was better suited to his own conception of his mission. That conception gave rhetoric the realistic
content which it had long been accused of lacking.[26] Through
it the teacher of rhetoric at last achieved the dignity which
put him on a level with the philosopher and made him independent of machine politicians—which actually gave him a
higher rank than they possessed, inasmuch as he represented a
higher interest than that of any separate state. The defects in
Isocrates' own nature—not only his physical weakness, but the
faults in his intellect and his character—and even the defects
of rhetoric itself were, through his programme, almost converted into virtues; or so it seemed. The rhetor, the political
pamphleteer and ideologist, has never since found himself in
such a favourable situation or commanded such a widespread
influence throughout an entire nation; and if his influence
lacked something in richness, power, and genius, Isocrates partially compensated for that by an exceptionally long life of
determined industry. Of course his determination does not affect
the quality of his work; but still it was a vital element in the
success of his mission, which, like that of the teacher, depended
on his relation to living men.

For centuries past, historians have seen in Isocrates nothing
more than a moralist, and have conceived him too exclusively
as a writer and publicist, too little as a teacher. They did not
fully realize that all his published writings, like those of Plato
and Aristotle, were ancillary to the educational programme of
his school. But the modern view of his career now does full
justice to the political content of his books, and understands
all their significance in the history of the fourth century. They
were of course intended to produce an effect even outside the
circle of his own pupils, and through them he often influenced
men who had never heard him teach. But at the same time his
political speeches were models of the new type of eloquence
which he taught in his school. Later, in the *Antidosis,* he himself exemplified to a wider public the special character of his
teaching, in a selection of passages taken from his most celebrated speeches. These speeches were intended to be models not

only of content but of form,[27] for in his teaching the two elements were inseparable. Whenever we try to re-create from the orations—which are our only evidence—the real character of the culture which he taught, we must always remember that dual purpose. Fortunately for us, he often expressed his views of his art and of his educational ideals; he often seized an opportunity to break off the thread of his argument, and to explain what he was saying, how he was saying it, and why. Indeed, at the beginning of his career he published several programme-works which clearly defined his position with reference to the other educational authorities of his time. We must start with them, if we are to comprehend the full extent of his activity, the true character of his paideia.

He had been a 'speech-writer', which in many respects corresponded to the profession of a barrister today; but we know nothing of the time when he abandoned that vocation for that of a teacher of rhetoric, or the reasons which led him to do so. Like Lysias, Isaeus, and Demosthenes, he had taken it up in order to make money—for his father's property had been largely destroyed by the war.[28] At a later time he was reluctant to mention that period of his career, although (as Aristotle humorously pointed out) volumes and volumes of the legal speeches he had written lay in the bookshops.[29] Only a few of them survive: his pupils, who had charge of editing his works after his death, had no more interest in preserving them than the master himself.[30] We can trace them no later than 390 or so.[31] Therefore, the foundation of Isocrates' school roughly coincided with that of Plato's.[32] In his introductory speech *Against the sophists,* it is clear that he has Plato's 'prospectuses', *Gorgias* and *Protagoras,* before him, and is deliberately trying to set up his own ideal of paideia in contrast to theirs.[32a] That takes us back to the same period. The incomparable value of that speech for us lies in the vividness with which it re-creates, blow upon blow, the first battle of the generation-long cultural war between the two great schools of education. And it is no less interesting for us to trace in it the immediate impression which Plato made on many of his contemporaries at his first appearance. Accustomed as we are to estimate his importance by the influence of his philosophy on more than twenty centuries of human history, we naturally imagine that he exercised the same powerful influence on the men of his own time. For that view Isocrates is a useful corrective.

He begins by saying that the representatives of paideia have a bad reputation, and he traces it to the excessive hopes which their self-advertisement excites among the public.[33] Thereby he steps forth to oppose the exaggerated estimates of the power of education that were customary in his day. And, as a matter of fact, there must have been something very bizarre in the revolutionary change from Socrates' loudly expressed doubts whether such a thing as education really existed, to the passionate educational conviction of Plato's earlier dialogues. Here as elsewhere, Isocrates represents the happy mean. He himself, of course, wants to be a teacher too; but he 'very well understands' the laymen who would rather do nothing about education at all than believe the enormous promises of professing philosophers.[34] How is it possible, he asks, to put any trust in their yearning for truth, when they themselves arouse so many false hopes? Isocrates names no names, but every word of his polemic is aimed straight at the Socratics, whom here and elsewhere he contemptuously calls 'disputers'.[35] In *Protagoras* and *Gorgias* Plato had presented dialectic as an art far superior to the long-winded orations of rhetoricians. His opponent makes short work of dialectic: he couples it with eristic—namely, argument for argument's sake. True philosophy always endeavoured to keep itself free from eristic,[36] although the methods of Plato's Socrates often seem to have much in common with it; and in fact there is a good deal of it in the earlier dialogues like *Protagoras* and *Gorgias*.[37] No wonder then that Isocrates does not see dialectic in the same favourable light as the Socratics, who thought it was a perfect panacea for all spiritual ills. The infallible knowledge of values (φϱόνησις) which they promise as the result of their teaching must appear to ordinary reasonable people to be something too great for mankind to attain.[38] Homer, who knew so well the frontiers that separate men from gods, claims that only the gods have such unerring insight, and he is right. What mortal man has the audacity to promise to give his disciples infallible knowledge (ἐπιστήμη) of everything they ought to do or leave undone, and to lead them through that knowledge to supreme happiness (εὐδαιμονία) ? [39]

In this criticism Isocrates has collected in a small space all the features which make Platonism repulsive to ordinary common sense: the peculiar technique of controversy by question-and-answer, the almost mythical importance which it attributes to phronésis (or knowledge of true values) as a special organ of reason, the apparently exaggerated intellectualism which holds knowledge to be the cure for everything, and the quasi-religious enthusiasm with which 'blessedness' is foretold to the philosopher. Obviously Isocrates is aiming some of his sharpest shafts at the terminological peculiarities of the new philosophical method: he tracks them down with the subtle instinct of the stylist for everything which seems odd or ludicrous to the average educated man; and by contrasting the Universal Virtue (πᾶσα ἀρετή), which is the putative aim of the Socratic knowledge of that which is 'good in itself',[40] with the trifling fees for which the philosophers sell their wisdom, he really makes the man in the street doubt whether what the young student learns from the philosopher is worth very much more than he pays for it.

He adds that the philosophers themselves cannot believe very strongly in the perfect virtue which they say they wish to release in the souls of their pupils, because the regulations of their school betray a far-reaching distrust of its members. They demand that the fees be paid into an Athenian bank in advance, before the pupil can be admitted.[41] They are justified, no doubt, in looking out for their own interests; but how can their attitude be reconciled with their claim to educate men to attain justice and self-mastery? This argument seems to us to be pitched rather too low; but it is not without wit. In *Gorgias* Plato had argued with just the same malice against the rhetors, who complain about the misuse their pupils make of the art of oratory, without seeing that they are accusing themselves—for if it were true that rhetoric improved its students, it would be impossible for those who had really learnt it to misuse it as they do.[42] Actually, the amoral character of rhetoric was the principal charge against it. In several different contexts, Isocrates supports the view represented by Gorgias in Plato's dialogue: the view that the teacher imparts to his pupil the art of rhetoric in order that he may use it rightly, and is not to blame if the pupil misuses it.[43] That is, he does not accept Plato's criticism, and maintains that Gorgias is wholly in the right. But he goes beyond that, and attacks the philosophers for distrusting their own pupils. That makes it probable that when he was writing the speech *Against the sophists* as an inaugural address, he knew Plato's *Gorgias* and deliberately set out to answer it.[44]

Plato's dialogue must have seemed particularly offensive to him as a pupil of Gorgias, and he must have felt himself arraigned in the person of his master: for, as we have shown, it was not only Gorgias himself but rhetoric in all its branches that Plato had impugned. All the typical doctrines of the 'eristics' which Isocrates ridicules in his inaugural speech *Against the sophists* had already been clearly enunciated in *Gorgias,* where they were analyzed with special reference to their significance for the new Platonic system of paideia.[45] (*Paideia* II, 126 f.) Plato and the Socratics are among the foremost of the opponents whom Isocrates attacks, and since he attacks them with special violence and completeness, it is clear that he fully understands the danger that threatens his ideal from their teaching. His invective is entirely realistic. He never makes it a theoretical refutation of his opponents' position, for he knows that if he did he would lose his case. The terrain he chooses is that of ordinary common sense. He appeals to the instincts of the man in the street—who, without comprehending the philosophers' technical secrets, sees that those who would lead their followers to wisdom and happiness have nothing themselves and get nothing from their students.[46] Their poverty did not harmonize with the traditional Greek concept of *eudaimonia,* perfect happiness, and other sophists—Antiphon, for instance—had already derided Socrates for exalting it.[46a] The man in the street sees that those who expose the contradictions in people's speeches do not notice the contradictions in their own acts; and that, although they profess to teach their pupils how to make the right decision on every problem of the future, they cannot say anything at all or give any correct advice about the present.[47] And when he further observes that the mob, whose conduct is based on nothing more than Opinion (δόξα), find it easier to agree with one another and to hit the right course of action than those who pretend to be in full possession of Knowledge (ἐπιστήμη), he is bound to end by despising the study of philosophy—concluding it to be empty chatter, mere hair-splitting, and certainly not 'the care of the soul' (ψυχῆς ἐπιμέλεια).[48]

This last point above all makes it certain that Isocrates is aiming his attacks at Plato and at the rest of the Socratics—Antisthenes in particular. He has deliberately—and in a way justifiably—mixed up their features into a composite portrait of 'the pupil of Socrates' which they all claimed to be.[48a] Nevertheless he knows very well that the pupils of Socrates are bitterly hostile to one another, and he converts their strife into another argument against professional philosophers—the favourite argument of common sense in every age. It was Antisthenes in particular who imitated his master's poverty and independence; while the abstract and theoretical aspects of Isocrates' portrait are principally drawn from Plato, and the description of philosophy as hair-splitting is obviously pointed at Plato's elaboration of dialectic into the art of logic.[48b] That was, as Isocrates rightly saw, a step into the sphere of theory and pure form. So he measures this new art of discovering contradictions—the art which attempts to conquer Opinion by Knowledge [49]—against the old Socratic aim of 'caring for the soul,' [50] and throws doubt on its ability to achieve that aim. Thereby he concludes his criticism precisely at the point where (as history shows) the real problem lies. And so, in the argument which we here witness between Plato and Isocrates, there is unfolded part of the long series of conflicts through which the ideal of culture has been developed—a dialectic process which still retains a deep and permanent value, independently of the small personal details of the dispute.

The second group of opponents attacked by Isocrates are described by him as teachers of politics.[51] They do not, like the philosophers, search for the truth. They simply practise their techné—their craft, in the old sense of the word,[52] whereby it implied no trace of moral responsibility. In *Gorgias*, Plato had asserted that true rhetoric ought, like the craft of the doctor, to entail such moral responsibility.[53] Isocrates could not deny Plato's claim; and the moral factor is especially prominent in his treatment of the third group of his opponents, the teachers of forensic oratory. But he did not assert its validity simply in

order to exalt Plato. His criticism of those who teach the craft
of making political speeches introduces us to a type of education
which was the absolute opposite of philosophy—the art of
extempore speechmaking. As typical of the specialist in this subject we must think of Isocrates' own fellow-student in the school
of Gorgias, Alcidamas [54]—who like him published several model
speeches, but whose forte was improvisation (αὐτοσχεδιάζειν).
One of his speeches, which has been preserved, is significantly
aimed against rhetors like Isocrates, who can write well enough
but are incapable of seizing the critical moment to say the words
demanded by the immediate situation.[55] There can be no doubt
that the constant practice of this technique was invaluable
training for the student who intended to be an active public
speaker, even although the actual teaching often degenerated
into mere routine instruction, and grossly neglected the higher
claims of art. This class of his opponents Isocrates charges with
lack of taste: they have, he affirms, no aesthetic sense.[56] In practice, their type of rhetoric turns out to be nothing more than a
collection of formal devices which the pupil gets off by heart
and can bring into play at any moment. It enlarges neither his
intellect nor his experience, but merely teaches him the patterns
of speechmaking as abstract forms to be learnt by rote, as the
elementary teacher teaches little children the alphabet.[57] This
method is a fine example of the contemporary trend towards
mechanizing both education and life itself as far as possible.
Isocrates seizes the opportunity to distinguish his own artistry
from this empty commercialized technique, and to clear himself
from the charge which he might well have incurred through his
distaste for the subtleties of philosophical education—the charge
of being narrow-mindedly practical. What he is looking for is
the middle way between highflown theory and vulgar penny-
chasing technical adroitness; and he finds it in artistically disciplined Form.[58] In this he introduces a third principle. Here again
we find that he explains himself and his ideal by contrast with
another point of view. But by thus waging war on two fronts,
he shows that his conflict with philosophical education, important as it is, expresses only half of his own ideal. He is just
as far removed in the other direction from rhetoric in the
accepted sense. For, in the sphere of rhetoric as well as in that
of philosophy, Isocrates' paideia was something perfectly new.

More than any other sphere of life, the art of oratory resists the effort of systematic reason to reduce all individual facts to a number of established *schemata,* basic forms. In the realm of logic Plato calls these basic forms the Ideas. As we have seen, he took this three-dimensional mode of describing them from contemporary medical science, and applied it to the analysis of Being. In rhetoric we can see the same process in operation at the same time, though we cannot definitely say that it was directly influenced by Plato's use of the term *idea.* Medicine and rhetoric were by their very nature the spheres in which this conception of basic forms or Ideas could be developed—for medicine reduces a number of apparently different physiological events to a few fundamental types; and rhetoric likewise simplifies what seem to be separate and distinct political or legal situations. The essence of both skills is to analyse the individual case into its general aspects, so as to make it easier to treat in practice. The comparison of these general patterns to the letters of the alphabet (στοιχεῖα)—which we find in Isocrates here, and later in Plato—was obvious enough. The act of reading is just the same as that of political or forensic or medical diagnosis: a large number of variously assembled shapes are reduced to a limited number of basic 'elements', and thus the meaning of each of the apparently manifold shapes is recognized.[59] In science too, the 'elements' which make up physical nature were first called by that name in the same period, and the same analogy, drawn from language and the letters of the alphabet, lies behind it.[60] Isocrates of course does not by any means reject the doctrine of a rhetorical system of Ideas. In fact, his writings show that he largely adopted that doctrine, and that he took as the foundation of his own teaching the mastery of the basic forms of oratory. But oratory which knew no more than these forms would be as sounding brass and a tinkling cymbal. The letters of the alphabet, immovable and unchangeable, are the most complete contrast to the fluid and manifold situations of human life, whose full and rich complexity can be brought under no rigid rule.[61] Perfect eloquence must be the individual expression of a single critical moment, a *kairos,* and its highest law is that it should be wholly appropriate. Only by observing these two rules can it succeed in being new and original.[62]

In a word, oratory is imaginative literary creation. Though
it dare not dispense with technical skill, it must not stop short
at that.[63] Just as the sophists had believed themselves to be the
true successors of the poets, whose special art they had transferred into prose, so Isocrates too feels that he is continuing
the poets' work, and taking over the function which until a
short time before him they had fulfilled in the life of his nation.
His comparison between rhetoric and poetry is far more than a
passing epigram. Throughout his speeches the influence of this
point of view can be traced. The panegyric on a great man is
adapted from the hymn, while the hortative speech follows the
model of the protreptic elegy and the didactic epic. And, in
these types, Isocrates copies even the order of his ideas from
the well-established traditional order which was a rule in each
of the corresponding poetic genera. More than that: the position
and prestige of the orator are determined by this parallel with
the poet. The new vocation must support itself on an old and
firmly-established one, and take its standards therefrom. The
less Isocrates hopes or wishes to succeed as a practical statesman, the more he needs the prestige of poetry to set off his
spiritual aims; and even in the educational spirit by which his
rhetoric is inspired, he is deliberately emulating what the Greeks
conceived to be the educational function of the poets of old.
Later, indeed, he compares his work with that of the sculptor
(as Pindar had done) and proudly puts himself on a level
with Phidias; [64] but that is more to illustrate the fact that there
are still some who, despite the loftiness of his art, consider
the rhetor's profession to be something second-rate. The classical Greeks had always tended to depreciate the sculptor's trade
a little, as resembling the work of a common artisan—and that
although the word *sculptor* could be applied to every worker in
stone, from the ordinary mason to the creator of the Parthenon.
But later, as the prestige of the plastic arts and their great
masters gradually rose in the post-classical centuries, the comparison of oratory to sculpture and painting seems to become
commoner. However, the dynastic succession of rhetoric to
poetry remained the true image of the spiritual process in which
rhetoric arose as a new cultural force: all late Greek poetry is
simply the offspring of rhetoric.[65]

Naturally, Isocrates' view of the educational value of rhetoric is defined by this conception of its true character. Being an act of creation, oratory in its highest ranges cannot possibly be taught like a school subject. And yet he holds that it can be employed to educate young men: because of his own peculiar view of the relation between the three factors which, according to the pedagogic theories of the sophists, are the foundation of all education. They are: (1) talent, (2) study, and (3) practice. The current enthusiasm for education and culture had helped to create and disseminate exaggerated views of their powers; [66] but that enthusiasm had been succeeded by a certain disillusionment—due partly to Socrates' far-reaching criticisms of the limitations and pretensions of education,[67] and partly to the discovery that many a young man whom the sophists had educated was no better than those who had never enjoyed such advantages.[68] Isocrates explains the exact value of education with great care. He asserts that natural talent is the principal factor, and admits that great gifts, untrained, often achieve more than mere training without ability—if indeed it is possible to speak of training when there is nothing there to train. The element second in importance is experience, practice.[69] It would appear that until then professional rhetors had theoretically recognized the trinity—talent, study, practice—but had in their own courses pushed study and training into the foreground. Isocrates modestly relegates training (*paideusis*) to the third rank. It can, he says, achieve much if it is helped by talent and experience. It makes speakers more clearly conscious of their art, stimulates their inventive faculty, and saves them much vague and unsuccessful searching. Even a less gifted pupil can be improved and intellectually developed by training, although he can never be made into a distinguished orator or writer.[70]

Rhetorical training, says Isocrates, can teach insight into the 'ideas' or basic patterns out of which every speech is built. He appears to mean that this phase of it, hitherto the only one which had been cultivated, was capable of far profounder development; and we would gladly hear more of his new doctrine of ideas, to be able to compare it with that of the older rhetors. But the real difficulty of the subject does not lie in that aspect of it—all the less so because it is taught so thoroughly. It lies in the right choice, commixture, and placing of the 'ideas' on each subject, in the selection of the correct moment, in the good

taste and appropriateness with which the speech is decorated
with enthymemes, and in the rhythmic and musical disposition
of the words.[71] To do all that correctly needs a powerful and
sensitive mind. This, the highest stage of training, assumes in
the pupil full knowledge of the 'ideas' of speech and skill in
their employment; from the teacher it requires the ability to
expound everything which can be rationally taught, and beyond
that—i.e. in everything which cannot be taught—it demands
that he should make himself a model for his pupils: so that
those who can form themselves by imitating him may at once
achieve a richer and more graceful style than any others.[72]

Plato, in *The Republic,* later declared that the highest culture
could be attained only if certain qualities which are rarely found
together were to coincide. Similarly, Isocrates asserts that it is
impossible for the teacher to succeed unless all the factors which
we have mentioned are brought into play at once.[73] Here the
general Greek idea, that education is the process by which the
whole man is shaped, is enunciated independently of Plato, and
variously expounded in such imagery as 'model' or 'pattern'
(παράδειγμα), 'stamp' (ἐκτυποῦν), 'imitate' (μιμεῖσθαι).[74] The real
problem is how this process of 'shaping' can be converted from a
beautiful image into a practical reality—that is, what is to be the
method of forming the human character, and ultimately what
is the *nature* of the human intellect. Plato seeks to form the soul
through knowledge of the Ideas as absolute norms of the Good,
the Just, the Beautiful, etc., and thus eventually to develop it into
an intelligible cosmos which contains all being within itself. No
such universe of knowledge exists for Isocrates. For him, rhetorical training is worked out simply by Opinion, not by Knowledge.
But he frequently claims that the intellect possesses an aesthetic
and practical faculty which, without claiming absolute knowledge, can still choose the right means and the right end.[75] His
whole conception of culture is based on that aesthetic power.
Plato's dialectic guides the young student step by step towards
the Ideas; but that still leaves it to him to employ them in his life
and conduct, and the way in which he employs them cannot be
rationally explained. In the same way Isocrates can describe only
the elements and the separate stages of the educational act. The
formative process itself remains a mystery. Nature can neither
be wholly banished from it, nor be put wholly in control of it.

Therefore, everything in education depends on the proper co-operation of nature and art. If we once decide that Isocrates' incompleteness (as Plato would call it) and his reliance on mere Opinion (which Plato called the vital force of all rhetoric) were imposed on him by his subject, then we must conclude that his resolute self-limitation, and his deliberate renunciation of everything 'higher,' everything which he felt to be obscure and doubtful, were a sort of constitutional weakness converted by him into a strength. This, in the sphere of culture, is the same thing that assured Isocrates' own personal success: he has made a virtue of necessity. He recognizes the empirical character of rhetoric; and, whether or not it is right to call it a true techné or art— Plato in *Gorgias* had claimed that it was not—Isocrates holds fast to its empiricism. Therein he clings to the principle of *imitation* established by his predecessors—the principle which in the future was to play such an enormous part in rhetoric and (as literature came more and more under the influence of rhetoric) in every branch of literature. Here we know more of his method of teaching than we do of his attitude to the rhetorical doctrine of ideas; for all his great speeches were meant to be models in which his pupils could study the precepts of his art.

He spends little time on the third group of educators, the writers of forensic speeches. Obviously he considers them his weakest opponents—although Plato attacked them a good many years later in *Phaedrus,* and therefore thought them fairly important even then. It is clear that Isocrates believes their rivalry far less dangerous than that of the new philosophical culture, in which he recognizes the real threat to his own ideals. The forensic speechmakers were out to make money, and their product was meant for practical use. We know their technique from the sample speeches published by Antiphon, Lysias, Isaeus, Demosthenes, and even Isocrates himself at the outset of his career. This type of literature is one of the most remarkable plants in the garden of Greek literature—and a native Attic vegetable at that. The Athenian mania for litigation, so delightfully satirized by the comedians, is the obverse of the firm legality of the Athenian state: of that foundation in Law of which its citizens were so proud. It produced a universal interest in *agones*— lawsuits and prosecutions. The model speeches written by the logographers served both as advertisements for their authors, as patterns for their pupils to copy, and as interesting reading-matter for the public.[76] Here too Isocrates manifests the more sensitive taste of the younger generation. Ironically he recommends that the logographers should leave it to the enemies of rhetoric (already numerous enough) to display this, its least attractive side, instead of proudly dragging it out into the glare of publicity; and he adds that anything that can be learnt in rhetoric is just as valuable in other spheres as in legal disputes. We need not question the sincerity of this attitude. It explains quite clearly why Isocrates abandoned the profession. He felt that the speechwriter was morally far below the philosopher.[77] Clearly he is thinking not only of the men who write speeches for use in law courts, but of all kinds of rhetors, since he includes them all under the name of 'teachers of political oratory'.[78] Doubtless the subjects investigated in philosophical education are not worth the trouble, and the arguers who 'wallow' in debates would get into serious danger if they applied their conclusions to real facts (here Isocrates is quoting Callicles in Plato's *Gorgias,* and taking his side too), but at least the fact that the rhetors talk about a better subject, politics, must not keep us from recognizing that in practice they generally misuse it and become interfering and ambitious busybodies. Thus Isocrates follows Plato in his criticism of the political orators, though he does not accept his positive conclusions. He does not believe that virtue can be taught, any more than the aesthetic sense. Plato refuses to grant the name of *techné* to any kind of education which does not teach virtue; and Isocrates frankly thinks it impossible to create such education. Nevertheless, he is inclined to concede that education of a political tendency might have some ethical influence if it were practised in the manner he recommends, not in the amoral way represented by earlier rhetoricians.[79]

The striking thing about Isocrates' conception of Plato's paideia, as set forth in his speech *Against the sophists,* is that he entirely overlooks the political content of his opponent's theories. From Plato's early dialogues he must have got the same impression as they made, until a short time ago, on most modern readers—that their author's sole concern was moral reformation, an ideal which is somehow strangely connected with dialectic reasoning. The superiority of rhetoric, as Isocrates conceives it, is that it is entirely political culture. All that it has to do to attain spiritual leadership in the state is to find a new approach to life and its problems. The older type of rhetoric missed many important opportunities because it was content to serve day-to-day politics as an instrument, instead of rising above it. From this we can see that Isocrates believed he could inspire the political life of his nation with a higher moral creed. Unfortunately only a fragment of the speech on the sophists now survives, without the principal section, which doubtless explained his new ideal. Isocrates must have changed his attitude to Plato's cultural plans as soon as he understood the political aspect of his philosophy. Actually, he had already been warned by Plato's *Gorgias* that Socrates was the only real statesman of his age, because he alone tried to make his fellow-citizens better.[80] That might well be interpreted as pure paradox—especially by Isocrates, who held that the moving impulse of all contemporary writers was to struggle for originality at all costs, hunting out hitherto unheard-of paradoxes on every subject, and who feared (with justice) that he could not rival Plato and the other philosophers in that exercise. But later, in his *Philip,* he reviews Plato's life-work not long after his death, and treats him as a very great political theorist, whose theories could unfortunately never be put into practice.[81] When did he first change his view of Plato's character and philosophy?

We can find the answer in his *Helen. Helen* is a model encomium, addressed to a mythical personage, and paradoxically praising her although she was generally reviled. The exact date of its composition is unknown, but it was obviously written soon after the speech *Against the sophists*—namely, while Isocrates' school was yet new. A lower limit for its date is fixed by the singular form which Isocrates, towards the end, gives to the praise of his heroine: it was she, he says, who first brought about national unity among the Greeks, in the war against Troy that resulted from her abduction.[82] Thus he makes Helen a mythical symbol of the political aspirations which he expressed more fully soon after that, in the *Panegyricus* (380)—of the great struggle to unite the Greek states in a national crusade against the barbarians. In this first decade Isocrates is still moving in the paths

beaten out by Gorgias. The relation between his *Panegyricus* and
Gorgias' *Olympicus* is the same as that between his *Helen* and
Gorgias' *Defence of Helen*. The little speech is (as he says [83])
a first-fruits offering suitable for a man of paideia. It is interesting because of its renewed polemics against the Socratic school
and its cultural ideal.[84] Here again, as in the speech on the sophists, he blends the features of Plato and Antisthenes in a composite portrait. His attack is aimed, not at one particular person, but at the entire tendency of the new movement. Isocrates says he cannot interpret their utterances as anything
more than attempts at paradoxical wit, when some of them
(Antisthenes) teach that it is impossible to make a false statement, or to make two contradictory assertions about the same
thing, while others (Plato) try to prove that courage, wisdom
and justice are one and the same, and that none of these qualities is implanted in us by nature, but that they are all attained
by one and the same knowledge (ἐπιστήμη).[85] Here Isocrates really
does distinguish the Socratics from those who are mere arguers,
who teach nobody, but only try to make difficulties for others.
He objects that all of them try to refute others (ἐλέγχειν), although they themselves have long since been refuted,[86] and that
their paradoxes are thrown into the shade by those of their predecessors the sophists: for instance, by Gorgias' statement that
no existing thing exists, or Zeno's, that the same thing is both
possible and impossible, or Melissus', that the apparently infinite
multitude of things is really one.[87]

With this pettifogging, Isocrates contrasts the simple effort
to find out what is true: which he conceives to be the effort to
get experience of reality and to educate oneself for political
action. Philosophers are always chasing the phantom of pure
knowledge, but no one can use their results. Is it not better to
spend one's time on the things which people really need, even
if we cannot achieve exact knowledge, but only approximate
opinions about them? He reduces his own attitude towards
Plato's ideal of scientific accuracy and thoroughness to the
formula that the smallest advance in our knowledge of really
important things is better than the greatest intellectual mastery
of unimportant trifles which are irrelevant to our life.[88] As a good
psychologist, he evidently understands how much young men
love dialectical disputation—for at their age, they have no

interest in serious private or public problems, and the more futile a game, the more they enjoy it.[89] But those who profess to teach them deserve reproach for allowing them to be charmed by it. They incur thereby the same guilt of which they accuse forensic orators—they corrupt the youth.[90] They do not shrink from preaching the absurd doctrine that the life of beggars and exiles, deprived of all political rights and duties, is happier than that of others—namely, of the full citizens who remain peacefully in their native land. (This is clearly an allusion to the ethical individualism and cosmopolitanism of the radical wing in the Socratic school—Antisthenes, Aristippus, and their followers.[91]) He finds the other philosophers to be even more ridiculous: those who think that their moral paradoxes really contribute something to the spiritual upbuilding of the state. This can only be a hit at Plato, who held that Socrates' moral evangel was true political science.[92] If we are right in this identification, it was as early as the 'eighties, soon after he wrote his speech *Against the sophists,* that Isocrates changed his views of Plato's cultural ideal, and recognized that it too had political implications. Only he felt that its concentration on individual morality and on dialectical quibbles—which seemed to him the distinguishing tendency of Plato's educational system—was absolutely irreconcilable with the universally useful purpose which it professed to serve.

Thus, as Isocrates and Plato appear to approach nearer and nearer to each other in the practical aim of their cultural theories, Isocrates' disapproval for Plato's abstract 'roundabout way' [93] becomes more and more pronounced. He knows only the direct route. There is in his system none of the inward tension that exists in the mind of Plato between the urgent will to action and the long philosophical preparation for action. True, he stands far enough away from the politics of his day and the activity of contemporary statesmen to understand Plato's objection to them. But, as a man who keeps to the middle way, he cannot appreciate the bold ethical claims of the Socratic system, which creates a gulf between the state and the individual. He does not look to Utopia for the improvement of political life. He embodies the rooted hatred of the propertied and cultured bourgeoisie both for the mad eccentricities of mob-rule and for the tyranny of individuals, and he has a strong admiration for respectability. But he has none of Plato's uncompromising passion for reformation, no thought of introducing such a terrific intensity into everyday life. Therefore, he does not realize the enormous educational power which lies in Plato's thought: he judges its value exclusively by its immediate utility for the particular political question which interests him. This is the internal condition of Greece, and the future relations of the Greek states to one another, after the great war. The Peloponnesian war had clearly demonstrated that the existing regime could not be permanent, and that the whole Greek world had to be rebuilt. When he wrote *Helen,* Isocrates was already at work on his great manifesto, the *Panegyricus.* Its purpose was to show the world that his school was able to state, in a new language, new ideals—not only for the moral life of the individual, but for the entire nation of the Hellenes.

3

POLITICAL CULTURE AND THE PANHELLENIC IDEAL

RHETORIC is, to begin with, an instrument of practical politics. But as soon as it is able to formulate ideals of statesmanship, it becomes the representative of a political form of culture. Isocrates discovered this through his rivalry with philosophy. For what Plato criticized most devastatingly in rhetoric was the moral indifference and the concentration on pure form which kept it from being more than a tool in the hands of greedy and unscrupulous politicians. That was why he believed philosophy to be the only true rhetoric. Isocrates saw that the great advantage of philosophy as an educational force was that it possessed a lofty moral ideal. And yet he believed neither that its ideal was the only one with any claim to respect, nor that the means chosen by the philosophers were likely to attain it. Accordingly, he determined to make rhetoric into the one true culture, by giving it 'the highest things' as its content.[1] No more than the sophists who had taught rhetoric before him, no more than Plato, no more than Aristotle, did he doubt that all culture which is more than specialist training for a particular vocation must be political culture. But still rhetoric lacked a great mission, some task which could release the formative forces latent within it. The sole reason that all previous rhetoric seemed jejune and affected was that it had always chosen the wrong starting-point. The improvement of style and language is not merely a matter of technique. The ideal of 'art for art's sake' is nowhere less possible than in the realm of literature. Again and again, Isocrates stresses the point that for the speaker or writer everything depends on the greatness of the subject with which he has to deal.

Therefore the subject of rhetoric must always be 'political'—although the word 'political' was, even as Isocrates wrote, changing its old simple meaning. Literally, it means 'concerning the *polis*'—i.e. that which helps or harms the community. But although ultimately the polis was still the frame for all public life, the great events of the fifth century had created new patterns and revealed new needs. The collapse of the Periclean empire had left open one urgent question. Would Athens slowly rebuild her shattered forces and then once more enter the path of imperialist expansion which had already led her to the brink of ruin? Or could some *modus vivendi* be established between Sparta, the sole ruler of Greece for the time at least, and the conquered queen of the seas?—some compromise which would give each of the two great states not only room to live but a common task which would transcend their individual interests? The professional politicians continued to think along traditional lines. They resumed their Machiavellian struggles for power: even in the 'nineties the Corinthian war showed that the Greek states were busy forming themselves into a new power-bloc, with a defence-system clearly aimed at immobilizing Sparta. But Isocrates strove to find an outlet for the surplus energies of the Greeks: some form of political or economic expansion which might at the same time resolve the internal conflicts of the exasperated Greek states. He was very far, of course, from believing that everlasting peace could be secured. But, seeing the destructive effects of war on the life of every Greek city, conqueror as well as conquered, no cultivated man could seriously look on and watch this noble nation slowly and incessantly hacking itself to death. Men 'of good will' and high intelligence felt that they were bound to discover some counter-charm to free the Greeks from the ghastly enchantment which lay upon them. Imperialism was inevitable. Then let it be directed against other peoples, naturally hostile to the Greeks and standing on a lower level of civilization. It could not continue to be exercised by Greeks against Greeks—the moral sense of the age felt that to be intolerable. Ultimately, it threatened not only the conquered state, but the entire Greek race, with complete annihilation.

For a long time harmony had been praised by poets and sophists as one of the highest of all goods; but since the time when Aeschylus in *The Eumenides* had presented the harmony of the citizens of one city as the divinely sanctified ideal of all political life,[2] the problem had become more complicated and its sphere had broadened. The only harmony which could be of any use now was one which embraced all the Hellenes. The feeling was growing in Greece that all its peoples spoke the same language (although in different dialects), that they were all members of an invisible political community, and that they owed one another mutual respect and mutual assistance.[3] There were of course some advanced liberals who saw no reason why this sense of solidarity should stop at the frontiers of Hellenism. They held that the bond of humanity itself was all-embracing, and was naturally stronger than the bond of nationhood. Plato makes the sophist Hippias advance this view in *Protagoras,* and Antiphon too expresses it in his *Truth.*[4] Still, it must have seemed highly abstract in an age when the Greeks had been suffering far more from one another than from other nations, and when the immediate problem was how to reconcile warring neighbours and quench the hatred of brothers. During the great war, tragic and comic poets had often raised their voices, not only in passionate utterances of hatred and vendetta, but in wise patriotic reminders of common origin and common nationality.[5] After the war, that idea must have spread more and more widely. It had once been almost entirely foreign to the Greek, whose thought limited itself to the narrow frontiers of the city-state; but conscious opposition binds neighbours closer together than peaceful isolation. Plato himself in *The Republic* is clearly affected by these new ideas. Their influence is shown in the ethical principles which he lays down for the conduct of war among Greek states.[6] And in his letters, he holds that the common interest of all the Sicilian Greeks justifies the concentration of all political power in the hands of the tyrant Dionysius, if he would only consent to give his state a constitution and abandon the arbitrary rule of despotism.[7] Aristotle, whose political theories do not transcend the old city-state frontiers, nevertheless declares that if the Greeks were united they could rule the world.[8] Therefore the idea of joint Greek action, if not of a permanent confederation of all Greeks, seriously occupied the minds of the men of the fourth century. In their political ideas, there was little to foreshadow a unified national state; and the conditions of the life which the Greeks called 'political', the life in which the citizen was at once free and actively engaged in serving the community, were too intimately connected with the narrowness of the city-state's spiritual frontier, to be transferred without difficulty to the looser texture of citizenship in a broader territorial framework. But with the growing consciousness of national solidarity there was growing up a system of ethical restraints which extended far beyond the city-state, and thereby limited the state's selfish devotion to egotistic power-politics. If we look for the origins of this new consciousness, we shall find they lie deep in the community of blood, language, religion, custom, and history. Yet, at an earlier time, these supra-rational forces would not have produced the same effect of conscious purpose. The Greek sentiment now awaking was created by education and culture. And, in its turn, Greek paideia was hugely stimulated and enriched by being filled with this newly-fermenting Panhellenic ideal.

The new partnership between culture and awakening national sentiment is immortalized in the *Panegyricus* of Isocrates. At the beginning of the speech, the current depreciation of intellectual culture is contrasted with the traditional exaltation of gymnastic contests.[9] And that itself is symbolic. For Isocrates chooses to disguise his essay as a rhetorical show-piece declaimed at one of the great Panhellenic assemblies, and at once the old contrast, first stated by Xenophanes [10] on a like occasion, falls naturally into place. For Isocrates, whose principles keep him from entering the arena of the people's parliament as a political debater, the festally ornate epideictic style is the natural one; and therefore the *panegyris,* the great formal assembly, is the natural milieu in which he can produce his greatest intellectual effect.[11] During the festivals of Olympia and Pytho the truce of God enjoined all the warring Greeks to lay down their arms. Where then could Isocrates have found a better atmosphere in which to advocate the unity of all Greece? From ages immemorial the gymnastic contests had been the most visible expression of the ideal unity of the whole Greek stock; but was the gift of reason not worth more to the community than all athletic feats? That was what Xenophanes had asked—comparing the services done to the polis by philosophical knowledge and by athletic excellence.[12] Isocrates now repeats his predecessor's question; but he is thinking, not of the polis, but of the community of Greece.[13] His theme is no less great in its opportunities for stylistic display than in its potential value to the

whole nation: for he is advising the Greek states to unite with
one another and make war on the barbarians.[14] As a true Greek,
he does not seek to excuse himself, but challenges all those who
think they know the truth better than he to come forward: he is
sure of himself, not because of the novelty of his theme, but
because of the completeness of his treatment of it.[15]

He attacks the subject at its core, the practical problem. At
the moment he is speaking, his proposals would seem to have
not the faintest chance of success. The first necessity is to lay
the groundwork. Sparta and Athens must be reconciled; and
these, the two strongest states, must share the hegemony of
Greece. That is what Isocrates hopes to attain through his
speech.[16] But even if it is impossible, he wants at least to make
the whole world realize who is standing in the way of the
happiness of the Greeks, and to establish once and for all the
justice of Athens' claim to naval supremacy.[17] For that is the
real point of dispute. He undertakes to trace the history of
Athenian leadership so as to show its continuity, and to fore-
stall the possible objection that every leadership must in time
change hands.[18] Athens acquired the hegemony earliest, and did
most to deserve it by her service to the rest of Greece.[19] That
is a theme worthy of Thucydides, and without that great model
Isocrates could hardly have worked it out as he does. Like him,
he makes the achievements of Athens culminate in her cham-
pionship of Greek unity during the Persian invasions. But
Thucydides saw Athenian power in the full light of the present:
he conceived it as built up in the latest stage of Greek political
development, the relatively brief period since the battle of
Salamis.[20] Isocrates substitutes for that a picture of Athenian
greatness which reaches back to the age of prehistory and
legend. There he sees reflected the pride of leadership to which
he summons Athens once again—as the asylum for political
refugees unjustly persecuted in their homeland, the bulwark
of Greece against the attacks of greedy barbarians, and the
protector of weak states threatened by powerful tyrants. This is
in fact exactly how Athens conceived her own role in the political life of Greece. Its ideology is more like that of British
foreign policy than anything else of the kind. Or, from another
point of view, this retrospective interpretation of Athens' early
history by her modern political aspirations can be best paralleled

by Treitschke's re-interpretation of the early history of Prussia in the light of her later leadership in the German Empire. But the pseudo-historical past of myth is more easily 'remodelled to the heart's desire' than a later period better known to history. At all times, the plastic world of legend had shaped itself to the artist's hand and symbolized his own ideas; and now, when the sagas of old Attica were remodelled by rhetoric to prove that since before the dawn of history Athens had been the champion and liberator of Greece, it was only the latest stage in an incessant poetic metamorphosis. That political legend had first taken shape in public speeches over the graves of the heroic dead, and on similar occasions, during the rise of Athenian supremacy in the fifth century. When Isocrates stood forward to preach the restoration of that supremacy, he found the legend an instrument ready to his hand.[21]

Thus, by interpreting the whole historical and legendary past of Athens as her gradual schooling for the task of Greek leadership, Isocrates takes a theme worthy of Thucydides, and actually used by him, but projects it into the past as Thucydides would never have done. And he does the same with another of Thucydides' great conceptions, one which he connects very closely with the ideal of Athenian hegemony—the mission of Athens as creatrix of culture. In Pericles' funeral speech [22] Thucydides had portrayed Athens at the height of her power and magnificence as the *paideusis,* the school of all Greece. This point of view combined her political with her intellectual and spiritual service to the Hellenic cause. Even in Thucydides the spiritual leadership of Athens is the real justification of her extension of political mastery.[23] But Isocrates goes beyond his model. He pushes the intellectual mission of Athens far behind his own age (in which it was still strong and gaining strength) and far behind the age of Pericles, into the legendary days of primitive Athens. He thus creates a static historical picture, conceived on this one plane alone. With an obvious allusion to the sophistic parallel between paideia and agriculture as the basis of all civilization, the activity in which man first put behind him the wild, bestial life of nomad and savage,[24] he begins his history of culture with the appearance of agriculture. The legend of the wanderings of Demeter asserted that it had originated in Eleusis, in connexion with the foundation of the Mysteries.[25] Thus mankind's progress towards a settled peaceful life and a higher moral code was associated with the origin of a nobler and more personal form of religion—for it was in that aspect that the Mysteries, with their strongly ethical tone, had awakened particular interest in the fourth century.[26] And at the same time, this journeying back into a legendary past allowed Isocrates to trace the origins of all culture to the soil of Attica, where (as he held) it was later to reach the highest stage of its development and spiritual power, in the form of paideia. Every national and cultural myth is created in the same way—by narrowing the field of vision and extolling one particular nation's achievements to the pinnacle of the absolute. It is meant to be accepted as a creed rather than judged true as a sober scientific fact. Therefore it cannot be countered by historical facts. It can quite well be combined with full knowledge of foreign nations and foreign cultures—it would be a mistake to think that Isocrates knew nothing of Egypt, Phoenicia, or Babylon. It is his faith in the unique mission of Athenian culture that is triumphant in his philosophy of history, and above all in his interpretation of the legendary past. Isocrates' nationalistic ideology (in which Athens is the founder of all civilization), along with all the other ideas implicit in his paideia, was later taken over by humanism as part of its general view of history.

The picture of Athenian civilization in the *Panegyricus* is a variation of that drawn by Pericles in the funeral speech. The stark lines of Thucydides' portrayal here melt into the lavish curves of rhetorical decoration—and yet not so fully but that they can be traced everywhere, shining gracefully through the overlay. Isocrates freely develops certain themes which he judges important, and adds others taken from the Attic poets. Thus, when he describes the act by which Athens set the model for all states based on law, the abolition of private vendetta and its replacement by the jurisdiction of the state's law courts, he is clearly modelling his description on Aeschylus' *The Eumenides*.[27] The rise of the arts (τέχναι), from the lowest stage where the skills necessary to life are worked out, to that which promotes comfort and pleasure—we should call it the progress from crafts to fine arts—is a favourite Greek idea, which meets us often in the fourth century.[28] Isocrates transfers to Athens this whole process of spiritual development, in which is implicit the origin of paideia itself.²⁹ Thus he sees the city, which had at all times been the refuge for every unfortunate, as at the same time the favoured home of those who sought the sweets of life. The essence of Athenian culture, in contradistinction to the exclusive Spartan attitude, is not to repel strangers but to attract them.³⁰ The economic exchange of goods by export and import is only the material expression of this spiritual principle. He makes the Piraeus the focus of the whole commercial life of Greece. And, similarly, he makes the Attic festivals the great social centre of the Hellenic world. In the immense throngs of strangers and in the many-sided intellectual intercourse which takes place there, both the wealth and the art of Athens and Greece are displayed and harmonized with one another.³¹ Besides the athletic contests of strength and agility which have, many centuries ago, set their mark on all Greece, contests of intellect and eloquence have grown up in Athens. They have made, out of the brief national festivals at Olympia and Pytho, one single uninterrupted panegyris.³² It is deeply interesting to see how Isocrates again and again conceives the essence of culture as a purposeless intellectual and spiritual activity—an ideal parallel to that of the gymnastic contests. Rhetoric does not define; it represents, through contrast and comparison. And so, although rhetoricians constantly extol its practical usefulness for the community, its real meaning continues to be *epideixis*—the speaker's display of his own intellectual powers: an activity of which no barbarian ever feels himself in need.

Philosophy—the love of culture and education—was the truly characteristic creation of Athens.³³ That does not mean that all the work of the spirit was done in that one city, but that it was there focused to a burning centre, and that its rays streamed out thence with increased vehemence. More and more powerful grew the feeling for that special atmosphere in which alone the strange and delicate plant of culture can live and grow. We have seen it described in poetry, in Euripides' *Medea,* and philosophically analysed in Plato's *The Republic.*³⁴ In the idealized picture at which Isocrates was gazing, there was no room for the tragic problems which made Plato keenly aware of the dangers of his milieu. It was this universal striving after intellectual possessions, after knowledge and wisdom, that made the Athenians what they were, and attuned them to that peculiar gentleness, moderation, and harmony that is the mark of civilization. Among the legion of human sufferings, the force of reason has learnt to distinguish those which are caused by mere ignorance from those which are inevitable, and has made us able to bear the inevitable with dignity. That is what Athens 'revealed' to mankind—and here Isocrates uses a word (κατέδειξε) which is usually kept for the founder of a mystery-cult.[35] Men are raised above the animals by their ability to speak their thoughts.[36] Neither courage, nor wealth, nor similar goods which characterize other nations, really distinguish the man who knows and is aware from him who is half-aware and half-conscious: nothing but intellectual culture, which can be recognized through his speech. Every useful attempt to raise the condition of mankind, whatever be its content, must take its form from language; and so the logos, in its double sense of 'speech' and 'reason', becomes for Isocrates the *symbolon,* the 'token' of culture. That was a happy conception: it assured rhetoric of its place, and made the rhetorician the truest representative of culture.[37]

The Isocratean ideal of culture is a national one. In the truly Hellenic way, Isocrates bases it on the fact that man is a free political being and part of a civilized community. But he extends it further and makes it universal. Through its intellectual culture, Athens has attained such superiority over the rest of mankind that her pupils have become the teachers of the whole world.[38] In this he goes far beyond the ideas of his model. Thucydides had called Athens the school of Greek culture. But, Isocrates boldly asserts, it was the spiritual achievement of Athens which brought it about that Greece henceforward meant, not a race, but a stage, the highest stage, of the intellect. 'The man who shares our paideia is a Greek in a higher sense than he who only shares our blood.'[39] Isocrates is not discarding the powerful ties of blood. They are dearer to him than to most of his fellow-citizens, because he is constructing a Panhellenic morality on the consciousness of racial unity, and by that new moral system he is endeavouring to set limits to the egotistic power-politics of the separate Greek states. But he believes that intellectual nationalism is nobler than racial nationalism, and when he states his views he knows exactly what they will mean for the political position of Hellenism in the world. When he

calls all the Greeks to help in his plan for conquering the barbarians, he is basing it much more on the Greek feeling of vast
intellectual superiority to other races than on the actual power
and resources of the Greek states. At first sight it looks like a
gigantic paradox for Isocrates to begin his proclamation of the
supra-national civilizing mission of Greece by an extravagant
utterance of national pride; but the apparent contradiction dis-
appears when we connect the supra-national ideal of Greece—its
universally valuable paideia—with the realistic political plan of
conquering Asia and settling it with Greek colonists. In fact,
that ideal contains a higher justification for the new national
imperialism, in that it identifies what is specifically Greek with
what is universally human. This is not actually said by Isocrates;
and some may object to our interpretation. But the only meaning
that can possibly be given to the universal exaltation of Greek
paideia which fills Isocrates' thought is this: the Greeks, through
the logos, over which they naturally have command, have revealed to other nations a principle which they too must recognize and adopt because its value is independent of race—the
ideal of paideia, of culture. There is a form of nationalism
which is expressed by keeping oneself apart from other races.
That is produced by weakness and self-limitation, because it is
based on the feeling that it can assert itself only in artificial
isolation. In Isocrates, national feeling is that of a culturally
superior nation which has realized that the efforts it has made
to attain a universal standard of perfection in all its intellectual
activities are its highest claim to victory in competition with
other races—since these other races have accepted the Greek
forms as the absolute expression of civilization. We might easily
think of modern analogies, talk of cultural propaganda, and
compare rhetoric to the modern machinery of press publicity
which grinds into action before economic and military conquest
begins. But Isocrates' faith grows from a deep insight into the
true character of the Greek mind and of Greek paideia; and
history shows that it was something more than political propaganda. From all his words we can feel the living breath of
Hellenism. The new era actually did fall into the forms which
Isocrates had thought out before its advent. Without the idea
which he here expresses for the first time, the idea that Greek
paideia was something universally valuable, there would have

been no Macedonian Greek world-empire, and the universal culture which we call Hellenistic would never have existed.

Isocrates did not make the deeds of Athenian heroes the chief topic of his *Panegyricus,* as was usual in the eulogies delivered over the graves of the fallen. He subordinated them to the spiritual achievements of the city,[40] and described them after exhausting that theme, in order, doubtless, to preserve a balance between the exterior and the interior life of Athens.[41] But in the tradition of the funeral speech there were dozens of patterns on which he could model this part of his oration. He obviously depends on them: he praises the great dead with far less freedom than he extols Athenian culture, where his personal enthusiasm and his deep conviction find utterance throughout. It was impossible for him to omit military glory in his speech, because without it the Thucydidean ideal, φιλοσοφεῖν ἄνευ μαλακίας ('love of culture without weakness'), would not be attained. He was bound to make that phrase real to his contemporaries in an age when intellectual interests had taken on exaggerated importance and the warlike virtues were dying away: for it was the most memorable expression of a harmony which they seemed to be forgetting. Recognition of this fact sounds through all Isocrates' works like a mournful ground-bass. Therefore he was compelled to try to create in Athens those qualities which men admired in Sparta. Thucydides himself held that Athenian superiority consisted not merely in an antithesis to Sparta, but in the combination of Spartan and Ionian characteristics.[42] But for the purpose Isocrates envisaged in the *Panegyricus,* the heroic aspect of the Athenian soul was all the more indispensable because he was proposing that Athens should be the equal partner of Sparta in leading the war against the barbarians.

This passage [43] ends with a defence of Athens against the criticisms of her imperialist methods in heading the first naval confederacy: for Sparta had used those criticisms to keep Athens permanently suppressed after her defeat, and to create moral obstacles to the restoration of her naval power. Isocrates uses a pun to bring home the point that Athenian naval primacy (ἀρχὴ τῆς θαλάττης) was for the rest of the Greeks the primal origin (ἀρχή) of all good. With the collapse of that domination began the decline of Greek prestige and the encroachments of the barbarian—who now, cries Isocrates, dares to enter Greece as arbiter of peace, and has set up the Spartans as his police.[44] The long list of Spartan acts of violence committed in recent years, and still fresh in everyone's memory, shows how little right the Spartans have to criticize Athens.[45] Thus his proposal that Greece should return to its former state, although that implies the re-establishment of Athenian power, becomes an urgent demand. The *Panegyricus* has been described as the programme of the second Athenian naval league.[46] However, that exaggerates the closeness of its relation to real political conditions, and underestimates the amount of Panhellenic ideology which it contains.[47] And yet it is accurate in one point—Isocrates declares that the restoration of Athenian power is indispensable for the attainment of his aim, the destruction of the Persian kingdom, and therefore he champions the right of Athens to head a second naval confederacy. In the light of the dream of national glory with which Isocrates surrounded it, that confederacy must originally have had something of the nobility of a great ideal, although in reality it never fulfilled the hopes which were here placed in it.[48]

But even although the actual execution of his proposal, in terms of practical politics, was to come rather from the united opposition of the Greeks to Sparta than from Isocrates' Panhellenic ideal, that did not detract from the new values which he had imparted to rhetoric in the *Panegyricus*. At one stride he had advanced before all Greece as the voice of a new kind of criticism of political facts and aspirations. The platform from which he addressed his country rested on no real power; but it was founded upon standards which were sure of recognition by very many of his fellow-countrymen, and which would bring to his school the wisest and best of the practical idealists in Greece. When philosophical educators preached that every activity must be subordinated to eternal values, that seemed to many to be too lofty an ideal; but there was a general demand that politics should be inspired by higher principles, and many of the younger generation must have felt that Isocrates' national morality was a happy and timely mean between the extremes of ethical scepticism on the one hand and philosophical retreat to the Absolute on the other. It is highly significant that the old city-state—to which even Socrates had entirely sacrificed himself—had not, in the next generation, the energy to produce this new political morality by itself.[49] Thus, the paideia of rhetoric, as conceived by Isocrates, has one feature in common with Plato's philosophical education: it sets its goal far beyond the limits of the traditional form of the state, in the realm of the ideal. Therein, it acknowledged that it was at odds with the political realities of its day; and yet, from that refusal to acquiesce in the dominant system, it drew a new tension and a new energy which had been unknown to the older Greek paideia. What had once been a culture drawing strength from the whole community was now replaced by a cultural ideal represented by great individual personalities. It was backed neither by a governing aristocracy nor by a united people, but by a chosen few, a spiritual crusade, an esoteric school. Such an association could hope to influence society only at second hand—by moulding the characters of great leaders who could either be, or seem to be, capable of transforming it.

4

THE PRINCE'S EDUCATION

ISOCRATES' speech *To Nicocles* was written some years after the *Panegyricus,* but belongs to a group of works closely akin to it. In content and structure it appears to be quite different from its famous predecessor; and yet the two are associated, because both are manifestly concerned with Isocrates' school and his educational programme. The date and the plan of *To Nicocles* connect it with *Evagoras* and with the other, slightly longer speech called *Nicocles.* All three relate to the royal house of Evagoras, king of Salamis in Cyprus. *Evagoras* itself is a eulogy of him published after his death. His son and successor Nicocles was himself a pupil of Isocrates, in that school from which (in Cicero's well-known phrase), as if it had been the Trojan horse, there came forth nothing but princes.[1] In *Nicocles* Isocrates makes the young monarch address his new subjects and explain his principles of government. Finally, the speech *To Nicocles* takes us to the source of his political wisdom: for it is addressed by Isocrates himself to the prince, who, although he has just ascended the throne, still feels himself to be his pupil.[2] One of the more charming aspects of Isocrates' vanity is his pride in his own pupils. He expresses it again and again, and goes into it at considerable length in the *Antidosis* speech; and we might well wonder whether, lacking this warmth of affection, the elegant surface of his prose would not often have seemed no more than cold and shallow smoothness.

These three works are all displays of the art of education as practised in the school of Isocrates. While the *Panegyricus* lays down the basis of his entire educational system—Panhellenic unity —the Cyprian speeches show more clearly the point at which his paideia has its practical beginning. If at first we find it hard to understand how, in the largely democratic Greek world of the fourth century, a school of political theory that was remote from the daily business of government could ever become effective, these speeches introduce us directly to a problem which must, in these circumstances, be of the very first importance— the possibility that *culture may influence the state by educating its leaders*. Throughout the literature of the fourth century, this question appears at the same time in writers and thinkers of the most diverse characters and attitudes—in Plato's philosophy, and in his practical endeavour to guide the tyrant Dionysius (an endeavour whose sad failure he himself, in the seventh of his letters, describes as the tragedy of paideia); in Isocrates' works about Nicocles, in his letter to Dionysius of Syracuse, in his *Archidamus,* in his *Philip,* and above all in his relation to his pupil Timotheus; in Xenophon's great educational novel, *The Education of Cyrus;* in Aristotle's philosophical friendship with the tyrant Hermias of Atarneus, and especially in his work as tutor of the future ruler of the world, Alexander the Great.[8] Those are only the best-known examples: it would be easy to add more.

This was not a new thing. In previous centuries there had been many wise men who had served the great as advisers, monitors, or teachers. As the philosopher now preceded the scholar, so the poet had preceded the philosopher in that part. The poets who haunted the courts of tyrants in the sixth century were not all greedy parasites and flatterers, who turned to glorifying democracy too when the opportunity presented itself, as Plato charges the poets of his own time with doing.[4] In Pindar's last great poems,[5] addressed to the new monarchs of Sicily, he abandons the pattern usual in his victory-odes. Instead of extolling the valour of bourgeois or noble prizewinners at the games, he turns to give counsel to princes; and these very odes are predecessors of Isocrates' speeches of admonition to contemporary princes. We may go further back yet, to the 'mirror of knighthood', Theognis' gnomic poetry, full of the aristocratic morality of early Greece.[6] Isocrates is fully aware of the fact that the sophistic prose of his time is the heir, in style and content, of those old poetic forms: in his *To Nicocles* [7] he expressly refers to the gnomic poems of Hesiod, Theognis, and Phocylides, and thereby stands forth as the inheritor of their tradition.

The three Cyprian speeches show different aspects of the education of a prince. The eulogy on Evagoras is a prose parallel to the Pindaric encomium—as is shown by Isocrates' deliberate introduction of the old name, *encomium*.[8] But Isocrates' encomium is more than a mere hymn of victory. It has become a glorification of the areté of Evagoras as it was displayed in his whole life, work, and character. Thus adapted, and with the original educative character of the poetic encomium greatly increased, the form became immensely popular among his contemporaries, and was soon imitated on every side.[9] Its essence was the ancient concept on which the poetic encomium was based—the noble Example.[10] Here the example of Evagoras is displayed to his son and successor. It is important to observe how Isocrates incorporates his Panhellenic ideal of political education in his description of the Cyprian monarch. He presents him not as an isolated phenomenon but as the champion of Greek areté and Greek character on the most easterly outpost of Hellenism against the Asiatic power of Persia.[11] We may compare this device of making a historical personage the embodiment of true areté with the strange blending of fact and ideal in Plato's portrayal of Socrates (which is similarly meant to serve as a great Example)—although Isocrates' glorification of Evagoras never attains the genuine individuality of Plato's character-drawing, but rather, in accordance with its purpose, makes its subject into a canon of all the political virtues, and above all of all the virtues of the monarch.[12]

Isocrates completes this picture of political paideia in his two speeches, *To Nicocles* and *Nicocles,* by adding to his description of the ideal monarch a deeper and more universal scheme of the principles on which a prince should be trained in politics. Ostensibly, the first of them is an exhortation in which he addresses his former pupil Nicocles on the true essence of the ruler's vocation; and in the second, its complement, Nicocles speaks to his people of Salamis.[13] It is assumed that they have previously heard Isocrates' speech to him—a touch which sets the political philosopher and teacher on a higher plane than the monarch himself. Thereby Isocrates is made the representative of a higher order of things, which deserves respect simply because of its moral truth. This must always be remembered by readers of the speech *To Nicocles.* It makes Isocrates an idealized lawgiver, and his position is expressly recognized by his relation to the young king. The Greeks usually thought that tyranny was

nothing but the arbitrary exercise of one man's will. Here, however, it is made part of a political ideal, and thereby legalized:
the tyrant's will is interpreted as being the will to rule his people
in accordance with established laws and a higher moral code.
Again and again in the fourth century, attempts were made to
transform tyranny into 'a gentler constitution'. In both these
speeches the problem occupies a great deal of space.[14] It is scarcely
necessary to recall the fact that in the fourth century gentleness
was often extolled as being the true characteristic of democracy.[15]
Thus, Isocrates, in his plan for educating princes, does more
than accept tyranny as a given fact in power-politics. He
brings it under an ideal standard; so that he can then fairly
explain that monarchy is the best form of constitution. This
he proves by showing that those states which were admired for
their political achievements (Carthage, for instance, and
Sparta) were oligarchies in peace and monarchies in war; that
Persia owed its long existence as a world-power to its monarchical regime; that even the Athenian democracy had always been
preserved in war-time by the leadership of one general; and
finally that even the gods in heaven formed a kingdom ruled
by a monarch.[16] Here as elsewhere, the standards which Isocrates
is striving to work out and establish are not based on ideals
alone, but also on historical examples and on experience. His
allusion to the absolute dominance of one *strategos* in Athens
during war-time seems to me to date the speech, with a good
deal of probability, to the years when his pupil Timotheus was
leading Athens in the war against Sparta after the foundation
of the new Athenian naval confederacy. The problem of internal
politics which we see here confronting democracy we shall meet
again, analysed at greater length, in Isocrates' later speech, the
Areopagiticus.[17] But Isocrates does not attempt to limit the
tyrant's power by written laws or constitutions. His subjects are
expressly directed to consider his word as their law.[18] Nothing
restrains him except the virtues of justice and self-control. These
—not the warlike qualities usually ascribed to great monarchs—
are the qualities which Nicocles describes as the pillars of his
rule, and he solemnly claims them for himself.[19] Their only source
is therefore the prince's paideia. Paideia brought to perfection
is areté, the highest of all goods.[20] He who has recognized it as
the highest of all goods will (so the king assures his subjects)

persevere in its practice all through his life.[21] The areté of the monarch is the basis on which his demand for obedience and loyalty from his subjects can be justified.[22] We need go no further into the social morality of the doctrine developed in this section of the speech, about the political duties of the good subjects of a good monarch.

But it is essential for us, before we turn to Isocrates' address to Nicocles on the monarch's duties, to glance at the proem of Nicocles' own speech. Here Isocrates has in his usual way taken the opportunity once more to defend and extol rhetorical culture. It is especially important that he should do so in this speech, for it means that he puts his praise of paideia into the mouth of the king, who is the ostensible speaker. He makes him attack the suspicion (natural enough when rhetoric had become so closely linked with monarchy) that the purpose of 'philosophy' and culture was not to bring men to perfection but to seize power.[23] We cannot tell from which side this criticism came. It can hardly have been from Plato: for he had seriously thought of realizing his political and educational ideals through the power of an absolute monarch, and had not shrunk from close association with the tyrant of Syracuse. Perhaps we should rather think of the practical politicians who surrounded Isocrates in Athens. To the charge of *pleonexia,* greed for power, raised against his rhetorical education, he replies that it would be truer to direct it against those who refuse to learn anything of the power of oratory, because they care for nothing but right action.[24] All striving after human areté is aimed at increasing and enhancing the goods of life, and it would be unfair to blame the things through which, with the help of moral principles, we attain that end.[25] The misuse of rhetorical culture cannot discredit it, any more than wealth, strength, or courage can be thought to lose their value because they are often misused by their possessors. Nothing could be more foolish than to blame things for the faults of men.[26] The only result of that attitude must be to reject all higher culture without distinction. Those who do so do not realize that they are robbing human nature of that power which produces the highest goods in life.[27]

And so the proem ends, and Nicocles appropriately utters a eulogy of eloquence as the power which makes all civilization.

This is a reprise of the theme stated in the *Panegyricus,* where Athens was praised as the original home of all culture.[28] The force which was there called 'philosophy' is presented here too as the faculty which distinguishes men from the beasts, and here too it is said to be based principally on the logos, the gift of speech.[29] The rivalry of rhetoric and poetry is nowhere displayed with such vividness as in this great encomium extolling speech as the one quality which truly gives man his humanity. I do not know whether it has ever been observed that it is actually a *hymn* written in lofty prose, and fully worked out in the severely formal patterns of poetry. If we closely examine the various statements made by Isocrates about the nature and effects of speech, we can see from their peculiar form that they are simply glorifications of an entity personified as a god.[30] The name of this entity appears part way through the encomium: it is Logos, the creator of all culture.[31] 'For in our other faculties we do not excel the animals. Many of them are fleeter or stronger or otherwise better than we. But because we were endowed with the power of persuading one another and explaining our thoughts, we were not only released from bestial ways of living, but came together and founded states and established laws and invented arts. It was speech which enabled us to perfect almost everything we have achieved in the way of civilization. For it was speech which laid down the standards of right and wrong, nobility and baseness, without which we should be unable to live together. It is through speech that we convict bad men and praise good ones. By its aid we educate the foolish and test the wise. For the ability to speak rightly is the surest sign of good sense; true, law-abiding, and just speech is the image of a good and dependable soul. With the help of speech we dispute over doubtful matters and investigate the unknown. For the same methods of proof which we use to convince others we employ in deliberating with ourselves, and we call men who can speak in public rhetoricians, while those who converse well with themselves we call men of sense. If we sum up the character of this power, we shall find that no reasonable thing is done anywhere in the world without logos, that logos is the leader of all actions and thoughts, and that those who make most use of it are the wisest of mankind. Therefore those who despise education and

culture must be hated just as we hate those who blaspheme
against the gods.'

We must recollect the emotion of this hymn to Speech and the
power of culture, in order to realize the immense influence of
Isocrates on his pupils, who are here represented by Nicocles.[32]
Thus conceived, rhetoric is raised high above the level on which
earlier experts treated it. All this does not give a satisfactory
philosophical answer to the problem raised by Plato in *Gorgias*
—that of the relation between rhetoric and truth and morality;
but that defect is for the moment hidden in the new glory
assumed by rhetoric as creatrix of culture and human society.
Of course, rhetorical training as it was in actual practice made
a miserable contrast to Isocrates' fine phrases. We must interpret them mainly as the expression of the ideal which inspired
him. But at the same time they are a form of self-criticism obviously designed to answer Plato's searching attacks by working
out a more profound conception of the purpose of rhetorical
education than had ever existed before. It is tacitly acknowledged that it would be a poor thing indeed if it had no more
to offer than was conceded by its philosophical opponents—a
purely formal technique of hypnotizing the ignorant masses
with persuasive talk.[33] From that connexion with demagogy
Isocrates endeavours to release rhetoric. Its essence, he holds,
is not a series of devices to influence the mob, but the simple
and fundamental intellectual act which everyone daily performs
in his own soul as he discusses his own welfare with himself.[34] In
that act it is impossible to make artificial distinctions between
form and content: on the contrary, the essence of the inner debate, 'prudence', consists in the ability to take the right decision
in every situation.[35] By saying this, Isocrates has deliberately
shifted the emphasis from style and form to the content of the
'advice' which the orator imparts.[36] For culture, as he conceives
it, is something more than language and rhetorical structure. In
it, form grows directly out of content. And the content, the subject of rhetoric, is the world of politics and ethics. The purpose
of Isocrates' rhetorical culture is to produce perfection in human
life, the state which he, like the philosophers, calls *eudaimonia,*
happiness. That is an objective good, the highest of all objective
goods. It is not the mere acquisition of influence over others to
serve subjective ends.[37] To hypostasize this cultural ideal in the

deified Logos, as he does, is a brilliant method of making his purpose clearer. For logos means speech, in the sense of rational speech and communication, which always rests ultimately upon the acknowledgment of common values. Isocrates strongly emphasizes this aspect of logos, and makes it the real core of all social life.[38]

On this philosophy of the logos is based Isocrates' position as a legislator and educator—a position which is not fully appreciated when we sum it up in the vague and flexible word rhetoric. We must now try to analyse its results, as shown in the speech *To Nicocles*. It begins by asking what is the best gift which can be offered to a prince.[39] According to Isocrates, that would be a right definition of the conduct that would enable a monarch to rule in the best possible way. Many factors (he goes on) combine to train the ordinary citizen: he cannot afford to be debauched if he has to make his living day by day, he must obey the laws of whatever state he belongs to, and he can be freely reproached with his faults by both friend and enemy. And poets of bygone days have left behind precepts teaching men how to live. All these things help to improve him.[40] But tyrants have no such assistance. Although they need education more than others, they never hear any criticism after they have acquired their power. They are entirely cut off from most people; those who do associate with them are flatterers and timeservers. And they misuse the great powers and possessions which they have, so that many men have come to doubt whether the life of a simple private citizen who behaves properly were not preferable to that of an absolute ruler.[41] Wealth, honour, and power make the monarch appear something like a god. But, thinking of the terror and danger in which the great live, and seeing that some have been murdered by their own flesh and blood, while others have been compelled to do violence to their best friends, men have come to think that any kind of life would be better than to suffer such disasters, even for the crown of Asia.[42] This last comparison is an obvious allusion to the remark of Socrates in Plato's *Gorgias* [43]: he says that he cannot tell whether the king of Persia is happy or not, because he does not know what degree of paideia and of justice he has reached. That was the first time that paideia founded on justice had been made the standard by which to judge the life and conduct of a great ruler, and the fundamental idea of the prince's education had been laid down. Perhaps even before Plato himself in *The Republic* went so far as to work out this principle into a complete educational system for training future rulers, Isocrates attempted, after his own fashion, to employ it in his speech to Nicocles.

He realizes, of course, that while an idea in itself may be splendid, its execution may be far beneath what its creator had hoped: just as many poems are magnificent in conception and fail entirely when they are put on paper.[44] But even to begin is noble. It is a fine thing to explore strange new territories in education, to make laws for kings. The ordinary teacher helps only a few citizens here and there. But if one could succeed in guiding the ruler of great populations towards the highest virtue, both the individual and the group would benefit: for that would more firmly establish the king's rule, and also make the citizen's life more tolerable.[45] Therefore the aim of Isocrates is (as we have said above) to halt or hinder the contemporary degeneration of the state from constitutional government to absolute monarchy, by binding the will of the ruler to higher moral standards.[46] In depth of philosophical reasoning, Isocrates' procedure cannot be compared with Plato's doctrine of the Idea of Good—the Idea which the perfect ruler must carry in his soul as a fixed pattern, or *paradeigma*, for his conduct; nor with Plato's description of the methodical way to dialectical knowledge, along which the soul must travel in order to contemplate absolute moral standards.[47] The roundabout way, by which (Plato says) the best of the best must be carried to that lofty goal, is entirely unknown to Isocrates.[48] He considers the position of the future ruler as a fact established by the chance of his birth,[49] and he seeks only to compensate, through his education, whatever defects there may be in his nature. Since he does not hold, like Plato, that a man's intellectual superiority or the dependability of his character qualifies him to rule,[50] his educational programme is bound to be more typical and more conventional. Yet he is quite aware of the danger lying in the lack of a general principle—that the high art of government may dissolve into technical details of administration. In such matters, he says,[51] the official counsellors of the king must advise him point by point. His own purpose is to try to describe the general outlines of the monarch's conduct.

He begins by asking what is the king's function: his 'work'.[52] We are reminded of Plato—and especially of the dialogue *Gorgias,* which must have made a lasting impression on him [53]— not only by this method of inquiry but by the description of the monarch's conduct as 'aiming' at right action.[54] Like Plato, he holds that it is essential to be clear about the ruler's ultimate purpose, since its parts can be defined only 'with an eye to the whole'. Like Plato, he starts from facts which are generally admitted—although he does not attempt to make a dialectical analysis of the goods which the ruler must try to attain, and merely accepts the views of the man in the street.[55] This method of laying down a supreme principle or aim of action he calls a *hypothesis,* a 'laying of foundations'—because all further arguments must rest upon it.[56] In several other passages in his speeches we can observe this effort to find a generally accepted hypothesis: it is an essential element in his political thought, and is to be explained by the influence of Plato's intellectual method. Ultimately, it is a procedure borrowed from mathematics.[57]

The hypothesis, then, is this. The good ruler must put a stop to the miseries of his state, maintain its prosperity, and make it larger and stronger. Separate problems arising day by day are to be subordinated to that end. Here it becomes quite clear that Isocrates does not believe like Plato that the task of the state is to *educate* its citizens and bring each of them as near to perfection as possible, but rather that it is to achieve material greatness and prosperity—an ideal which corresponds more than anything else to the practical statesmanship opposed so violently by Plato in *Gorgias* and followed by the great Athenian politicians of the past, Themistocles, Pericles, and others.[58] Thus, his conception of the ruler's duties is not specially characteristic of monarchy. Monarchy is only that form of the state in which Isocrates believes they can be most easily performed.[59] It was the Athenian democracy of the era following the Persian war which had so boldly advanced on the path of imperialism. Isocrates now transforms its powerfully materialistic idea of well-being into the ideology of an enlightened despotism, not without making some concessions to contemporary philosophical morality.

The ideal he sets up for Nicocles is a compromise between the Periclean tradition of practical politics, the fourth-century trend towards dictatorship, and the ethical criticisms of the philosophers. In any case, Nicocles is not thought of primarily as an Athenian statesman, but as ruling in the more colonial conditions of distant Cyprus. There, even the Athenians would consider it justifiable for all political power to be concentrated in the hands of one man, since that was the only way in which the Greek cause could be defended against Persian encroachment. If there is anything in our suggestion that both this speech and *Nicocles* were composed at the time when Isocrates' favourite pupil Timotheus was admiral of the entire fleet of the new Athenian naval confederacy, then the allusion in *Nicocles* to the quasi-monarchical position of Athenian generals in war-time is more than a chronological coincidence,[60] and the two speeches are Athenian propaganda. They are clearly intended to bind the Cyprian state of Salamis closer to Athens (with which Nicocles' father Evagoras had allied himself against Persia in 390) by giving it a 'gentler form of government'.[61] Between the families of Timotheus and Nicocles there had been close ties of friendship ever since the time of their fathers, Conon and Evagoras; and this personal and political connexion had prepared the way for Evagoras' alliance with Athens. It went right back to the time when Conon was admiral of the Persian fleet, and, after the naval victory at Cnidus, restored the Long Walls of Athens. For it was on Evagoras' advice that the Persian king had appointed Conon his admiral.[62] And now their association seemed to be resumed in their sons. Perhaps Nicocles and Timotheus had actually met and known each other in Isocrates' school. Accordingly, Isocrates' speeches can be placed, with some probability, in the period when Timotheus was Athenian strategos for the first time; and they would fall between the death of Evagoras (374) and the dismissal of Timotheus from his post (373-2). The remark in *Nicocles* that Athens had always prospered in war when guided by one supreme leader, and had always lost when generalled by committees,[63] is very probably an allusion to the impending disputes which ended in Timotheus' fall when his conduct had become too arbitrary. Timotheus was always a statesman-like general: he helped his country to victory quite as much by diplomatic successes as by feats of arms. His friendship with the kings whom he made allies of Athens is well known; and Isocrates' attempt to make political use of his influence over Nicocles seems logically to be another link in the chain. There is express evidence for the fact that during the war Isocrates backed Timotheus in other ways; and in the field of internal politics we shall see it proved by the *Areopagiticus*.[64]

After this glance at the historical background of the speech *To Nicocles*, let us return to our analysis of its subject-matter. If the ruler's tasks are as great as Isocrates says they are, surely the success of any monarchy will depend on the intellectual ability of the monarch. Therefore no athlete needs to train his body so constantly and carefully as the future ruler must train his mind.[65] For none of the prizes offered at any competition is as important as the stakes for which he will play every day. The exceptional honours he enjoys as king can be justified only if he excels all others in intellectual and moral qualities.[66] There is almost a Socratic ring about the next adjuration to Nicocles: 'do not believe that attention and care (ἐπιμέλεια) are useful in everything else, and powerless to make men better and wiser.' [67] In his speech *Against the sophists* Isocrates had energetically attacked Plato's educational ideal, and affirmed that virtue could not be taught.[68] Here, however, it is clear that he does not intend to assert that man cannot be taught anything whatever. The two problems are not identical for Isocrates, as they appear to be for Plato. In the earlier speech, his eagerness to oppose Plato's exaggerated estimate of the value of pure knowledge had led him to depreciate the value of learning in comparison with natural ability [69]; but in the speech *To Nicocles* we find a more positive estimate of the power of education. Even here he does not go so far as to assert that 'areté can be taught'. But he does fall in with the optimistic ideas of the earlier sophistic theorists, who believed that man was not worse equipped by nature than the unreasoning beasts, whose souls can, after all, be tamed.[70] However, this shift in emphasis does not mean that Isocrates' views have been essentially changed: it has been caused by the change in the opponent he is fighting. Theoretically, he is a pessimist with regard to the philosophical paradox that virtue can be taught. But practically, his will to teach remains unbroken. With remarkable energy he devotes himself to the new task of educating a monarch. That energy and optimism make him treat paideia in this speech as one of the greatest benefactors of human nature.[71]

Like Theognis in his plan for rearing the young nobleman, Isocrates attaches the greatest importance to the right kind of friendships. (In that he is obviously under the direct influence of the old gnomic poets.) The king must associate with only the wisest men of his court. Other advisers must, if possible, be sent for from abroad. This is clearly a hint of the position which Isocrates conceives himself to hold in the life of his young pupil. Plato had gone to Syracuse only after the most urgent invitations and entreaties from his friends and from the prince himself. But Isocrates invites himself to Cyprus. In the next sentence he makes his advice more general: he counsels the king to associate with poets and scholars, and to become the auditor of some and the pupil of others. That, he says, is the training-ground, the *gymnasion,* in which he can best fit himself to fulfil the ideals imposed on him by his great vocation.[72] Both here and in *Nicocles,* Isocrates lays it down as the highest axiom that the better should not be ruled by the worse, nor the wise be governed by the foolish. In association with others that means that the prince must criticize the bad and vie with the good. The essential thing is that he who wants to rule over others must apply that principle to himself, and be able to justify his position by his own true superiority to them all.[73] Hence, Isocrates does not believe that the principle of legality on which monarchies are usually based is enough to ensure a man's right to succeed to a throne and give orders to other men. That purely constitutional idea, which is accepted without question by the citizens of most monarchical states, was never widely approved by the Greeks. Believing as they did in the rights of nature, they always expected that a ruler's power should be based on his true areté, on personality rather than automatic rules and institutions. Isocrates himself shows very strikingly that this attitude did not mean the idolization of might without right. Of course the lack of legal safeguards for the liberty of the citizens of a state like Salamis was a serious defect, which was scarcely remedied by the Greek faith in the power of education. But one of the great services rendered to the world by Greek paideia is that in a situation dominated by might, not law, it demanded that morality and the rights of man should receive all that was due to them.

The ruler must be both patriot (says Isocrates) and philanthropist: he must love both mankind and the state.[74] He is, as it were, to be both Creon and Antigone. The first problem in the art of government is to unite these apparently contradictory qualities. For it would surely be useless for the ruler to devote himself to that abstraction, the State, if he did not *like* the actual living beings whom he was engaged in caring for. Philanthropy is a conception which was becoming more and more prominent in the literature of that era.[75] Inscriptions too tell us how much it was prized in communal life: again and again it is mentioned in decrees passed to honour distinguished public men. Service to the polis was not really admired unless it was inspired by that general love of humanity. Isocrates does not forget to add the fact that it is not mere weakness to try to win public affection. The best popular leader—and even a king must be a popular leader (δημαγωγός) in that sense—is he who allows the masses neither to become unruly nor to be oppressed.[76] That was the great merit of Pericles, as portrayed by Thucydides: and to Thucydides can be traced the doctrine of harmony between opposites which Isocrates makes the criterion of statesmanship throughout this speech.[77] In the funeral oration of Pericles, Thucydides had constructed a picture of Athenian culture and the Athenian constitution out of many such skilfully harmonized oppositions.[78] From that speech, Isocrates now takes the idea that only the best have the right to be honoured, but that the rest of the citizens must be protected against wrong. He calls these two principles—whose reconciliation Pericles terms the true secret of Athenian democracy—the 'elements' of every good constitution.[79] Thucydides boasted that the Athenian constitution was not borrowed from others, but was an original creation. Isocrates now recommends King Nicocles to invent good measures as far as he can, and, where he cannot, to imitate the best things in other countries.[80] He is, of course, adapting his advice to circumstances; but it is the same principle of reconciling opposites. Originality and imitation are both necessary. The most essential thing is to create a stable system, and just laws that harmonize with one another. Legal disputes must be kept as few as possible and settled as quickly as possible.

For it is not enough for laws to be good in themselves: the administration of justice is quite as important.[81] Business must bring in fair profits; but litigious people must be made to suffer for being busybodies (here Isocrates is plainly thinking of the Athenian law courts, which had encouraged the Athenian passion for lawsuits). The same standards should be applied to all citizens; and the king's legal decisions must be firm and consistent, just like a good code of laws.[82]

The rest of this educational treatise for princes is not so systematic as we should expect from its beginning, and from Isocrates' statement that he intends to lay down only the general principles of monarchy. Based (by its author's own admission) on the gnomic poetry of Hesiod, Theognis, and Phocylides, it is like it in form too—for it consists chiefly of separate precepts which follow one on another without a close logical connexion. But we must not be led by its apparent informality to imagine that the speech is only a list of practical tricks.[83] There is an underlying connexion between the separate precepts. They add up to form a portrait of the ideal ruler—a portrait whose unity lies in its ethical consistency, and thereby is completely typical of the spirit of the new era. At the end of *Phaedrus* Plato makes Socrates say of the young Isocrates that there is something philosophical in his nature. To take this remark as irony is to misunderstand it completely. Within the obvious limits, it is absolutely just, and every careful reader of Isocrates cannot but be impressed by its truth. In this particular speech Isocrates shows his philosophical character by the way in which he transforms the usual conception of the monarch, feature by feature, into a new ideal: changing the personification of arbitrary will into a dominant personality whose will is bound by higher laws.

In each of his separate precepts it is obvious that the deeply-based intellectual and spiritual culture, which we have shown to be the foundation of the speech, is the guiding principle of Isocrates' ideal of monarchy. He keeps the name *tyrant,* but he entirely changes the character of tyranny. One after another, he takes up the characteristics which form the traditional ideal of a monarch, and in neat epigrams transforms them to fit his ideal. This can be shown by a series of examples, which could easily be lengthened. 'Honour the gods,' he says,[84] 'whose cult your ancestors introduced; but be assured that the finest sacrifice and the noblest worship is to make yourself as good and as just as you can. Hold your surest bodyguard to be the virtue of your friends, the good will of your citizens, and your own moral insight. Take care of the property of your subjects, and believe that those who waste their money are wasting yours, while those who work are increasing your own possessions.[85] Make your word more reliable than the sworn oaths of other men. Free your citizens from constant fears, and do not allow people who are doing no wrong to be harried by terror: just as you behave to them, so will they bear themselves towards you.[86] Do not try to make yourself a ruler by harshness and heavy punishments, but through the superiority of your mind and the conviction of all that you can care for them better than they can themselves. Be warlike in knowledge and preparation; but be peaceful by making no unjust claims. Treat weaker states as you wish stronger states to treat you.[87] Be ambitious, but only in those things in which it will benefit you to be first. Do not think that those are weak who accept defeat with profit, but those who win costly victories. Do not hold those noble who grasp at more than they can hold, but those who strive for noble things and achieve what they attempt.[88] Do not copy him who has the greatest power, but him who makes best use of what power he has.[89] Choose not those who wish, but those who deserve, to be your friends; and not those whose company you enjoy most, but those who will best help you to rule. Test your associates carefully, knowing that all who do not meet you will judge you by them. When you choose men to do state business which you yourself cannot manage, remember that you will be responsible for all they do.[90] Do not think him loyal who praises all you say and do, but him who exposes your errors. Let sensible people talk freely, so that they can help you to decide doubtful questions.' [91]

The monarch's paideia culminates in the rule of self-control. It is not fitting for a king to be the slave of his own desires. By mastering them he will learn to rule others.[92] Everything that has been said about the choice of friends is based on the importance of friendship to self-education. But even the monarch's work and the tasks he imposes on himself must be estimated by their influence in developing his character. The real standard by which to judge the attitude of the people to its ruler (and therefore the standard by which to judge his areté) is not the honour they pay him under duress, but what they think of him in their hearts, and whether they have more admiration for his brains or his luck.[93] The king's self-control is not important merely as a proof of his worth, but also as a model for his subjects: since the character of the whole polis copies that of its ruler.[94] Here, as in Plato, a conception which we know from the aristocratic paideia of early Greece—the idea that great men are models for others to copy—reappears on a higher plane, and is transferred to the problem of educating the whole population of a state. But whereas Plato changes the paradeigma into the Absolute, into the Idea of Good, namely into God, the measure of all things, Isocrates still believes that the example to be copied must be a person. He makes the ideal monarch the representative of his people's culture, the visible embodiment of the character of his state. By making the idea of monarchy serve the education of mankind (at least as worked out in one state and one people), he attempts to inspire it with new life: since, for his age, the conception of paideia is the only living thing, the ultimate meaning of human existence. Every good thing, every realm of life, religion and worship, state and community, individual and family, each is justified by its contribution to the great task of culture. At last Isocrates sees his ideal of monarchy personified before his eyes. He defines it as a harmonious balance between the two forces, in uniting which he considers the hardest part of his prince's education to lie—amiability of character and serious virtue. Either of these qualities is by itself insufficient for a king. Virtue is regal, but chilling. Charm and refinement make it easy to associate with others, but draw one down to their level.[95]

In the realm of the intellect, just as in that of morality, there are two contradictories which can reveal their full significance in building the prince's personality only if they are balanced against each other—experience and philosophy.[96] The formula is obviously a summary of Isocrates' own political paideia—as is shown by remarks in his other speeches about the method of imparting this type of education, and above all by his own acts and thoughts. Experience he defines as knowledge of the past, which constantly shows its value as a source of historical examples.[97] Nicocles (he continues) must learn from it what happens to individuals and to rulers—that is, he must find out the universal and permanent conditions which govern their lives and conduct. If he studies the past and remembers it, he will be better able to judge of the future.[98] Isocrates does not then, like Plato, think that rulers should be trained by studying the lofty abstract conceptions of mathematics and dialectic, but by knowledge of historical fact.[99] Here for the first time historical writing begins to influence political thought and the general culture of the whole era. Even without taking into account the many smaller borrowings from Thucydides which we have pointed out here and there in Isocrates, we must acknowledge that it is Thucydides' influence which is responsible for this, for it was he who created the science of political history. It was produced by the impact upon the Greek mind of the agony and collapse of Athens in the Peloponnesian war; and, describing it in that connexion,[100] we treated it chiefly as the achievement of a new type of objective political thought, and therefore potentially an important factor in the paideia of the future. Thucydides himself, of course, did not put it to any practical use: the most that he did was to call it in general terms a source of political understanding for future generations, a 'possession for ever'.[101] And now in the paideia of Isocrates—especially in his programme for educating the future monarch—this mighty new intellectual instrument is fully employed for the first time, and becomes, as it was fated to, one of the most powerful tools by which man shapes his destiny and his character.

Here we may shortly survey the part played by history in the development of Greek paideia. In the old-fashioned system, made up of music and gymnastic training, there was no such thing as independent historical knowledge and historical thought. The past was known, of course, since it was part of poetic tradition; but it was known only as narratives of heroic deeds done by single nations or great heroes, and there was still no clear distinction between history and myth.[102] These traditions were kept alive to provide heroic models to be imitated, as the sophist Protagoras expressly says in Plato's dialogue [103] when he is describing Athenian education in the Periclean age. But he says nothing of studying history in the deeper sense,

for the political study of history did not yet exist. The philosopher was educated by investigating the eternal laws of nature
or of morality, but in his training there was no place for history.
Even after Thucydides' work had been published, in the first
ten years of the fourth century, the situation did not immediately change. In Plato's plan for a comprehensive system of
scientific paideia, the most up-to-date branches of mathematics,
medicine, and astronomy are included, but the great new science
of political history is wholly neglected. We might think from
this that the real effect of Thucydides' work is to be found only
among specialists—namely, in the few historians who imitated
him directly. The problem, important though it is, has not yet
been adequately investigated. But in considering it we must
certainly not overlook the other great representative of contemporary paideia—rhetoric. Just as the educational value of
mathematics is fully recognized only in philosophical culture, so
the new educational force of historical science, revealed by
Thucydides, really finds its true place within the rhetorical system of education. That fact was of the greatest importance
in the development of historical writing, because it meant that
history came under the influence of rhetoric.[104] But we must also
remember that the perspective can be reversed. Our point here
is the influence exercised by historical thought upon the rhetoric
of Isocrates. In fact, that influence must have been all the more
powerful because rhetoric was no longer a matter of specialist
education in forensic oratory, but now aimed at training men to
occupy the highest posts in public life, as statesmen and monarchs. Political experience was an indispensable part of such
training,[105] and Thucydides was an especially good source from
which to draw it—for his work contained many different models
of epideictic and deliberative oratory, the styles which were
then becoming more and more important in Isocratean rhetoric.
In later rhetoric this interest in history survives in frequent
allusions to historical *paradeigmata*—a trick which reminds us
of the fact that the two arts were first connected in the field of
education. But by that time real political oratory had perished:
nourished by the life of the Greek city-state, it died when that
died. Historical examples in what remained of rhetoric after
that are no more than lifeless ornaments. However, Isocrates'
rhetorical system of education had been nourished by the ener-

gies of great and living political disputes; and in it serious historical study found its rightful place.[106]

We have no time for a more detailed study of Isocrates' use of historical examples in political argument.[107] Nor can we trace how his political preconceptions altered his view of the historical facts which he used to support them, although it would be extremely interesting to see how, when historical knowledge comes into contact with his political interests, it is always history which is altered, to suit his wish. The incorporation of history in his system of paideia meant, among other things, that history was now affected by a new passion for argument, for praise and blame, which had been foreign to earlier historians. His pupils did not only study existing histories, but wrote new ones—so that his point of view spread throughout contemporary historiography. This is clearly shown by the works of Ephorus and Theopompus, which are represented by good tradition as coming from his immediate circle, or at least influenced by his teaching. He also transformed the local history of Attica. His pupil, the Athenian statesman Androtion, rewrote it in accordance with Isocratean political ideals; and either Isocrates himself or Androtion exercised a decisive influence on the Peripatetic view of Athenian constitutional history, which is now the chief source of all our knowledge of the subject.[108] His transformation of Athenian history was part of his educational programme as it affected internal politics: we shall deal with it at greater length in discussing the *Areopagiticus*.

In the last part of the speech *To Nicocles* Isocrates asks, with characteristic earnestness, what will be the effect of this new literary type, the idealized 'mirror of a monarch'. Here we can see the rhetorician, with his passion for artistic effect, at grips with the educator, who wants only to produce positive and lasting results. He compares himself with the ancient bards who composed didactic poetry (ὑποθῆκαι) [109], which everyone praises as full of good advice, but no one reads: people would rather read the cheapest comedy than the most carefully written aphorisms of thoughtful poets.[110] Books are like food; most of us enjoy what tastes sweet more than what does us good. It is best to imitate Homer and the early tragedians—for they saw through human nature, and made their wise words palatable by mixing them with myths and legends.[111] In this, Isocrates is expressing very plainly one of the great disadvantages of the new art of rhetoric in its effort to supplant poetry as an educational instrument. The real masters of *psychagogia,* the art of 'leading hearts', are the poets like Homer, to whom we will always turn back after hearing the new teachers—simply because they are more entertaining. They lead our hearts by a light chain: by our enjoyment of the beautiful. But didactic speeches contain no paradoxes, no exciting novelties, nothing unknown or unusual; and the best orator in that field is he who can best collect what is scattered through the minds of all men and say it most neatly—as Hesiod, Theognis, and Phocylides did.[112] Form (Isocrates believes) is one of the greatest problems of paideia. Whatever its educational intentions or effects might be, the poetry of old drew its true strength from form. Although their ideals of paideia are in many ways fundamentally opposed to each other, Plato and Isocrates are both well aware of this fact; and the discovery of a new form is one of their chief educational interests. In later ages, when rhetorical conquered philosophical education (at least in the wider circles of culture), its victory was due to its constant formal superiority. Plato and Aristotle ensured a stylistic victory for philosophy in their own time; but thereafter philosophy and science abandoned the contest, and deliberately surrendered to formlessness—in fact, lack of style became synonymous with scientific method. In the time of the great Athenian thinkers, it was far different. Between the lines of the speech *To Nicocles* we can easily read Isocrates' fear of the influence of philosophy. But he does not close on a polemical note. Although (as he says [113]) the great educators of his day have widely different views of the true methods of culture, they are all agreed that it should make men capable of judging and making right decisions. Theoretical disputes should therefore be abandoned. It is better to watch the facts, and see whose education stands the test of emergency—for even the philosophers agree that the aim of all their work is practical.[114] This is a strong appeal to the young king to show himself worthy of his master's teaching, and to remember that its value will be measured by his deeds. All eyes are on him: and the sharpest are those of Isocrates' critics. And Isocrates is thinking of himself when, in his closing words, he exhorts Nicocles to honour and cultivate men of sense and superior insight, because a good adviser is the most useful of all possessions, and best befits a monarch.[115] Thus, Isocrates once more repeats his claim to see further into things than others do—including ordinary politicians. That is the real basis for his authority.

5

FREEDOM AND AUTHORITY:
THE CONFLICT WITHIN THE RADICAL
DEMOCRACY

EVER since the rediscovery of Isocrates' political works, his essays on foreign policy have attracted the greatest interest of them all: for the Panhellenic ideal expounded in them is rightly considered to be, historically speaking, the most important of his contributions towards solving the question of the survival of Greece. But in this another aspect of his political thought has often been passed by or underestimated—his attitude to the internal structure of the contemporary state, which of course means Athens for him, first and foremost. Every discussion of politics which was published in the decades following the Peloponnesian war started more or less directly with the problem of Athens. But whereas Plato soon turned entirely away from the contemporary state,[1] Isocrates always remained keenly interested in his native city. His principal work on internal politics is the *Areopagiticus*.[2]

Even in the last of all his writings, the *Panathenaicus*, we can see how closely and inseparably his life was bound up with the destinies of Athens. There too it is the internal structure of Athenian constitutional politics which concerns him. In his early essay, the *Panegyricus*, his interests were naturally different: during the long and laborious resurgence of Athens after her defeat and the loss of her naval empire, it was her relation to the other Greek states which chiefly exercised his attention. But the problems of domestic and of external politics were too closely interconnected for us to believe that it was only later in his career that Isocrates began to think about the internal affairs of his city. We must say, rather, that the *Panegyricus* is simply a one-sided expression of his attitude to the problems of statesmanship. It is the speech in which he expounds his new Panhellenic national ideal; and therefore he was bound to place his chief emphasis (both in interpreting the past history of the city and in appraising its task for the future) on the contributions made by Athens to the cause of Greece. Even the way in which he approaches the problem of internal politics proves that external policy held the foremost place in his thought: for in the *Areopagiticus* the standard by which he examines the Athenian democracy of his day is its effect on the relations of Athens to other countries. This is shown even in the starting-point which he chooses. He begins with a survey of the actual position of Athens as a Greek power at the moment when the speech was written. That makes it particularly important for us to understand the state of public feeling at the time when it appeared. In order to make the work look like an actual speech,[3] Isocrates conceives himself to be addressing the Athenian people, to warn it at a critical moment in its history. (For that role he could find famous prototypes in Solon's political poetry and in the speeches in Thucydides' history.) He starts by admitting that the majority of the citizens and the counsellors of the state are full of confidence. They will be unable to understand his anxiety, and will point to all the circumstances which seem to justify them in taking a favourable view of the external power of Athens. The separate elements of the optimistic picture which he now sketches seem to belong to a period when the second Athenian naval league (created since he wrote the *Panegyricus*) was still strong. Athens possesses a large fleet; she is mistress of the seas; she has many allies who are ready to help her whenever necessary, and many more who willingly contribute to the league's war-chest. There is peace on all sides of the Athenians' territory; and, instead of fearing the attacks of enemies, they seem to have good reason to believe that their enemies are anxious for their own safety.[4]

Opposite this cheerful picture Isocrates places a gloomier one of his own. He foresees that his ideas will be met with contempt, since many of the facts on which they are based are less obvious than those which point in the other direction. One of his chief concern is the general feeling of optimism, in which there are always implicit dangers. The majority of the Athenians believe that, with their power at its present height, they can become masters of all Greece. Isocrates on the other hand fears that power, like a will-o'-the-wisp, may lead Athens over the brink of the abyss.⁵ This idea stems from Greek tragedy. Isocrates believes that the political world is subject to the fundamental law of tragedy, whereby wealth and power are always conjoined with infatuation and licentiousness, and are threatened with destruction by these cancerous inward growths. It is poverty and abasement which really teach men, for they inculcate self-control and moderation. Thus, experience shows that it is usual for the lowly to be exalted, since humility leads them to higher things, while the mighty are easily cast down.⁶ Isocrates asserts that this law is true, not only in the life of individuals, but in that of the state. He chooses only two of the numerous examples at his disposal: the histories of Athens and of Sparta. Athens, destroyed by the barbarian invader, raised herself to the leadership of Greece because fear made her turn all her energies to the task of recovery. But from the height she had thus reached, she fell headlong down in the Peloponnesian war, and only just escaped being utterly enslaved. By living a life of soldierly self-denial, the Spartans, starting long ago from small and humble beginnings, achieved the mastery of the whole Peloponnese. But thereupon their power made them arrogant, and after they had won dominion on both land and sea they fell into the same danger as Athens.⁷ Isocrates is alluding to the Spartan defeat at Leuctra, which had made a very deep impression on the Greeks, and not least on the whole-hearted admirers of Sparta —as can be seen from the change in the estimates of the Spartan character and constitution which appear in fourth-century political writings. Not only Plato and Xenophon and Aristotle, but Isocrates himself alludes again and again to the overthrow of the Spartan domination; and they all explain it by the fact that Sparta had not been able to use her power wisely.⁸ These, then, are the examples by which he supports his political theory of historical change (μεταβολή).⁹ We can with justice assume that in his school for statesmen this problem was examined far more fully than is apparent from this brief passage in the *Areopagiticus*. The violent vicissitudes of the past two or three centuries had forced it on the Greeks much more immediately and impressively than before. He did not, then, choose his examples at random. The events on which they were founded were really those which had moved his generation to serious thought. Plato and Aristotle, like him, held the problem of political change to be of prime importance, and Greek thinkers grew more and more deeply concerned with it as time went on. In view of the experiences of his time, Isocrates holds that any exaggerated confidence in one's own security is simply self-deception. Of the two examples he cites, the Athenian disaster is obviously the more remote in time. The collapse of Sparta is expressly described as parallel to the misfortune which Athens had already sustained.[10] For that reason it is impossible to interpret his reference to the Athenian disaster as meaning anything but the fall of the Athenian empire at the end of the Peloponnesian war. Isocrates is reminding his hearers of the violence of that overthrow, and of the power possessed by Athens before it was overthrown—power far greater than that which it now holds.

The speech on the Areopagus has usually been dated to the period after the loss of the Social war (355 B.C.), whereby the second Athenian naval league collapsed just as the first had done, and the unexpectedly swift recovery of the years after the *Panegyricus* was just as swiftly nullified and reversed.[11] If this were a correct conception of the situation assumed in the *Areopagiticus,* it would be pointless for Isocrates to detail the hidden dangers in the position of Athens, and there would have been no need for him to give examples to prove that great power often harbours the seeds of its own destruction. Instead of warning his fellow-citizens of the possible threats of the future, he would have had to analyse the catastrophe which had just occurred; and he would have tried to teach them not by pointing to terrifying examples from the past, but by reminding them of what could be learnt from the experience of the immediate present. He would not have proved his point by quoting the destruction of the first Athenian empire in the Peloponnesian war, but would necessarily have alluded to the destruction of the second. And in describing the Athenian optimists, he could hardly have said that they believed Athens still owned great financial and military power, commanded a strong fleet and a large number of willing allies, and was undisputed mistress of the seas. The chief support for a later dating of the speech is found in a few allusions to contemporary events which scholars have felt must belong to the period during or immediately after the Social war. In their eagerness to identify a few events mentioned by Isocrates with already known historical facts, readers have lost sight of the general situation which is presupposed, and have therefore been misled in interpreting the individual events.[12]

Isocrates picks out various symptoms which should be taken as warning signals. He speaks of the growing hatred and mistrust which the other Greek states feel for Athens and her naval league, and of the renewed hostility between Athens and the Persian monarch. These, he concludes, are the two factors which overthrew Athens at the time of the first naval confederacy.[13] Now, this description is usually taken to apply to the situation after the Social war. It suits it, certainly; but in that case it would be pointless for Isocrates to foretell a repetition of the first disaster, since it had already been repeated. And, according to his views, the statesmanlike quality of his speech lies in the fact that, even before the catastrophe, a watchful observer could, under his guidance, perceive the symptoms he describes—the growing hatred of the Greeks (and he means, first and foremost, the other members of the naval league) and the growing enmity of Persia. Most of his allusions are general and typical rather than individual, and are appropriate to various situations of the years between 370 and 350—for instance, the gradual estrangement of the allies, and the renewed threats of the king of Persia.[14] The more concrete events which are mentioned point to the time before the outbreak of the Social war (357) [15] rather than to the period after it ended in the final collapse of the naval league, and the destruction of Athenian naval supremacy.

If these arguments are cogent, then Isocrates' speech on the Areopagus is not a post-mortem report after the expiry of the naval league, but a last attempt to prevent its decease. It is from this point of view that we must consider its proposals for the transformation of the Athenian democracy. All the dangers which he sees threatening Athens spring (he believes) from the internal structure of the Athenian state. By good luck or by the genius of one man, he says, we have at times won great successes; but we have been unable to keep our winnings. Led by Conon, and by his son Timotheus, we gained the mastery over all Greece; but we soon frittered it away again, because we do not have the kind of constitution which would enable us to keep it.[16] The soul of a state is its constitution. It is to a state what reason is in a man. The character both of individual citizens and of political leaders is modelled upon it, and so is their conduct.[17] We have met this idea already, in the speech *To Nicocles*.[18] Here it is repeated in its negative aspect. Isocrates affirms that all the Athenians agree in believing that they have never been worse ruled under democracy than they are at present. People sitting and gossiping in the shops talk of nothing else; and yet no one is ready to make any change, and all the citizens prefer the present degenerate form of political life to the constitution created by their ancestors.[19]

This sharp criticism prompts us to ask what was the origin of these contradictions in the thought and conduct of the Athenians. Obviously, the state was for most of them—even for those who felt it needed reform—a convenient means by which to satisfy their selfish aims. It compelled each of them to restrain his desires somewhat, but at the same time it kept others from encroaching. In fact, it established a sort of equipoise among the many individual selfishnesses, which ultimately allowed each man to satisfy a fair number of his own wishes, and was therefore indispensable to him. It is at once obvious, and it was admitted by political thinkers of every kind, that in such an age the factors which really form men's lives and men's souls are those desires (chiefly material desires) which men are exercised in satisfying through this kind of communal life. Then paideia sinks to become mere education. It is engaged in trying to change conditions from outside, without being able to set up a real counterpoise to the forces opposing it. If it attempts to do more, it must give up the attempt to mould the nation as a whole, and withdraw into the cloistered life of school and sect: that was what nearly all the philosophers did; otherwise it can merely endeavour to influence a few dominant individuals —or, in democratic communities, to influence the whole state by altering certain parts of its organization. The latter alternative is Isocrates' educational ideal. In his address *To Nicocles* on the duties of the monarch, he had pursued the first of these courses. In the *Areopagiticus* he takes up the second.

Believing that the central problem of politics is to discover how men can be changed, Isocrates makes a genuine attempt to attain this end by changing the structure of the state they live in. He decides that men were different in the times of Solon or Cleisthenes. Accordingly, the only way to set them free from their exaggerated individualism is to restore the constitution of that long-past century.[20] As the 'soul' of the state changes, the separate citizens will change too. But his fine epigram, 'the soul of the state is its constitution',[21] conceals a serious difficulty. Granted that in the sixth century, for the ancestors of Isocrates' contemporaries, their constitution had really been the soul of the state—or, in other words, the spiritual expression of the real life of man, the form of their communal life which was not imposed from without, but grew, as it were, from within—was it so in the time of Isocrates? Did he not think of it simply as the means to an end, as a legal arrangement by which he could re-create the social pattern destroyed by any harmful forces? According to this altered conception of the constitution, it was no longer to be life which formed the character of the Athenian citizen, but rather education; and thereby the state was to take over the task of educating its members. Paideia now became something merely mechanical; and this defect is all the more noticeable because of the contrast between the highly technical way in which Isocrates tries to realize his paideia, and the romantic picture of the past which he hopes thereby to restore. In this the whole contrast between him and Plato is evident. In Plato's ideal state too, life seems to be romantically simplified and limited; yet it starts out from a perfectly realistic point of view, because it places all the emphasis on the task of forming the human soul. Everything in *The Republic* is aimed at doing that. Isocrates, on the other hand, believed that he could form the souls of his own contemporaries in the Athenian state of his time simply by restoring the rights of the Areopagus. And therefore, in accordance with his conception of paideia, he makes the state simply a supervising authority.

It is instructive to see how this idealistic picture of the past, through which he characterizes the spirit of the education he wants Athens to pursue, turns, unknown to him, into a wish-fantasy in which all the problems of the present are solved and

all its sorrows ended. We can best understand this strange attitude to history if we realize that all his praise of past virtue
is the negation of a corresponding evil in the present. For large
circles of critical observers, the radical form which Athenian
democracy had reached in the fourth century presented an in-
soluble problem: the problem of mass-rule, as it is vividly de-
picted in the *Areopagiticus* and other speeches of Isocrates,
with all its epiphenomena—demagogues, informers, arbitrary
and tyrannical exercise of power by the majority over the cultured minority, and so on. In the time of Solon and Cleisthenes,
the fathers of their democracy, the Athenians did not believe
that democracy meant licence, that freedom meant anarchy, that
equality under the law meant freedom to say anything one
wished, and that the highest happiness was the power to do
what one wanted without hindrance: instead, by punishing men
of that type, the state tried to make its citizens better.[22] The
equality they strove to achieve was not mechanical equality
among all men, but proportional equality which gave each man
what was due to him.[23] And the elections too were not mechanized
by the introduction of the system of lots, which substituted sheer
chance for the sane judgment of worth. The officials, instead of
being elected directly from the entire population, were selected
by lot from a previously elected group of really qualified citizens.[24] The watchword of the city still was 'Work and save', and
no one left his own property to look after itself while he got
rich out of other people's. The citizens were not then accustomed to live off state revenues; on the contrary, they con-
tributed to the state's funds from their own possessions whenever necessary.[25] It was not then a matter of good business, but
rather an obligation, to take part in the government.[26] To keep
all this praise of the past from sounding anti-democratic, Isocrates adds that in those days the demos was still lord and master:
it appointed its own officials; it chose its servants from among
those who had the necessary leisure and property to let them
serve.[27] A man's understanding of business was more likely to get
him elected than his sound party views.[28]

These sentences read like the programme favoured by the
moneyed conservative minority of Athens at the time when the
second naval league collapsed. We know the character of their

criticisms of contemporary Athenian politics mainly from remarks made by the opposition which came into power after the
Social war ended in defeat. At that time, the rich financier Eubulus, by introducing his new fiscal system, remedied the mistakes
made by demagogues in the previous decade, and won the confidence of the great majority of the population for many years
thereafter. The principle 'Work and save' suits this political
attitude admirably; and those reproaches against the aberrations
of mob-rule and demagoguery must have come from the moneyed
classes that had had to bear the cost of the radicals' war-policy
without being able to keep the state from downfall.[29] Several
times, especially in the speeches written when the Athenian naval
league was dissolving, Isocrates hints that he is deeply concerned about the cause of the property-owning minority.[30] He is
cautious, of course, about expressing this feeling; and yet, again
and again, he defends that class against the attacks of demagogues. He says it is wrongly suspected of being anti-democratic,
although it contributes more to preserve the safety of Athens
than most of the loud-mouthed orators.[31] But he believes it necessary to defend himself too against the suspicion of anti-democratic tendencies. This is doubly necessary at the moment when
he is making the unpopular proposal to restore greater rights
to the Areopagus.[32] The re-establishment of the authority of the
highest court, especially touching the supervision of public morality, had for long been an essential point in the conservative
platform; and, in Isocrates' picture of the classical era of Athenian democracy, it is the central tone and the finishing touch.[33]

The slogan which had been so important in Athenian constitutional disputes during the latter half of the Peloponnesian war,
'Return to the ancestral constitution' (πάτριος πολιτεία), is not
expressly used by Isocrates. But, by and large, his retrospective
admiration for the democracy of Solon and Cleisthenes agrees
best with the programme of the party whose ideal that was. In
the Peloponnesian war, and during the oligarchy of the thirty
'tyrants', its chief representative had been Theramenes, leader
of the moderate democrats. Aristotle tells us in *The Constitution of the Athenians* that one of the first steps taken by the
Thirty, when they came to power in 403, was to repeal the laws
by which, under Pericles, the authority of the Areopagus had
been decisively diminished and its guiding influence on the state

definitely abolished.[34] This restoration took place in the early part
of the rule of the Thirty, when Theramenes and the moderate
conservatives still exercised a major influence on their policy.
When the democrats returned after their overthrow, they obviously reversed these measures; and even the fact that Theramenes, the inventor of the slogan, was executed by Critias and
the radical wing of the oligarchs did not make the moderate
democrats and their spiritual heirs any more beloved by the restored democracy during the succeeding decades. It is easy to
understand therefore why Isocrates deliberately omits or para-
phrases the notorious phrase, 'the ancestral constitution', in order to avoid giving offence. Still, it is perfectly clear that he is a
supporter of Theramenes' programme, which must have had
adherents even after the restoration of the democratic constitution in Athens. This assumption, based on the resemblance between Isocrates' essay on the Areopagus and the ideals of Theramenes, finds welcome confirmation in the fact that biographical
tradition names not only the sophists and Gorgias, but the statesman Theramenes, among the teachers of Isocrates.[35]

It is impossible, then, to deny the continuity of political
thought between the two statesmen. Once recognized, it is simple
to trace it far beyond the *Areopagiticus,* both in the literature of
political philosophy and in the constitutional history of Athens.
Hence, it is improbable that the proposals of Isocrates in this
speech are simply the utterances of one man, looking nostalgi-
cally back from an hour of crisis to the constitutional reforms
proposed during the Peloponnesian war. On the contrary, Isocrates' whole attitude to the demagoguery and radicalism of his
time makes it clear that, on questions of internal quite as much
as of external policy, he was closely allied to the political group
whose ideals he is upholding. As we have seen, the speech declares that all the power and fortune of Athens are bound up
with the personality of Timotheus and his work as military
leader of the second naval league.[36] Isocrates holds that every
Athenian set-back and every Athenian defeat began after this
great man was dismissed.[37] He was never weary of singing the
praises of Timotheus: even after his death, despite his final overthrow and condemnation, he still defended him valiantly.[38] If we
are right in dating the *Areopagiticus* to the critical time before
the outbreak of the Social war, it was written in a situation

which makes it all but impossible to assume that in such a vital question Isocrates was a lonely pioneer in internal politics, and had taken no steps to ensure agreement with his great pupil—who was nevertheless living in retirement in Athens, and must have watched the career of his incompetent successors with growing concern.[39] Without doubt he held, like Isocrates, that the new government had in a short time destroyed everything he had laboriously built up;[40] and his re-entry into Athenian politics and Athenian war councils, after the affairs of the naval league came to a crisis, shows that he had expected his hour to come again. Isocrates drives home the necessity of constitutional reform by pointing out the effect it will have on foreign politics: and that is the best evidence that his views were shared by Timotheus, whose sole aim was, not the internal interests which bulked so large in the minds of the mass-leaders, but the assertion of Athenian power and prestige in the world.

Therefore we cannot escape the conclusion that, in the *Areopagiticus* and elsewhere, Isocrates is speaking in the name of a real political party, which, in the face of impending danger, was making a last effort to regain its share in moulding the destinies of Athens, after its enemies had brought her to the extreme verge of ruin. We know that its attempt failed: it could not prevent the disastrous collapse of the second naval league. The profound gulf between that party and its left-wing opponents, which is so obvious in Isocrates' speech, was not bridged over even by the appointment of Timotheus to share the command of the fleet. It can be seen yawning widely throughout the Athenian strategy of the following years. Isocrates himself tells us that his ideas on the revision of the constitution were by no means new in his mind when he resolved to advocate them publicly. He had expounded them several times to his friends; but he had always been warned against putting them in writing, because they would expose him to the charge of anti-democratic sentiment.[41] We may infer that he did not explain his views in casual conversation, but as a regular part of the political paideia in his school. This also casts a clear light on his relation to Timotheus, and fits in with the fact that his ideas originated in the circle of Theramenes: that is, during a considerably earlier period.[42] Isocrates must have been deeply moved by the intellectual struggles of the last years of the Peloponnesian war (when he was already a grown man), even although he had refrained from taking any public part in political activity. This interpretation is made even more probable by the resemblance between the attitudes of Isocrates and Plato during this period.[43]

Now that we understand the political background of the *Areopagiticus,* we can not only account for the remarkable impression of reality which is conveyed by Isocrates' description of the better days of Athenian democracy, but see in his vivid picture of the past a great number of direct allusions to contemporary history. The picture is meant to have an educational effect: to be an example. From this point of view, read (as well as the sections on public affairs expounded above) the passage on religious festivals and the treatment of matters of ritual, as they had been and as they were in Isocrates' time, and you will find that every word is a bitter attack on the lack of culture in contemporary Athens. He accuses his contemporaries of disorderliness and vacillation between two bad extremes in the practice of religion. At one time, he says, the Athenians pompously offer three hundred steers to the gods, and at another they let the rites handed down from their ancestors fall into disuse. Now they celebrate some newly-introduced festival with great magnificence, if it entails a public entertainment; and now they have to pay contractors to carry out the holiest ceremonies.[44] The Athenians of earlier days, he goes on, had none of the levity with which nowadays people abandon long-standing rituals or add new ones. They believed that piety consisted not in extravagant display, but in the will to change none of the traditions of their forefathers.[45]

In this connexion we may remember how carefully (to judge from its extant fragments) a new type of history just then coming to its perfection, the Athenian Chronicle or *Atthis,* studied and recorded the objects of religious worship and the origins and rituals of all divine festivals and pious celebrations. In Roman history there is an analogy for this backward-looking attitude: it is Varro's *Antiquitates rerum humanarum et diuinarum,* a grand compendium of cultural history and theological learning. It was created in a situation inwardly analogous to Isocrates' period. In Isocrates' school also there must have been a new kind of understanding for that particular phase of the past. In order to write sentences like those quoted above, he must have made a detailed study of the sacrificial rites and festivals of old Athens—and that is true even if we allow for his tendency to make rapid generalizations. When he wrote them, he had already seen the first attempts at composing Attic chronicles. On the other hand, we should surely not be wrong to assume that both his interest in these matters and his study of the political history of Athens were factors which impelled his pupil, Androtion, to write his own *Atthis*. The religious conservatism voiced so clearly in the *Areopagiticus*, by his criticisms of the degeneracy of festivals and of the worship of the gods, cannot be considered separately from the political conservatism which aspires to return to the ideal 'constitution of our ancestors'.

He devotes particular attention to the social problem in earlier Athenian history, in order to counter a possible objection. It might be said that his picture of the past had a dark side, in the relation of rich and poor, noble and humble. He holds that it had not: that the social body was then in perfect health. So far was the poor man from envying the well-off, he says,[46] that he cared quite as much for the welfare of the great as for his own, thinking that their prosperity meant his own livelihood. He who had property certainly did not despise the less fortunate, but considered their impoverishment as a disgrace to himself, and helped them in their need by giving them employment. Compared with Solon's description of the state of Athens in his day,[47] this seems a very rosy picture—even although there may have been periods in the history of Athens when such a relation between rich and poor was commoner than in Isocrates' day. We may, for instance, recall Cimon's social attitude, which was based on patriarchal views.[48] As long as there was a landed aristocracy of his type in Athens, it was more possible for such a relationship to exist than in a period of growing industrialism, growing capital, and growing poverty. In those times wealth was not being relentlessly accumulated: people put their money out in productive investments, not thinking that every such venture was inevitably dangerous. In business matters there was mutual confidence. The poor valued security in economic conditions just as highly as the rich. A man did not hide the

amount of his wealth; he endeavoured rather to make practical
use of it, in the conviction that it would not only help the state's
prosperity but increase his own possessions.[49]

Isocrates does not believe that the sound health of the early
Athenian state was due to some external cause or causes; it
was brought about by the way in which the citizens were educated.[50] From this point he moves quite naturally on to his main
idea, the need for a strong Areopagus—for he looks at the
Areopagus essentially from the point of view of education
rather than of legal administration. What is wrong with the
system in Isocrates' time is that the Athenians limit paideia to
paides: to children,[51] who have many people to keep them in
order, while every one can do exactly what he wants as soon
as he grows up. In the past, grown men were looked after even
more carefully than children. That was why the Areopagus was
set to supervise the orderly behaviour (εὐκοσμία) of the citizens.
No one could be a member of it but men of good family and
praiseworthy life. That principle of selection made it the finest
tribunal in Greece.[52] Although it had since those days lost much
of its power, its moral authority was still so great that anyone—even the worst rogue—who came in contact with it felt
involuntary respect for it.[53] It is on that moral authority that
Isocrates wishes to rebuild the education of the Athenians.

His greatest emphasis [54] is on the fact that good laws alone
will not make good citizens and a good state. If they did, it
would be easy for all the Greek states to borrow the letters of
the law from one another, and therewith the spirit of virtue.
It was common enough for one state in Greece to copy some
of the provisions of another's laws; and the philosophers who
worked out codes of law either for one definite country or for
the betterment of all states in general were moved by the same
admiration for good legislation. But, as we have already seen,
Plato's thought was penetrated by the realization that laws, as
such, are useless when the spirit of the state, its *ethos,* is not
good.[55] For the particular ethos of each community, which deter-
mines the education of its citizens, forms the character of every
individual on its own model. The most important thing therefore is to inspire the state with a good ethos, not to fill it with
an ever-increasing swarm of special laws covering every aspect

of life.[56] Many pointed out that in Sparta there were few written laws, but the behaviour of the citizens was excellent. In his ideal state Plato had thought it needless to have any specialized legislation, because he assumed that in it education would, through the free will of the citizens, produce the effect which in other states laws vainly attempted to create by compulsion.[57] That idea was taken over from Spartan life as it was then conceived to be, and as it was described by contemporaries, especially Xenophon. Isocrates, however, does not use Sparta as a model. He sees the ideal life rather in ancient Athens, where a strong Areopagus still supervised the conduct of all the citizens, and especially of the young.[58]

He describes [59] the young men of his time as being very gravely in need of education. Youth is the time of great spiritual chaos and of a multitude of desires. The young ought to be educated by 'good occupations which are laborious but enjoyable'—for no others will hold their interest for long.[60] Also, their activities must be varied to suit the differences in their stations in life: everyone must engage in something appropriate to his social class. Since young men belong to different classes, it is impossible for them all to have the same kind of education. Isocrates believes it is absolutely necessary to adapt paideia to the economic situation of each individual.[61] This point of view was of considerable importance in Greek educational theory as long as there was any call for higher education. We meet it as early as Protagoras—in Plato's dialogue he makes the length of each youth's education dependent on the wealth of his parents.[62] And it is still alive in 'Plutarch' 's essay on education, which is based on older works now lost to us.[63] It is only in Plato's *Republic* that it is eliminated, for there all higher education is a state concern, and is enjoyed by pupils specially chosen by state officials. Isocrates, of course, with his own special political attitude, could not possibly take that view. He was bound to believe that state control of education was merely the wild dream of extreme radical theory, which in practice would not create an intellectual élite, but rather mechanically level down all social distinctions. Isocrates believed such distinctions to be an inevitable and irremovable fact of nature. Therefore he wanted to abolish any unnecessary hardships, but not to destroy property distinctions themselves. For him, the goal of all education lay beyond them.

'Our ancestors,' he writes, 'assigned to each a type of training suited to his wealth. Those who had less property they put to farming and trade, knowing as they did that poverty comes from idleness and crime from poverty. Thus, by destroying the root of evil, they thought they would get rid of all the errors which arise from it. Those who had sufficient property they compelled to engage in riding, gymnastics, hunting, and intellectual exercise (φιλοσοφία), seeing that these pursuits make some men distinguished and keep others from most kinds of wickedness.' [64] Notice how he puts intellectual culture on a level with different types of sport. That is characteristic: like the aristocrat Callicles in Plato's *Gorgias,* Isocrates conceives paideia as a noble game. It was from that point of view that one particular social class was most likely to acquire a taste for the intellectual interests of the new era. He is not in the least afraid to acknowledge this to a wide circle of readers. He assumes that Greeks and Athenians of all classes can appreciate this way of describing intellectual education, perhaps better than they would if it were presented (as by Plato in conformity with the ideals of knowledge) as a too earnest and brooding concentration on problems of the mind and spirit.

Isocrates believes that the real defect of education in contemporary democracy is the lack of any kind of official control. It had existed in the earlier and healthier periods in the life of Athens—mainly in and because of the smaller local units: parishes in the country and wards in the city (δῆμοι and κῶμαι). In these it was easy for each individual's way of life to be watched. Cases of disorder (ἀκοσμία) came before the council on Ares' Hill, which used a system of discipline divided into various grades. The mildest of these was a warning; next to that was a threat; and the gravest, to be used when both the others failed, was actual punishment.[65] Thus, with the complementary principles of retribution and supervision working together, the Areopagus 'controlled' (κατεῖχον) the citizens. (This word appeared long before Isocrates, as early as Solon, and often recurred in discussions of legal methods of disciplining the citizenry.[66]) *Then* young men did not waste their time in gambling-dens and among flute-girls as they do now, says Isocrates. Everyone stayed at his own occupation, admiring and imitating those who were best in it. In their conduct to their elders young men observed the rules of respect and politeness. Their demeanour was serious; they had no ambition to be known as wits and buffoons. A young man's gifts were not estimated by his versatility in society.[67]

In bygone days the entire life of Athenian young men was imbued with *aidôs*: that was the honourable feeling of holy shame, and, since Hesiod, no age had more loudly lamented its disappearance than that of Isocrates.[68] The central elements of his description of old-fashioned discipline remind us of Aristophanes' contrasting pictures of the old and new paideia in *The Clouds*.[69] But in details also they harmonize to a surprising degree of accuracy with the ideal set up by Plato in *The Republic,* which may well have been another source of inspiration for them. The concept of aidôs was inherited from the aristocratic moral code and the aristocratic educational ideal of early Greece; and, although it had lost more and more of its meaning during the intervening centuries, it had played an enormously important part in the thought of the Homeric and Pindaric Greeks.[70] Shame or respect, it is difficult to define it. It is a complicated spiritual inhibition, induced by many different social, moral, and aesthetic motives—or it is the feeling which causes that inhibition. Under the influence of the democratic trend, which endeavoured to embody all moral standards in the rational form of law, it had for a time retreated into the background of Greek sentiment. But if we think of Isocrates' conservative outlook, we can easily realize how his paideia went back to the old aristocratic morality, not only for separate rules and for the principle of imitating great models, but also for the sense of honourable shame, aidôs, as the basis of ethical conduct.[70a] Both in his 'mirror of princes', the speech *To Nicocles,* and in the ideal system of education which he sketches in the speech on the Areopagus, Isocrates is deliberately striving to revive the discipline and the standards of the old Greek aristocracy. In the period which he so much admires, the spring of the Athenian democracy, that discipline had still been fully active, and had added much strength and firmness to the social structure. Isocrates was fully aware of the importance of that factor, and he believed it even more important than law, which was the very keystone of the democratic way of life. His scepticism about the educational value of legislation *per se,* and his admiration for the moral force of shamefast respect, condition each other reciprocally.

After his penetrating critique of democracy in its existing form—radical mob-rule—Isocrates feels that he must anticipate the charge of being an enemy of the people. He could expect this accusation to come from the leaders of the demos, and he does well to answer it now; for he takes the wind out of his opponents' sails by ruling out the obvious misinterpretation that he was joining the side of the oligarchs, who were opposed to the democratic constitution on principle.[71] The charge of oligarchic sympathies was freely thrown about by orators in the Athenian assembly to cast suspicion on their political adversaries. Now Isocrates makes his own use of this custom to show that, of all possible charges, he is least open to that of exchanging political views with those of the thirty tyrants, who in the eyes of every Athenian democrat embodied all the wickedness of oligarchy for all time to come. How could anyone who idealized Solon and Cleisthenes, the fathers of Athenian democracy, ever be suspected of wishing to impugn the liberties of the citizens, which were the foundations of the Athenian state?[72] Isocrates could point to the fact that in every one of his writings he had condemned oligarchy and praised *genuine* equality and democracy.[73] His choice of instances to exemplify genuine freedom shows that here he makes the concept of democracy essentially a broader thing than most democrats of his day. He considers it to be most completely embodied in old Athens and in Sparta, where true popular equality had always been dominant in the selection of the higher officials and in the regulation of daily life and conduct.[74] Much as he holds the radical mob-rule of his time to need reform, he far prefers it to the tyrannies of oligarchy, which Athens had experienced under the Thirty.[75] He elaborates this comparison to impressive length, partly to remove all shadow of doubt from his own democratic attitude, but also to show what he holds to be the ultimate standard by which every constitutional theory must be judged.[76] His speech had started by laying down that the political life of Athens needed reform, and his argument had been based on a gloomy criticism of the position of Athens in relation to other states in

Greece.[77] It is therefore only logical that he should derive his respect for radical democracy, in comparison with oligarchy, from a comparison between the abilities which Athens had shown, under these two constitutional systems, to assert herself against her external enemies.

It is almost as if, in this part of the essay, the old Isocrates—the Isocrates of the *Panegyricus*—had spoken once again, in order to test the results of both these policies by his own criterion; but here the Panhellenic ideal is thrown into the background by Athenian nationalism. Isocrates is eager to show that he is not merely blaming the faults of the demos, but is prepared to glorify its services to the nation wherever he can find them. In the *Panegyricus* he had given powerful expression to his wish that Athens would recover her naval supremacy, and he had used the plan of a war by all the Greeks under the dual leadership of Sparta and Athens against Persia to show the need and justification for such supremacy. Accordingly, in the *Areopagiticus,* he estimates the political achievements of the demos and the oligarchy by the amount which each has done to establish Athenian sea-power. In this comparison, the oligarchs cut a poor figure, for they were the heirs of defeat and of the broken empire: they were wholly dependent on the Spartan conqueror, and ruled only by his favour. The only laurels they won were in domestic politics, where they triumphantly crushed out freedom and efficiently served the victor in conquered Athens.[78] They exercised their despotism over none but their own countrymen, while the victorious demos, during the decades of its supremacy, had garrisoned and held the citadels of other Greek states.[79] It was the demos that had made Athens the mistress of Hellas; and, despite all the anxiety with which he gazes into the future, Isocrates still believes that she is destined to be the ruler, not only of the other Greeks, but of the whole world.[80] This is the last time in Athenian history that Periclean imperialism (revived in the second naval confederacy) raises its voice to demand, in the name of Athenian claims to hegemony, a reformation (μεταβάλλειν) in the political education of the citizen body—a reformation which will make the country and the people capable of successfully maintaining the historical role which they have inherited from their forefathers.[81]

By this just apportionment of blame and praise Isocrates

wishes to appear to be a true educator;[82] but he does not want, by acknowledging the great deeds of the Athenian democracy, to allow his readers to imagine that his acknowledgments are so whole-hearted that the Athenians can be perfectly self-satisfied. They should not compare themselves with a few crazy degenerates, and be proud because they have kept the laws better; but ratner with the greatness (areté) of their ancestors, of which they themselves at present fall far short.[83] He wants his criticism to make them discontented with themselves, so as to raise them up to their true task. Therefore, in conclusion, he holds up before them the ideal of the *nature* (φύσις) which is the heritage of the Athenian people, and which it must use to its fullest potentiality. He explains this concept by a brief comparison with the nature of particular crops and trees which are at their best in particular countries: in the same way (he goes on) the soil of Attica is able to bring forth men far superior to those of other lands—not only in the arts, in active life, and in literature, but in manliness and character.[84] The whole history of Athens is simply the unfolding of the Athenian people's national character. In adapting the concept of *physis,* nature, to the realm of intellect and history, Isocrates is obviously following Thucydides. For, in Thucydides, as well as the idea of a nature common to all men (ἀνθρωπίνη φύσις), there is also the conception that separate races or cities have each a special physis: this corresponds to the medical uses of the term, for medicine also distinguished between a universal and an individual human nature.[85] But the peculiarity of Isocrates' argument is the special normative sense he gives to the idea of nature. In medicine it is usually universal nature which is the standard, while the individual physis simply manifests it weakened and modified in some way; but Isocrates' concept of the Athenian nature embodies both a universally applicable standard and a unique individuality. The educational message he wants to convey is that the Athenian people must bring to light the true Athenian physis, its better self, which is for the time being obscured and hidden, but which was clearly displayed in the great exploits of its ancestors.

Later, when Athens is in even more urgent danger, during the critical struggle with Philip of Macedon, this idea reappears in the speeches and harangues of Demosthenes. That is not

the only such tribute paid by him to Isocrates, widely as he
differs from him in other respects about the Macedonian problem.[86] The new generation which had dedicated itself, after the
collapse of the second naval league, to the task of remaking
the life of the Athenian state, was deeply influenced by Isocrates' criticisms. And no one repeated his attacks on tyrannous
demagoguery and the materialism of the mob with greater conviction than Demosthenes, the champion of democratic liberty
against its foreign oppressor. No one more whole-heartedly
supported Isocrates in his protests against squandering public
funds to amuse the proletariat, and in his stern admonitions
against the growing effeminacy and spiritlessness of the bourgeoisie. Finally he actually took over the idea with which the
Areopagiticus culminates—that the Athenians owed it, not only
to themselves, but to their character as defenders and champions
of all Greece, to rouse themselves from the torpor of mis-
management and *laisser-faire*, and to submit to a more drastic
type of education which would make them capable once more
of fulfilling their historical mission.[87]

But the tragic aspect of it all is this. At the very time when
Isocrates' thoughts were taking root in the hearts of his successors, he himself was finally abandoning his belief that Athens
could ever rise again to be an independent power and the leader
of a great federation of states. In his speech *On peace* we can
see how he resigns all his plans for the spiritual revival of
Timotheus' great political creation, the new Athenian empire
based on the second naval league. It is impossible to read the
educational programme he sketches in the *Areopagiticus* without thinking how, in the Peace speech, he seems to bid farewell
to the allies who had seceded after the Athenian defeat. The
fundamental thought of the *Peace* is his conviction, expressed
with great emphasis, that Athens has now no choice, except to
give up all her claims to mastery of the seas, and, therewith,
the idea of a naval confederacy on which Athenian imperialism
is based. Now he advises her to make peace—not only with her
rebellious allies, but with the whole world of her enemies.[88] She
can do so only if she extirpates the ultimate cause of conflict:
and that, says Isocrates, is her ambition to rule others.[89]
If we are to understand how his views could change so radi-

cally as this, we must try to realize how terribly the situation of Athens had changed since the collapse of the naval league. The league's sphere of suzerainty had shrunk to about one-third of what had been its greatest extent under Timotheus. The number of its members had dwindled correspondingly, since the most important of them had left it altogether. Its financial situation was desperate.[90] The numerous financial and political lawsuits and trials which we know from Demosthenes' early speeches cast a lurid light on the degenerate morality of the age, and on the dubious devices adopted by politicians to save the situation.[91] The great men who had carried the second league up its triumphal ascent, Callistratus and Timotheus, were dead. The only conceivable policy for Athens seemed to be this: she must trim her sails adroitly to the storm, abandon all active foreign politics whatever, and slowly build up her internal security, especially in the sphere of finance and economics. In that situation Isocrates advised her to return to the Peace of Antalcidas and found her foreign policy on it: [92] that is, to give up the dream of Athenian naval empire for ever. That programme shows close resemblances to Xenophon's pamphlet *On the Revenues,* which appeared about the same time, and was intended to point a way out of the crisis.[93] The group which had now taken command was the conservative bloc led by the political financier Eubulus, and their thoughts were running in the same channel.

The speech *On peace* goes more deeply than the *Areopagiticus* into the problem of providing a political education for the Athenian public.[94] Today it is customary to date both of them to the end of the Social war, or later. But, after what we have said above, it is clear from the changed attitude of Isocrates in the speech *On peace* that the two cannot belong to the same period. Obviously they both criticize contemporary Athenian democracy in the same way: hence the close parallelism in argument between the two. But they express widely different views of the problem of Athenian naval supremacy. If we accept the current view that in the Peace speech Isocrates was driven to advise the abandonment of Athenian naval ambitions by bitter experience at the secession of the allies, then that too will confirm our conclusion that the *Areopagiticus* belongs to the epoch before the crisis became acute: for in it (as has been shown above) he supports his proposal to increase the educational influence of the Areopagus by showing that that is essential for the maintenance of the naval empire.

In the speech on the Areopagus Isocrates never expresses the slightest doubt that Athenian naval domination is an admirable thing, a great benefit both to Athens and to Greece. And in that he is still the old Isocrates of the *Panegyricus*. There, he had preached that it was necessary for the sake of Greece to restore Athenian sea-power, destroyed in the Peloponnesian war.[95] That destruction he called 'the origin of all disasters' for Greece. The pessimism of the *Peace* is a complete reversal of this: the beginning of the naval empire is now called the beginning of all evil.[96] From one to the other of these two poles Isocrates' political views had travelled; and the *Areopagiticus* stands, not at the negative extreme (the abandonment of naval empire) but between the two.[97] Corresponding to this reversal of his views on Athenian imperialism, from the *Panegyricus* to the *Peace*, we can observe two contrasting views of the Peace of Antalcidas in the two works. In the *Panegyricus* it is savagely condemned: it is used as an image of the shameful dependence of Greece on the Persians—a disgrace which could only have been possible after the collapse of Athenian sea-power.[98] In the *Peace* (along with the hope of Athenian sea-power) this nationalist attitude is abandoned: the Peace of Antalcidas is presented as an ideal programme to which the Greeks must return in order to reorganize their decaying political life.[99] Any reader of the *Panegyricus* can see that this renunciation of his earlier views must have been extraordinarily painful for Isocrates, and we can readily understand how his anti-Persian sentiments sprang up again in his *Philip,* as soon as a new 'champion' of the Greek cause appeared in the person of the Macedonian king.

But one thing made it easier for him to abandon the thought of naval empire. That was his morality, which had at first made an uneasy alliance with his imperialism, and which at last triumphed over it in the Peace speech. Imperialism is justified in the *Panegyricus* on the ground that it benefits the whole Greek people. In the *Peace,* empire (ἀρχή) and aggrandisement (πλεονεξία) are utterly condemned, and the rules of private ethics are expressly declared valid for the relation of state to

state.[100] Isocrates is careful not to rule out all possibility of a
return to the creation of large federal groups, but against the
principle of domination founded on force he sets up that of
hegemony—which he here conceives as leadership by the most
worthy.[101] Hegemony means, for him, that other states will volun-
tarily annex themselves to Athens; and such a relationship he
thinks not impossible. He compares it with the position of the
Spartan kings, who also held an authority resting not on power
but on honour; and he suggests that that type of authority ought
to be set up between great and small states. (He forgets, for the
moment, that in Sparta the authority of the kings was always
guaranteed by the power of the state.) He describes the craving
for power and empire as the source of all evil in Greek history;
it is, he declares, essentially the same as tyranny, and therefore
incompatible with the spirit of democracy.[102] As he says, he wrote
the speech *On peace* in order to change the ideas of his countrymen about power.[103] Once again, as in the *Areopagiticus,* he shows
that the political situation cannot be improved unless the basic
morality of Athens is entirely reformed—although here we cannot help feeling that the pressure of fact and historical necessity
was partly responsible for his attitude.[104] It is not so much that
he has renounced allegiance to his old ideas, as that he is always
ready to learn from experience. We have seen that already, in
the lessons which, in the *Areopagiticus,* he drew from the first
collapse of Athens in the Peloponnesian war and from the defeat
of the Spartans at Leuctra. And now we see it again when he is
eighty years of age, in the Peace speech after the naval league
has been broken up. In the *Areopagiticus* he had used bitter
experience to warn his countrymen against tragic hybris; in the
Peace he uses it to justify the complete renunciation of all purely
imperialistic attempts to gain power. Imperialism, of course,
means no more than the domination of one Greek state over
others: for not even at this time, when he was sadly turning
away from his early dreams of empire, did he give up the idea
that the Greeks were destined by nature to rule the barbarians.
From the point of view of supra-national morality, this limita-
tion makes the ethical preachments of the *Peace* weak and difficult to defend. But even though Greek political life remained
far from the ideal, the moral code of Isocrates is an important
symptom of the changing attitude of Greek states to one another.

In that respect we must compare it with such phenomena as the new code of morality for war between Greek states laid down by Plato in *The Republic*.

Isocrates is convinced that the problem is ultimately an educational problem. The lust for power is deeply rooted in human nature. To uproot it needs a violent effort of the spirit. He seeks to show that power (δύναμις) has led men into licence. It is, he thinks, not his own contemporaries who are responsible for the degeneration of the citizens under its influence, but their fathers —the brilliant generation of the first Athenian naval empire, its brilliance shadowed now by the darkness of the present.[105] Just as in the *Areopagiticus* he maintains that the law-abiding character and carefully controlled life of the early Athenians had educated them to all kinds of virtues, so in the *Peace* he ascribes all the wickedness and disorder of the present to the fact that the people and its leaders have been corruptly educated by power.[106] In that he is well aware of the factors which are actually making the life of the Greeks of his time. The character of the individual is not formed by the innumerable plans and devices which are employed under the name of education to annul and weaken evil influences, but by the whole spirit of the political community. It is greed, the passion for power (πλεονεξία), that shapes the characters of men. Whenever it dominates the state and its actions, it soon becomes the supreme law in the conduct of the individual. He calls on the spirit of democracy to oppose this dynamism—the true tyranny, which has become pre-eminent in every type of state.[107] For many years democracy has paid more whole-hearted allegiance to power than all others, without seeing that thereby it is sacrificing its own self.[108]

Thus, democracy is defined as the renunciation of the struggle for power. But does this not mean that the only important democracy still in existence ought to eliminate itself from the struggle with other types of polity, which are striving to reach the same goal by the direct road, unhampered by the constitutional rights of individual citizens? It is a terrifying question. But we are bound to acknowledge that Isocrates called upon Athens to abandon the arbitrary power of her imperialism only after events had begun to force her to do so willy-nilly.[109] His ethical appeal to free will simply acted as a justification after the fact, appeasing the consciences of those patriots who still thought in terms of traditional power-politics. He wanted as far as possible to lighten the task of those hard-working statesmen who were picking up the pieces of the second empire. And he was justified in using his intellectual prestige to educate his country-men into accepting this new resignation, because he had for so long upheld the ideal of Athenian sea-power. The spiritual revo-lution through which he had passed was symbolic of the histori-cal process which worked itself out during his life; and it is almost incredible that the Athenian state, which he endeavoured to usher into peaceful retirement, could once again, under the leadership of Demosthenes, rise in its might to enter a last battle. This time the battle was not to be a contest for the acquisition and control of power, but a struggle to retain the only thing Athens had left after the loss of its empire—liberty.

6

ISOCRATES DEFENDS HIS PAIDEIA

ISOCRATES often mentioned himself in his speeches; but in one of his latest works, written when he was over eighty,[1] he gave the fullest play to this autobiographical impulse, and composed an entire oration about his own character and his own work. This is the speech about the exchange of property—*antidosis,* as it is called in Attic law. In Athens the expenses of equipping the fleet had all to be borne by a small and heavily taxed group, the richest of the citizens. To ensure equal distribution of burdens, a law was passed, by which anyone chosen to be a trierarch and pay for a warship could (if he held it to be an unfair imposition) name a richer citizen who should with more justice be called upon to take the post; and he could challenge the wealthier man to exchange his entire property with him, as a proof that he was really poorer than the substitute whom he had named. When Isocrates was an old man, he was challenged in this way; and during the case his opponent made many attacks on his character and his teaching. They were not strictly relevant —except that he was reputed to have made a huge fortune by his work as a teacher and publicist.[2] His widespread unpopularity in political circles must have been known to him even before it was voiced in his opponent's speech: for both in the *Areopagiticus* and in the speech *On peace* (that is, in both his utterances on internal politics) he tried to answer the charge of being an enemy of the people.[3] It is easy to see how it arose —from his repeated attacks on demagogues. And now, in the Antidosis speech, he takes it up again.

The speech on the Antidosis as we have it is not what he really said at the lawsuit. Like most of his political speeches, it is more than it pretends to be.[3a] Ostensibly in order to vindicate himself against this public attack, he composed a long essay in which he 'defended' his life, character, and teaching—that is, he gave them what he held to be the correct interpretation. In the speech he himself called attention to this peculiar blend of forensic oratory, self-defence, and autobiography,[4] and let it be understood that he thought this 'mixture of forms' to be a particular refinement of his rhetorical skill.[5] It allowed him, under the pretence of self-justification, to say things which would have been repulsive if uttered as self-glorification.[5a] Plato, with the *Apology*, was the first to convert the speech of defence into a literary form in which a great man could defend his 'activity' (πϱᾶγμα) and thereby utter a confession of faith.[6] The egotistical Isocrates must have been deeply impressed by this new autobiographical pattern, and in the Antidosis speech he adapted it after his own manner. Of course, his life had none of that background of heroic struggle which sets off the noble and steadfast figure of Socrates in the *Apology;* and yet he clearly felt that his position was closely similar to Socrates', for he took every opportunity to remind the reader of it by verbal imitations of Plato's words and of the accusation aimed at Socrates.[7] He admitted quite freely that his challenger and the danger which was supposed to be threatening him were only stage properties; and he himself thought the speech, the longest of his works, was also the weakest.[8] Still, it has a good deal of charm as the first real example of autobiography,[9] or rather of the self-portraiture of a great man's life and thought; [10] but, besides that, it is deeply interesting as the most detailed of all presentations of the aims and the success of Isocrates' paideia.[11]

The charge which Isocrates pretends to be answering is that he corrupts the young by teaching them to gain unjust advantage in law courts.[12] This was the obvious charge against every professor of rhetoric, and in defending himself against it Isocrates begins by distinguishing himself from the general run of speech-writers who merely trained their pupils for practice at the bar. In the earliest of his programme-speeches, *Against the sophists,* he had expressly attacked these hacks,[13] and he always took special offence when his political and moral teaching was confused with their dreary forensic exercises.[14] Compared with them (he says) he felt like Phidias compared with the workmen that stamp out clay statuettes, or like Parrhasius and Zeuxis compared with the commercial painters who turn out cheap daubs.[15] Again and again he voices his proud sense of being a great artist. It is partly due to the fact that in content his speeches are

unlike all others, being about the interests of the entire Greek
nation, instead of the affairs of private individuals.[16] But in
form also they are closer to poetry than to the ephemeral
speeches pronounced in ordinary legal disputes, and their effect
is more comparable to that of the rhythmical creations of poetic
fantasy.[17] The atmosphere in which they are created breathes
not the restless urgency of daily life, but a noble leisure.[18] That
(he goes on) is why his art attracts many pupils, while none of
the practical speech-makers can really form a school.[19]

He explains the content and form of his speeches by quoting a
selection of fine passages from them. This is done to set his
written orations in the proper light.[20] The selection, as he presents it, is the clearest possible proof that his influence depended
on teaching his pupils to admire and imitate great examples,[21]
and we are safe in concluding that, as he speaks here, so he
actually taught. In his school, as here, he did not merely discuss
the technique of language and composition—the final inspiration
was derived from the art of the master himself. In this connexion he uses the word 'imitation' in his very earliest programme-speeches,[22] and it must have grown to be the central
principle of his method. His teaching implied that actual perfection was capable of being attained and recognized: so now, in
the Antidosis speech, the aged Isocrates presents himself to the
world of literature as a perfect classic, and his own works as
models to be imitated. This, be it noted, is the root from which
all classicism sprang. He sets his *Panegyricus* above all his other
works,[23] both because of the excellence of its form and because
it best shows his patriotism. In his comments on this oration, he
stresses his Athenian sentiment rather than his Panhellenism,[24]
obviously because his fellow-citizens had suspected it. But since,
two years earlier, he had openly described the Athenian naval
empire as the root of all evil,[25] he could not quote the *Panegyricus* (in which he had expressly supported it) without some alteration. So, in the short summary of that speech which introduces
his selection from it, he substitutes the neutral word 'hegemony'
for what he had originally called sea-power.[26] It was hegemony
that he had recommended in the speech *On peace*, as a mild
type of honorary leadership which would be preferable to a
naval empire based on force, if ever the naval states of Greece
could be re-united.[27]

Isocrates, himself an Athenian patriot, feels sure that his *Panegyricus* will still be applauded by patriotic feeling in Athens; and yet it is significant that, immediately after citing that glorification of Athenian history and Athenian power, he counterbalances it by quoting a passage from his newest work, *On peace* —and he chooses the section in which he calls for permanent peace and the abandonment of Athenian naval ambitions.[28] He could easily have been charged with changing, or rather with reversing, his attitude;[29] so the easiest defence for him was to present the two ideals recommended in the *Panegyricus* and the *Peace* as two different expressions of the same educational policy. He himself, after citing the *Panegyricus,* says that many of his readers might think that Athens as she then was needed blame more than praise, and he deliberately adduces the speech *On peace* as an example of his intention to educate her by criticism.[30]

The third selection he takes is from his speech *To Nicocles.* It is clear that, in certain circles, he had been particularly criticized for his friendship with the Cypriot king and had been charged with accepting large presents from his royal pupil.[31] He replies that he certainly did not get them for doing what his opponents charged him with—training the future monarch, the supreme judge in his own land, to practise the eloquence of an advocate at the bar.[32] He reminds his public that in the speech *To Nicocles* he had struck a new line by maintaining that the education of powerful men was a special necessity, and had himself provided a worthy example of the art.[33] As for enmity to the people, he points out that he had urged the king to make the welfare of his people his chief interest. He wishes his hearers to infer from this that he held that to be even more the duty of a democracy like Athens.[34] And this we must accept as true, interpreting 'democracy' as it is described in the *Areopagiticus.*[35] Still, it was very diplomatic of Isocrates not to cite that speech (although it is particularly characteristic of his educational outlook) among the others quoted in the Antidosis oration. Some have concluded from this omission that the *Areopagiticus,* although all indications show that it was earlier, had not yet been written; but the self-justificatory motive which controls the whole Antidosis speech makes that conclusion quite untenable.[36] It would have been very inappropriate at that moment for Isocrates to recall his own unsuccessful attempt to limit the democracy of Athens by bringing it under the sway of a small moral and educational authority.

He rounds off this selection from his speeches with some remarks on the importance of his work as a teacher of politics, which they have exemplified. It is, he says, more important work than that of the legislator, whose influence is confined to the sphere of business and the internal affairs of one city. On the other hand, Isocrates' paideia, if it were followed, would benefit the entire Greek nation.[37] In this he uses his faith that the interests of Greece are the highest moral law, to justify all his work as an educator: for, since there is no Panhellenic state to realize something of his aims by legislation affecting all Greece, the only instrument which can bring about any such political situation is the spiritual force of education and culture. We cannot be sure whether, among the legislators, Isocrates meant to include Plato. The old man was writing his *Laws* about the same time; and all the intellectuals in Athens must have known about it. That book cast a new light on Plato's educational ideals, at the very end of his life. But although with it he took his place at the end of the long series of Greek lawgivers, Isocrates could not admire him for it: for, as he says, 'men love the oldest laws and the newest speeches'.[38] And that was his own purpose—not to rival the great legislators of Hellenic history, but to be the political counsellor of the whole Greek nation and in its present crisis to speak the word of deliverance.[39] But his work as a teacher (he goes on) is also more important than that of philosophers or sophists who exhort people to self-control and justice: for their summons to *phronésis*, moral knowledge, and action in accordance with it, is directed only to individuals, and they are content with winning the agreement of a few men.[40] But Isocrates' education is meant for the whole polis; he tries to persuade its citizens to undertake enterprises which will make themselves happy and free the rest of the Greeks of their present troubles.[41]

The speech on the Antidosis is a monument raised by Isocrates to commemorate and glorify his own paideia. In it his doctrines are embodied in a group of his own writings, and over against them he sets a group of his greatest pupils, from the beginning of his career down to the date of his speech. Modern readers have more interest in the literary side of his memorial: as we look at it we seem almost to hear his own voice speaking to us. But for the Athenians, especially those who did not know his speeches, the long line of statesmen and great public figures who had gone through Isocrates' school must have meant more than the written word. For they were a living witness to the force which had flowed from his teaching all through the life of his native city. In them anyone could see what he meant by paideia; and there was no near rival to the work he had done in training them to be the leaders of their states. Later, this kind of test was extended to his competitors. Alexandrian scholars tried to measure the political effectiveness of the great philosophical schools, especially Plato's Academy, by following the public careers of various pupils of Plato.[42] Many of them had a brief and violent life as political experimentalists and revolutionaries. In an earlier chapter we have explained this fact as due to their extreme interest in theoretical problems, which led them so often to become thoughtful recluses; but from the standpoint of the real state of their day, most of them were characterized by their inability to do any real service to it and exert any real influence upon it. Isocrates obviously felt that, when he wrote the history of his school in the Antidosis speech, and in the eyes of his fellow-Athenians he must have been partly vindicated by the fact that his pupils had done so much to help their own cities.

But this once more raises the old question: how far is education responsible for its products? In *Gorgias,* Plato had indicted the older type of legal rhetoric for teaching its adepts the black art of making the worse cause appear the better. Isocrates had protested against this indictment at the outset of his career, maintaining that when bad men misuse any of the goods of this world, it is the fault of the men, not of the goods.[42a] But at the end of his career he is ready to take full responsibility for his pupils, provided that now, when their good actions are so apparent, he is not denied all share in what they have done.[43] He leaves the decision to the reader; but he is obviously thinking of the discussions which had started after Socrates' death, about his relation to his pupils Alcibiades and Critias. The Socratics had taken great pains to absolve their master from responsibility for the deeds done by these two men during the grimmest period

of Athenian history. But Isocrates, as he himself says, had no
need to conceal the guilt of any pupil of his who had injured
Athens.[44] This would remind all his readers of the most famous
of all his pupils, Timotheus son of Conon. A few years before
the publication of this speech, he had twice served as admiral
and statesman in the second naval confederacy, and had twice
raised Athens to the summit of her power. Then, because of his
conduct in the Social war, he had been impeached, deprived of
his office, and condemned to pay an exorbitant fine; and had died
in self-imposed exile soon afterwards. He had naturally been
put down to Isocrates' discredit; for everyone knew how closely
the two men were associated. And everyone knew that their association had been more than mere friendship: it had been an
acknowledged political sympathy. Isocrates had admittedly acted
as Timotheus' publicist on several occasions,[45] and Timotheus
owed his political principles to the teaching of Isocrates. So
when Isocrates now says he is ready to accept full responsibility
for the acts of all his pupils, he is challenging public opinion—
which is sufficiently startling in a man who is generally scrupu-
lously careful about offending the susceptibilities of the demos.

The motives which led him to address the Athenian public in
this way were rather complex. He may well have been seriously
disquieted by the irresponsible criticisms which were in the air—
charges that he was the intellectual father of the political reaction embodied in his pupil Timotheus. Since he fully endorsed
Timotheus' views on the failure and collapse of the second naval
league, he was bound to feel it important to keep his friend's
name unspotted, at least in the memory of those whose judgment he respected. Also, much of the reputation of his own
school and his own teaching seemed to be at stake in this case;[46]
and he feared that his whole life-work might be threatened by
the very connexion between his paideia and actual politics of
which he was so proud and which he had tried from the first
to establish and maintain. All these facts were so closely connected that he decided he must throw the whole weight of his
reputation as a writer and moralist behind the cause of his great
pupil. His fear of the charge of anti-democratic tendencies, his
insight into the true facts of the case, and above all his knowledge of Timotheus' character gave him the courage to make this
attack—which is unique in all his writings. The speech displays

to us the whole tragedy of his career—outwardly such a record
of success: and that tragedy is for Isocrates the tragedy of the
Athenian state as well. Ultimately, it is the old problem of
the relation between a great personality and the masses, as they
interacted within the framework of Greek democracy.

Isocrates draws a picture of Timotheus' great character, and
sets it against the glorious background of his deeds as general
and leader of the second naval league. Still, the eulogies he
lavishes on him are not exaggerated, but appropriate to the magnificence of his exploits. He counts up the cities captured by him,
compares them with the victories of all earlier Athenian generals, and finds that Timotheus has far surpassed them all.[47]
The names of his most important victories are like symbolic
figures grouped around the pedestal on which his monument is
reared: Corcyra in the western sea, Samos in Ionia, Sestos and
Crithoté on the Hellespont, Potidaea and Toroné on the coast
of Thrace, the battle of Alyzia, the peace imposed on Sparta
which broke her domination and led to her downfall at Leuctra,
and finally the overthrow of the Chalcidian league.[48] Timotheus
who won these victories was still, despite his renown, a surpris-
ingly human person, and had none of the heroic poses of earlier
generals. He was not a muscular bravo hardened by countless campaigns, but a man of delicate health and sensibilities. Compared
with the battle-scarred swashbuckler Chares (the idol of the
radical party, whom Isocrates obviously has in mind although
he does not name him) he was the very model of a modern
general. Men like Chares he used as subordinate officers, while
he himself was great in all the arts of military strategy.[49] He
saw each war as a whole, its elements being the enemy and the
allies. He always looked at it as both a political and a military
problem. In all his operations, he managed to remain unaffected
by influences behind the front, and yet he carried his campaigns
to a successful conclusion.[50] He was a master in the art of moulding an army to answer every purpose, and knew how to live with
it and enable it to sustain itself.[51] His strength did not lie in the
mailed fist. He was a moral conqueror. By winning friendship
and confidence he gained everything that his successors lost by
awaking the hatred of Greece. He cared more for the popularity
of Athens among the Greeks than for his own among his soldiers.[52]

This whole character-sketch was obviously written with an eye on the collapse of the second naval league, which had been brought about by the mistrust and hatred that the Greek states felt for Athens.[53] Without saying so expressly, Isocrates traces all the misery of the Athenians to the fact that they did not recognize their real leader. He compares Timotheus to another much admired leader of modern times—the Spartan Lysander— and gives Timotheus the preference. Lysander won his position through one stroke of phenomenal luck. Timotheus always kept his head in handling all sorts of difficult problems, and always proved to be right.[54] The Athenians (he says) were bound to feel that such a eulogy of the general whom they had thrice deposed was a severe indictment of themselves. From the stand- point of absolute justice, Isocrates cannot resist the conclusion that their behaviour to their greatest citizen was simply shame- ful. And yet it was only too easy to understand, considering the stupidity of human nature, the envy which darkens every great and splendid thing, and the confusion of the times.[55] Not only that, but Timotheus had helped to create some of this misunder- standing about himself. With that admission Isocrates leaves the lists of political argument and moves onto his own ground, that of education. Timotheus (he points out) was an enemy neither of the people nor of mankind. He had neither arrogance nor any similar bad quality; but his loftiness of soul, so useful to him as a general, made him difficult in ordinary social intercourse, and made him seem to be arrogant and harsh.[56] And here Isocrates makes an admission which is of the greatest importance for a proper estimate of his relation to his pupil, for it shows that his educational influence on Timotheus lasted long after he had ceased to be *in statu pupillari,* and continued until he had reached the peak of his career. 'He has often heard me say this: a states- man who wishes for public approval must choose the best and most useful deeds and the truest and most righteous words—but he must also take the most elaborate care by all he says and does to get the reputation of amiability and benevolence.' [57]

At this point Isocrates puts in a whole hortatory speech addressed to Timotheus. It is not intended to be a large-scale repetition of anything actually said, so much as an impressive demonstration of the kind of teaching Isocrates used to give. In vivid direct speech the reader is shown how the master tries, by the power of personal address, to control the proud soul of the hero. No one can fail to think of the Homeric prototype which Isocrates must have been remembering when he composed this mixture of truth and fantasy—the warning speech of Phoenix to Achilles in the ninth book of the *Iliad*. The problem there was the same: how can the feelings of the *megalopsychos,* the 'great soul', be bound down, how can the man of might be fitted into the framework of human society, which is not always ready to give thanks and gratitude when they are due? The tragic failure of the attempt—which, in Homer as in life, is due to the hero's own proud nature—casts a cold and ominous shadow on this scene between Timotheus and Isocrates.[58]

Isocrates explains to him that the masses love pleasure and think more of men who flatter them than men who do them good. They would rather be betrayed by a genial man who smiles on everyone than be helped by a man who proceeds with pomp and circumstance. Timotheus has never paid any attention to this fact. If he is successful in the conduct of the state's foreign relations, he believes the politicians at home will be friendly to him too.[59] He does not see that they judge his acts not by their true nature, but by the good feeling they themselves have for him. If they like him, they will overlook all his blunders and magnify all his successes mountains high.[60] But he does not realize the importance of this factor in internal politics, although in external politics he is expert in judging the psychology of the other side.[61] He cannot bring himself to make concessions to the demagogues, although he realizes the power of these men who have the confidence of the public.[62] In other speeches Isocrates agrees perfectly with Timotheus in his estimate of the demagogues.[63] Here, he seems to be inclined to take back some of it, in order to help Athens and Timotheus; and he blames the uncompromising pride with which Timotheus rejects these proposals. 'When I said this, Timotheus agreed that I was right; but he could not change his nature. He was a gentleman, well worthy of our city and of Greece—but he was of a different stamp from these men who dislike all their superiors.'[64]

The form of the speech on the Antidosis makes it possible for Isocrates to insert, besides vignettes of such profound historical importance as this, a discussion of business-matters—the size of

his property and his lecture-fees: for he is pretending to answer
a challenge to exchange possessions with another Athenian, and
therefore it is 'inevitable' for him to refer to the material aspect
of his profession.[65] He passes over to it lightly, almost chattily.[66]
We cannot fail to notice the self-complacency with which he
handles it, although all his remarks are couched in a vindicatory
tone. This is justified by the attacks on him which he mentions
in the introduction, with reference to the gifts he received from
his pupil, the late King Nicocles of Salamis.[67] His great wealth
was almost bound to awaken the envy and greed of the multitude; for whereas in earlier times people were proud to show
off their property, in Isocrates' day everyone tried to hide what
he owned, for fear of losing it, even if it had been honourably
acquired.[68] He does not treat the question of money as a side-
issue. It is clearly a point to which he wishes to direct the
reader's close attention—for the material profits of his teaching
were, both in his own eyes and in those of most of his contemporaries, a final standard by which to judge its success.[69] He
tells us it is wrong to compare a professor's salary with the
wages of an actor, and suggests we should compare the salaries
of men who hold the same rank in the same profession.[70] The
first example he gives is his own teacher Gorgias, who taught in
Thessaly when the Thessalians were the richest people in Greece,
and who was considered to be the wealthiest man in his line.
Even he left only 1000 staters. This is a discreet hint about the
approximate size of Isocrates' own property.[71] He adds that he
always spent much less on himself than on his public duties.[72]
The money he made came not from Athenians but from foreigners who were attracted to Athens by his reputation, and had
therefore helped the prosperity of the city.[73] In this point it is
easiest for us to see the practical bourgeois character of Isocrates and of his teaching. Only compare it with the high-minded
attitude of Plato, who never made a business of philosophy!
Every one of Isocrates' writings shows with perfect frankness
how much he valued money for its own sake.[74] In judging him,
we must remember that therein he followed a path well trodden
by sophists and rhetors before him. Like doctors, they had
always charged their clients as much as they saw fit. We must
never forget that Plato's feeling about the matter was an exception to the rule.[75]

As we have pointed out, the speech on the Antidosis is Isocrates' autobiographical account of his life and work, in the form of a defence of his paideia. He explains it first by giving examples of his speeches, then by listing his pupils and telling their exploits, as well as by pointing to the high estimate in which the public held his teaching—as evidenced by its eagerness to share it and the high fees it paid him. Finally, in the last part of the oration, he gives a general account of his educational work, and expounds the principles on which it is based.[76] He starts by saying that public opinion about the value of philosophy and higher education is so uncertain that it is hard for him to make himself understood.[77] From his early programme-works on education—the speech *Against the sophists* and the introduction to *Helen*—we know that he was always careful to make his own position clear by distinguishing himself from others. And so the last of these vindications turns into an attempt to keep his contemporaries from confusing his type of teaching with others. While disowning ideals to which he does not subscribe, he takes occasion to judge and condemn them. Much depends on the kind of education we choose, for he who has the young has the state.[78] Isocrates' argument is inspired by that belief, and he deliberately makes it his first point in order to awaken the interest of all, even those who professed to be unconcerned by such problems. He considers that the influence teachers have on the young is not important for their own private aggrandisement so much as for its influence on the safety and welfare of the polis. If it were really true that culture corrupted the young, (as frequently maintained ever since the trial of Socrates and now stated in the charge Isocrates pretends to be answering), then it ought to be rooted out. But if it is beneficial, then the slanders against it should be stopped, and the sycophants who threaten it with lawsuits should be punished, and young men should be encouraged to give it more time than any other occupation in the world.[79]

Isocrates assumes that all higher education of the intellect depends on cultivating our ability to understand one another. It is not an accumulation of factual knowledge in any sphere; it is concerned with the forces which hold society together. These are summed up in the word *logos*.[80] Higher education means education to the use of speech in this sense—speech full of meaning, about the essential affairs of the life of society, which were called by the Greeks 'the affairs of the polis', τὰ πολιτικά or 'politics'. Man is a being composed of soul and body. Both his soul and his body need care. That is why bygone generations created a dual system, gymnastics and intellectual education.[81] Here Isocrates does not call the latter *music,* as was customary, but philosophy, 'the love of wisdom'—for, as a Greek, he naturally understood the relation of poetry and the other 'musical' arts to the formation of the spirit.[82] There is, he continues, a far-reaching parallelism between the two forms of paideia, gymnastics and philosophy. Both of them naturally consist of *gymnasiai,* exercises. The trainer teaches the positions which have been worked out for wrestling. The teacher of philosophy explains the fundamental patterns used by the logos. Here, as in the *Sophists* speech, Isocrates is talking of his doctrine of the 'Ideas' or forms of speech, although only allusively, as is natural in a general description of his method.[83] As we have already shown, Plato treated the technical side of his doctrine of Ideas in just the same way when expounding his paideia in *The Republic.* Not only in this doctrine of the Ideas of language, but in everything that concerns the relation of knowledge, exercise, and perception of the *kairos,* the Antidosis speech is simply restating the views developed by Isocrates in the speech *Against the sophists.*[84] Therefore no change had taken place in the basic principles of his rhetorical system. That applies also to his estimate of the importance of the separate factors in education— nature, practice, and training.[85] He quotes a long section from that early programme-piece, to show that at that early date he had clearly formulated the relatively modest view of the value of paideia which he still upholds at the end of his long educational career.[86]

He now turns to attack those who despise paideia.[87] They fall into two classes. The first class doubts in principle whether it is possible to educate men both to mastery of speech and to right action.[88] The second class concedes that the intellectual and rhetorical part of the programme is possible, but claims that it makes men morally worse—because it tempts them to misuse the intellectual superiority they have acquired.[89] Both these questions are obviously among the topics which the sophists used to discuss as an introduction to their teaching. An obvious case is Protagoras' speech about the possibility of education, in Plato's dialogue *Protagoras*.[90] Isocrates refutes those who deny its possibility by arguments some of which reappear in the essay on education attributed to Plutarch. In an earlier chapter we traced this line of thought back to the educational theories of the earlier sophists. From them Isocrates seems to have taken it over.[91] Just as bodies, even the weakest bodies, are strengthened by care and attention (so goes the argument), just as animals are trained and altered in character by taming, so there is a type of schooling which moulds the soul.[92] Laymen easily underestimate the importance of the time-factor, and become incredulous unless they see results within a few days, or at least within a year.[93] Here Isocrates repeats his doctrine that there are various degrees in the effectiveness of paideia.[94] But even granting that, he still maintains that its effect can be seen in all who have a certain amount of ability. All, in a lower or higher degree, bear the mark of one and the same intellectual education.[95]

Against the second group Isocrates points out that no human motive, neither pleasure nor profit nor honour, could induce a teacher deliberately to pervert his pupils.[96] His greatest and finest reward is when some of them attain *kalokagathia* and become fully developed personalities both morally and intellectually, honoured by their fellow-citizens. They are his best recommendation, whereas bad pupils are bound to set people against him.[97] Even supposing the teacher himself lacked self-control, he would not therefore wish his pupils to be debauchees.[98] But when the pupils have a bad character to begin with, it would be unfair to make the teacher responsible for that. Education ought to be judged by its good and worthy representatives, not by the degenerates who cannot make any use of culture.[99] Isocrates does not go any further into the question posed by Plato—whether it is even possible for *real* culture to be badly or unscrupulously used. He thinks of it rather as a means than as an end. It neither claims nor endeavours to change the whole nature of man, but presupposes that the pupil already has a sound moral sense. Later, we shall show that Isocrates still has something to say on this topic.[100] But now he asks: why did his pupils journey all the way from Sicily or the Black Sea to Athens to get an education? Not because there was any scarcity of bad men to corrupt their character in their homeland, but because the best teachers lived in Athens.[101] Rhetorical culture in itself does not make people greedy and malevolent, as is shown by the large number of statesmen who helped Athens to reach the height of her power—for they all possessed that one gift and through its help they achieved their aims. Isocrates names as examples not only Solon and Cleisthenes, who created 'the ancestral constitution', but the great figures of the imperialist era, Themistocles and Pericles.[102] These men were typical of the same rhetorical culture and state policy which Plato had condemned in *Gorgias,* and whose supposed knowledge he had stigmatized in *Meno* as mere opinion resting on 'divine dispensation'.[103] Of course Isocrates knows these objections. But he regards Pericles and the others just as they were regarded by the Athenians before Plato and most of the Athenians after Plato—they are the highest standard of all areté. So nothing is left of the charge against rhetoric except that it can be misused: and so can any art.[104] That does not alter Isocrates' faith in the civilizing power of the logos. And, as all the basic principles of his thought reappear in this final and fundamental exposition of the nature of his teaching, to form a huge and comprehensive synthesis, he closes this part of his apologia with a word-by-word repetition of the lofty hymn to Logos which he had made Nicocles utter in the speech that bears his name.[105]

Clearly this defence of Isocrates' paideia is not aimed so much against public opinion in general as against other representatives of paideia who are opposed to rhetoric. In the concluding section of the speech, his opposition to Plato's Academy comes clearly into the light. He charges its members with one error in particular: they, who know the power of the logos better than anyone else, still depreciate it just as heartily as the uneducated, in the hope of making their own type of education appear more valuable.[106] There is a good deal of personal feeling in this; but Isocrates is evidently anxious to suppress it, although he makes no secret of his dislike for the Platonic school of philosophy. He says he would be more justified in speaking bitterly of them than they of him. But he will not lower himself to the level of men warped by envy.[107] These words do not rise merely from the old professional rivalry of rhetoric and philosophy, which was so fully set forth in *Helen* and *Against the sophists*. They harbour a tone of personal rancour which is not difficult to explain. There is a tradition that when Aristotle was a teacher in Plato's Academy (that is, during Plato's old age) he introduced instruction in rhetoric. In his lectures he parodied a line of Euripides, thus—

'Twere shame to hold our peace, and let Isocrates speak! [108]

His purpose in giving the course was to answer the demand for formal education: he was adding instruction in rhetoric to complement the existing courses in dialectic. But it was also an attempt to put rhetoric on a more scientific footing.[109] For both of these reasons his course must have hurt Isocrates' school and provoked his resentment. One of Isocrates' pupils, Cephisodorus, wrote a large polemic work against Aristotle, in four books, which there is some evidence to show was composed when he was still teaching in the Academy.[110] Aristotle had such a malicious wit that his new lectures probably contained some shrewd hits at Isocrates, even though he often cited the old man's speeches as models to be imitated. Their pupils probably did what they could to exasperate the conflict. And yet Isocrates here tries to keep his tone impersonal, and is even ready to make certain concessions to Plato's ideal of culture. We must interpret this as an attempt to forget the bitterness which had arisen between his pupils and Plato's, in the dispute with the Academy, and to address himself directly to the master. Despite his dislike for school-rhetoric in general, Plato had concluded *Phaedrus,* his most recent work on the subject of rhetoric,[111] with a eulogy of Isocrates and a tribute to his philosophical nature.

That is the best explanation for the way in which Isocrates avoids polemics in the Antidosis speech.[112] What he says makes a neat counterpoise to Plato's qualified praise of him in *Phaedrus.* He does make certain concessions—for he has altered his estimate of the importance of theoretical studies. He is now willing to admit that dialectic (or 'eristic', as he still persists in calling it) and the mathematical sciences like astronomy and geometry do not harm young men, but benefit them, although the good they do is not so great as their teachers aver.[113] By this he obviously means the Platonic Academy, for it had always (but especially in the last decades of Plato's life) been distinguished by teaching these two subjects together.[114] 'Most people', he says, think they are hair-splitting and verbiage, because they cannot see their value in practical life.[115] We may recall how he himself expressed that opinion in his early writings, and actually used these very words in his attacks on Plato.[116] Now he is on the defensive; and also, perhaps, he has learnt how to look at things from a different angle. He is willing to acknowledge that logical and mathematical studies are of considerable value in intellectual education, although he still emphasizes their practical uselessness.[117] Certainly, he says, that kind of culture must not be called *philosophy,* because it leads neither to correct speech nor to right action; but it is training for the intellect, and a preparation for true philosophy—i.e. for political and rhetorical education.[118] It is similar, therefore, to training in literature, music, and poetry, which serves the same purpose and makes the student able to learn greater and more serious subjects.[119] Like Callicles in Plato's *Gorgias,* he believes that it is desirable for young men to spend some time on the 'philosophy' of the Platonic school, provided that their abilities are not dried up and fossilized by it,[120] and that they do not run aground on the paradoxical arguments of the old sophists (he means the pre-Socratics). These false and juggling tricks, admired only by fools, ought to be entirely abolished from the curriculum.[121] But during these same years they had gained even more prestige in the Academy than before, as is clear from Plato's *Parmenides* and *Theaetetus* and the writings of his pupils. Therefore even Isocrates' last thrust was really a hit at the Academy. He always felt that metaphysical theorizing about Being and Nature (typified by the names of Empedocles, Parmenides, Melissus, etc.) was mere vanity and vexation of spirit.[122]

Now at last Isocrates turns to define the nature of true paideia, and to contrast it with the false or half-true culture. But just at this point it becomes clear how much his thought owes to his great opponent. Plato's philosophical study of education had brought the main problems so clearly into the light that Isocrates is compelled to state his dissent simply by denying what Plato had said. What *is* education—or rather, what *is* philosophy (in the true sense, not in the theoretical, Platonic sense)? Once again he takes up part of his earlier writings and strives to make it clearer.[123] The decisive point for him is that human nature is not capable of achieving a real science (in the strict sense which Plato applies to the word *epistémé*) of what we ought to do and say. (Note, by the way, that Isocrates always thinks of speech and action together.) Therefore there is only one wisdom (σοφία). Its essence is to attain, in most cases, what is best for man, simply by the use of opinion (δόξα). So we should apply the name 'philosopher' to a man who studies such things that he can acquire this practical wisdom or *phronésis*.[124] Isocrates seems to agree with Plato in holding τὸ φρονεῖν (the knowledge of good and evil) to be the purpose and the epitome of human education and culture. But he insists on giving it the practical interpretation which it had had in the ethical thought of pre-Socratic Greece. He empties it of all its abstract and theoretical meaning. Now it does not connote knowledge of virtue or of Good, in the Platonic sense, for according to Isocrates such knowledge is impossible—or at least impossible for human beings.[125] This means that we must not strive to acquire an art of politics, like that recommended in Plato's *Gorgias*— based upon that knowledge of the Good, in the manner demonstrated by Plato in *The Republic*. In *Gorgias* Plato had severely censured the great statesmen of the past for not possessing the sure standard provided by this art. But Isocrates holds that that accusation falls back on the accuser, because he demands that men conform to a superhuman standard, and thereby wrongs the best among them. Later, in his *Meno,* Plato said that the virtue of these famous statesmen was produced not by real knowledge but only by right opinion, which came to them by 'divine providence' (θείᾳ μοίρᾳ)—and Isocrates would consider that to be the highest praise a mortal could obtain.[126] Whereas for Plato the higher plane of areté and paideia lies beyond the success brought by instinct and inspiration, Isocrates deliberately, from a fundamental scepticism, confined his teaching to the realm of opinion and belief. He held that right opinion was not a part of exact knowledge, but of genius—so that it was inexplicable and could not be produced by teaching.

He felt that Plato and the Socratics insisted on overestimating the power of paideia. That is why he was so unjust as to accuse his opponents of professing to make even bad natures acquire virtue and justice.[127] It is in his criticisms of Plato's theory of paideia that his intellectual limitations are most clearly seen. For all his hatred of the hair-splitting abstractions of dialectic, he is ready to admit its educational value as formal training; and he ultimately came to do the same for mathematics too, although it was even further from his conception of 'philology' (the love of speech).[128] But on the other hand he was quite unable to understand the connexion between the intellectual cleansing and purification effected by dialectic and the moral regeneration of the soul which followed; and his purely practical mind never rose high enough to reach the clear vision of absolute standards which was for Plato the proof that education actually was possible. He judged Plato's lofty conception of paideia by the standard of wide applicability: since it could not be imparted to most people, it was, he concluded, an illusion. His ultimate standard is always ordinary common sense; and, judged by that standard, Plato's bold attempt to unite the absolute Ideas with the realities of state and education must appear simply a bridge of clouds.[129]

However, the attention which the Academy was now paying to rhetoric must have had a positive interest for him, quite apart from the criticisms of his school which it produced. By taking up rhetoric, the Academy had admitted that careful training in the use of language was indispensable. And perhaps it was that admission which made him write, in the Antidosis speech, these words, which would otherwise be so difficult to explain: 'Those who busy themselves with ethical education [of the type recommended by Plato] would be better men if they became ambitious to speak well and fell in love [eros] with the art of persuasion.' [130] Here it would seem that he is not thinking merely of the training of the intellect, but of the improvement of the moral character. There is, indeed, as he has said, no infallible knowledge leading to virtue—but it is possible for the whole nature to be changed and gradually and involuntarily improved by concentration on a worthy object of study. And it is rhetorical education which can bring that about.[131] Plato, in calling it morally neutral or even tending to misuse, entirely misapprehended its true character, according to Isocrates. It is not concerned with the private commercial interests which used to be the subjects of rhetorical training, but with great and noble matters which concern all society. The actions to which it directs attention are the most fitting and salutary, and the speaker who is accustomed to contemplate and judge such matters is bound to acquire the ability to think and speak correctly, not only about the subject in view but about all his conduct: and that ability is the natural result of serious study of the oratorical art.[132] Isocrates maintains that the orator's task is not the abstract one of making eloquent speeches and mastering the necessary technical preliminaries (namely, the various devices used in the art of persuasion), but rather to make others feel the power of his personality. For the personality behind the words is what really makes a speech convincing.[133] Plato had charged rhetoric with leading its practitioners into *pleonexia*—selfish greed, the satisfaction of every impulse—because it was merely a means without an implicit moral end.[134] Isocrates takes up this charge, and thereby lets it appear once again that his definition of true education is in every point an answer to Plato's.[135] When arguing against the power-politics of the Athenian imperialists in the speech *On peace,* he had been careful not to condemn their 'aggrandisement' *en bloc,* but to point out that they were misunderstanding a fundamental human instinct and therefore going seriously wrong.[136] What he had urged there as the proper policy for the state, he now urges as the right aim of the individual. In the earlier speech he had maintained that a policy of moral conquest and strict justice was the only real pleonexia; and here he rejects Plato's identification of pleonexia with injustice and violence, and maintains that such pleonexia does not really profit those who practise it. This is a return to the old Greek belief that honesty is the best policy. He declares that the effort to reach the high aims of moral and intellectual culture is the true and genuine fulfilment of the basic impulse to gather power and possessions for one's own self. What the so-called philosophers now call philosophy is not really philosophy; and in the same way that is not real pleonexia which they blame as being the evil fruit of rhetoric. True rhetoric, which is true philosophy and culture, leads to a higher kind of self-enrichment than that achieved by greed, theft, and violence—namely, to the culture of the personality, which is its implicit aim.[137] Isocrates declares that this theory is realized in the young men who have been pupils in his school, and he contrasts them and their enthusiastic studies with the unrestrained debauchery practised by the uncultured Athenian youths, wasting their energies in drink, gambling, and lust.[138]

Isocrates suggests two reasons for the criticisms levelled against his educational system: the slanders of false educators (i.e. philosophers) and the political calumnies of demagogues. He slips unawares from confuting the first into confuting the second, when he complains that in Athens people preferred young men to waste their time rather than to study and work hard, because that kept them politically harmless and uncritical. This remark leads him to conclude his account of his own teaching by examining it with reference to the real nature and mission of the Athenian people. Once, in the *Panegyricus,* he had thought it the highest eulogy of Athens to say that she was the home of all higher culture, whence the Greek spirit streamed out all through the world, and that she had sent her pupils forth to teach other states.[139] Now he converts that idea into the decisive proof that rhetoric is necessary and vital to the nation. He had always regarded rhetoric as the quintessence of the instinct which is at the basis of civilization, 'philology', the love of the logos.[140] Now both the political leaders and the masses in Athens often despise the logos and hate intellectual culture; and this symptom of degeneracy he holds to be an un-Athenian thing. That is an ambiguous description, of course, and anyone could interpret 'un-Athenian' almost as he liked; and yet there is an objective standard for true Athenian character. The essential and permanent contribution of Athens to world history, in the eyes of all Greeks, had been its culture.[141] If the Athenians had sunk so far that they could no longer realize that, it was time to remind them of the thing which upheld the fame of Athens in all countries—the Athenian spirit. Surely, he asks, it is impossible for the people to believe that the tough and violent demagogues who have made them hated by many of their neighbours love them more and are more useful to them than the true upholders of culture, who fill everyone they meet with love for Athens? If the Athenians persecute the leaders of intellectual culture, they are doing the same as if the Spartans were to punish all who practised war, or the Thessalians to penalize everyone engaged in horse-racing.[142]

In those years after the collapse of the naval confederacy, it must have been quite necessary to make this kind of political defence of culture. The demagogues whom Isocrates and his spiritual comrades had stigmatized as responsible for the disasters of Athens had, it is clear, counter-attacked. The radical wing in democratic Athens was becoming more and more anti-cultural, as the Athenians gradually realized the connexion between culture and political criticism. Actually, the chief representatives of culture, divided as they might be on the character of true paideia, were all spiritual opponents of the contemporary Athenian state. It was that feeling of opposition that had produced the plans for political reform expounded in the *Areopagiticus* and the speech *On peace*. And now the opposition is openly acknowledged in Isocrates' great defence of his educational ideals.[143] The one thing which the masses most disliked, the creation of a new intellectual élite to replace the old aristocracy of birth (which had now lost its importance for good), was the conscious purpose of Isocrates' teaching. The culmination of his defence is the assertion that true culture is impossible in a society dominated by demagogues and sycophants.[144] Still, he is anxious to prove that culture is not naturally alien to the spirit of Athens, and he turns once again to the example of the great Athenians of earlier ages. The statesmen who made Athens great were men of a different calibre from the demagogues and agitators who rule her now. Men of high culture and superior mentality drove out the tyrants, and set up the democracy, and conquered the barbarians, and freed the Greeks and united them under the leadership of Athens. They were not ordinary men. They were far superior to those around them. And the last counsel of Isocrates to his fellow-citizens is to honour such superior men, to love them, and to cultivate them.[145] Nevertheless, it is difficult not to see the deep pessimism which broods over all his words. They were ostensibly spoken to a jury, before the whole people of Athens; but actually they came from an ivory tower, from a distance so great as to render them ineffectual. The chasm between the individual and the mass, between culture and its opposite, had now become too wide to cross.

It is only with this in mind that we can understand why Isocrates and the party he represented were discarding their allegiance to the traditional Greek city-state and turning to a new Panhellenic ideal. And we can also understand why the most cultured of the Greeks 'made the great refusal', and failed to play their part in the last battle to save the city-state. In the rising star of the Macedonian King Philip, which seemed an omen of doom to the defenders of the polis, Isocrates saw the harbinger of a happier future; and in his *Philip* he hailed the great enemy of Athens as the man chosen by Tyché to realize his Panhellenic dreams. He urged Philip to take up the task which, in the *Panegyricus,* he had planned for Athens and Sparta,[146] and to lead the Greeks against the barbarians. Of the Athenians like Demosthenes, who organized the opposition to Macedonia, he said no more than that they could do the city no good.[147] By this time, state and culture—which had complemented and strengthened each other in the fifth century—were drifting further apart every year. Then, poetry and art had transfigured the life of the political community. Now, philosophy and culture bitterly criticized it, and they were supported by many of the politically disaffected. The last of all Isocrates' works, the *Panathenaicus,* shows him still occupied with the same great problem that he had handled in the *Areopagiticus:* what is the best constitution for Athens? In his rhetorical school the content of oratory—namely, politics—was being more and more emphasized.[148] Evidently the influence of Plato had something to do with this; for he had pointed out that empty formalism was the worst weakness of rhetorical education. But it was also the compulsion of external events and the attitude of Isocrates to the political situation of Athens which drew him in that direction. He had always admitted that it was necessary for rhetoric to have some content, so it was not difficult for him to take another step and define the content. His rhetorical gymnasium became, quite openly, a political research-institute. It discarded the spirit of panegyric for the spirit of criticism. Panegyric revived for the last time, in the *Panathenaicus,* written when Isocrates was ninety-eight; but in the old man's farewell eulogy of Athens,[149] there is none of the lofty and hopeful exaltation of his maturity. The speech breaks down into theoretical disquisitions on the best kind of constitution—which, according to Isocrates, is the correct mixture of the chief forms of polity.[150] The ideal he settles on finally is a democracy with strongly aristocratic elements, and he declares that this has already been tested in the great age of Athens, when the city had just such a constitution. That point among others he took from Thucydides, who had made Pericles, in the funeral speech, describe the Athenian state as an ideal combination of the good elements in all sorts of constitutions. The same theory influenced the Peripatetic statesmen; and through them it shaped the historical work of Polybius—particularly his description of the spirit of the Roman state—and the political ideal expounded by Cicero in his essay *De republica*.

7

XENOPHON: THE IDEAL SQUIRE AND SOLDIER

IT is not mere chance that the work of only one writer of the Socratic circle—apart from the supreme genius Plato, whose works were preserved by his school—has survived in any considerable quantity. This is the outsider Xenophon. The others, Antisthenes, Aeschines, Aristippus, and so forth, who simply imitated the moral sermons of their master, are scarcely more than names. Xenophon has always been a favourite of the reading public: both because of the multiplicity of his interests and the variety of his style, and because of his personality, which, with all its limitations, is still vivid and likable. The classicists of late antiquity were justified in looking on him as a characteristic representative of Attic grace and charm.[1] If we do not take him simply as the first Greek prose-writer to be read (as children still do at school, because of the transparent clarity of his style), but read him after the great authors of his century, Thucydides, Plato, and Demosthenes, we shall feel him to be the purest embodiment of his age, and we shall see in a different light many aspects of his work which, in spite of his pleasant style, appear to be intellectually trivial.

But even Xenophon, in spite of his homely respectability, was not merely an average man of his age—the 'man in the street'. He was an individual in his own right. He had his own strange destiny, arising logically out of his nature and his relation to his environment. He was born in the same Attic deme as Isocrates, and had the same unhappy experiences as Isocrates and Plato during the last decade of the Peloponnesian war, while he was growing to manhood. Like many young men of his generation, he was attracted to Socrates; and although he was not strictly a pupil of Socrates, the old man made such a deep impression on him that in later life, after he returned from his Persian expedition, he made more than one lasting memorial to him in his books. But it was not Socrates that moulded his fate. It was his own burning passion for adventure and for war, which drew him to the young prince Cyrus, that romantic rebel, and made him join the mercenary army fighting under his banner.[2] This enterprise, which he described in his most colourful book, the *Anabasis* or *Expedition of Cyrus,* brought him suspiciously close to Spartan political influences,[3] and he was compelled to pay with banishment for the inestimable military, ethnological, and geographical experience he had gained on the Asiatic campaign.[4] In the *Anabasis* he tells of the estate the Spartans gave him at Scillus, in the farming country of Elis on the northwest of the Peloponnese. It became his second home.[5] He stayed there for many peaceful years, living as a gentleman farmer, and writing books. His love for the varied life of the farmer is as strong a characteristic of his nature as his memory of Socrates and his interest in history and in soldiering; and, like them, it is an important element in his writing. His bitter political experience with the democracy of his own Athens impelled him to go over to Sparta. His increased knowledge of the leading men and the internal structure of Sparta (then the almost unchallenged leader of Greece) drew him to write his essay *The Lacedaemonian Constitution* and his eulogy of Agesilaus. But his 'Greek History', usually known as the *Hellenica,* marked a widening of his interest to take in the whole of contemporary history; and the 'Education of Cyrus', or *Cyropaedia,* reflected the impression made on him by Persia. During the period when Athens, with her second naval confederacy, was regaining some of her old power, Xenophon still remained far from home. He did not return till after the fall of the League, which had been the last great political achievement of Athens; and then he attempted to play his part in the reconstruction of the army and the Athenian economy with a few practical essays on a small scale. Not long after the end of the Social War (355) we lose sight of Xenophon. He was over 70 by then, and may not have lived much longer. His birth and death, therefore, coincided fairly closely with Plato's.

As his varied career shows, he was one of the men who felt incapable of getting on within the narrow limits imposed on them by their city-states, and who felt alienated from them by the experiences of their time. It was his exile (which he can scarcely have expected) that really made the gulf too deep to bridge. When he left Athens, the great war had been lost, and disruption within and the collapse of the empire without had thrown the younger generation into a crisis of hopeless doubt. He determined to make his own life. When he wrote his defence of Socrates—which now appears as the first two chapters of a later work, the *Memorabilia* or *Memoirs,* but which was probably written between 393 and 390, during the literary dispute started by the publication of the sophist Polycrates' attack on Socrates and the Socratics ⁶—it was mainly for political reasons that he joined the defenders of Socrates. He spoke from exile against the idea that Socrates could be identified with the ideals of Alcibiades and Critias ⁷—the men whom the opponents of the new Socratic school were trying to prove to be Socrates' pupils, in order to discredit everything connected with him as anti-democratic.⁸ Not even Socrates' accusers had done such a thing, when he was being tried for his life. Besides, it was dangerous for Xenophon to be thrown into such a category once and for all, if he ever intended to return to Athens.⁹ One might even infer from the essay itself, which is to be read as a separate pamphlet against Polycrates' political pasquinade on Socrates, that when Xenophon wrote it he was still hoping to return.¹⁰ In order to understand why it was embodied in the larger *Memorabilia* after it had gone out of date,¹¹ we must think of a parallel situation later in Xenophon's career. That was when he was actually recalled from exile between 360 and 350: for then it was of immediate interest once again, as a proof of his permanent love for his native city. Through his eulogy of the perfect loyalty of Socrates, he was also proving his own often questioned support of the Athenian democracy.¹²

A large part of his literary work was concentrated in the decade from 360 to 350 B.C.¹²ᵃ (His return to Athens evidently brought a new stimulus to his mind.) It is then that he must have finished his *Hellenica:* the book ends with the battle of Mantinea (362), and contains an effort to explain the collapse of the Spartan system, which he so greatly admired.¹³ His essay, *The Lacedaemonian Constitution,* also belongs to the period after the collapse of Spartan hegemony: this is made absolutely certain by the final comparison and criticism of Sparta as she had been and as she then was.¹⁴ The alliance between Sparta and Athens in 369 brought Xenophon closer to Athens, and finally he was summoned home from exile. Then, between 360 and 350, when Athens too lost much power, and her second naval confederacy was destroyed, the national tragedy inspired a new and intense educational purpose in the later books of Plato and Isocrates—*The Laws,* the *Areopagiticus,* and *On Peace.*[15] Xenophon was sympathetic to the ideals of this movement, and took his part in it with the *Memorabilia* and some smaller works.[16] We must certainly place among his latest books, written after he came back from exile, the treatise on the duties of a good cavalry officer, *Hipparchicus* (which expressly refers to Athenian conditions), the essay *On Horsemanship* (which is connected with the *Hipparchicus*),[17] and the essay on political economy dealing with the public revenues (if, as now believed, it is genuine).[18] His book on hunting, the *Cynegeticus,* which is explicitly devoted to the problem of the best paideia, should probably be placed in this period too, because it contains violent attacks on mere rhetorical and sophistical education.[19] He would not have felt like that in the country quiet of Scillus, where some have thought—because of its subject—that the book must have been written. Of course, the experience on which it is based goes back to that period; but the book itself belongs to the active literary life of Athens.

All Xenophon's books are more or less dominated by the desire to educate. That characteristic is not merely a concession to his age. It is a spontaneous expression of his nature. Even in the exciting story of the part he played in the expedition of the ten thousand Greeks, there are many touches which are purely and simply educational. The reader is meant to learn how he ought to speak and act in certain situations. Like the Greeks in their desperate straits, surrounded by threatening savages and hostile armies, he must manage to discover and develop the areté within himself. Xenophon often emphasizes the fact that many characters and actions are *models* to be imitated—to say nothing of the specialist knowledge and skill which he displays quite frankly, particularly in military affairs. But in reading it we are not so much influenced by his intentionally educational touches as by the exciting adventures of Xenophon and his comrades in a situation which would have been serious, perhaps hopeless, even for seasoned troops. He has absolutely no intention of showing off his own brains and bravery. The book is even more interesting and sympathetic because the single story it tells, how an army corps of 10,000 Greek mercenaries, after most of their officers were killed or captured, made their way through incessant dangers and battles from the Euphrates to the Black Sea, is the only bright touch in the gloomy history of Greece during those years.

What moves us most deeply is not the influence Xenophon tries to exercise on us, but the lasting impression the strange foreign peoples make on him. It appears on every page. The first place we notice it is in his ingenuous description of the Persian noblemen and their manly virtues. We cannot appreciate how much he admired their life until we examine his description of it against the idealized background of the *Cyropaedia*. Of course his admiration is not unmixed. He has nothing but bitter contempt for the treacherous conduct of the degenerate Persians with whom the Greeks had to deal. But we scarcely need his assertion in the *Oeconomicus* that if the younger Cyrus had lived he would have been as great a ruler as his famous ancestor,[20] to understand how we are to look on Cyrus' portrait in the *Anabasis*.[21] It is drawn by an enthusiastic admirer, not only lamenting the tragic death of the heroic young prince, but respecting him as a last brilliant revival of the areté of old Persia. At the close of the *Cyropaedia,* Xenophon declares that the Persian power was started on its decline by the lax morality of the court of Artaxerxes Mnemon—the king whom his brother Cyrus tried to dethrone.[22] If the enterprise had succeeded, Cyrus would have initiated a rebirth of the old Persian ideals in cooperation with the best forces of Hellenism;[23] and perhaps the whole history of the world would have been different. The character of Cyrus, as Xenophon draws it after narrating his gallant death in the battle of Cunaxa, is a perfect pattern of the noblest *kalokagathia*.[24] It is intended to impel its readers to imitate it; and also to show the Greeks that true manly virtue, fine conduct, noble feelings are not the exclusive preserve of the Greek race. Again and again Xenophon's national pride and his belief in the superiority of Greek culture and courage break through his words. But still he is far from thinking that true areté is given to every ordinary Greek at birth like a gift from heaven. In his description of the noblest of the Persians, it is good to see how constantly he realizes what his association with them had taught him—that anywhere in the world true *kaloka-gathia* is a rarity, the flower of good manners and high culture, which is fully present only in the best representatives of any stock.

The Greeks of the fourth century were in danger of losing sight of this truth, in their lofty but often impractical efforts to claim an equal share in areté for all human beings alike, as though it inhered in them along with equal civic rights. Xenophon found by repeated experience that the average Greek was superior to the average barbarian in his capacity for independent initiative and responsible action. But the greatness of the Persians was due to the impressively high level of culture and character-training which their élite attained; and the alert Greeks were well aware of this—all the more so because contemporary writers like Plato and Isocrates, in discussing education and culture, laid it down clearly that the problem of the élite was the central problem of every civilization. So Xenophon's interest in the great people of Persia and its strange way of life revealed to him the secret of higher culture—a secret often overlooked by idealistic educators. The noble Persians had a paideia of their own, or something like it;[25] and it was because they had it that they were so receptive to the highest achievements of Hellenism.[26] In Xenophon's portrait of Cyrus, two features are closely conjoined: his philhellenism, and his lofty Persian areté. Cyrus is a Persian Alexander. Only his fortune, his tyché, was different from his Macedonian parallel. The spear which pierced him might have killed Alexander.[27] If it had not taken Cyrus' life, the Hellenistic age would have begun with him, and would have followed a different course.[28] But because of that, Xenophon's *Anabasis* was the book which, by recording the expedition of the Ten Thousand, reminded the Greeks of the fourth century that any brave Greek general could do what the Greek mercenaries would have helped Cyrus to do if he had not fallen at Cunaxa. Thenceforward the Greeks felt that the Persian empire was at the mercy of the first Greek to conquer it. Xenophon had convinced all thoughtful men of that —Isocrates, Aristotle, Demosthenes.[29] Moreover, the *Anabasis* was the first book to emphasize the possibility that the Oriental culture of Persia might be fertilized by Greece, for it pointed to the paideia of the Persian nobles as a determining factor in the field of cultural relations.[30]

Greek culture, through its intellectual content and its form, always imparts to every other élite something which that élite does not possess, but thereby helps it to develop itself too. In Xenophon Cyrus is not presented as an insipid cultured personage, a thin imitation of the Greeks, but as the purest and finest type of Persian.[31] This view fits in very well with Isocrates' remark that many Greeks had no Greek paideia, whereas the best citizens of other countries were often deeply imbued with it.[32] These two Greeks, and others like them, saw, however dimly, the possibility that Greek culture might extend its influence beyond the Greek race itself, and the conditions under which this might occur. It must be linked onto the best of each country's civilization. Accordingly Xenophon came to realize that the knightly Persians, hereditary enemies of Greece, had a system of paideia closely akin to the fine old Greek ideal of *kalokagathia.* And indeed the comparison affected his view of the Greek ideal in its turn, so that he blended some traits drawn from the Persian aristocracy with his picture of Greek areté. That is the only way to explain a book like the *Cyropaedia,* which presents to Greek readers the ideal of statesmanlike and kingly virtue embodied in a Persian monarch.

Although it has the word *paideia* in its title, it is a disappointing book from our point of view. Only the first part really deals with the education of Cyrus.[33] It is not a classical 'novel of education', but a complete, although romantic, biography of Cyrus, the founder of the Persian empire. Still, it is paideia in the sense that its educational purpose appears clearly on every page. Cyrus is the model monarch who gradually conquers his position both by his own fine character and by right conduct.[33a] The very fact that the fourth-century Greeks could view such a person sympathetically shows how times had changed. And so, even more perhaps, does the fact that it was an Athenian who wrote it. We are entering the age when one of the greatest and most urgent problems was the education of young princes. To narrate the exploits and the successes of a monarch famous in history was one way to educate such pupils. Plato and Isocrates tried other ways—one chose dialectic training, and the other offered his collected maxims and reflections on the duty of the prince.[34] Xenophon is chiefly interested in the soldierly prowess of the prince. He describes it from the moral as well as from the strictly military point of view, and adds touches drawn from his own experience. Xenophon thinks the soldier is the ideal man: fresh and healthy, honest and brave, disciplined not only to resist the elements and the enemy but to conquer his own weaknesses. In a world where the framework of politics and civil security is collapsing, he is the only free and independent man. Xenophon's ideal soldier is not an arrogant domineering fellow who tramples rough-shod over conventions and laws, and violently slashes through every Gordian knot. Thus, his Cyrus is a pattern of justice, ruling his nation through the love of his friends and the trust of his people.[35] Xenophon's soldier is a man of simple faith in God. In his essay on the cavalry officer's duties he once says that the reader who wonders why he so often adds σὺν θεῷ, 'God willing', would soon understand if he had to spend his life in constant danger.[36] But also he thinks of soldiering as the best education for a truly noble man. The conjunction of soldier and ruler in Cyrus is for him a natural ideal.[37]

The education of the Persians interested Xenophon as a splendid school for such nobility and such courage. He wove a description of it into the biography of his hero. It was probably not Socrates who first drew his attention to the subject. Good society in Athens and elsewhere had long been keenly interested in the constitutions and educational systems of other nations.[38] Xenophon could give new details about Persia from personal experience and investigation—that particular aspect of Persian life had perhaps never been so well documented before. But even his account of it does not go very closely into details. He thinks Persian education is better than that of other states,[39] by which he means the Greek system as described by Plato. The Greeks are not very much concerned with education—except in Sparta, which Xenophon does not mention, and which he does not put on the same level as the rest of Greece.[39a] Everyone, he says, lets his children grow up as he likes. When they are grown up, the law takes them over and imposes its prescriptions on them. But they prove badly trained in the obedience to law, of which the Greek states are so proud, and which they call Justice. The Persians, on the other hand, begin when they are very young to teach them justice as Greek parents teach their children the alphabet.[40]

The place where they are educated is the 'free forum' or freemen's meeting-place, beside the king's palace and the other public buildings. Trade and commerce are banished from it, so that their rude bustle will not interfere with 'the orderly behaviour of educated men'.[41] (The contrast to Athens, and Greece in general, is obvious. There the market-place and the official buildings around it were full of shops and booths, ringing with loud excited talk and business).[42] This localization bound the Persian paideia firmly to the community: in fact, it placed it right in the centre of society. The superintendents of children's education were elderly men chosen for their suitability to the task; while carefully selected men in the prime of life were put in charge of educating the youths of military age, the *ephéboi*.[43] Just like adults in Greece, children in Persia had a court to which they could bring charges of theft, robbery with violence, assault, fraud, or insulting speech.[44] Wrongdoers were punished according to the law, and so also were those who accused innocent persons. Xenophon points out one peculiarly Persian feature in this code—the severe penalty for ingratitude. Ingratitude was considered the root of shamelessness, and therefore of crime.[45] This reminds us of the emphasis laid by Plato and Isocrates on aidos, honourable shame, as the basis of education and of the maintenance of any society.[46] Xenophon holds that the real foundation of the Persians' educational system is the imitation of great examples. It is by example that young men learn to comply willingly with the supreme law, which is obedience: for they see their elders always fulfilling the same duty punctiliously.[47]

Young Persians live as simply as possible. They take their bread, and their cardamon-seeds for relish, and a cup for water, to school with them; and they all have their meal together supervised by the schoolmaster. Their education goes on till they are seventeen. Then they enter the cadet corps, as ephéboi, and serve there for ten years. Xenophon praises the system of compulsory military service in youth, for that is the age which needs particular care. The cadet corps is the school of discipline. Young men in it are constantly at the orders of the officers, and a detachment accompanies the king as his bodyguard when he goes out to hunt—which he does regularly several times a month.[48] Xenophon thinks the high importance the Persians attach to hunting proves how healthy the Persian system is. He eulogizes the hardening effects of hunting, and calls it an essential part of good paideia—as in *The Lacedaemonian Constitution* and *Cynegeticus*.[49] To these two features of Persian education—the practice of justice, and the hunt—he adds one more in his *Oeconomicus*, farming.[50]

Persian society is divided by age into four classes: children, cadets, men, and elders. The cadets are only those young men whose parents can afford not to make them work, but to send them into the school of *kalokagathia;* and only those youths who have completed their term in it join the ranks of adults (τέλειοι) and later become elders (γεραίτεροι).[51] These four classes form the élite of the Persian nation. The whole country depends on them, for it is through them that the king rules the land. All this must have looked very strange to the Greek public, with the possible exception of the Spartans, who would notice many Persian institutions that were parallel to their own.[52] Modern readers will be reminded of the cadet schools of military states like Prussia, which supplied the army with a constant flow of young officers, and trained the boys up from childhood in their own spirit. The comparison is justified by the fact that the social foundations of both systems were the same. They were feudal states. And although Xenophon's description makes it seem that financial independence had replaced good birth as the entrance-qualification for the cadet corps,[53] the boys who went into it must have nearly all belonged to the landowning Persian aristocracy.

Xenophon's admiration for a soldierly aristocracy, which corresponded to the Spartan system more nearly than anything else in Greece, found a second model for him to admire in this strange Persian system. We might well ask whether his purpose in writing the *Cyropaedia* was purely theoretical, or he actually wanted to spread and realize the ideal he was describing. In such an age, it is unlikely that even a historian like Xenophon would have had a purely historical attitude to the subject. It is

tempting to suggest that he conceived the book at a time when
Sparta still held her hegemony, and that he felt he should, as
a refugee from Athens, show the educated Athenians what the
soldierly spirit really meant by depicting it as it was in Persia.
His work on the Spartan state serves the same purpose. Nevertheless, we must not think he wanted to write pure propaganda.
That is ruled out by the concluding observation he appends to
both books. At the end of the *Cyropaedia,* he emphatically condemns contemporary Persia, and explains why it has declined.[54]
He does the same for contemporary Sparta at the end of his
Lacedaemonian Constitution.[55] This would scarcely have been
possible during the lifetime of King Agesilaus, whom he praised
in an encomium written after his death in 360, as the embodiment of true Spartan virtue. The conclusion of both books, with
the historical allusions therein, tends rather to place them in the
later period of Xenophon's career, when the domination of
Sparta was past and gone.[56] And yet a man with ideas like
Xenophon's might well have wished to immortalize the spirit
of Persian education quite apart from any consideration of contemporary politics. He tried several times to anticipate the objection that he was advocating Oriental manners and a barbaric
despotism: he took care to draw a distinction between the degenerate Persians of his own day and the knightly warriors of
the age when the Persian empire was founded. He held that the
luxurious Oriental ways which were often considered Persian
were really Median.[57] They were one of the main reasons for
the defeat and annexation of the Median empire by the Persians, as soon as they realized their own superiority. The Persians of Cyrus' time were not slaves, but free men with equal
rights;[58] as long as Cyrus reigned, that spirit lived on unchanged
in the institutions of the new state. It was his successors who
disowned it, and so hastened their own downfall.[59] Xenophon
holds that the paideia of the Persians is the last relic, and the
only existing representative, of the areté of their early days. And
even if contemporary Persia is degenerate, he believes it is
worth immortalizing it, along with the founder of the empire
and the past greatness of Persia.

Xenophon's essay, *The Lacedaemonian Constitution,* is the
closest parallel to the *Cyropaedia.* Although its subject is not

the history of one man but the description of a whole political framework, the two are comparable in the fact that they both begin with paideia, and thereby bring out the particular point of view from which they approach their theme. Education in the strict sense covers only the first few chapters in both of them; but Xenophon holds it is the foundation of both Persia and Sparta, and he constantly alludes to its influence.[60] But the other institutions of both nations also bear the stamp of one single educational system worked out to its logical conclusion— if we take the word education to cover the kind of supervision of adult life which was customary in those states.

We have already worked out the Spartan ideal of civic virtue from the earliest available documents, Tyrtaeus' poems (see *Paideia* I, 87 f.). Tyrtaeus wrote in the age of the Messenian wars, during which, under the pressure of frightful danger, the new Spartan ideal was asserting itself against older and more aristocratic principles. In brief, it was that the citizen's greatest contribution to the common good was to join in the defence of his country, and that his rights in the state should be measured, not by privileges of rank or wealth, but by his valour in fulfilling this supreme duty. Since the Spartan community always had to fight, or to be ready to fight, for its life, this basic conception of the relation between individual and state was never challenged. In the course of centuries it developed its own peculiar system of communal life. (We have no information about the various stages of the development. In the age of Xenophon and Plato, and indeed long before them, the Spartan cosmos was finished and complete. But it is entirely because of the interest in Spartan paideia which was felt by writers like Xenophon that any valuable historical information about Sparta has survived).[61] The rest of the Greeks saw with astonishment and admiration how every institution in Sparta served the same purpose, to make Spartan citizens the best soldiers in the world. They understood very well that this was not done by incessant drilling and manoeuvring, but by moulding the character from earliest childhood. This education was not only military. It was political and moral in the broadest sense; but it was directly opposed to everything meant by political and moral education elsewhere in Greece. In every Greek state there were, besides the friends of Athenian democracy, convinced admirers of the

Spartan spirit. Plato is not typical of them, for he is very critical of the Spartan ideal as such. What he admired was the logical thoroughness with which one guiding principle was carried through every sphere of Spartan life, and their recognition of the fact that education is essential in forming the spirit of the community.[62] Xenophon much more than Plato is the representative of the out-and-out pro-Spartans, who were to be found particularly among the aristocracy.

His criticism of contemporary Athenian democracy often comes out in the *Memorabilia,* despite his patriotic loyalty to his homeland; and it makes him admire many things in Sparta, the political opponent of Athens, which he holds to be wise solutions for problems left unsolved in Athens. All the woes of the democracy of his own time seemed to him to flow from one source, the exaggerated self-assertion of individuals, who appeared to think that citizens of a democracy had no duties, only privileges, and who believed that the essence of liberty was to have these privileges guaranteed by the state. With his ideals of strict soldierly discipline, Xenophon must have found this lack of a sense of duty and responsibility particularly repulsive. His political thought started not with the individual's claims to attain his own personal ideals, but with the external conditions that made it possible for the community to exist. The fault for which so many contemporary thinkers criticized the Athenian democracy, the reluctance and inability of its citizens to fight for their country in the midst of a world full of hostility and envy, must have looked to him like preposterous and childish folly, which would soon deprive Athens of the liberty she vaunted so proudly. Spartan discipline had of course not been introduced by the free decision of a majority of the citizens. It was built into the legislative structure of the state, which, according to Xenophon, was the work of one single genius, the half-mythical Lycurgus.[63] Xenophon knew very well why the Spartans had maintained their old type of life as a sort of permanent garrison dominating an alien and conquered race, in a state of war which had lasted more or less continuously for many centuries. But he does not mention these historical facts. He treats the Spartan cosmos as a political work of art complete in itself; he praises its originality, and believes it is a model for others to imitate.[64] He certainly did not mean it to

be slavishly copied in every detail. Plato's political works are
the best key to understanding what the Greeks meant by imitation. They were much less inclined than we are to take a logically constructed work of art or thought, with its own particular nature and conditions, and to treat it as a unique individual thing. As soon as they were compelled to recognize the
virtues in any system, they would try to imitate whatever seemed
good and useful in it. Sparta was for Xenophon the embodiment
of the soldierly virtues of Cyrus' camp, in a whole great Hellenic
state.

Xenophon knew very well that the individualists and lovers
of liberty who were so common in his day were bound to think
that the Spartan way of life and Spartan education were a complete paradox.[65] He is usually careful to conceal his approval
of the institutions of Lycurgus by leaving it to the thoughtful
reader to decide whether his legislation benefited the country or
not. He must have foreseen that his readers would differ, and
that many of them would think the price to be paid for those
benefits was too high.[66] And yet he evidently expects most of his
contemporaries to approve, and that not only in cities and
states where such literary interests as those presupposed by his
book itself were counted superfluous—as they probably were
in Sparta.[67] This question was not a matter of pure ideology.
Xenophon has been called a romantic for upholding such an
untimely ideal in an enlightened democratic environment. But
he was not a poet: he was a practical man. The sympathy he
felt for Sparta because of his early career as a soldier must
have been increased by his political outlook as a squire and a
farmer. He knew the city and its people. He saw clearly that
any attempt to solve the social problem that started from the
city proletariat was useless for the country and for farmers.
Even while he was farming in a remote corner of Elis, he took
part in the political struggles that existed there as elsewhere.
We know this from the accurate knowledge of Elean party
politics he betrays in the closing books of the *Hellenica:* he
gives disproportionate space to the subject, and speaks with
the authority of an eyewitness.[68] The influences of conservative
Sparta and democratic Arcadia played their part in those social
struggles, and Xenophon had a good opportunity to study the
effects of both. In the agrarian Peloponnese, the democratic

movement (fostered by Thebes after the Spartan defeat at Leuctra) was something comparatively new. It was a departure from the fixed patterns in which the Peloponnesians had lived for hundreds of years under Spartan guidance. Even after the Messenians and Arcadians seceded from that political system, the conservatives still sided with Sparta. In Elis the new expansionist influence of Arcadia was unwelcome. Xenophon considered it highly fortunate that Athens, in her anxiety over the sudden rise of Thebes, allied herself to the humiliated Spartans. This tended (especially after Athenian troops had fought several times by the side of Spartans against Thebes) to make Athenian readers more receptive for a quiet but critical description of Spartan conditions, and it did not as before expose him to political suspicion for describing the hereditary enemy, Sparta.[68a]

The details of the *agogé*, the Spartan educational system, are too well known to be transcribed here from Xenophon's account. Its essential features are these:

1. Official supervision of the education of healthy children began very early—during, and even before, conception and pregnancy.
2. Great attention was paid to keeping up the quality of the race by eugenic breeding.
3. Children were educated by state-appointed teachers, not by their parents or by slave-nurses and -tutors as in other countries.
4. There was a supreme governmental authority in charge of all education, the *paidonomos*.
5. Boys and youths were organized in military units, the youths being kept separate from the younger boys.
6. Each class was independently governed by its more reliable members.
7. The boys had their bodies toughened by being given rough and scanty food and clothing.
8. Education was continued by the state right into early manhood.

Much of this will appear exaggerated and crude to modern readers; but the Athenian philosophers recognized the soundness of its underlying principle—that education ought to be taken over by the state or city, and superintended by publicly appointed officials. By putting it into their plans for ideal states, they helped it to conquer almost the entire world.[69] The postulate that *education should be the concern of the state* is Sparta's real contribution to the history of culture, and its importance can scarcely be overestimated. The second main point in the Spartan system is compulsory military service for young men, which counted as an essential part of their education. This service lasted far longer in Sparta than in the democratic Greek states, and was continued into mature life by the drills and communal meals (the *syssitia*) shared by all men. This point too, as we have seen, was adopted by Plato.

For a man with Xenophon's ideas, it must have been a violent shock when the Spartan system received a mortal wound at Leuctra, where the invincible Spartan army was defeated. In the concluding lines of his essay, *The Lacedaemonian Constitution,* he accuses the contemporary Spartans of greed, ambition, and voluptuousness, hinting that these vices destroyed their hegemony.[70] In his history of Greece, the *Hellenica* (which was meant not only to be an external continuation of Thucydides' history, but to continue its spirit by explaining the necessity behind historical events), he criticizes the Spartans severely for the faults they committed during their domination of Greece. With his religious outlook, he could not interpret their tragic fall from such a height of power except as the working of divine nemesis: retribution for too lofty aspiration, the reflex action of the overstrung bow. Despite his admiration for Sparta, he had clearly remained enough of an Athenian to feel alien to the harsh tyranny of the Spartans. That did not keep him from writing his book on Spartan paideia after the fall of Sparta; but it did make him regard it with the same qualified admiration as he gave to Persia in the *Cyropaedia.* It is in fact his admonitory attitude which is the most truly educational thing in that educational book. And it is in the same sense that we may treat his *Hellenica* as part of the great structure of Greek paideia. What it teaches is not immanent in the facts themselves, as in the History of his incomparably greater predecessor Thucydides. He offers his teaching frankly and personally, with a sort of evangelistic zeal. The defeat of Sparta at Leuctra, and the fall of Athens at the end of the Peloponnesian war, were the two greatest historical experiences of his life. Together, they moulded his belief in a divine world-order founded on justice.[71]

Xenophon's books about Socrates—dialogues and personal reminiscences of the master—fall into a special group among his works. It is needless to point out their connexion with the subject of education. Xenophon naturally tended to see the ethical, the thought-provoking aspect of things, and it was Socrates who gave his character the strongest impulse to develop as it did.[72] We have already appraised his reminiscences, the *Memorabilia,* as historical evidence for our knowledge of Socrates; we cannot go over them again as a reflection of Xenophon's ideas about paideia.[73] Our criticism of their value as historical evidence implies a judgment about Xenophon's mind. It is quite delightful to see how he makes Socrates put forward his own pet theories, to make him potentially the teacher of the age of Athenian restoration which Xenophon hopes for.[74] Socrates offers specialist military advice on the duties of cavalry-officers and on the teaching of tactics. He meets the younger Pericles, later one of the commanders at Arginusae, who is in a state of deep depression during a series of Athenian setbacks; and he tells him of his faith in her future power, provided she introduces severe military discipline and once more recognizes the moral authority of the Areopagus.[75] These ideas were obviously borrowed from the programme of the Conservative party, and were put forward in the period when we find Isocrates giving them public support—[76] the period when the second naval league was breaking up, and when thinking men naturally remembered a parallel series of events, the collapse of Athens in the last phase of the Peloponnesian war. But Xenophon uses Socrates even more freely to voice his ideas in his *Oeconomicus.* This dialogue deserves our special attention here because it develops Xenophon's general principles of education with particular reference to one point he considered essential: the relation between culture and agriculture.

The sophists often based their theory of education on a comparison between teaching the young and cultivating the land.[77] But although they recognized that civilization began with tilling the land and gathering the crops, their teaching still remained a product of the city. They were far from the days when

Hesiod made country life and its rules the starting-point of his own ethical code in his *Works and Days*. The city-state had dominated Greek civilization. By Xenophon's day 'countrified' had come to mean 'uneducated and uncultured'.[78] It seemed scarcely possible for farming to keep any of its former dignity. Xenophon himself was city-born; but he was inclined by nature and by destiny to life in the country. He must have felt the necessity of finding some spiritual relation between his literary culture and the hard and skilful vocation which supported him. This was the first time the full impact of the conflict between city and country had come out in literature. The Old Comedy of Athens had touched on the problem, but only to show how impossible it was for the new-fangled sophistic education to fit the traditional ways of country life.[79] There is a new spirit in Xenophon's *Oeconomicus*. The world of farmers and peasants has realized its own worth, and has become capable of showing forth its own very considerable contribution to civilization. The love for the country which comes out here is equally far from the sentimental rusticity of the Hellenistic idylls, and from the yokel farce of Aristophanes' peasant scenes. It is quite sure of itself. It does not need to exaggerate the importance of its own world. Although we need not generalize the phenomenon of the literary farmer, it is still true that Xenophon's book shows *the land* to be the imperishable and eternally young root of all human life. Behind the narrow, excited foreground, jostling with the activity and civilization of the city, stretches the quiet, broad, comfortable world of the country. Xenophon's book also shows how truly alive and permanent Socrates' educational ideal was: it was able to penetrate the world outside the city walls, the world which Socrates himself, a townsman through and through, would not enter because the trees could not teach him anything.[80]

The introductory conversation about the nature of 'economy' or household administration takes Socrates and Critobulus to the theme of farming (γεωργία). The discussion of this theme forms the main part of the book. Critobulus asks Socrates to explain to him which types of practical activity and knowledge are the noblest and the most suitable for him as a free citizen.[81] They readily agree that what the Greeks call banausic trades are unsuitable, because they are not highly respected in the various states; they weaken the body by long unhealthy hours of sitting at work, and dull the mind.[82] Socrates recommends the farmer's life, and in the course of the discussion shows such an astonishing amount of specialized knowledge of agriculture that Xenophon feels bound to give a special reason for it. In order to give a broad justification for his interest in farming, and to show that it is not socially despicable, Socrates cites the example of the Persian kings, who hold there is only one vocation worthy of them, besides soldiering—the cultivation of fields and gardens.[83] Xenophon of course takes this from his own acquaintance with Persia. But in Socrates' mouth a long detailed description of Cyrus' wonderful park sounds rather strange.[84] Xenophon adds a personal reminiscence of the Spartan general Lysander, who, on a visit to Sardis, was escorted by Cyrus through his gardens, and heard from his own mouth that he worked there every day, having himself planted all the trees and shrubberies, and planned their situations. Lysander told all this to a friend in Megara, from whom Socrates is supposed to have heard it.[85] This transparent invention is meant to imply that Xenophon, who is here speaking through the mouth of his teacher (as Plato often does), heard the story himself from Lysander. Xenophon was probably presented to him as the gallant officer who had led the ten thousand Greeks on their retreat through Asia. They were both friends of Cyrus, and no one would have enjoyed Lysander's reminiscences of the dead prince better than Xenophon. Later, when Xenophon himself became a farmer, he must have felt that this combination of soldiering and the love of the land [86] was a new reason to admire the Persian tradition.

Xenophon finds it harder to give reasons why Socrates should be interested in the details of agriculture. He gets out of it by making Socrates repeat a conversation he has had with a distinguished country squire, to whom he gives the significant name of Ischomachus, Staunch in Battle. Socrates himself says he has heard of Ischomachus on all sides as the embodiment of true *kalokagathia*. When Critobulus asks him to define the nature of *kalokagathia*—the word which everyone uses for the epitome of virtue and nobility, but generally without having a clear idea of its meaning—the best answer Socrates can give is to describe Ischomachus, whom he has actually met.[87] In the conversation which he now repeats, Ischomachus is of course the protagonist. Socrates only puts the questions which draw him out. What proves to be true *kalokagathia* is simply the life of a good farmer, who practises his vocation with real pleasure and full understanding, and has his heart in the right place. Some of Xenophon's own personal experience comes into this description. It is combined with a portrayal of his ideal man and ideal farmer in such a way that, as we can easily see, Ischomachus is a self-portrait of Xenophon himself, idealized into poetry. Xenophon certainly did not claim that *he* was such a model man. In the same way as the Persian nobleman is a combination of soldier and farmer, so throughout the dialogue Xenophon implies that the lessons taught by farming are the same as those taught by soldiering. That is shown in the name of his ideal farmer. The blend of the ability and devotion of farmer and soldier is Xenophon's ideal of culture.

Paideia is much discussed in the *Oeconomicus*. Success in farming always appears to Xenophon to be the result of proper education not only in the farmer himself but in his wife and his labourers, especially the housekeeper and the foreman.[88] Therefore Xenophon thinks one of the farmer's chief duties is to *teach* his household; and we may assume that this is his own personal idea of what farming means. The farmer's most important pupil is his wife,[89] who is described as the personage of chief interest in the farm, the queen-bee of the hive.[90] An inexperienced girl of fifteen, she is brought straight from her mother's care, to become the lady of the house and the estate:[91] the course of education which her husband is to give her is obviously very necessary.[92] Ischomachus is rather proud of the curriculum he maps out. He assumes that the young wife and mother expects to learn everything from his superior knowledge and character:[93] he sets out to describe to her the duties she must fulfil, making her proud and happy to start working at her difficult new tasks. The passive wife of the townsman, who, with her servants, goes through the same little daily round of household tasks and spends her leisure on clothes, and making up her face, and exchanging gossip, would be useless in a big farmhouse. Our idea of Greek womanhood would lack many of its finest and most essential features if we did not possess Xeno-

phon's picture of the education of the wife of an important
country squire. When we think of the emancipation and education of women in that period, we usually go no further than the
eloquent female intellectuals of Euripidean tragedy.[94] But between these two extremes, the wise Melanippe and the average
Athenian woman with her narrow and deliberately restricted
range of interests, there lies the ideal of a woman thinking and
acting for herself, and having her own broad sphere of influence, as described by Xenophon in the best traditions of country
life and civilization. All that he himself did for it was probably
to rationalize and explain its traditional duties. But the educational content in the tradition was as old as farming itself.

In Xenophon the wife is her husband's true helper.[95] She is
the mistress of the household, while her husband directs the
labourers in the fields. He is responsible for everything that
comes into the house from the farm, and she is in charge of
storing and using it. She has to bring up and educate the children. She must superintend the cellar and the kitchen, and ar-
range the baking and the spinning. All this has been planned by
God and nature, who destined men and women for different
work.[96] Women, being timid, are better fitted for safeguarding
the crops, while men, who are courageous, are needed when
faults or failures occur in the work out in the fields.[97] The care
and love of new-born children is innate in women.[98] A man can
more easily bear heat and cold, make long arduous journeys,
and take arms to defend his home soil.[99] It is the wife who
allots each of the servants her work, and sees that it is carried
out; she also looks after the food, and is the doctor for anyone
about the farm who is ill.[100] She teaches inexperienced maids
spinning and other household skills, and trains a good housekeeper to help her.[101] Ischomachus attaches great importance to
teaching his wife to love order, which is particularly important
in managing a large household.[102] He describes the arrangement
of the rooms, the various kinds of cooking- and table-utensils,
and the linen for daily use and for special occasions, with a
thoroughness which provides a unique opportunity to see the
inside of a Greek farmhouse.[103] The end of this system of
paideia for the young wife is a course of instruction on methods
of preserving her own health and beauty. In this respect too,
Ischomachus' ideal country wife is different from the fashion-

able ladies of the town. Assuring her that powder and make-up are unnecessary, he makes her aim, instead, at having the beauty of a fresh and supple body—which she can acquire more easily than any city woman, from constant exercise at her work.[104] In the same way Xenophon explains the education of the other important elements of the little organism which is the farm household. The housekeeper must be trained to be dependable, self-controlled, faithful, not forgetful or careless,[105] the foreman to be unselfishly and devotedly loyal to his master, careful, and capable of directing others.[106] If the master wants to teach him to be tirelessly devoted to the household under his charge, he must begin by setting the example.[107] He should never slacken off in his work, no matter how richly his fields and herds produce. He must rise early, and take long walks over the fields.[107a] Nothing should escape his notice.[108] The special knowledge needed for his work is more simple than that of many other vocations; [109] yet the farmer's life demands not only soldierly order but the soldier's ability to lead and to command. If, when the squire himself appears, the labourers do not involuntarily tauten their muscles and work in a more regular rhythm, then he lacks the one ability which is vital for his job, which is the cause of all success in it, and which alone can make his position truly a kingly one within his own sphere.[110]

In order to supplement and complete the cultural ideal personified in his gentleman-farmer of the *Oeconomicus,* we should read Xenophon's book on hunting, the *Cynegeticus.*[111] It is not merely a specialist handbook giving the rules for one particular type of activity in an increasingly technical civilization. It is full of specialized knowledge, indeed, and something of the specialist attitude and purpose can be seen in it; but Xenophon's real purpose is something higher. He was an enthusiastic huntsman, and believed that hunting had a valuable influence on his whole character and attitude to life.[112] He puts the same high value on hunting in his *Lacedaemonian Constitution,*[113] and describes it as part of the Persian paideia in the *Cyropaedia.*[114] Plato too in *The Laws* made his laws on education contain certain provisions for the practice of hunting. The passage in which he deals with it is loosely added at the end, after the laws about teaching mathematics and astronomy, far away from the regulations for gymnastic and military training—from which we might infer that it was inserted later.[115] It might even have been the appearance of Xenophon's book that directed Plato's attention to this gap in his educational system. However that may be, the *Cynegeticus* was published in the period when Plato was actually writing *The Laws*.[116]

At this point we may digress briefly to *The Laws*. In the concluding passage of his legislative programme for education, Plato discusses whether he should recognize hunting as a legitimate form of paideia or not. His discussion seems to imply that some literary exposition of hunting similar to Xenophon's *Cynegeticus* already existed, and that he is inclined to accept its assertion of the value of the hunt in training character.[117] But he feels that if he is to accept it, he must clear up the meaning of the word 'hunting' (ϑήρα) which covers several very different types of activity, and cut away from the concept everything unworthy of the name.[118] He refuses to admit that everything called 'hunting' is paideia. However, he does not lay down a law about it. Instead (as often in *The Laws*), he inserts praise and blame of various kinds of hunting in the legislation.[119] He severely condemns all kinds of fishing, by net or by rod, and likewise fowling—these sports do not strengthen the character.[120] Nothing is left but hunting animals, and that too must be done openly and in daylight, not at night, and not with nets or traps.[121] Hunters must ride, and have hounds with them, so that they are compelled to make some physical exertion. Plato goes beyond Xenophon in forbidding nets and traps, although Xenophon also ignores fishing and fowling. Xenophon gives elaborate directions for the training and use of hounds. One argument sometimes used to prove the *Cynegeticus* a forgery is that it does not say men should hunt on horseback. For that was how all Athenian gentlemen hunted; and it seems particularly queer that an ardent horseman like Xenophon should not mention horses.[122] But in the first place, the book is not meant to describe how Xenophon himself hunted, but to popularize hunting among the general public; and besides, it is too difficult for us to lay down the law about what the squire of Scillus considered correct form, or to demand *a priori* that he conform to Plato's theories.

Anyone who wished to, and who could afford it, might ride to hunt. It was not the art of hunting that taught him how to ride, but the art of riding, which Xenophon had treated in a separate book. But the training of hounds is entirely appropriate to a book on hunting; and in the *Cynegeticus* Xenophon set down the results of his experience in that art, with many fascinating details that show he was a man who knew and loved dogs.

Xenophon too claimed that his book was a contribution to the contemporary discussion of paideia. In the introduction he says that hunting was invented by the divine twins Apollo and Artemis, who taught it to the centaur Chiron as a way of honouring his righteousness.[123] In early legend Chiron appears as the teacher of all the heroes, particularly Achilles—[124] Pindar tells how he learnt hunting as Chiron's pupil.[125] By going back to this mythical model, in the manner of the sophistical rhetoricians, Xenophon contrives to embody in Chiron the close connexion between hunting and the training of young men in *kalokagathia,* and so to make it seem something very old, original, and worthy. He gives a long list of famous heroes taught by Chiron's paideia,[126] and says that they all owed their training in the highest areté to 'the practice of hunting and the rest of paideia', which he proves by telling a separate story about each hero.[127] This is the best proof that the catalogue of heroes is not taken over *en bloc* from some real mythological poetic tradition, but composed by Xenophon himself from his own knowledge of the sagas, to strengthen his thesis that hunting had been one of the foundations of genuine paideia since the beginnings of the heroic age. Apparently he feels that his claim that hunting helps to mould the character is against the general trend of contemporary thought, and it is this that makes his pleasant little book really interesting. We cannot go into its technical details here. Its charm is in the rich hunting experience which lies behind it all. The centre of interest, of course, is hunting the hare: that takes up most of the book.[128] Apart from it, Xenophon spends some time on discussing the Greek sports of hunting the stag and the wild boar. He says that in his day beasts of prey—lions, leopards, panthers, and bears—were hunted only in Macedonia, Asia Minor, and central Asia.[129]

Here we should take the conclusion of the *Cynegeticus,* and

connect it closely with the introduction, because it once more emphasizes the link between the book and the subject of paideia.[130]
The author takes issue with the ideal assumed by the sophists,
which is that men can be educated by the word alone.[131] As
always, his standard is an ethical one. His chief interest is
character-building. The basis of this is physical fitness. Hunting
makes a man healthy, makes his eye and ear keen, keeps him
from growing prematurely old.[132] It is the best training for war,
because it makes him accustomed to do long marches carrying
his weapons, to bear rough weather, and to sleep out of doors.[133]
It teaches him to despise low pleasures, and, like all 'education
in truth', it makes him just and self-disciplined.[134] Xenophon
does not say what he means by this, but it is obviously the compulsion to learn discipline that he values most highly; and he
calls that training, which is enforced by reality, 'education in
truth'. This gives a realistic and practical turn to Socrates'
ideal. The whole book is inspired by his admiration for *ponos*,
exertion and hardship, without which no man is properly educated.[135] Historians of philosophy think this comes from the influence of the moralist Antisthenes, who put that interpretation
on Socrates' teaching. Yet Xenophon was a man who naturally
liked hard exercise, and who put out all his strength wherever
necessary. Here, if anywhere, he is speaking from personal experience. *Ponos* is the educational element in hunting. The lofty
areté of the ancient heroes, taught by Chiron, was built up by
ponos.[136] The books which the sophists use to start the education of their pupils are devoid of any real content (γνῶμαι), and
fit the young men for nothing but useless fancies.[137] Xenophon
cannot believe that true *kalokagathia* can ever grow out of that
seed. He knows that he is speaking only as a layman; but his
experience teaches him that in everything we learn what is good
only from nature herself: or next to her from men who have
knowledge of something truly good and useful.[138] Modern education tries to show off with artificial phraseology. Xenophon
assures us he knows nothing of that.[139] He says that not words
(ὀνόματα) but content (γνῶμαι) and thought (νοήματα) are the
real food of areté.[140] By this he does not mean to rule out all
true love of culture (φιλοσοφία), but only the sophists—by which
he means all those who 'are clever with words'.[141] The good

huntsman is also best educated to take part in the life of the community.[142] Selfishness and greed do not fit in with the spirit of the chase. Xenophon hopes his own companions in the hunt will be healthy and holy, and so he is sure that the work of the hunter is pleasing to the gods.[143]

8

PLATO'S *PHAEDRUS*: PHILOSOPHY AND RHETORIC

NONE of Plato's books has been more variously judged in the last hundred years than his *Phaedrus*. Schleiermacher thought it was the programme of the Academy, written early in Plato's life. It was long taken to be the natural starting-point for the study of the ultimate aims of Plato's method of writing and teaching. It contains the shortest summary of his views on the relation between writing, speech, and thought. Therefore it used to be the customary approach to his philosophy. The dithyrambic ecstasy into which Socrates (as he himself ironically remarks) allows himself to fall in his speeches about Eros [1] was taken to prove that it was written while Plato was a young man. Critics in antiquity described its style as bad, or as 'youthful'—by which they originally meant not that a young man had written it, but that it was like a young man's work: it was an aesthetic condemnation of its extravagance.[2] But later this was interpreted as a sign of the lack of balance and youthful excitement of the author, which of course overlooked the facts that the dithyrambic style is not characteristic of the whole dialogue, but only of the speeches about Eros, and that Plato marks it out as a symptom of the exceptional frame of mind in which Socrates happens to be. Plato's readers expected him to give some explanation of his attitude to the vocation of writing in general, and on the value of the written word for philosophy in particular, at the very beginning of his literary career—all the more so because they realized the particular difficulty of understanding the form of Plato's writing, and its importance in grasping his philosophical meaning. Schleiermacher had, with the help of *Phaedrus,* mastered this connexion between Plato's form and his meaning, which is absolutely essential for the study of his books. Naturally enough he decided that Plato had meant *Phaedrus* to be a sort of introduction to his whole work.[3] Then, when Platonic scholars in the nineteenth century began to take up the idea that Plato's works might represent the historical development of his thought, and to make careful chronological studies of the separate dialogues, they began to find reasons for thinking *Phaedrus* a later work. At the same time, they turned away from Schleiermacher's theory of the pedagogical purpose of all Plato's dialogues, which he supposed Plato to have announced in *Phaedrus*.[4] Platonists now looked for the real meaning of *Phaedrus* either in the speeches about Eros in the first part, or in the psychological theories and the doctrine of Ideas put forward in Socrates' great speech, along with the stimulating remarks in the second part about dialectic method. Finally, they realized that the rich language and complex style in which Plato here clothed his thoughts must mean that the book was written when he was fully mature; and they discovered more and more features in it which connected it with the dialogues written towards the end of his life. *Phaedrus* had at first been put with *The Symposium,* in the middle of Plato's career, after he had founded the Academy. But now scholars felt they must place it in his old age.[5] His interest in theoretical descriptions of the dialectic method was now taken to prove that *Phaedrus* belonged to the group of what were termed dialectic dialogues, which meanwhile had been incontrovertibly proved to belong to his later life.[6]

The structure of *Phaedrus* is a very difficult and much vexed problem. The Eros speeches in the first part, rising to a pitch of wild excitement, are hard to fit into a unity with the abstract theorizing on the nature of true eloquence which occupies the second part. Of course a good deal of the difficulty in the structure of the book is created by the obvious but false comparison with *The Symposium.* The latter is entirely concerned with Eros, and it is natural to take *Phaedrus* along with it, and call them Plato's two great dialogues about Eros. But as far as *Phaedrus* is concerned that is an incomplete view: it neglects the second part entirely, or treats it merely as an appendix. The gap between the two parts becomes even wider if one emphasizes the praise of the Platonic method of dialectic in the second part. But all these difficulties vanish as soon as we understand the intellectual situation in which the work was created, the background against which Plato expressly puts it.

It derives its unity from its concern with the subject of rhetoric. Both the first and the second parts deal with oratory. Most of the perplexities of its readers have been caused by their failure to see this connexion. The first part, sometimes called the 'erotic' section, begins with the reading and criticism of a speech by Lysias, who is taken as the leader of the most influential rhetorical school in Athens, standing at the height of his reputation in the age of Socrates.[7] Then Plato contrasts with it two speeches by Socrates on the same theme, the nature and influence of Eros, to show how one could either (a) treat the same subject better on the basis of Lysias' false assumptions, or (b) speak properly about Eros, if one knew his true nature. In harmony with this, the second part, which is more general, first discusses the faults of rhetoric and the rhetorical systems which were current in Socrates' time; and then points out the advantages of Socratic dialectic as a method of attaining true eloquence. The question whether such an art of rhetoric will ever exist or not remains unanswered. But Plato makes Socrates say he has great hopes of young Isocrates, and with this complimentary reference the dialogue ends.

The eulogy of Isocrates is meant to be a contrast to the hostile criticism of Lysias with which both parts of *Phaedrus* begin.[9] It shows that at the time Plato was writing the book he was once again keenly interested in the problem of rhetorical education which he had already discussed in *Gorgias,* and that something of his new interest must have been due to the great new developments in rhetoric which are associated with the name of Isocrates—although we may feel inclined to minimize the generous praise given to him here. If modern research is correct in placing *Phaedrus* late in Plato's career, then this expression of his attitude to the school of Isocrates is surely most important. It is difficult to say *a priori* what period of Isocrates' career Plato is actually thinking of when he makes Socrates praise him. But it is clear that Socrates' prophecy of his future greatness would have had no point in Plato's youth, when Isocrates had as yet no school, and it was impossible to distinguish him from the general run of speech-manufacturers. It was only after his new rhetoric had proved the quality of his talent that Plato could have thought of offering the praise of Socrates, like a laurel wreath, to the leader of his own Academy's powerful competitor.⁹ᵃ Isocrates' school was founded somewhere between 390 and 380: but it is not likely that Plato would express himself so favourably then, just after Isocrates had sharply condemned Plato's paideia in his programme-essay *Against the sophists,* and in *Helen.* But in the changing intellectual relations between the schools of Plato and Isocrates, there must have been a point when they approached each other—probably before Aristotle organized classes in rhetoric in the Academy, and started a competition with Isocrates which was to degenerate into a public literary squabble.¹⁰

Phaedrus can be understood only as a new stage in Plato's developing attitude to rhetoric. In *Gorgias* he hates the whole thing: it is the typical education which is based not on truth but on sheer appearance. Yet even there, if we read carefully, we can see an occasional allusion to what might be called Plato's sense of his own rhetorical powers.¹¹ The man who, in *The Symposium* and *Menexenus,* had brilliantly demonstrated his ability to imitate and surpass every type of contemporary eloquence, would not simply turn his back on rhetoric and say he had no interest in it.¹² He had put his native gift of style at the service of philosophy. But that did not mean he was to refrain from expressing his thoughts in the most attractive way possible: on the contrary, it meant that he was strongly drawn to do so. Isocrates tended to deride the hair-splittings of dialectic and call them educationally barren, compared with the practical utility of his own art, eloquence.¹³ Accordingly, Plato felt bound to make a public statement explaining the value of dialectic education for the same purpose. He could with justice point out that precision and clarity in logical and psychological distinctions are the preconditions of all rhetorical art. He could easily show that, unless he cultivated these intellectual faculties, no orator or writer would be able to convince his audience and his readers; and that the technical tricks taught (then and now) through handbooks of public speaking were no substitute for this type of intellectual training. Plato wrote *Phaedrus* to illuminate this aspect of his paideia, and to justify its claims to represent this tendency. It is extremely probable that it was this manifesto which prompted young Aristotle (Plato's pupil, and then a new teacher on the Academy's staff) to bring in rhetoric

as a fresh subject in the Platonic curriculum. No doubt he meant
to show what a *new* rhetoric could be, if built on the philosophical foundation laid down in *Phaedrus*.[14]

We must not be led to think that Eros is the real subject of
Phaedrus, by the fact that Plato discusses it in such detail at the
beginning. The significant point is that the dialogue begins with
the discussion of one of Lysias' speeches, which the great orator
had given his pupils to learn by heart.[15] This striking detail
would have no significance unless Plato's main purpose had been
to criticize Lysias' rhetorical treatment of his subject. But why
was Eros chosen? Mainly because it was a favourite theme for
such exercises in rhetorical schools. Among the titles of Aristotle's lost works, there is a collection of such rhetorical disquisitions on Eros.[16] It must have been much older than Aristotle; it was obviously an attempt to excite the interest of the
students. For that matter, it goes far to explain why Plato himself chose the subject.[17] It would be practically impossible for
any such school to pass completely over a subject which interested young men so much, although Plato went further into it
than any rhetorical declamations like those of Lysias ever could.
The discussion of Eros gave Plato the opportunity to treat not
only the form of the speech, but the question of truth or falsity,
which was his chief concern as a philosopher. The rhetorical
schools tried to excite interest by using this sensational theme
without really understanding it. Plato takes it up as if in play,
brings in all his profound philosophical speculation on the nature of Eros, and constructs a rival speech that reveals by contrast all the ambiguity and triviality of the rhetoricians' artificial orations.
    He shows that the speech of Lysias is full of repetitions, and
does not define the subject clearly.[18] This concrete example reveals the practical importance of Platonic dialectic in rhetorical
education—the central theme of the second part of the book.
But at the same time the attempt of Socrates to improve Lysias'
logical treatment of the subject shows the real errors on which
it is based. This is not the place to examine them in detail. What
we have to do here is to concentrate on the main theme of
Phaedrus, rhetoric. Young Athenians often discussed whether,
and in what circumstances, it was permissible to give way to a

lover's pleadings: by which they meant physical surrender. We have met the question before, in Pausanias' speech in *The Symposium*.[19] Lysias outargues those who held it permissible, by the perverse argument that it would be better for the beloved to surrender to a friend who is not overpowered by Eros but keeps his passions cool.[20] Such a friend would not, like the lover, be driven back and forward by emotional tempests, and injure the beloved by selfishly forcing him into isolation from all other men and trying to keep him exclusively for himself. In his first speech, which he delivers with his head covered because he realizes the blasphemy of the subject, Socrates adds to and confirms these arguments by a neat logical definition and distinction of the various kinds of desire. Like Lysias, he describes Eros as a subspecies of sensual desire, and builds his proof on that definition.[21] According to it, the lover is a man who prefers the pleasure of the senses to good. He is selfish, jealous, envious, despotic. He cares nothing for either the physical or the spiritual welfare of his friend. Just as he subordinates his beloved's physical welfare to the satisfaction of his own desires, so, intellectually, he keeps him as far as possible from 'philosophy'.[22] He is not honestly interested in his independent spiritual development. His conduct is a contrast in every point to the educational Eros glorified in *The Symposium*.[23]

This contrast makes it perfectly certain that the speech does not seriously express Socrates' conception of the nature of Eros. The speech is serious enough: but it is about an Eros which does not deserve the name. The views expounded here with every resource of dialectic are worlds apart from the lofty view of the nature of Eros put forward in Diotima's speech. The reason they are worked out in such clear detail is to explain clearly what Lysias (without knowing it) means by Eros. This close dialectic treatment of the subject necessarily goes beyond the definition of Eros, and rises to the heights of philosophical contemplation. It impels Socrates to make a second speech on Eros, a 'palinode' or recantation, in which he tries to make amends to the god in his real nature, beginning with an unforgettable description of divine madness, and distinguishing it from the ungodly and injurious form of madness.[24] Eros is put on the same level as the gifts of poetry and prophecy, and inspiration is described as the common nature of them all. The creative emo-

tion of the poet is recognized directly and necessarily as an educational phenomenon in the highest sense; [25] and the same educational element is recognizably active throughout the true Eros.
Then Plato gives a deeper proof of the theory that Eros educates, by connecting it with his doctrine of the nature of the
soul; [26] and illustrates that doctrine by comparing the soul to
an earthbound and a heavenly horse guided by a charioteer,
Reason.[27] With growing excitement, the speech soars on the
wings of inspiration into the regions high above heaven, where
the soul possessed by Eros rises to follow the god to which it
is most akin, and is thought worthy to look on pure Being.[28]
Socrates excuses himself for speaking in such a poetic style by
saying that he does it to suit Phaedrus.[29] It is the only way to
talk to a student and admirer of rhetoric. But Socrates proves
that the philosopher can easily beat the rhetoricians at their
own game, if he wishes. The dithyrambic sweep of his words is
not artificial and mechanical as the affected elevation of the
rhetors often is, but flows from a living spring in the heart—
from Eros, to whose spiritual dominance he pays tribute in his
speech.

From this oratorical competition between rhetor and philosopher the discussion moves freely and easily to the general
question: what is the best way to write and speak? [30] This is
obviously the fundamental problem of all rhetoric. Plato is
mainly concerned to discuss whether the knowledge of truth is
requisite in order to put a thought into beautiful words.[31] That
is the parting of the ways between philosophical and rhetorical
education. Here, as in *Gorgias,* Plato builds the discussion
around the concept of techné, skill or art. He declares rhetoric
is not an art in the strict sense of the word, only a knack with
no solid basis of special knowledge.[32] It cannot grow into an art
unless it is founded on the knowledge of truth. In practice it is
generally defined as the art of convincing people in law-courts
or public meetings.[33] Conviction is attained by speeches and
counter-speeches delivered on both sides of a question: what
might be called antilogic, or argumentation. This antilogic is
not confined to these occasions, but extends to all spheres of
thought and speech.[33a] Ultimately it consists in the ability to
compare everything with everything else.[34] The process of proof

used by rhetors is mainly the demonstration of resemblances.[35] In his later years Plato was much interested in the logical problem of method and particularly of proof; and he appears to have started at this point to study the rhetorical methods of persuasion from a quite new angle. While *Phaedrus* was being composed, his pupil Speusippus wrote a long book on dialectic entitled *Similarities,* dealing with the classification of all existing things.[36] To define anything, we must know what it is like and what it is not like. Now, if we assume that the purpose of rhetoric is to deceive the audience—to lead them to false conclusions by resemblances alone—that makes it imperative for the orator to have exact knowledge of the dialectic method of classification, for that is the only way to understand the varying degrees of resemblance between things.[37] It is not easy to confuse iron and silver, but it *is* easy to confuse good and bad.[38] Nobody can understand clearly what men agree or disagree about unless he learns how to define the *eidos* methodically. Therefore Socrates begins his argument when speaking about Eros by defining the concept he is using.[39]

Now, after finishing his speeches, he takes the opening of Lysias' speech once more, and shows that it begins where it ought to end.[40] He goes on to general criticism. The speech has no solid structure. It ought to have an organic body like a living thing: lacking neither head nor feet, but possessing a proper middle, beginning, and end; and all these parts ought to stand in the right relation to one another and to the whole. Judged by this standard, Lysias' speech is a total failure.[41] These are penetrating discoveries about the nature of literary composition, which were taken up by later writers, and became fundamental principles of classical poetic and rhetorical theory.[42] It is important for us to realize this: the principle that a work of literature must be an organic unity was laid down by a philosopher, not by a rhetorical critic of art, not by a poet; and its enunciator was a philosopher who was also an artist, who admired natural organic unity and was also a logical genius. His realization that every speech must be divided into logical parts was a consequence of the great discoveries he made through systematic research into the relations between various concepts—the kind of research carried on 'for practice' in the 'dialectical' dialogues of his later period, as concrete examples of his technique. What led

Plato to write *Phaedrus* was to some extent his increasing insight into the connexion between the difficult and apparently abstract theoretical problems which he found, late in life, in his doctrine of Ideas, and the simplest rules of practical skill in writing and speaking, which was much desired and much discussed at that time. But Plato was particularly attracted by the subject because he could make a positive contribution to it, enough to disprove the rhetor's objection that philosophy was useless. Instead of copying the spiteful or derisive tone of rhetorical polemic which even Isocrates had originally used against him, Plato praised his distinguished opponent, and added to his praise an allusion to the deep spiritual bond between their two spheres of teaching.

Plato himself points out that the three speeches in the first part (one by Lysias and two by Socrates) are patterns to show the relation between rhetoric and dialectic.[43] After the criticisms mentioned above, he leaves Lysias' speech alone, and turns to the two speeches of Socrates, which demonstrate the fundamental dependence of rhetoric on dialectic.[44] He gives a complete guide to understanding his purpose in writing them, and the ideas they are meant to embody.[45] In spite of their poetic language, they are a model of logical division and combination. These two processes condition each other, and together they form the whole of dialectic.[46] Plato makes this clear in the second speech, by briefly recapitulating the course and result of the process of logical classification.[47] His explanation of the synoptic and diairetic function of dialectic method is the clearest and most detailed statement he ever made on the subject. We cannot make a separate study of it here, but it is important that in this very passage Plato describes it as the epitome of everything that is 'technical' (in the higher sense) in oratory.[48] The remainder of rhetoric—what men like Lysias teach their pupils—can never constitute a techné in itself. It might be called the pre-technical part of rhetoric.[49] With deliberate humour Plato lists all the various terms for separate sections of the speech described in the handbooks of the rhetors.[50] He gives all the names of the early rhetoricians, and sometimes adds the particular inventions that made each man famous—they show a tendency to become more and more complicated. Plato does not despise these things. He merely assigns them to a subordinate position. All these men worked out valuable methods to improve the artistic form of speech.[51] But they could not use them to teach anyone how to persuade an audience and compose an artistic whole.

In his introductory essay on rhetoric, Isocrates always declared that natural talent was the most important thing, and gave only a comparatively modest place to practice and knowledge.[52] In *Phaedrus* Plato discusses the relation of these three factors, which the sophists had marked out as the three essentials in building up perfect skill in oratory.[53] He affirms that what Isocrates called the two minor factors are definitely important, chiefly knowledge, epistémé,[54] but also to some extent practice—evidently he is thinking of the curriculum at the Academy, where logic was taught not only as theory but as a practical exercise too. Isocrates always emphasizes the important part played by the creative artist's intuition.[55] Of course, the knowledge or learning (epistémé, mathésis) which he belittles is merely the formal teaching of the old-fashioned sophists who drummed in rhetoric by rules. In its place Plato puts the logical training given by philosophy, which is also a matter of teaching. It is absolutely indispensable in learning anything else. And thus Plato's criticism of the rhetorical teaching of his predecessors and contemporaries grows into a positive ideal of rhetoric which is entirely his own, and which if realized would make rhetoric into a true art. This ideal is the conjunction of

rhetoric	and	philosophy
form	and	intellectual content
power of expression and		knowledge of truth.

Whenever any classical school of philosophy paid any attention to rhetoric at all, it always revived this programme.[56] It was not till comparatively late that rhetoricians took it over, and then it was in a less strictly logical and more general sense: it was interpreted to mean the combination of style with the philosophical training of the intellect. It was Plato's synthesis which moved Cicero to formulate the ideal of culture put forth in his book *De oratore*;[57] and its influence worked through him to form Quintilian's *Institutio oratoria*. Plato searches for a model of this type of rhetoric in the history of practical oratory; and finds one in Pericles. His greatness as an orator was due (Plato affirms) to his profound intellectual culture. It was the philosophy of his friend and protégé Anaxagoras that filled his thought and gave his eloquence a sublimity unequalled by any other statesman.[58]

Plato gives another explanation to show why the orator must have a thorough specialist training. The orator's function is psychagogy: his real art is not so much dressing up words as influencing souls.[59] The obvious parallel is the profession of the physician, which Plato had already compared with that of the orator in *Gorgias*.[60] In the earlier book, he used the example of the doctor to show the nature of a true techné. In *Phaedrus*, he uses it to show the meaning and procedure of correct method. He cites Hippocrates himself as the embodiment of the true medical art.[61] It is, he thinks, the essential characteristic of the doctor's intellectual attitude that in treating the human body it always considers the whole of nature, the entire cosmos (see p. 22 f.). So also, if a writer or orator wishes to guide his hearers and readers correctly, he must know the world of the human soul with all its emotions and powers.[62] And again, as the doctor must know accurately whether the nature of anything is simple or manifold, and how it works—or how its various forms work upon one another—so the orator must know the forms of the soul and their origin, and the corresponding forms of oratory.[63] Rhetoric had already been teaching these patterns, or *ideai,* of oratory,[64] but the novelty in this outline of Plato's scheme of rhetoric seems to be that the forms of oratory are deliberately referred to forms in which the soul acts, and interpreted as their necessary expression.[65] This puts the entire emphasis of rhetorical training on psychology.

It is remarkable how well Plato knows the particular strength of his own mind. That was (here as elsewhere) his insight into the soul and its powers. After realizing that certain forms of expression are determined by certain functions of the soul, he makes the practical inference that men of a certain emotional type or a certain permanent disposition of character can be moved and persuaded to certain acts only through oratorical methods chosen to correspond to them.[66] To discover these psy-

chological bases of the art of influencing people through speech
was a task for which Plato was uniquely well fitted by nature.
It is significant that he is not content with the theoretical activity
of working out a comprehensive system of psychological cate-
gories for use in rhetoric, but lays just as much emphasis on
testing these discoveries, by applying them in practice to concrete cases and actual occasions.[67] We should expect him to do
this, after giving the same time and importance to practical
experience and character-training in *The Republic* as to purely
intellectual education.[68]

But his real innovation here lies in the method he recommends
for training the orator's mind. *Phaedrus* adds a new branch of
learning to the paideia described in *The Republic*. This new subject is rhetoric; but he fits it into the outlines he traced in the
larger work. In *The Republic* the aim of his paideia was to train
future statesmen; in *Phaedrus* it is to train orators and writers.[69]
The peculiarity of both books is their insistence on a type of
intellectual training which does not appeal to purely practical
men.[70] *Phaedrus* is the programme of philosophical training for
the orator; and it repeats in so many words the fundamental
idea of *The Republic,* that a long 'detour' is necessary to reach
the goal.[71] This is a deliberate allusion to the educational theory
of *The Republic*. Both here and in *The Republic* the detour is
the journey through dialectic.[72] It will probably seem dispropor-
tionately long and difficult to anyone who expects it will be
enough to learn a few tricks. Plato's educational philosophy,
however, is always aimed at the highest and not the lowest; and
from the height it is clear that there is no primrose path to
learning the orator's job. There can be no doubt that Plato
thinks of the function of the orator as a moral one. But even
if we think that aim is set too high, the philosophical detour is
still inevitable, as we have already recognized.[73] Teachers of
rhetoric are, in principle, content with probabilities and with
plausible evidence, instead of trying to find out the truth.[74] In
this book Plato is not trying to convince them that it is necessary to speak the truth. Instead, he takes his opponent's standpoint (as he so often does) and proves even on that basis that
knowledge is indispensable for him. In *Protagoras,* he proved
the value of knowledge by showing that, if the masses are right

in taking pleasure to be the supreme good in life, then knowledge is needed as a standard to distinguish larger from smaller
pleasures and near pleasures from distant ones.[75] Similarly in
Phaedrus he proves the necessity of knowledge for the orator
by showing that if he is to discover the probable (εἰκός), which
is the usual basis of rhetorical argument, he must first know
what is true. For the probable is that which looks like truth.[76]
The true purpose of rhetoric, of course, is not speaking to please
men, but speaking to please God—and this is what Plato admits
at the end.[77] This is the doctrine we know from *The Republic,
Theaetetus,* and *The Laws.* In the strictly theocentric character of the paideia taught by Plato in his later period, all the
unanswered problems (the *aporiai*) of his earlier books are
solved at last.

Plato is perfectly willing to recognize the literary skill of the
professional orators. But, brilliant though it may be, it is not
therefore pleasing to God. The legend of the discovery of writing (i.e. of the alphabet) by the Egyptian god Theuth will
make that plain.[78] When the god took his new invention to
Thamous of Thebes, and boasted of providing an aid for the
memory, and so for the knowledge, of mankind, Thamous answered that the invention of writing was more likely to make
people neglect their memory, and to produce forgetfulness in
their souls, because they would rely on the written word instead
of keeping their memories alive.[79] So the new invention would
produce sham wisdom instead of true knowledge. All Plato's
greatness is revealed in this attitude to books and writing—
which affects his own work as an author no less than the reputation of the rhetors. It is difficult after reading *Phaedrus* not
to see that Plato is criticizing himself in the closing portion of
the book quite as much as others; but if we doubted it, the
seventh Letter shows quite clearly that he saw the full difficulty
of putting *any* thought adequately into writing. Some comments
on his teaching had been published by unqualified persons; and
this led him to the paradoxical conclusion that it was impossible
even for himself to put his doctrine into writing, and that therefore there was no written version of his philosophy.[80] Students
of Plato soon connected the similar statement of his attitude in

Phaedrus with the peculiar form in which he wrote, the Socratic dialogue, and took the connexion to be one of the main grounds for holding *Phaedrus* to be an early announcement of his programme (see p. 182). But in fact it is difficult to believe that if Plato had been so sceptical about the value of books in his youth, he would ever have written such a huge quantity of them; whereas if he turned against all his books late in life, we can explain it as an assertion of his own freedom, which he would not surrender even to his own books. He refused to be bound by what he had written.

Having reached this attitude late in life, Plato is inclined in *Phaedrus* to concede only limited value to the art of writing, even in its higher rhetorical application. A book goes into everyone's hands; some understand it, and some do not; it cannot explain or defend itself, if it is wrongly accused. It needs another book to defend it.[81] The truest writing is written in the soul of the student, for it has the strength to defend itself.[82] The only value of the letters traced in ink is to remind someone of what he knows already.[83] Contemporary rhetoric was turning more and more into a written art, 'graphic speech'; and so Plato proves the educational superiority of philosophical dialectic to rhetoric by the fact that dialectic acts directly upon the mind, and moulds it. The sophists had compared education with agriculture.[84] Plato takes up the comparison. Anyone who cares about seed, and wants it to grow into a crop, will not plant a 'garden of Adonis' and be pleased when it shoots up in eight days, but will prefer proper agriculture, and be glad when the seed finally bears fruit after eight months of laborious care.[85] The images of sowing and planting are applied by Plato to the dialectic training of the mind. Anyone who cares about the true education of the intellect will not be content with the scanty and trifling early crops produced by the rhetorical garden of Adonis, but will have the patience to wait till the crops of the true philosophical education come to ripeness. We know this method of defending philosophical culture, from *The Republic* and *Theaetetus*. It is based on the principle of the 'long detour'; and it is important to see how Plato comes back to it again and again.[86] The seed of Plato's paideia can grow only in months and years of life together (as the seventh Letter says), and not in a few terms of academic training.[87] To show that this, which his opponents considered its weakness, was really its strength, is Plato's chief aim, here and elsewhere. It could develop its full strength only in a few chosen pupils.[88] For the general mass of 'cultured people', rhetoric was the broad and easy way.

9

PLATO AND DIONYSIUS: THE TRAGEDY
OF PAIDEIA

RECENT philological criticism has at last succeeded in proving
that the seventh and eighth Letters, which were long discarded
as forgeries, are Plato's own work, records of his own thoughts
and feelings. This at once added an important chapter to the
history of Plato's paideia.[1] The external truths, of course, could
not be changed. We should still know that Plato had been
friendly with the most powerful tyrant of his age, even if those
Letters (the seventh in particular) were not autobiography of
the first rank, but sensational inventions by some clever literary
swindler, who thought it would be exciting to work the great
Plato into a melodramatic political story. For the basic facts
around which the seventh Letter (our chief concern here) is
written have never been disputed even when everyone thought
the Letter itself was a forgery.[2] But it is enthralling for the
student of history to read Plato's own account of the tragedy
of Syracuse; and the elaborately dramatized version of the
story given in Plutarch's life of Dion does not debar us from
comparing it with the authentic, vividly alive detail of its chief
source, Plato's seventh Letter.

Even without the Letter, we should have known that the man
who wrote *The Republic* and *The Laws* was inspired by a great
and genuine passion for politics—a passion which at first impelled him to action. This does not merely illuminate Plato's
psychology; it is expressed even in the structure of his conception of knowledge. For he held that knowledge (*gnosis*) was
not contemplation of truth, divorced from life, but became skill
or art (*techné*) and reasoning (*phronésis*) about the right way
to take, the right decision to make, the true aim, the real good.
This remains true even of its most abstract form, the doctrine
of Ideas in Plato's later dialogues. The real emphasis for Plato
lay on action, on *bios*, even when this sphere of action moved
away from the realization of the ideal state and concentrated

into the 'state within us'. But here, in the seventh Letter, Plato himself describes the development of his mind down to his first journey to Magna Graecia, which took him to Syracuse, and to the court of the tyrant; and throughout the account it is clear that his practical interest in politics was the dominating force in his early life. This is confirmed not only by the attitude to politics which appears in his major works, but by intimate details of his own family life which are part of the background of *The Republic* as well as of *Timaeus,* which belongs to the same trilogy. He put them in to cast an indirect light on himself—although, as the author, he had to remain out of sight—and on his relation to Socrates. His brothers Adeimantus and Glaucon are put forward in *The Republic* as representative members of the Athenian younger generation, with all its enthusiasm for politics. Although Glaucon is only twenty, he is anxious to enter politics, and it takes a great deal of trouble for Socrates to hold him back. Plato's uncle Critias is the notorious oligarch who led the revolution of 403. Plato makes him appear several times as an interlocutor; and intended to dedicate to him the dialogue bearing his name, which was meant to complete the trilogy that begins with *The Republic,* but which remained only a fragment. Like many others, Plato had become Socrates' pupil because of his interest in politics. Xenophon says the same was true of Critias and Alcibiades, although he adds, doubtless correctly, that they were soon disappointed when they found out what kind of 'political' teaching he gave.[3] But that teaching fell on fertile soil in Plato: the fruit it bore was his philosophy. It was Socrates who inspired Plato to see a new link between the state and education—in fact, almost to identify them. But it took Socrates' conflict with the state and his death to prove to Plato that a new state could be started only by giving men a philosophical education which would change the whole structure of society from the ground up. With this conviction implanted in him early, and later transformed into the axiom he lays down in *The Republic,* he went to Syracuse. (According to the seventh Letter, this was about 388, when he was 40.) There he converted and inspired the noble and fiery Dion, a close kinsman and friend of the powerful monarch of Syracuse.[4] Dion's endeavour to convert Dionysius I himself to his ideal was bound to fail. The great and moving confidence which the cool politi-

cian showed for the grave young enthusiast, and which encouraged him to introduce Plato himself to the tyrant, was due
rather to Dion's absolute loyalty and the purity of his motives
than to his ability to see the world of practical politics with the
same eyes as the tyrant. In the seventh Letter Plato tells us that
on his instigation Dion asked his uncle to give Syracuse a constitution and govern it by the best laws.[5] But Dionysius did not
think the situation which had produced dictatorship in Syracuse
would justify such a policy. Plato held that it, and it alone,
would give a genuine firm foundation to the power of Dionysius
in Italy and Sicily, so as to give it real meaning and a chance
of becoming permanent. Dionysius, on the other hand, was convinced that it would soon destroy his dominion, and deliver the
Sicilian city-states into which it would dissolve into the hands
of the Carthaginian invaders. That episode was a prelude to
the real tragedy, in which the actors were Plato, Dion, and
Dionysius II, son and successor of the elder tyrant. Plato therefore returned to Athens, enriched by his experience, and shortly
afterwards founded his school. But his friendship with Dion
outlasted the disappointment which must have strengthened his
resolution (announced in the *Apology*) to withdraw from all
active public life. The two men became friends for life. But
whereas Plato now gave himself entirely over to his work as
a teacher of philosophy, Dion clung to his ideal of reforming the
Sicilian tyranny, and awaited a favourable moment for realizing it.

The moment seemed to have come after the death of Dionysius I in 367, when his son, still a youth, inherited his power.
Plato's *Republic* had appeared not long before, between 380
and 370. It must have strengthened Dion's convictions, for it
set down with perfect clarity and force the ideas he had once
heard Plato teach by word of mouth. The book was still quite
new, and was hotly discussed. In it Plato had mentioned the
obvious question whether his ideal state could ever be realized,
but he had judged it to be irrelevant for the practical *application*
of his philosophical paideia. Perhaps (he had written)[6] the perfect state existed only in heaven, as an ideal pattern; or perhaps
it had already been in existence somewhere far away among barbarians (i.e. foreigners) of whom Greece knew nothing.[7] (In
the Hellenistic age, when new Oriental peoples became known

to the Greeks, and others became more familiar than before, some scholars suggested, on the basis of Plato's remark, that the perfect Republic had been the caste-state of the Egyptians, or the hierarchic theocracy of Moses.)[8] Plato proposes that education should aim to create the perfectly just state within each of us—after all, that is how actually existing states are created.[9] He had given up the contemporary state as incurable.[10] It could do nothing to help his ideals to realization. From a theoretical point of view he thought it would be simplest to take the educational system which he had suggested for the rulers of his Republic, and which he held was the basis of any improvement in the state, and to try it on one man—assuming that that one man was really sent by heaven. It is obviously easier to change one man than many.[11] This idea was not inspired by considerations of political power. In *The Laws,* at the end of his life, Plato came out against the concentration of power in the hands of one individual.[12] When he recommended giving the power in his Republic to one tyrant, of high moral and intellectual calibre, he was impelled solely by educational motives.[13] It is surely just as easy to spread a good spirit all through the population of a country by the instrumentality of one man, as for the one powerful ruler to corrupt the entire people so that it follows his bad example. The latter was what Plato saw happening in Syracuse under Dionysius I; and indeed the gloomy picture of the tyrant in *The Republic* obviously has several features that belong to him. It is discouraging. It seems to refute all Dion's plans of reform. But why should one grant that the dreadful human weakness shown by Dionysius I must be characteristic of all men in his position? Such an indictment against humanity would make a better future for ever impossible. At least, so thought the ardent ethical idealist Dion. After the tyrant's death he pelted Plato with letters and messages beseeching him to seize the opportunity, come to Sicily, and realize his ideals of the perfect state with the new ruler's help.[14] In *The Republic* Plato said that his ideals could not come true until power and moral knowledge (δύναμις and φιλοσοφία), which are usually hopelessly separated, could be brought together.[15] This, he said, could happen only through a special act of providence, a divine tyché.[16] Dion now tried to convince him that the accession of the younger Dionysius was in fact this far-off divine event, and that it would be a betrayal of his ideals not to grasp the moment.[17]

Even the idealistic Dion realized that Plato's plans were the work of a single exceptional individual. It was hopeless to expect them to be realized in the contemporary state by the unconscious energies of the subordinate masses, whose efforts tended in the opposite direction.[18] He expected nothing of the masses: because they were no longer the organic people of old, but a rash and passionate mob: it was they who had most loudly hailed the tyranny of Dionysius I. Only a few, with the help of a favourable tyché, could be won over for the supreme purpose; but Dion thought the new monarch might be one of them—and if he were converted, then Syracuse would be the home of perfect blessedness.[19] In Dion's plan, the only fixed factor was the unlimited power of the tyrant; and it must have been uncanny to think of this, because no one knew what use he would make of it. But Dion was enthusiastic enough to rely on Dionysius' youth. Youth is the plastic age. Although the inexperienced young monarch had none of the mature moral and spiritual judgment that Plato expected in his ideal ruler, he seemed to be one, and indeed the only possible, means of converting Plato's ideal into fact.

Plato too, in *The Republic,* saw no other way to achieve the ideal state than by educating a perfect ruler to rule it. And he had assigned to himself—that is, to the creative philosopher— the task of fixing the fundamental lines of education, and establishing them as the ideal to be striven for. But who was there, apart from Plato himself with his incomparable and dominating personality, who would be capable of taking on the work of educating the ruler as he had foreseen it, and putting it into action, and carrying it to success? In *The Republic,* of course, the process is quite different. But there the education of the future rulers is completed by a patient lifelong process of selection and testing, both in philosophical understanding and in practical life. The candidates are all the best of the younger generation. The choice narrows down from stage to stage, until at last only a few, or one, remains, whose task is to complete the great work as it is pleasing to God. A ruler trained in this school would be the absolute opposite of a tyrant. He would carry the good of the whole community, seen by the light of eternal truth, in his

soul as his supreme law; and that would take him beyond any
one-sided individual wish or belief. The tyrant of Syracuse
might well be willing, talented, and educable; but he was chosen
for his task only because he was the heir on whom a historical
accident happened to drop the mantle of power. In that respect
the situation which confronted Plato in Syracuse was not very
different from that which faced Isocrates in educating his
princely pupils.[20] But Dion held that it was necessary to make
the grand endeavour at any cost, not only because, if it succeeded, Dionysius' vast power promised greater success, and not
only because he himself held a unique position in that mighty
empire,[21] but mainly because he had felt the utterly transforming force of Plato's personality and teaching, and was therefore
inspired by Plato's belief in the power of education.

Looking back on all this in the seventh Letter, Plato reviews
the principal events in Dion's life, and the separate stages of
his association with his noble and gifted friend, whose recent
death still saddens him. Not one, but two attempts to educate
the tyrant, begun immediately after his accession, had failed.
And then the powerful monarchy of the Dionysii collapsed too;
for after his educational plans fell through, Dion was banished
by the tyrant, resorted to force, conquered him, and then died
himself. After a brief reign he was assassinated, as a result of
a feud within his own retinue. What we call Plato's seventh
Letter is a pamphlet, meant for publicity, and written after
Dion's murder. It describes and justifies his career; but it is
couched in the form of an advisory speech addressed to his son
and his adherents in Sicily, encouraging them to be loyal to the
dead man's ideal. If they do, Plato promises he will aid them
with advice and influence.[22] This means that he is publicly siding
with Dion, and reaffirming his original belief. Dion, he says,
tried neither to capture the tyranny nor to overthrow it; he was
driven to expel the tyrant by the wrongs he had suffered. The
entire blame falls on the tyrant himself, although Plato recognizes that his own first visit to Syracuse, by converting Dion to
his philosophy, had ultimately brought about the fall of the
tyranny.[23] Just as in *The Laws* (which he was writing at that
time) he traces God's pedagogy in history, so he sees in all these
great events the power of divine tyché. Looking back on his

past, he sees the hand of providence equally clearly in the way his own life has been linked up with the history of his time. Nothing but divine tyché could bring it about that a ruler should become a philosopher, or a philosopher a ruler: so Plato had said in *The Republic*. Surely it was the hand of divine tyché which brought Plato and Dionysius together; and which closed the whole series of events in a tragic climax, when the monarch refused to recognize its power and thrust it away. Common sense would lead to the conclusion that Dion's enterprise (and so indirectly Plato's, who backed him) was doomed to failure, because it was based on an error in psychology, a faulty understanding of the weakness and baseness of the average human nature. But Plato does not think so. After his teaching had once set in motion a force like Dion, it was for the weaker character, Dionysius, a betrayal of his instincts as a ruler to reject this opportunity to fulfil his task in the highest possible way.

Accordingly, Plato's role in the drama was not that of a spontaneous actor. He was the tool of a higher power. The philosophical basis of this idea appears in *The Laws*. There Plato repeatedly declares that man is a plaything in the hands of God, a puppet in a toy theatre.[24] But the puppets have to learn their parts; and their desires and passions are not always ready to obey the strings as God pulls them. At bottom, this is the primitive Greek view of human life. In Homer and in tragedy, the life of man is always played beneath a larger stage, the life of the gods. Invisible threads run down from heaven to earth, moving what we call events. The poet sees them everywhere, sees them controlling the acts of humanity.[25] In *The Republic* there seemed to be a huge gulf between actual human life and the divine principle of the universe, the Good. But Plato's interest was turning increasingly towards the form in which it manifested itself in the visible world—that is, in history, in life, in the concrete. Not only in his theory of Ideas, but in his description of the ideal life, the bios, metaphysics begin more and more to penetrate the realities of sense-perception. From that point of view too the seventh Letter is important. It shows us that Plato's efforts to determine and shape his own career actively moulded his interpretation of the world. This personal factor he intentionally concealed, but it can be traced in *The Republic*, where he says that it is the intervention of divine tyché which preserves the 'philosophical nature' in a corrupt environment.[26] Unless we keep this in mind we cannot understand what he means in *The Republic, The Laws,* and the seventh Letter by saying that even the conjunction of power and intellect (embodied in the ruler and the wise man) is an individual act of this heavenly providence. This connects his Sicilian adventure with the description in *The Republic* of the situation of the philosopher in his own day. It becomes more than a mere fact in his biography. It becomes a direct illustration of his thesis in *The Republic* that the general belief in the philosopher's helplessness and uselessness is really not an accusation against philosophy, but an indictment of the world.

When Dion invited Plato to come to Syracuse, he said it would be his function to realize the ideal of political philosophy proposed in *The Republic,* in the new situation created by the death of Dionysius and the accession of the new ruler. We might think this would entail changing the whole constitution; but in the seventh Letter Plato expressly says he was not called in as a political adviser with carte blanche, but with the clearly defined duty of educating the young tyrant. This way of stating his function shows more plainly than anything else that Dion was taking *The Republic* very seriously: for there Plato described the ideal state quite simply as the ideal paideia fulfilled. The ruler was now already in existence, and had to be taken as he was. So Dion was bound to start with a chief 'guard' who was to be trained for a job he already had. This was a serious restriction on Plato's original claims. Instead of building from the ground up, he had to begin at the top and work down. In his letters to Plato Dion described the tyrant as a gifted youth 'yearning for paideia'.[27] Plato had said in *The Republic* that the most important thing about education is to create a favourable environment in which it can be carried on. This remark must have inspired gloomy forebodings: for right at the beginning of his seventh Letter (as if in the exposition of a drama), he vividly describes what he thought of the manners of Syracuse and the spiritual climate at the tyrant's court.[28] He explains his fear of the risk Dion was taking, and justifies it by the fact he has learnt in long years of experience as a teacher, that young men are easily gripped by enthusiasms that do not live very long.[29] He realized that Dion's character, mature and tested, was the only fixed fulcrum on which he could lean. But there was a more important reason for him to accept the invitation. If he refused it, it would mean he was abandoning the possibility of realizing the theory which he had said would change the whole life of man. He had not gone so far in *The Republic* as to abandon it; although he had said it would be difficult to realize it. He shrank from drawing this last conclusion from his pessimistic theory. He refused to admit he was acting, not because he really believed in the success of his mission, but because he was ashamed to look like 'talk instead of action' (λόγος μόνον κτλ).[30] The resignation he had already expressed so movingly in *The Republic* was virtually a refusal to leave his isolation.[31] He now risked his reputation on the chance to controvert his well-justified pessimism by his own work. He left his activity as a teacher in Athens, which, as he says, was 'entirely worthy' of him, and put himself under the power of a despotism which was out of tune with his views.[32] But still he believes he kept his name free from offence against the God of friendship and hospitality, and ultimately against his own philosophical vocation, which did not allow him to choose the easier way.

In the seventh Letter, Plato's relation to the tyrant is all described in this light. Plato is presented as a teacher who went to instruct a pupil. As soon as he arrived he found his worst fears were justified. Dion had been so slandered to the tyrant that there was in the court an atmosphere of impenetrable uncertainty and distrust. This was so deep that the strong impression Plato made on Dionysius only increased the jealousy the courtiers felt for Dion.[33] Dionysius I had been kind to Dion and trusted him; but had tried to destroy Plato's influence on him by sending the philosopher back to Athens. His son, a weaker spirit, believed the whispers of those who hated and envied Dion, being competitors for his favour: they said that Dion wanted to depose him, and to make himself tyrant under the cloak of philosophical reform, while Plato had been brought in simply to make the young monarch a pliable instrument in Dion's hand. Dionysius II did not question Plato's loyalty, and was flattered by his friendship. So he did the opposite to his father. He banished Dion, and sought friendship with Plato. But (as Plato writes)[34] he shrank from doing the only thing that would have ensured their friendship: which was to learn

from Plato, become his pupil, and listen to his political dis-
courses. Court slander had made him afraid that he might grow
too dependent on Plato, and so, 'his mind enchanted by paideia,
neglect his duties as a ruler'.[35] Plato waited patiently for the
awakening of a deeper desire in his pupil, the desire for a philosophical life; but 'he managed to resist successfully'.[36] So Plato
returned to Athens. Still, he had to promise to come back after
the end of the war which had just broken out. Mainly for Dion's
sake, he was reluctant to make a complete break with the tyrant;
he hoped his friend would be called back from exile. But his and
Dion's plan to take the young monarch who had hitherto been
'out of contact with paideia and intellectual conversation suitable to his rank',[37] and to 'teach him and train him into a king
worthy to rule',[38] had ended in failure.

    It is not easy to understand why, a few years after the failure
of his first mission, Plato accepted another invitation from Dionysius. He says he did so because he was constantly urged by
his friends in Syracuse, and also, in particular, by the Pythagoreans in southern Italy, with the great mathematician Archytas,
the ruler of Tarentum, and his adherents.[38a] Before leaving
Syracuse Plato had established a political alliance between them
and Dionysius II, which would be endangered if he now refused
to go.[39] Dionysius sent a battleship to Athens to make the difficult journey easier for Plato,[40] and promised, if he accepted the
invitation, to summon Dion home from banishment.[41] But the
deciding factor for Plato was that Archytas and friends at
Dionysius' court reported his intellectual attainments had improved.[42] Pressed by his pupils at home and drawn on by his
friends in Sicily and Italy, Plato determined, in spite of his age,
to make the journey.[43] It was to bring him the profoundest disappointment. This time, Plato's account passes swiftly over his
reception and over political conditions in Syracuse, to concentrate on the educational situation he found when he arrived.
Since his last visit, the tyrant had been associating with all sorts
of bogus intellectuals; he was full of the ideas he had picked up
from them.[44] Plato thought nothing would be gained by continuing that kind of instruction. Experience had taught him that
the sure and certain test of a pupil's enthusiasm was to explain
to him the difficulty and toilsomeness of the task, and observe

the results.[45] If he were filled with a genuine love of knowledge he would really be strengthened by realizing the obstacles in his way; he would use all his energy, and all the energy of his spiritual guide, to reach the goal beyond. But the unphilosophic type shrinks from the trouble involved, and the arduous life he must lead; he is incapable of pushing on against obstacles. Some convince themselves they have understood the whole thing already and do not need to bother about it any further.[46]

Dionysius belonged to the latter type. He posed as a great mind, and showed off the knowledge he had got from others as if it were his own.[47] At this point Plato mentions that afterwards Dionysius did the same thing with what he had learnt from Plato himself: he even wrote a book on it, expounding it as if he had worked it all out for himself. This trait is rather important: it shows that the young fellow had a certain intellectual ambition. But it was the ambition of a dilettante. Tradition tells us that after his overthrow the tyrant lived in Corinth and taught there. Plato knows about the plagiarized book only by hearsay: he never saw it. But the mention of it allows him to bring in an explanation of the relation between his books and his teaching which is not really surprising after what he has already said in *Phaedrus*,[48] but which is remarkable for the form in which it is couched. It is certainly not mere chance that in his old age he speaks more frequently of the impossibility of putting the essential parts of his teaching satisfactorily into a book. If what he says in *Phaedrus* is true, and a book is useful only to recall what has been already learnt, without being able to impart new knowledge, then every book Plato wrote was important for him only as a reflex of his word-of-mouth teaching. This must be particularly true of a form of knowledge which cannot be communicated by words alone, like other kinds of knowledge, but can only be brought slowly into being by a gradual growth of the soul. He means that apprehension of divine things from which everything in his philosophy ultimately derives its certainty, and towards which everything in the world strives. Here Plato touches the final questions, on the answer to which his teaching, his influence, and his conception of the value of education all depend. We do not possess, and we never shall possess, any written statement by him about the supreme certainty whereon his work was founded.[49] Aristotle's theology, at least in conception, is a didactic thing: it is the noblest and highest science (or educational discipline) among a number of others. Plato of course believes it is possible and necessary to purify the mind of the sensuous elements which cling to it, by putting it through the gradually ascending system of knowledge which he describes in *The Republic* as philosophical paideia, and so to guide it closer and closer to the Absolute. But this process is long and tedious. It can succeed only through a great deal of shared dialectic research (πολλὴ συνουσία) on the subject in a sort of philosophical community. At this point, Plato brings in the image of the spark which jumps across between two pieces of wood rubbed together: that is how the spark of knowledge kindles a soul which has gone through the long rubbing process of dialectic.[50] The apprehension by the light of which it is kindled is a creative act of which few are capable, and they only through their own strength, with a little guidance.

This process is a gradual transit from sense-perception to the spiritual apprehension of true reality. After describing the education of the tyrant in the seventh Letter, Plato gives an account of the process of approaching dialectic apprehension, in an excursus on the theory of knowledge. He uses a mathematical metaphor, the image of the circle.[51] It is a difficult passage, much discussed in recent times, and never quite cleared up. It is the climax of Plato's description of the character of learning and teaching as he conceived them.[52] Apprehension of the Good in this sense means becoming like it, at the highest point where man and God meet and touch. But the vision which is the final aim of the process of 'becoming like God'[53] is never described by Plato; it remains an *arrhéton,* unspoken.[54] Similarly *The Symposium* had described the soul's vision of eternal beauty as the process of initiation into the mysteries, a *mystagogia*;[55] and *Timaeus* says, 'It is hard to find the creator and father of the universe, and when he is found, it is impossible to describe his nature publicly'.[56] If Dionysius had understood Plato, the reve‹ lation would have been as holy for him as for Plato himself.[57] To publicize it was an act of profanation, to which he was impelled by contemptible ambition, either because he wanted to claim those ideas as his own, or because he wanted to pretend he possessed a paideia of which he was unworthy.[58] The allu-

sions in the seventh Letter make it clear that the princely education which Plato meant to give Dionysius was not merely technical instruction in various types of government. It was meant
to change the whole man, and his whole life. The knowledge on
which it was based was the apprehension of the supreme paradeigma which Plato in *The Republic* says must be the ruler's
standard and measure: the apprehension of divine Good.[59] The
way to reach it was the same as that described in *The Republic*
—mathematics and dialectic. In his conversation with the tyrant,
Plato does not seem to have got beyond defining the outlines of
his paideia; but he was evidently determined to give up none of
his rigorous principles. There is no royal road to learning the
royal art of government. By his attitude to what Plato told him,
the young prince showed his mind was incapable of penetrating
to the depths where lie the true roots of the vocation he was
vainly trying to follow.

The last part of the Letter is very dramatic. It describes
Plato's break with Dionysius, and the monarch's tyrannical behaviour to him. These scenes make a violent and effective contrast to the description of Platonic paideia which forms the central part of the Letter. Long before, in *Gorgias,* Plato had set
his philosophy of paideia up against the philosophy of violence
and power.[60] Now Dion's property, which had kept him alive in
his exile, but which he had not been able to take out of Syracuse,
was confiscated; his promised recall was denied. Plato himself
lived for some time as a prisoner, incommunicado in the palace
of the tyrant; and was then transferred to the barracks of the
bodyguard, which hated him and threatened to kill him. Finally,
Archytas of Tarentum was secretly informed of the situation,
and obtained Dionysius' permission for Plato to return home.
On the way, he met the exiled Dion at the Olympic festival, and
heard his plans for revenge, but refused to take part in the
preparations.[61] In another passage of the Letter, he describes
his association with Dion as a 'community of free paideia'
(ἐλευθέρας παιδείας κοινωνία).[62] But this community did not oblige
him to follow his friend into violence. He was ready, however,
to try to reconcile Dion with Dionysius, and promised to do so.[63]
But he did not forbid Dion to recruit volunteers from among
his students to form his corps of liberators. Even though the

tyranny in Syracuse could scarcely have been overthrown without the active assistance of the Academy, Plato regarded the whole affair as a tragedy; after the two protagonists fell, he summed up their lives in Solon's phrase αὐτοὶ αἴτιοι, 'theirs was the guilt'.[64]

Really, the Sicilian drama was a tragedy not only for Dion and Dionysius, who fell, but for Plato too, although externally he seemed to stand quite outside the catastrophe. Doubtful as he was of its success, he put his whole strength behind the adventure, and thereby made it his own. It has been said that his mistake arose from a complete misunderstanding of the 'conditions' of political life and action—a misunderstanding which is implicit in the very nature of his political ideal. Isocrates had already spoken humorously in *Philip* of people who wrote Republics and Laws which could not be used in real life.[65] That was in 346, soon after Plato's death, when he thought he had said the last word on Plato's work in politics. He himself was very proud that his principles, although they went far beyond the purview of ordinary hack politicians, were politically practical and useful. But his criticism does not really hit the mark. There is indeed a profound gulf of principle between Plato's ideal state and political reality, but he knows the gulf exists, and constantly points it out.[66] Only some miracle could conjoin this wisdom with earthly power. The failure of the attempt in Sicily which he had undertaken with so much compunction must have made him doubt whether his ideal could be fulfilled during his own lifetime, or ever. . . Yet it still remained his ideal. It is a mistaken idea that if Plato had known more about mass-psychology or courtly suppleness, he could have made the idea which was for him the highest and holiest thing acceptable to the world—the world which he regarded as a doctor regards a patient seriously ill. In this sense, his interest in the state was not 'political' at all. This has been shown beyond all doubt by our analysis of the intellectual structure of *The Republic,* and of Plato's conception of the perfect statesman. Therefore the Syracusan disaster did not destroy his life's dream, or even his 'life's lie', as some have called his lifelong interest in the state and his assertion that it should be governed by philosophy.

As we have seen, Plato gave up all active participation in politics some time before he began to write. This is asserted with complete clarity in the *Apology*. There he was thinking merely of Athens. But although Dion, on becoming acquainted with Plato, may have tried to convince him on theoretical grounds that his ideals would be more easily fulfilled in a state ruled by an absolute monarch, Plato's disbelief in the possibility of their practical fulfilment remained the same in *The Republic*. He was driven by the enthusiasm of his pupils and friends, particularly Dion, to give up his resistance; but the failure which resulted, and which he had foreseen, could scarcely alter his conception of human society and of the central position held in it by paideia. And still what happened in Syracuse was a tragedy for him. It was a blow to his paideia—not because it controverted its philosophical truth, but because it misapplied his practical skill in education. The persons chiefly responsible were his friends, who had taken the responsibility of persuading him to make the experiment.[67] It is not probable that Dion dragged Plato into the adventure for selfish reasons, to help on his own ambitions, although he was directly interested in Plato's intervention in the political situation. Plato's knowledge of men, however, was so great that he must have known what the tyrant's character really was, and he cannot have been entirely wrong about one of his closest friends.

So the difference in the attitudes of Plato and Dion, which emerged during the episode, only serves to distinguish Plato's far-sighted and heroic resignation from the bold and adventurous but shallow and credulous idealism of Dion. In the seventh Letter, despite his declared agreement with Dion's aim, the creation of a constitutional monarchy for Syracuse, Plato takes care not to identify himself with his means, and thereby tells us more about himself. Every observant reader must have noticed this. On principle, Plato rejects revolution as a political technique.[68] But after the Syracusan adventure, he must have believed even less than before that his ideal could be fulfilled by legal means either. A Christian must feel that Plato's honourable disappointment was due to the fact that he tried to find the spiritual kingdom which he had been working to build up, not in the next world, but in this. His correction of current errors about the events in Syracuse and the part he played in them is due to a profound and impressive sense of his own rightness and superiority to such things. This sense comes from the long-trained strength of his soul, which enables him magnificently to represent himself as an embodiment of the divine equilibrium which reasserts itself in every error of the world. It is impossible not to compare this very personal document with Isocrates' justification of himself in the *Antidosis* speech. It is certainly an important sign of the times that two such men should end by taking the public into their confidence about their personal aspirations and defeats. It is a valuable proof of the authenticity of the seventh Letter that it makes us feel with overpowering clarity the dominating personality which lies behind it.

PLATO'S *LAWS*

THE LAWGIVER AS EDUCATOR

WRITTEN in Plato's old age and published after his death, *The Laws* had few readers and still fewer commentators even in late antiquity. The scholarly Plutarch is proud of knowing it;[1] and the fact that all our manuscripts go back to one single archetype shows that it was almost lost in the Byzantine period.[2] In the nineteenth century, classicists did not know how to approach it. Eduard Zeller, the representative historian of philosophy in that period, declared in an early work that it was not by Plato at all.[3] Later, when discussing Plato in his history of Greek philosophy, he treated *The Laws* in an appendix—[4] which means that he thought it was genuine enough, but was unable to fit it into the general picture of Plato's philosophy which he had drawn from the other dialogues. Since *The Laws* is by far the largest of Plato's books, covering more than one-fifth of his entire work, this shows how little real attempt has been made to reach any *historical* understanding of Plato's philosophy.[5] Scholars tend to reconstruct it in accordance with their preconceived ideas of what philosophy ought to be. Now, *The Laws* contains neither logic nor ontology. Therefore philosophers hold it is not a central work, but a sort of offshoot of Plato's thinking. Nevertheless Plato thought that what he said in it was of central importance: it contains most profound discussions of the state, of law, of morals, and of culture. But all these subjects Plato subordinates to paideia. Therefore *The Laws* is a book of major importance in the history of Greek paideia. Paideia is Plato's first word, and his last.

Just like *The Republic,* which is the culmination of his earlier work, *The Laws* is a broad, comprehensive account of human life (βίος). But it is remarkable that after he finished *The Republic* he still felt the need of composing the same kind of gen-

eral survey once again, in another form, and of constructing a
second state, after once making the perfect state, the ideally just
Republic. Still, as he says in *The Laws,* the Republic is a state
for gods and their children.[6] In writing about it, he said he
would pay no attention to detailed legislation. The perfect system of education on which the Republic was founded was to
make the laws that overload most contemporary states quite
unnecessary.[7] In *The Statesman* too, he is critical of the traditional Greek reverence for *nomos,* and says the perfect monarch
would be preferable to perfect legislation, because rigid laws
could not be rapidly adapted to changing situations, and would
not allow the necessary measures to be taken at once.[8] But Plato
called the last of his political books *The Laws,* and filled it with
legal regulations for every detail of civic life; so it is obvious
that he was applying different standards.[9] This is shown also by
his increasing tendency to appeal to experience. In ethical and
educational matters this new attitude is shown by the shift of
his interest from concentration on pure knowledge of the norm
to history and psychology.[10] The central portions of *The Republic* were concerned with the theory of Ideas and the Idea of
Good. But these theories are mentioned only briefly in *The
Laws,* towards the end, where they are recommended as subjects for the ruler to study;[11] and the design for higher education, which was the main interest and filled most space in *The
Republic,* is superseded in *The Laws* by a plan for educating a
much wider group, including even small children. After Plato
died, Philip of Opus, who was his secretary and his Boswell,
edited *The Laws* from his incomplete draft on wax tablets, and
divided it into twelve books. He noticed the gap created by the
absence of any system for educating the ruler, and tried to compensate it by defining in greater detail the special wisdom which
the ruler ought to possess. These supplementary ideas he recorded in the treatise which still exists as the *Epinomis* or *Appendix to the Laws* at the end of the book itself.[12] The Academy
must have entrusted him with this task because he knew the
manuscripts Plato had left and the plans he had had in mind,
so that we cannot call the *Epinomis* a forgery. It is rather a
supplement to *The Laws,* which Plato's own school therefore
considered to be incomplete.

The Laws is such a gigantic book that we have no space to

discuss every part of it in detail. It is difficult even to give an outline of it, as we did with *The Republic:* because its composition
and its structural unity present a problem of great difficulty,
and because its special charm lies in the originality with which
the old man tackles a number of important special problems,
and gives a new turn to every one of them. It is difficult too to
give a general explanation of the relation between *The Republic*
and *The Laws,* although many have tried to do so. We might
say that by dialectic standards *The Republic* represents the
plane of reality on which are the Ideas, and truth grounded in
that higher reality, whereas *The Laws* represents the lower
plane of opinion. That is the only solution of the riddle given
by Plato himself.[13] In the development of philosophy, *The Laws*
is in many respects much closer to Aristotle, as far as method
goes. Plato is trying to control a larger and larger mass of material and to inform it all with his principles, instead of making
the gulf between Idea and phenomena wider and deeper, as he
did in his youth. Much of *The Laws* is occupied by discussions
of education—the first two books and the seventh contain nothing else. But that is not the only importance of the book for the
subject of paideia. From Plato's point of view the entire work
is devoted to constructing a powerful system of education. Its
relation to the problem of paideia is most clearly set forth in
a passage of the ninth book, which takes up and develops a
theme already introduced in the fourth.[14] This is the comparison
of a bad legislator with a slaves' doctor, hurrying from one
patient to another and prescribing treatment quickly and dicta-
torially without giving reasons or making a complete diagnosis,
simply by following the practice of others or working on his own
experience. Compared with him the free men's doctor looks like
a philosopher. He talks to his patients as if they were pupils
whom he had to help to conscious understanding of the cause
of some phenomenon. The slaves' doctor would not understand
that detailed and comprehensive method of instruction; if he
heard his colleague doing it, he would say, 'You are not treating your patient; you are teaching him (παιδεύεις), as if you
wanted to make him a doctor instead of curing him'.[15]

All contemporary legislators are on the same level as the
slaves' doctor. They are not real healers, because they are not
teachers. And that is the purpose of Plato in *The Laws.* He is

trying to be a legislator in the highest sense, which means to be the teacher of the citizens. The difference between this attitude to legislation and that of the usual type of lawgiver can be seen in his contempt for the usual type of law—which simply prescribes a definite punishment for definite actions. This means that the lawgiver has begun far too late. His main duty is not to avenge wrongs which have been done, but to prevent them from being done. Here Plato is following the example of medical science, which then had a growing tendency to regard not sick men but healthy men as the proper object of its care. Hence the dominant influence of dietetics in medicine. That was the art of keeping people healthy by prescribing the right way for them to live. For *diaita* in Greek medicine means not only 'diet' in the modern sense—the proper menu for invalids—but the general pattern of life to be followed by healthy persons. We have shown above that the Greek doctors' increasing interest in diet shows the influence of educational thought on medicine.[16] Plato's purpose in *The Laws* is to take the parallel established by him in *Gorgias* between the care of the body and the care of the soul,[17] medicine and politics, and by working out its logical consequences to make the ideal of paideia victorious in the realm of legislation. In *The Republic* he tried to make education so perfect that legislation would be superfluous.[18] In *The Laws* he assumes that laws are normally indispensable in the life of the state; and now sets out to subordinate legislation to the educational principle, and make it its instrument—as in *The Republic* he had converted the entire state into an educational institution.

He does this through the prefaces (*prooimia*) to the laws themselves. He clearly took particular care to define the concepts used in the prefaces, and to polish every detail of them. In his statement of principles in the fourth book, he distinguishes between those utterances of the legislator which are persuasive and those which are directive.[19] The function of the persuasive part, which occupies the prefaces, is to state and give reasons for the standard of right conduct.[20] This part, he says, must be elaborated in great detail, and is intended not only for the judge, but for all citizens. The sophist Protagoras, in Plato's dialogue named after him, remarks that when a new generation leaves school and enters life, a new phase of life begins: from now on the law of the state becomes their teacher in the conduct of practical life.[21] So law is the real vehicle of education for those who have grown up and are to acquire civic virtue. This is not a new idea of Protagoras'; he is describing the facts of life in any Greek state. Plato starts by assuming this, but by reforming the style of legislation he intends to give particular stress to the educational force of law. From the very beginning he thought of his own life-work as education, and made his philosophy the centre and focus of all positive educational forces. He had already made Socrates' dialectic, and Eros, and the symposium, and the state, all parts of that vast spiritual and intellectual structure; and now at the end of his life he emerges as a legislator, the last of that mighty historical procession to which Minos, Lycurgus, and Solon belong, and he promulgates his ordinances in a dignified archaic language specially designed for its function.[22] The Greeks always thought that legislation was the work of the superior wisdom of one divine person. So the highest philosophical virtue of Plato's Republic, Sophia, which is wisdom, is ultimately manifested in the promulgation of laws; and that is how it does productive work in the life of the community, from which it at first seemed to set its possessor far apart. The philosopher becomes a legislator. In almost every respect he resembles the great old Greek lawgivers. The only difference is that he takes what had been latent and potential in their work and makes it a consciously informing principle. That is the idea that the lawgiver is the prototype of the teacher. This is made clear as early as *The Symposium,* where Plato puts the lawgiver in this sense beside the poet; [23] other Greek writers had done the same. It was because Plato's philosophy had been from beginning to end a work of education, and because he had realized the deepest meaning of that concept, that he was bound to end as a legislator.

TRUE EDUCATION AND THE SPIRIT OF THE LAWS

As *The Republic* begins with the general problem of justice, so *The Laws* begins by discussing the spirit of the laws, which inspires every single thing in a real state with its ethos. Plato's concept of the spirit of the laws was the origin of Montesquieu's famous essay, *L'esprit des lois,* which influenced the development of modern politics so powerfully. To illustrate it, Plato

chooses one particular kind of political life which had long interested him: the Dorian state. Accordingly, he introduces as
interlocutors two representatives of that particular Greek stock,
a Spartan and a Cretan. It is a happy idea—not only because
it is a good example of the influence of a strongly individual
political character on the natural details of legislation, but because it at once raises a philosophical question. Which is the *best*
political ethos? In Plato's day, political theorists mostly held
that Sparta and Crete had the best constitutions in Greece.[24]
Besides the two typical Dorians, who are intellectual twins, as
it were, Plato introduces as principal interlocutor an 'Athenian
stranger'—a person of powerful, though mysterious, superiority,
which is willingly recognized by the two Dorians, despite their
strong dislike for the average Athenian. Megillus says he is convinced that if, in an exceptional case, an Athenian is good, he
is usually very good indeed.[25] Plato makes this objectivity in the
Spartan credible by telling us that Megillus had been Athenian
consul (*proxenos*) in his own city, and had for a long time been
sympathetically interested in the problem.[26] He is an Athenised
Spartan, just as the 'stranger' is an Athenian admirer of Sparta.
This choice of characters is symbolic. More concretely than any
other of his books, *The Laws* shows Plato's lifelong endeavour
to join the Dorian and Athenian natures in a higher unity. We
might compare it with the efforts of later humanists to marry
the spirit of Greece and the spirit of Rome in a harmony of
contrasts. In Plato's synthesis here we can see the same philosophical attitude to history, which starts with imperfect historical
facts and tries to rise on them to something perfect and absolute. This ought to assure the interest of all humanists for *The
Laws,* even apart from the question which it discusses, the question of the best education. These two racial stocks embody the
fundamental powers of the Greek nation—perhaps one-sidedly,
but each of them with all the strength and independence of
primitive nature. Each of them attempted to dominate Greece
and destroy the other; and now Plato tries to reconcile them by
pointing out their common origin. It is a Panhellenic ideal; but
Panhellenism for Plato did not mean a general planing down of
all differences, and a resolution of all individuality into a flabby
average Greekness, so that it would be easier to manage. He
thought the *worst* thing that could happen was the mingling of

all Greek stocks with one another.[27] He held that that was just as bad as the mingling of Greeks and barbarians.

The Athenian stranger is staying for a while in Crete, and is drawn by the two Dorians into a discussion of the best kind of law—an urgent problem for them because they are about to found a colony. It is a new Cretan city, and it is to have the very best possible constitution. So they inevitably start by discussing the nature of the state and of human areté—and, because of their Dorian surroundings, by defining them in terms which fit Dorian ethics and politics. Every reader of *The Republic* will welcome this, because the earlier work showed so much Spartan influence that we want to have Plato's exact attitude to the Spartan ideal defined. In *The Republic*, when Plato was constructing the ideal state, he made scarcely any reference to Sparta, because he was solely concerned with the ideal world. But in the series of degenerate constitutions he described the Spartan timocracy as the real constitution which came closest to the ideal; [28] and many features of the ideal Republic were taken directly from the model of Sparta, or were Spartan institutions moved by Plato to a higher, more spiritual plane. Judging by external things only, we might think that there was relatively little to differentiate the Spartan political ideal from that of Plato. The idealized Sparta of Plato's *Republic* seems to cast a ray of heavenly light upon the earthly state which was its pattern.

But all this appears in a clearer light in *The Laws*. Although everything Plato says about the Dorian idea of the state and Dorian traditions is full of respect, he is still fundamentally opposed to them. He was bound to be opposed to them as soon as he embarked on a philosophical analysis of the spirit pervading the concrete, contemporary Sparta. It is impossible to accuse him of being a one-sided admirer of Sparta: as far as that goes, *The Laws* is the best commentary on *The Republic*. No one could be more convinced of the value of the Dorian contribution to the ethical and political culture of Greece and of humanity. But as soon as he examined it as a historical phenomenon in itself he was bound to judge it merely as one stage in his philosophical cosmos of values, and to give it only limited approval. Instead of the simple contrast between historical fact and absolute ideal which we find in *The Republic*, *The Laws* gives a scheme of real human perfection broken up into several stages, each of which corresponds to definite historical phenomena, and which range from lower to higher in a sort of dialectical process. *The Laws* therefore contains the elements of a philosophy of history, although Plato's scheme of contrast may not be judged adequate for the refined historical sensibilities of to-day, when we attempt to understand the individual peculiarities of each historical factor. In any case, we can clearly see that he is now anxious to concentrate on concrete historical fact, and to blend it in a higher unity with knowledge of ideal standards. That is the result of an attitude like that of Plato in *The Laws,* which treats the historical expressions of the spirit in literature and poetry as representative of human areté, and tries to fix their value within the whole universe of paideia.[29]

In Plato's day, the Spartan ideal of paideia was represented by the poems of Tyrtaeus. They were its standard expression both for the Spartans themselves, who learnt them by heart at school and were 'crammed' with them,[30] and for the other Greeks, who thought of them as the embodiment of Spartan areté.[31] They had held that position for centuries, and continued to hold it as long as the Spartan element in Greek civilization persisted. This is shown by a Hellenistic poem lately discovered. It is an inscription over the grave of a teacher who died for his country, which says that he preserved in action 'his paideia' as described in the poems of Tyrtaeus.[32] Plato thinks of the works of the Dorian poet in exactly the same way, as documents and laws of areté. But although he asserts he fully agrees with the introduction of the Spartan commandment which makes it the citizen's sacred duty to defend his country, in *The Laws* he is interested in something greater and more fundamental. That is the ultimate standard of human virtue and perfection which is at the bottom of Tyrtaeus' admonitions to courage.[33] In the first two books of *The Laws* he starts from an analysis of Tyrtaeus, to criticize the ethics and ideals of Sparta, and then bases his practical attitude to Spartan and Cretan institutions on his criticism. In other words, when Plato, as a lawgiver, tries to inspire all the lives of all the citizens with an ideal of areté, he must get that ideal from the poet, who is the supreme lawgiver of human life. Plato's educational ideals are rooted in historical fact—that is where his thought is most genuinely humanist. He always treats the poets as classical representatives of ideal standards. But he therefore thinks they ought to be judged by a supreme standard, and the dialectical examination of that standard is the contribution of philosophy to the making of paideia.

It is simple enough, the Dorian ideal of areté taught by Tyrtaeus' poems and by the Spartan and Cretan institutions. It is this: Life is War. All forms of social life, every moral attitude dominating it, are assimilated to that ideal.[34] Plato begins his philosophical criticism of Sparta by pointing out this general feature pervading every detail of Spartan life and making us fully aware of its existence. Wherever men think victory is the only thing worth living for, courage inevitably becomes the only virtue.[35] We have already traced, in the first volume of this work, the dispute about the canon of virtues from the days when Tyrtaeus proclaimed the supremacy of the Spartan ideal of manhood, right through Greek poetry, where it is one of the richest and greatest themes. Now we look back on the entire development once again, from a new standpoint. Plato takes up the old dispute between Tyrtaeus, who praised courage, and Theognis, who taught that all virtues were comprised in justice; and he decides in favour of Theognis.[36] The foundation of the constitutional state governed by law was indeed a decisive advance on the old Dorian ideal. Men had to learn the difference between courage justly and unjustly employed, and realize that courage in connection with the other virtues—justice, self-control, and piety—is better than courage alone.[37] So Tyrtaeus must be 'corrected' by Theognis. Legislation must be directed to producing *the whole of virtue* (πᾶσα ἀρετή).[38] But there is one thing we can learn from the Dorian legislators: namely, that it is necessary to start with a definite ideal of human character, a fixed conception of areté. That makes them the model for any future legislator.[39] Human goods, such as health, strength, beauty, and wealth,[40] are to be subordinated to the four virtues of the soul, which Plato calls divine goods.[41] Where divine goods are cherished, human virtues appear of their own accord. Those who try only for the latter, lose both.[42] The higher virtues (as Theognis said of justice) contain the lower in themselves.[43] But the true unity, which includes them all, human and divine, is phronésis, the areté of the mind.[44] With this statement Plato transcends all the concepts of virtue which had been established, one after another, by the early Greek poets.

Plato shows how legislation can bring out and cultivate one particular virtue, by describing how courage had been cultivated in Sparta and Crete by the institution of meals in common for men, *syssitia* or 'messes', by physical exercise for military purposes, by hunting, and by all sorts of hardening methods.[45] Yet the Spartan system of training courage teaches its pupils to resist fear and pain, but not the temptations of pleasure.[46] This logical error causes them to surrender weakly to lust. In fact, the Dorian system has absolutely no institutions to cultivate temperance and self-discipline.[47] The influence of the syssitia and organized games in this direction is doubtful.[48] The Athenian speaker attacks the Dorian love of boys as an unnatural and degenerate form of normal sexual life, and criticizes the sexual looseness of the Spartan women.[49] The Spartan prejudice against wine and drinking-parties does not seem to him the right way of teaching self-control, but rather a shamefaced way of turning one's back upon Spartan lack of self-control. Love of wine, like so many other things in life, is in itself neither bad nor good.[50] Plato suggests that there should be rigid discipline at banquets, supervised by a good chairman to bind the wild and chaotic elements into a cosmos.[51]

The character and length of this polemic against the Spartan prejudice about drinking-parties obviously means that certain enthusiastic supporters and admirers of Spartan education had praised the abstemiousness of the Lacedaemonian youth at such functions. Plato's own uncle, the tyrant Critias, was one of the philo-Spartan writers of the Athenian oligarchic party; and he had sung the praise of Spartan abstinence in an elegiac poem on the Lacedaemonian constitution, which Plato must have read as a young man.[51a] The poem is different, of course, from his prose book on the Spartan state, used by Plato elsewhere in *The Laws*. In this elegy Critias eulogized the Spartan custom of not drinking the healths of individuals and calling them by name at the symposium. He gave a long description of the good effects of this tradition on the health and character of young men. According to him, the Spartans were very far from being teetotalers; they were just the proper mean between that extreme and Athenian licence. Against this judgment Plato tries here to prove his point that symposia are beneficial if they are conducted in a fine academic spirit.

What good does a 'well-educated drinking-party' of a few individuals do to the state?[52] The advantages it brings about are quite unknown to the Spartan legal system, because Sparta has no experience of such things.[53] Plato makes a long examination of teetotalism, which lasts all through the first two books of *The Laws,* and allows him not only to criticize Spartan legislation but to elaborate his own thoughts about paideia—in particular about the training of the desires. It is the work of an old man, as is shown by the almost pedantic elaboration with which it treats the one special problem from which Plato intends to move on to more general truths. The value of the drinking-party is the same as that of any paideia, such as the training of a chorus.[54] The education of the individual is not decisively important for the community, but 'the education of all educated men'[55] together is vitally important for the polis, for it makes them into men of real ability who do everything properly. They are also capable of beating the enemy, which Sparta counts the supreme test of areté.[56] For it is culture (παιδεία) that produces victory, not victory culture; in fact, victory often produces unculture (ἀπαιδευσία)![57] A victory that increases hybris in man is a Cadmean victory, where more is lost than was won; but there has never been a Cadmean paideia.[58] To prove the educational power of drinking-parties, Plato has to fit them into the general frame of paideia and connect them with 'musical' education.[59] So he is led to define the nature and influence of paideia; and he adds, 'Our discussion must make its way through it till it reaches God'.[60]

This link between the philosophy of education and the supreme being recalls *The Republic,* where paideia was based upon the Idea of Good.[61] But in *The Republic* the entire emphasis was placed upon the highest stage of paideia, and Plato did his best to cut the word and the concept away from *pais* (child). In *The Laws,* on the other hand, he begins with earliest childhood.[62] He is increasingly interested in tracing how the rational and conscious aspects of paideia (its truly philosophical elements, one might say) lead straight into the pre-rational and subconscious, or half-conscious, levels of the life of the soul. This idea was potentially present in *The Republic,* as we showed; [63] but it is interesting to note that Plato in *The Laws* concentrates very hard on discussing *how* it is psychologically possible. The principal necessity in paideia, he now holds, is proper pre-school training.[64] As if in play, it should arouse in the child's mind the desire for those things which he will attain when he is grown up. We have met the concept of trophé or early rearing in *The Republic,* and seen that it is characteristic of Plato. He stated as clearly as need be that complete areté in any field was made easy or difficult by the way in which a man or animal or plant grew up.[65] We described it as the *plantlike* element in ethical or biological perfection. This doubtless led Plato to investigate the development of desire in childhood, and to enquire how the pleasure-pain principle which is particularly strong in children could be used in the service of education.

Paideia is used to mean training in many different kinds of activity, Plato explains; and we can say men are trained or untrained in shopkeeping or navigation or any other work.[66] But when we look at it from our standpoint—that is, from the standpoint of an educator who wishes to implant a particular ethos or spirit in the state—we must take education to mean the teaching of areté, which begins in childhood, and makes us wish to become perfect citizens, knowing how to command and to obey in accordance with law.[67] No type of training in special activities can strictly be called paideia, culture, or education. They are banausic, aiming at making money or at cultivating one particular skill which is devoid of a governing spiritual principle and right aim, and is merely a tool, a means to an end.[68] But Plato does not wish to argue about the *word* paideia. What interests him is that the proper conception of its nature should be taken as the basis of all legislation. For he is convinced that those who are properly educated are in general distinguished men. True education must not be despised, since for the best of men it is the highest of all ideal values (πρῶτον τῶν καλλίστων). If it ever dies out, and if it is capable of being restored, everyone must try throughout his life to restore it.[69]

In these words Plato describes himself and his life-work. He has explained clearly how he saw the position in which he found himself. True paideia, which had always been the education of men for 'the whole of areté', had collapsed into purely specialist skills with no dominating aim in view.[70] His philosophy is meant to put that purpose back into human life, and so give a new meaning and unity to all the disjointed activities of our existence. He must have felt that his era, in spite of all its astonishing wealth of specialist knowledge and ability, was really marked by a decline in culture. What he means by restoring true paideia [71] he has shown by the opposition between the true culture he is trying to attain and the specialist or vocational culture he decries. To restore wholeness in areté—that is, in life and the human soul—was the most difficult of all tasks, incomparably harder than any specialized investigation that philosophical thought could carry out. We can see the kind of solution Plato envisaged if we read *The Republic*: for it is built around the fundamental principle of all values, the Idea of Good, which is placed in a dominating position in the centre of the cosmos. The whole nature of education is changed by the realization that it must start from that conception of the cosmos, and move around the Idea of the Good like a planet round the central sun. So we find that in this passage of *The Laws* also the true paideia, as Plato puts it, depends on the divine.[72]

It is characteristic not only of *The Laws* but of all Plato's books after *The Republic* that he talks a great deal about God and the divine. He may originally have been reluctant to call his basic principle divine, and slowly abandoned his reluctance; or he may be using the concept rather loosely, on the plane of opinion rather than thought. But here too, and all through *The Laws,* he shows himself deeply interested in the psychical processes by which the supreme principle actually *works* in the human soul. He illustrates it by the image (eikon) of a marionette theatre, in which man is the puppet playing on the stage of life.[73] Now, whether he was made as a toy for God to play with or for some serious purpose—we cannot tell which—it is clear that his desires and beliefs are the strings which pull him in one direction or another.[74] The expectation of pleasure or of pain moves our desires in the guise of courage or fear, while reasoning (λογισμός) tells us which of these impulses are bad, which good. When reasoning of this kind becomes the common resolution of the whole city, we call it Law.[75] The soul must obey only the golden cord by which logos guides it, not the hard iron wires of

lust. The more gently and peaceably reason guides our soul, the
more co-operation it needs from within.[76] But the cord of logos
is, as we have seen, simply what law commands in the state.
God, or someone who knows God, gives logos to the state; and
the state raises it to be a law regulating its intercourse with
itself and with other states.[77] The soul's obedience to the logos
we call self-control. That explains the nature of paideia. Paideia
is the control of human life by the cord of logos, moved by a
divine hand.[78] But here we observe an essential difference between *The Republic* and *The Laws*. In *The Republic* Plato said
the Idea of Good was the model which the philosophical ruler
carried in his soul.[79] In *The Laws* he tries to be more concrete.
He assumes a type of man who wishes to know exactly *what* he
must do, and *why,* and *how,* and who needs laws for every detail of conduct. The question therefore arises how the divine
logos is to make its way down to men and become a political
institution. Plato seems to think that this happens whenever any
kind of public agreement is reached,[80] but he insists that one
single man who knows the divine should be the lawgiver for the
city. In this he is following the pattern set by the great lawgivers of past history. The Greeks used to call them 'divine
men', a title which was soon given to Plato himself. Even in
Plato's day, more than one Greek city asked some famous philosopher to give laws to the state. The prototype of this lawgiver who is intermediary between gods and men is Minos, who
'talked with God'. The 'wisdom' of the Greek lawgiver comes
closest to revelation.[81]

With this in mind, we can understand what Plato means by
the educational influence of the custom of drinking-parties, and
why he criticizes Sparta for banning them.[82] His ideal of paideia
is ultimately self-control, not control by the authority of others,
as in Sparta.[83] As an educator, he wants to find a test for the
ability he values so highly, and he finds it in drunkenness. Wine
intensifies feelings of pleasure, weakens mental energy, and
brings back childish ways.[84] Therefore it tests the power of the
unconscious control exercised by shame and modesty. We can
teach men to be fearless only by exposing them to danger, and
so the soul must be exposed to the temptations of pleasure if it
is to harden itself against them.[85] Plato does not elaborate the
list of pleasures involved in this test, he merely hints at them; [86]

but he takes the greatest care to emphasize the connexion of paideia and *pais,* 'the child'.[87] In *The Republic* he traced the development of all the forces of paideia up to the topmost branch of education and culture. In *The Laws* he follows it down to its roots, the subjugation of the desires by reason. In early childhood education is almost exclusively concerned with control of pleasure-pain feelings. They are its real material. Considered in this light, paideia becomes pedagogy.[88]

It is needless to say that this interpretation does not exclude the other, loftier conception of paideia. It is a new and promising shoot rising straight from the roots of Plato's philosophy of paideia. Plato now believes more and more that the success of all later education depends on the results of those first attempts to mould the ethos in childhood. That was inevitable; yet had he not taken, as the starting-point of his paideia, Socrates' belief that virtue was knowledge?[89] Plato did not, as we might expect, abandon the belief that virtue is knowledge, but he moved the beginning of education further and further back. It began fairly early in *The Republic*—but there he was simply trying to start training the child's *intellect* young enough.[90] But here he is trying to mould the *desires* as early as possible, so that the child may begin by learning, as if in play, to love right and hate wrong.[91] No one, he thinks, can get the best out of his own logos unless he has been unconsciously prepared by the logos of someone else, teacher or parent. All areté (in so far as it is areté of the ethos, or what we should call moral culture) is based on the harmony of intelligent insight and habit. Paideia is the training of the pleasure-pain feelings, upon which that harmony is based in its turn.[92] Plato has here reached the point at which Aristotle's *Ethics*—also primarily concerned with ethos—starts.[93] Socrates' doctrine that virtue is knowledge developed into the elaborately detailed late Platonic and Aristotelian doctrine of ethos, and that doctrine became the foundation of all modern systems of 'ethics'. The whole development was conditioned by the fact that Socrates was not teaching an abstract theory of moral conduct but seeking a way of paideia. It begins by finding out moral standards, and moves on to an enquiry into the nature of the soul and methods of treating it. Plato at first held that the most important thing was to get more and deeper *knowledge,* in the Socratic belief that it would improve the entire moral culture of the personality; and now in his old age he seems to be concentrating on the earlier Greek idea that the most important thing is to mould human *character*. This makes him see truth in a new light. This seeming return from ideals to historical fact is not unnatural. Plato had gone as far upward to the ideal world as he could; now the wish to realize the ideal as far as possible, and make it part of everyday life, leads him back to the real world. Like Prometheus, he becomes a moulder of men. The general idea that the philosopher's duty is to mould character is expressed in *The Republic*.[94] But he is found to be much more concerned with it in *The Laws,* where he turns to the problem of moulding the irrational forces of the soul. Here he is dealing with character-building in the narrowest sense of the word: he is regulating gestures, movements, and every expression of the ethos of the soul. He began by a concentration on the pure intellect which looks quite Protestant; and now he discusses the importance of these visible expressions of the spirit which Catholic education always tries to mould as early as possible.

Certain elements of ancient Greek culture with which we have long been familiar are thus brought once more into the focus of importance. Singing and choral dancing used to be the musical education of early Greece. They had lost this function in the new intellectualized world, and survived (particularly in Athens) only as highly elaborate forms of art. But as soon as Plato set about discovering how to mould the ethos in early youth, he felt there was nothing in contemporary education to replace them. So in *The Laws* he declared that the ancient Greek round dance should be revived and made one of the fundamental elements in education. Children are never still. They are active all the time, and they cannot be kept in one place—their movements can only be guided.[95] Unlike other animals, man has a sense of order and disorder in movement, which we call rhythm and harmony. This is a perfect example of the delight in good and beautiful activities which is to be developed in play at an early age, as a powerful stimulus to the development of the moral and aesthetic sense.[96] A man is not properly educated unless he has come to feel pleasure in rhythmical movement and the harmony of choral singing when he was at school. The educated man is a fine dancer.[97] He has the right standard within him, an unerring sense for beauty and ugliness—by which Plato means both ethical and aesthetic beauty and ugliness.[98] In contemporary art the unity of ethics and aesthetics was almost extinct. But Plato was eager to reintroduce it into dancing, which he takes as the model art. This assumes that there is an absolute standard for beauty,[99] which is the gravest of all problems for an educator who tries to found everything on that artistic basis. If we believe that education and culture mean making the ethos of the city (especially of its young people) resemble heard melodies and danced rhythms, then we cannot afford to leave everything to the poet's whim or inspiration, as we do 'to-day'.[100] Plato wanted to live in a country where art was confined within fixed hieratic forms, and was free from all interference by reform, renovation, and personal inclination or taste. Egypt was the only such country he could find. There art seemed never to change, never to develop. A monumental respect for tradition preserved all the patterns of the past. From his new standpoint he had a new understanding of this fact, just as he had for Sparta in another connexion.[101]

The future of art depended (according to Plato) on its power to free itself from the hedonistic and materialistic taste of the public. Cicero says that the refined taste of the Athenian people was the standard which maintained the perfection of Athenian art; and he adds that lack of taste in other countries was due to their lack of such a standard.[102] Plato was living in the age which Cicero admired as classical, but he took a very different view of the matter. He held that the contemporary public wanted nothing but pleasure, and corrupted all art.[103] A true art-critic—and Plato is thinking of the state commission which gave prizes for the best plays performed each year in Athens—must not follow the audience. That spoils both the poet and the audience. He is to be a teacher, not a pupil, of the polis. The noisy applause of the mob and its lack of culture are opposed to good judgment and good taste.[104] We have already seen that the public's only standard for judging the artistic merit of any work is the amount of pleasure it gives. But if we once worked out what people of different ages understood by pleasure, and what type of art they preferred, every age would choose a different type. Children would prefer conjurors to any other kind of artist, and the taste of grown-ups is no better.[105]

In Greece only Crete and Sparta had a fixed poetical tradition. There, the public still clung to old Tyrtaeus.[106] But, as

Plato has pointed out already, we cannot use him in our state until he is 'rewritten', with justice inserted as the supreme virtue instead of courage.[107] To explain this, Plato chooses the particular poem in which Tyrtaeus compares courage with all the other merits a man can have and adjudges it the best.[108] Plato then argues that it is really not heroic valour but justice which makes other virtues valuable, and without which they are worthless.[109] Since the poet's duty is to educate the young, all true poetry must start by setting up a proper scale of values.[110] Poetry and music, if they do that properly, can truly be called paideia.[111] One-sided this view may be, but it contains a good measure of truth, in so far as it concerns early Greek music and poetry. Anyone who has read so far will not find it hard to see what Plato means. Early Greek poetry had been concerned for centuries with the dispute about the highest areté and the greatest good in life. Plato is consciously taking up that dispute in *The Laws:* he is using the odes of poetry as *epodai,* 'enchantments' to cast on the hearer's soul and make it, by their secret magic, willing to assimilate their serious meaning as if in play. It is like a pill covered with sugar.[112] Plato wants to make his city hunger and thirst after such sweets.[113] The only thing that really shows it is a Greek city is that Plato uses its native enjoyment of Beauty, and blends it in a new unity with the desire for Good. It is only that love of beauty that can take the Greek soul and forge it into a permanent form in the fire of youth and enthusiasm;[114] even old men and women lose their hardness and inflexibility when their spirits are thawed, softened, and warmed by the gifts of Dionysus.[115] So the legislator forms and moulds (he is a πλάστης) the souls of men.[116]

Plato adds a note on gymnastic exercise at the end, but it is obviously only for form's sake.[117] He does not linger on it—even in *The Republic* he gave it much less space than music. Taking up the question of drinking-parties once again, he discusses their educational value. That was the point with which he started, and which he seemed to have forgotten for the time. He now concludes his discussion of it by a long study of the exact amount of wine which should be drunk by people at various ages, and so, with some remarks on the special importance of wine for old men like himself, he ends this, his first large enquiry into paideia.[118]

THE CAUSES OF THE STATE'S DECLINE

After this discussion of paideia and the spirit of the state, which fills the first two books of *The Laws,* Plato passes on to examine the problem of the origin of the state. The transition to the new topic looks rather abrupt, but that is only as far as form goes. Before legislation can start, the foundations of the state must be laid; and before that can be done, the spirit of the state must be defined. It must inspire all the state's institutions to express it. The Dorian states are good examples of this, but the spirit of the state described in *The Laws* is radically different from theirs. The new state is to be a large-scale educational system. But the standard determining the type of education in it is the *whole* nature of man, the fullest development of the personality.[119] In its range of values, the Spartan virtue, courage, is not to stand first, but fourth and last.[120] The progress of the discussion shows that Plato is not simply issuing a stern moral commandment to substitute self-control and justice for the ideal of strength, without reference to the actual facts of political life. He does so because he thinks it will prolong the life of the state. We shall return to this point shortly.

His theory of the origin and transformations of the state, and of the periodical destruction of civilization by great natural disasters, shows that he had thought earnestly and intelligently about the history of mankind.[121] He believes that what we call history goes back not much further than yesterday or the day before, in comparison to the dark prehistoric ages in which the human race developed slowly, slowly, with a snail's pace.[122] There were huge floods, pestilences, et cetera, from which only a small portion of mankind survived into a new period, to recommence the gradual ascent from primitive life.[123] The world was not yet thickly populated. Men knew nothing of the use of metals, and nothing of war—which is produced by the advance of technical civilization.[124] Plato conceives those primitive ages as essentially peaceful, with no wealth or poverty, and a high standard of morals, because of the kindly simplicity of human character.[125] There was no need of legislators—there was not even any writing.[126] In Plato's day there was no archaeological excavation, so he has to rely on literary tradition, especially

Homer. Here he admits that the earliest poetry is (at least partially) valuable as a source for historical fact. The historical
and aesthetic attitudes to poetry, which seem so natural to us
now, began to develop more and more as the paideutic (i.e. the
absolute) value of poetry became doubtful or lost its original
sense. With Homer as evidence, Plato describes the transition
from the lawless life of the Cyclopes to systematic union in society and patriarchal government.[127] When various families and
clans joined to form a town, it became necessary to strike a
balance between the various kinds of law which were current.
That was the task of legislation.[128] Like the contemporary historian Ephorus, Plato puts the return of the Heraclidae just
after the Homeric era, when the Achaeans made their expedition to Asia Minor. That event began the earliest history of the
Peloponnesian states, offshoots of the Dorian immigration which
came in upon the ruins of the Achaean empire.[129] This brings our
historical survey to the point at which our dialogue begins, when
the Dorian states were being founded and the Dorian legislators
were, allegedly, at work.[130]

Between 370 and 350 B.C., when Plato was writing *The Laws*,
every thinking man in Greece was conscious of the tragedy of
the Dorian race, which had once been so powerful and so distinguished, and then had been brought so low by the catastrophe
of Leuctra.[131] After defeating the Spartans there, the Theban
statesman Epaminondas had summoned the Messenians out of
centuries of serfdom to liberty, in order to stir up dissension
within the Peloponnese and complete the enemy's overthrow.
All Greek friends of the Dorian stock must have asked, with
deep foreboding, what would have been the course of Greek history if the Dorian states of the Peloponnese, Sparta, Argos, and
Messenia, had grown into a political unity instead of doing their
best to exterminate one another.[132] It was the same question, with
reference to the past, which was even then being asked about the
future of the whole of Greece; in fact, it was the great contemporary problem projected onto the past. When the Dorians settled the land, conditions were ideal for the development of what
Plato calls 'the system of Dorian states,'[133] the league of the
three sons of Heracles, immediately after the settlement. They
were not forced to take any of the measures advocated by social
reformers and revolutionaries in Plato's day, and endanger the

state by redistribution of land and abolition of debts. They could start clear. They took the land just conquered and divided it into equal shares, and thus built up the state on a fair and just social principle.[134] We see later how serious Plato is about the problem of distributing the land: he suggests an actual return to the settlement of the Peloponnese by the Heraclidae.[135] But what had caused the fall of the Dorian kingdoms although (Plato believes) they were much stronger, more unified, and better governed than the Greeks before Troy?[136] They could have united Greece and ruled the world;[137] but they destroyed one another in hopeless feuds. Plato's historical imagination, looking back to the almost legendary distance of the eighth and seventh centuries, thought of that strife as the real, the irretrievable tragedy, the wonderful opportunity to 'dominate the world' which the Greek nation had missed—obviously a cruel satire on Isocrates' Panhellenic programme![138] He thinks of Sparta as the best proof of the Dorian ability to build states—the Messenians and the Argives were lesser breeds.[139]

The cause of their fall was not, as a Spartan might think, lack of courage or ignorance of war. It was ignorance (ἀμαθία) of the most important things in human life.[140] It is this profound lack of culture, he says, which destroyed those states then, which is destroying them now, and which will continue to destroy them in the future.[141] If we ask in what it consists, he directs our attention to the nature of paideia as we have studied it in long and elaborate enquiries. Paideia depends on the proper agreement of desire and intellect.[142] The mighty Dorian states fell because they followed their desires and not their rational insight.[143] Thus the recognition of the political blunder which ruined the Dorians leads back to the problem with which the dialogue opened: the question of finding the right ethos for the state, an ethos which is based on the healthy structure of the individual soul. In *The Republic* Plato had criticized the spirit and the education of the Spartan state. His criticism seems to be confirmed in *The Laws* by the overwhelming failure of the Dorian stock (as seen from Plato's own day) to win the leadership of Greece, the prize which it seemed certain to gain. These pages appear to contain Plato's final conclusion on the question which had occupied him all his life: the political ideal of the Dorians. It is, it must be tragic. As a young man he had lived among the aristocrats who composed the Athenian opposition, and there he had heard Sparta eulogized as the absolute ideal. In his prime he had learnt much from the Spartan model; but even when the enormous and unchallenged success of Sparta appeared to justify all its most uncritical admirers could say, he had been pointing out its hidden weaknesses in several prophetic passages of *The Republic*.[144] When he wrote *The Laws,* the weakness was plain for all the world to see.[145] Plato had only to point out that what was described in *The Republic* as 'the second best state' was bound to be overthrown because it was not the best—that is, because it did not have true paideia and the best ethos. The Spartan 'kings' had obeyed the mob in their souls (the desires for power and honour, which are *pleonexia* or aggrandisement) instead of following their true guide, which is reason. Plato held that paideia was more important than practical politics— a preference which is shown here too, in the bold and stimulating antithesis between the outward form and the inward spirit of the state. To outward appearance, these states had been governed by kings; but spiritually they were governed by the mob of desires and lusts that ruled their kings' souls.[146] Similarly in *Gorgias,* Plato compares democracy, if it is ruled by the whim of the mob, with tyranny, which is closest to it by nature.[147] In the words of *The Republic,* the collapse of the state within the soul [148] of the ruler confirmed the outward overthrow of his power. A state is never power alone, but always the spiritual structure of the man whom it represents.

So if the decline of the state is due to lack of culture, lack of harmony between desire and reason in the ruler's soul (be he one or many), uneducated people must be prevented from influencing government. But in this deeper sense those whom the public thinks of as cultured may well be uneducated: for instance, the clever calculating fellow, the man of quick intellectual reflexes, the witty talker. In fact, Plato seems to think that the latter quality is a symptom of the preponderance of desires in a man.[149] So the central question comes to be: Who shall rule? In *The Republic* Plato had answered it by saying that the better should always rule the worse, and the higher rule the lower.[150] In *The Laws,* however, he makes a new attempt to answer it, obviously because he feels it is the decisive question in politics both as a science and as a practical art. If we think of politics as the science of government, it needs a principle to regulate all its details; and that principle must give to the question 'Who ought to rule the state?' a general answer which every reasonable person will find self-explanatory.

At this point in *The Laws*, Plato lays down seven 'axioms' of government, to which he refers several times, both in criticizing actual states of his own day and in founding institutions for his own state.[151] The meaning of the word 'axiom' is 'claim to own' in the juristic sense; and that is how all commentators have taken it here, since that is the problem under discussion. But towards the end of Plato's life it had already acquired the scientific sense in which we now use it: an assumption which cannot be proved but does not need proof, and which is used as a point of departure in a scientific train of reasoning—particularly in mathematics, where (according to Aristotle) that use of the word first appeared.[152] We know how Plato tried to make mathematics the model of all scientific and philosophical method. He pushed his endeavour very hard, particularly in his later years: and Aristotle thinks of it as characteristic of the whole Platonic school.[153] So we must take the mathematical meaning of 'axiom' here, because Plato is discussing the general principles on which politics is based. That does not exclude the first sense, 'claim to possess'.[154] For 'axiom' in the mathematical sense too is a claim or a demand, which is self-explanatory: that is, the original legal sense is still alive in the word. The same sense is implied by the fixed number of the axioms which Plato lays down, and which he points out by numbering them 1 to 7, thus limiting their number [155] just as Euclid's axioms are limited. They set forth the following principles:

1. Parents must rule children
2. The noble must rule the ignoble
3. The old must rule the young
4. Masters must rule slaves
5. The better must rule the worse
6. Thinking men must rule the ignorant

And the seventh axiom is the democratic principle that

7. The man chosen by lot must rule him who is not chosen.

Here, and throughout *The Laws,* Plato treats the lot as a divine institution, instead of calling it a senseless piece of machinery, as he often does in his earlier books when criticizing democracy.[156]

According to these axioms, the kings of Messenia and Argos were justly deprived of their rights, because the powers they controlled were too great and too irresponsible to be handled by one individual who did not have all the qualifications involved.[157] Many points in *The Laws* and *The Statesman* might lead us to think that Plato admired monarchy as a form of constitution. But in *The Laws* he comes wholeheartedly out against any such concentration of power in the hands of one man: he calls it a degenerate form of the lust for power, pleonexia.[158] Isocrates too held that pleonexia in the usual sense was the root of evil. The example of Sparta shows that the mixed constitution is the most durable. For in Sparta the prerogatives of monarchy are restricted by the dual kingship, by the Elders' College, the Gerusia, and the Overseers, or Ephors.[159] It is not Messenia or Argos, but Sparta, that Greece has to thank for her purity of blood. Without Sparta the Greek tribes would have mingled with one another and with the barbarians in utter confusion, like the population of the Persian Empire. For Plato, that is the real meaning of the freedom won in the Persian war.[160] The aim with which the lawgiver starts should not be the accumulation of huge unorganized powers in the hands of one person, but the freedom, reason, and harmony of the polis.[161] Persia and Athens show the fundamental elements of all political life exaggerated as far as possible in one direction and the other.[162] Both elements, in fact, are indispensable; and the merit of Sparta is that she has been trying to blend them, and has therefore maintained herself for a long time.[163] Here Plato inserts a long criticism of the Persian monarchy, based on the idea that the great men who built it up—Cyrus and Darius—did not know how to educate their sons.[164] The paideia of the Persian princes was carried on by ambitious and newly rich queens.[165] Therefore Cambyses and Xerxes soon wasted away everything their fathers had won.[166] Indeed, their fathers had no understanding of their most important duty, the education of their successors, and thus had spent no time on it.[167] According to Plato, the warning which Aeschylus' Darius rises from the tomb to give the Persians after their defeat came far too late.[168] Actually, neither Darius nor Cyrus could educate their sons because they themselves possessed no paideia.[169] With that one stroke Plato obliterates Xenophon's book *The Education of Cyrus*. He finds in Persia nothing that can be a model for Greece.[170]

But Plato's deepest interest is in his own city, Athens.[171] The praise he gives it for its part in liberating Greece [172] seems to be contradicted when he blames it for pursuing liberty in excess.[173] But his picture of Athenian history is neither all bright nor all dark. In that too he resembles the aged Isocrates, who criticized Athens of his own day very sharply, but eulogized many of the great qualities shown by Athens in the time of the Persian war.[174] In the heroic dawn of Athenian democracy, Plato holds that much of the traditional respect for law was maintained, although it has since then disappeared.[175] In his description of this aidos (honourable shame), which is the force that really holds the social structure together from within, he speaks in just the same tone as Isocrates, who was writing the *Areopagiticus* at the same time as *The Laws*.[176] From the standpoint of the political educator, he held that to be the main problem. That is why those two very different minds, the philosopher Plato and the rhetor Isocrates, agree on this point. Plato sees the degeneration of the Athenian democracy entirely from that educational standpoint— just as he attributes the fall of the Persian empire entirely to its lack of paideia. This is chiefly noticeable when he traces the degeneracy of Athens to the decline of music and poetry into licence and lack of discipline.[177] That is really one of his greatest historical judgments. It was taken over from him by the Peripatetic school, through which it passed into the poetic and musical theory of the Hellenistic and Imperial ages.[178] It illustrates in full detail the statement in *The Republic* that musical education is the citadel of the perfect state.[179]

The character of the separate poetic patterns—hymn, dirge, paean of triumph, dithyramb, and nomos—was kept pure for many years. This ensured the maintenance of the fixed musical traditions that had existed in earlier centuries; [180] neither the shouts and whistles nor the applause of the masses had any influence whatever on art. Those who were experts in paideusis could listen undisturbed to the end, while the mob was kept in order by the steward's staff.[181] But then there came a new age

in which some composers, who had great creative talent but no
sense of how to preserve the ethical standards of art, were carried away by Bacchic ecstasy and utter sensuousness: they mixed
dithyrambs with paeans, hymns with dirges, and they tried to
play the lyre so as to imitate the noisy effects of the clarinet.[182]
These people obliterated all artistic frontiers. They thought
anything was permissible if it gave pleasure to the senses somehow or other, for they were too ignorant to believe in existence
of standards of right and wrong in music.[183] Libretti of the same
type were written to their music. So lawlessness was introduced
into the realm of the muses, and encouraged the mob to the
crazy idea that they could pass judgment on such matters—which
they then did, with loud applause or disapproval.[184] The utter
silence of the theatre changed into an uproar. Instead of the
gentlemanly manners which had hitherto been customary there,
there arose a theatrocracy, the rule of the uneducated public.
If it had really been a democracy of free men, it would have
been tolerable; but everything was now ruled by the craze to
appear knowledgeable and the hatred of all discipline, those
bold passions which halt at nothing.[185] What will follow after
this illimitable liberty? Plato thinks that spiritual self-discipline
will gradually break down into complete licence, and finally into
the savagery of the Titans, who were the monsters before the
cave-men.[186]

THE DIVINE STANDARD IN FOUNDING THE STATE: THE PREFACES TO THE LAWS

The discussion began with a historical fact: the spirit of the
Dorian states and of their legislation. But Plato immediately
introduced a philosophical element. He brought in the absolute
ideal of areté and of human character, and with it his own conception of paideia; from that lofty standpoint he criticized the
Spartan tradition of paideia.[187] That appeared to clear the way
for the foundation of the new state, which we were awaiting.
But history intervened once more. Instead of starting at once on
the practical task before him, Plato asked how, in actual fact,
the state had originated.[188] After we had followed the various
stages in that historical process, it returned to the foundation
of the Dorian states. Their brilliant promise and their tragic

failure brought us back once more to consider the previous
criticism of the Dorian spirit and its ideal of character. Historical fact was used to confirm philosophical analysis. For a
while it seemed that Plato's critical analysis of history was to
lead to the foundation and systematic description of an ideal
state, for Plato laid down the axioms from which any such enterprise must start.[189] But once again historical perspectives opened
up, to an even broader horizon. Plato now uses history to ensure
the proper application of these axioms. According to him they
lead to the ideal of a *mixed constitution,* such as that of old
Sparta.[190] Persia and Athens in their present form, on the other
hand, embody the two extremes of tyranny and arbitrary whim,
which arise from lack of paideia.[191]

Here, for the first time in the dialogue, one of the interlocutors mentions the intention of the Cretans to send out a new
colony. He is the Cretan Cleinias; and he informs the Athenian
that the city of Cnossus, which has been entrusted with the duty
of superintending the new settlement, has authorized him and
nine others to do what must be done.[192] This turns the discussion to practical matters—which here are equivalent to problems
of method and system, because a philosopher is assisting in the
construction of the city. For Cleinias asks the Athenian to give
them the benefit of his advice. The actual directions which are
laid down for the construction of the state cannot be described
here with all their technical details, although in a deeper sense
every one of them springs from the idea of paideia, and is meant
to embody it. The very first ordinance, that the city is not to be
a seaport, is inspired by Plato's educational ideals.[193] In *The
Constitution of the Athenians* Aristotle asserts that the drift of
the Athenian democracy towards mob-rule was due to the state's
transformation into a naval power.[194] That idea started in the
moderate conservative group of Athenian democrats, which was
bidding for new power after the fall of the second naval confederacy [195]—just at the time when Plato was writing *The Laws*
and Aristotle was forming his opinions in the Academy. Plato
agrees both with Aristotle and with the aged Isocrates in his
dislike of Athenian sea-power and his admiration for a mixed
constitution.[196] Isocrates too was an outspoken admirer of the
moderate policy which preached a return to the 'ancestral constitution'.[197] The rise of Athenian naval power and the diminu-

tion in the authority of the Areopagus are connected by Aristotle as the causes of the degeneration of Athenian democracy.[198]
That idea too is part of the conservative criticism levelled at
Periclean Athens, the imperialistic democracy with the powerful
navy. In fact, it goes back beyond Pericles. In Aeschylus' *The
Persians* the old conservative members of the council of the Persian empire criticize the policy of the young king Xerxes, and
their criticism shows the dislike of noblemen for big fleets and
naval hegemony.[199] Aeschylus did not learn about that feeling
in Persia, he learnt it in Athens, and he understood it remarkably well. We must not forget that he was himself a country
squire from Eleusis. In *The Persians* what really and finally
overthrows the barbarians is the land battle of Plataea.[200] Plato
goes still further. He says that the sea-battle of Salamis, which
was Athens' proudest title to national glory, was not of decisive
importance. What saved Hellas from slavery was the destruction of the Persian land-power at Marathon and Plataea.[201]
Plato's political views cohere very closely with his ideal of
paideia, just as do those of Isocrates with his. At this point in
The Laws the connexion between politics and paideia becomes
especially clear.

Plato understands that we do not simply make laws to suit
ourselves. War, economic necessity, epidemics, and misfortunes
bring in change and revolution.[202] Tyché dominates human life—
political life included. God rules everything; and after him tyché
and kairos; and third comes skill or art, techné—still, a very
useful thing, like helmsmanship in a storm.[203] If Plato as lawgiver could have one wish to ensure the happiness of the future
state, he would choose that it be ruled by *a teachable tyrant*.[204]
Tyché must bring him together with the great lawgiver in order
to produce the coincidence of mind and power which Plato hoped
for in *The Republic*, and which he still thinks the quickest possible method to realize his ideal.[205] From his experience with the
Syracusan tyrant, Plato knows that one man of that sort can
easily change a whole nation's ethos by bestowing praise and
punishment.[206] Only it is rare and difficult to find such a man
dominated by a divine passion for justice and self-control.[207] In
his old age, Plato thinks that difficulty is more formidable than
ever. And yet, as long as it is not surmounted, that way of realizing the ideal state is only 'a myth'.[208] He holds that other types

of constitution are different from tyranny in degree only, not in kind. They are all tyrannies, and the law by which they are ruled is only the expression of the will of whichever class happens to be in power.[209] But it is not the nature of law to be the right of the stronger.[210] Plato applies his axioms to this problem, and comes to the conclusion that those are fittest to rule who obey the *true* law most thoroughly.

Obedience to law in that sense is simply obedience to God, who, as the old saying goes, holds the beginning, end, and middle of everything.[211] When a godless man is leader of the nation, he leads it straight into the abyss.[212] God is the measure of all things. God is the aim which all should strive to reach.[213] This thought, fundamental in Plato's ideal of the state, is put most simply and clearly in *The Laws*. In *The Republic* it is philosophically modified and expressed in such concepts as the 'Idea of Good' and the 'conversion' of the soul to it, since it is the source of all being and all thought.[214] The Idea of Good was the new Platonic aspect of the divine to which everything else must be subordinated. Earlier Greek thinkers had given the name 'divine' to the single inexhaustible unity which is the universe, or to the original force which started the motion of the world, or to mind which shapes everything that is. But Plato started with an educational or ethical point of view, and he therefore thought the divine was the standard of all standards, the supreme norm. If thought of in that way, the idea of God becomes the centre and source of all legislation, while legislation became its direct expression and its realization on this earth. God is made manifest, and acts, in the cosmos of the state as he does in that of nature. For Plato, the two are related: for the universe too is ruled by the supreme standard and its harmony.[215] Law becomes an instrument by which men are educated to that harmony. When they are so educated, they have attained areté, and in their areté they achieve their true nature. Plato's thought finds a fixed point of rest in this new concept of nature (physis) as implying standards.[216] As the discussions of the soul in *The Laws* show, Plato considers not matter and its chance distributions, but the soul and its order, to be the ruling principle of the world. From the stars down to the plants, everything is united under the rule of the soul: soul, meaning reason and a standard.[217] In such a world, the standard of mere belief and opinion has ceased to be valid. Plato's ideal of education and politics is expressed by inverting Protagoras' epigram that Man is the measure of all things. Plato substitutes God for man, and says that God is the measure of all things.[218] (This is not the first time we have seen a Greek poet or philosopher expressing his main ideas by correcting some famous predecessor.) Ultimately Plato is only setting up once more the relation of state, law, and God which obtained in early Greece. But the essence of divinity has been changed. Instead of the individual gods of the city-state, Plato has introduced the 'standard of all things', his Good, the prototype of all areté. The cosmos has become a teleological system, and God is the 'teacher of the whole world'.[219] In the other great work of his old age, *Timaeus,* which was written at the same time and expressed parallel ideas, he showed how the divine demiurge reproduces the world of eternal Ideas in the natural world of phenomena. Thus, the Ideas are the 'models fixed in the realm of Being'.[220] By his work in making laws, the legislator becomes the demiurge of human society, which must be made a part of the greater cosmos; and the rule of God perfects itself in conscious accomplishment of the divine logos, by man as a rational being.[221] In this sense the un-Homeric description of God as the world's *teacher* is justified. In fact, it illuminates more emphatically than any other phrase the origin of the new Platonic attitude to God. Plato considered it to be the most important fact about the stars that—as discovered by the astronomer Eudoxus—they move around heaven in simple and meaningful mathematical patterns.[222] Similarly legislation is an attempt to take the random movements of the physical creature, man, and in so far as he has any insight into that higher order, to stop his purposeless wanderings and to guide him into noble and harmonious courses. The march of the stars, 'the army of unalterable law', is reflected in the human soul and in the steady movement of pure thought within it.[223] Plato's pupil Philip, who edited *The Laws,* is certainly echoing his master's thoughts when he says in the *Epinomis* that mathematical astronomy, the knowledge of the 'visible gods', is an image of the supreme wisdom manifested in them.[224]

After laying down the theological foundation, Plato goes on to erect the laws themselves upon it. This is the point where he describes and explains his view of the true nature of legislation. Legislation is education. Law is its instrument. So Plato reaches the principle expounded in detail above, that the lawgiver should not only lay down the law, but explain it and guide men to right conduct by the preface to each law.[225] There are many things that need saying and yet cannot be said in the usual brief legal paragraph.[226] The real meaning of this principle is that the power of law alone, which says peremptorily 'Thou shalt not!' has become subordinate to philosophy, which works in general principles. For philosophy cares less about the content of the law than the rational principle, the moral standard involved. That fact was bound to create practical difficulties for the philosophical legislator. He tries to overcome them by philosophizing, as it were, between the lines of his ordinances.[227] This naturally entails an enormous increase in the size of each law: so that it is impossible for all the laws to be given and treated with the same fullness. But Plato is more interested in giving examples of how it should be done. As a test case, he takes the marriage-laws. He gives them first of all in the usual form, a prohibition + a threat; and then in the new bipartite form, combining persuasion and command.[228] Of course the preface turns out to be longer than the law itself. In it Plato recalls the theory advanced in *The Symposium* that copulation is intended to perpetuate the race. He thinks of humanity as a single thing, an unbreakable chain of generations stretching down from age to age. That is a kind of immortality. When a man wishes that after death his name will not be forgotten, but will be famous, he is wishing for the same immortality in another way.[229] This is an echo of the old Greek ideal of the 'famous name', *kleos*, which is the social expression of the individual's areté.[230] It is the family, which, in the narrowest sense, possesses this fame and carries on the name. It cannot be an act of piety (ὅσιον) to rob oneself of this immortality.[231] Therefore marriage is a duty. Plato fixes the age of marriage at 30-35 for men; and lays down that anyone who is not married after 35 is to be fined every year, so as to deter everyone from living a gay bachelor life and profiting by it. He is also excluded from the honours paid by young men to old men in the city. In the social sense, he never becomes 'an old man'.[232]

Plato leaves it to the judgment of the lawgiver to determine which laws, long or short, require a preface.[233] He says that all the previous discussion is such a preface in a sense,[234] and asks that the rest of the enquiry should be taken in the same sense.[235] Most important of all is the preface which deals with the citizen's duty to God and his parents, and the honour he must pay them. After that Plato thinks an explanation of the nature of the soul is absolutely necessary, because it is of vital importance in education.[236] After the discussion of prefaces is complete, the promulgation of the laws proper begins. They ought to start with laws about administrative offices and the basic political structure of the new state. For before offices can be created and the authorities attaching to them be defined, the laws by which the officials are to administer the state must be written.[237] Here Plato makes a preliminary remark which is important for the organization of paideia. He says there are two elements in the state, warp and woof. The warp, which must be the stronger of the two, is the élite which is destined to rule. Their areté must be superior to that of the other citizens; they must therefore hold aloof from those who have had only a little paideia (σμικρὰ παιδεία).[238] In book twelve, just before the end of the work, when Plato mentions the rulers and their education, he says they have a more careful paideia (ἀκριβεστέρα παιδεία).[239] The remark seems a little out of place in book 5, because he is discussing paideia neither in the higher nor in the lower sense, but different problems altogether. But Plato has obviously been thinking of education all the time, and one whole book, the seventh, is taken up with laws about it. They are apparently equivalent to the 'little paideia' which is mentioned in the preliminary hint (5.735a). That is the general education given to the main citizen body, in contrast to that of the future rulers of the state. In the version of the book which we have, this elementary education is thrown into the foreground; but that is perfectly justified. One of the principal charms of *The Laws* is its detailed and careful examination of a problem which is not only entirely overlooked in *The Republic,* but is never seriously discussed in any of the arguments about right education which began with the heyday of the sophistic movement.[240]

Actually, Plato's creation of a complete system of elementary education, to be the paideia of the people and the basis of the higher education with which he had been concerned in his earlier works, was one of his boldest innovations, well worthy of his enormous educational genius. It was the final step towards a full realization of the programme of the Socratic movement—a step which was bound to have the most far-reaching effects, even although no legislator of his time ever felt tempted to translate Plato's ideal of a general education for the masses into reality. As the history of Greek paideia has shown, it started (as it does wherever education aspires to be more than mere technical and vocational training) from the early aristocratic ideal of shaping the entire human character, man's whole personality. This ideal of areté was transferred to the education of the citizens who wished to participate in the kalokagathia of the most cultured groups under the modified social and political conditions of the classical Greek city-state. But the task was entirely left to the private initiative of the individual, even in democratic Athens. The revolutionary step taken by Plato in *The Laws,* which is his last word on education and politics, is the institution of a genuine system of popular education by the state. In *The Laws* he gives this problem the same importance as he gave in *The Republic* to the education of the rulers. Indeed, where should the problem find the attention which it deserves, if not in the educational state of *The Laws,* built on the ideal harmony of guidance and freedom?

LAWS CONCERNING THE EDUCATION OF THE PEOPLE

Plato knows that it is harder for the lawgiver to influence people's lives in matters of education than in any other sphere. A great deal of paideia takes place at home, within the family. Therefore it escapes public criticism.[241] Still, home influence is extremely important. Plato thinks he can do more to improve it by advice than by laws.[242] As things now stand, private education is differently managed in different homes. The differences are usually in small, almost imperceptible things; but the lawgiver can do nothing to overcome them. Nevertheless, the fact that so many families have different ideas about the right kind of education makes it doubtful whether any written laws are useful at all.[243] So it is hard to make laws for this situation—but it is impossible to do without them. That is Plato's criticism of Athens and most of the other Greek city-states, which had no

legal way of regulating education.[244] With his laws on marriage
and child-rearing, Plato laid the foundation for those about education, which come right after them.[245] The two partners in a
marriage are to believe that its highest social purpose is the creation of as good and beautiful children as possible.[246] Plato does
not say that the bridegrooms and brides should be chosen and
paired off by the state, as he did for the guards in *The Republic*.
He does not even attack marriage as such. But he does recommend that both partners should be specially careful about these
matters; and sets up a committee of women to supervise them,
with an office in the temple of Eileithyia, goddess of birth.[247]
They have a consulting-room there, and give advice. Their
supervision of marriage extends over the ten-year period which
is the proper term in which to beget children. They intervene
when a husband or wife does not show the correct interest in
having children, or is incapable of it. In the latter case there is
a divorce.[248] The members of this committee visit and advise
the younger wives, so that they can avoid mistakes arising from
ignorance. If any of them deliberately or contumaciously opposes
their superior wisdom and their advice, she is liable to an elaborate system of punishments, particularly degradations of various
kinds.[249]

Plato is here copying Spartan law, and carrying it further.
From Critias and Xenophon, both of whom wrote books on
Sparta and Spartan discipline, we learn that Spartan couples
began to take measures for the improvement of their children
during conception and pregnancy.[250] This eugenic ideal had great
influence on the philosophical literature of the fourth century.
Plato and Aristotle both introduced it into their political utopias,
while 'Plutarch' and other late writers on education borrowed it
from them. It is characteristic that Plato is much more careful
in *The Laws* than in *The Republic* to describe the physiological
and eugenic methods that will make the younger generation
better and healthier. Similarly, it is in *The Laws* that he says
the decisive years for moral training are those of early childhood.[251] Obviously his beliefs had been strongly influenced by the
science of dietetics. When he says that the baby should get exercise, even in its mother's womb,[252] that is only an extension of
the system of physical exercises which interested the physicians
of his day so profoundly. He uses an odd example. He points

to game-cocks and other birds trained for fighting, which are made fit by being carried about in their masters' arms, or under the armpit, on long walks.[253] Movement and shaking of the body, with or without effort on its own part, strengthens it—as is shown by such diversions as walking, swinging, boating, riding, et cetera.[254] So Plato advises expectant mothers to take long walks, and, after the baby is born, to 'shape it like wax' with massage, and bind it in swaddling-clothes up to the age of two. The nurse is to carry the baby in her arms on country walks, and to church, and to visit relatives, until it can stand by itself.[255] Plato expects the mothers and nurses to object. Still, he believes the parents should be given this advice, to make them understand their duties and realize the consequences of neglect.[256] After they grow a little, children are to be kept in constant movement, not put to sleep in perfect quietness: that is unnatural for children, who ought to be in rhythmical motion day and night as if on board ship.[257] The right thing to put children to sleep is not silence but singing and rocking, which release mental anxiety and bring repose.[258] Plato gave these problems, which are really medical problems, a good deal of attention, because he knew that physical health and discipline were vitally important in moulding the ethos, the character. All he says about the physical care of babies passes into directions for their psychical education. When we give a child comfort and abolish discomfort by the movement of its body, we have taken the first step to moulding its soul. It is because Plato thought that all education was moulding the soul that he was the first to establish an educational system for early childhood.

The first step towards making the child brave is to set it free from fear. That is what Plato thinks will be attained by giving it exercise when it is still very young. Depression and anxiety help to create fear.[259] Plato says we must find the happy medium between coddling and bullying. Coddling makes the child hypersensitive and sulky; bullying makes him slavish, sneaking, and misanthropic.[260] As we should say, it brings on an inferiority complex, which the teacher must try very carefully to avoid, because it very easily results from over-education. The real aim is to make the child cheerful. The foundation for the harmony and equilibrium of the character must be laid down at an early age. The golden mean can be reached by neither depriving the child

of pleasure nor giving him pleasure exclusively.²⁶¹ Habit is a
powerful thing. Plato actually says ēthos, character, is derived
from ĕthos, habit.²⁶² The child must become accustomed to this
equilibrium in his first three years, during which time he is pretty
well dominated by pleasure and pain.²⁶³ Plato regards these
measures not as laws but as unwritten customs (ἄγραφα νόμιμα).
He considers them vitally important, calling them the ties that
bind the state together (δεσμοὶ πολιτείας). They hold the whole
structure fast, and if they are taken out, it collapses.²⁶⁴ The
standards of paideia essentially consist of these fixed customs
(ἔθη) and habits (ἐπιτηδεύματα). They are more important than
written law (νόμος). Anyone who wants to construct a new city-
state and bind it firmly together needs both elements.²⁶⁵ Later,
in his books on ethics and political philosophy, Cicero often
speaks of *leges et mores* or *leges et instituta maiorum,* to cover
the whole complex of standards written and unwritten on which
human life is based. The dichotomy goes back to the classical
Greek city-state, from whose social structure Plato borrowed
those ideas, to pass them on to the philosophical thought of later
generations. He himself raises the objection that customs and
habits strictly should not be handled in a work called *The Laws.*
If, despite that, he wrote a great deal about custom,²⁶⁶ it is not
because he did not accurately distinguish it from law, but because his main interest is paideia. He thinks legislation is wholly
an educational process; and so he makes his conception of it
broad enough to take in plenty of customs and folkways too.
After all, *The Laws* is not simply to be carved in bronze and
set up on the citadel. It is a literary work. The many interesting
references to the customs (νόμιμα) of foreign peoples in it show
that that part of the work is based on quite as extensive study
of Greek and barbarian 'nomima' as the passages which compare actual laws found in different lands.²⁶⁷ At this period the
Greeks were more interested than at any time before or since
in the culture and customs of their own and other peoples. Aristotle carried on this kind of research, which had obviously been
done at some length in the Academy.

Plato divides the education of children into periods. From
three to six, they ought to do nothing but play. Only if a child
is too sensitive or cowardly, he should be punished, in such a
way that he does not harbour resentment but does not get off

scot free.[268] They should not have games shown them, but make up their own when they play together. Plato thinks the children of every district (κώμη) ought to meet in the local church. (This anticipates the modern kindergarten.) Nurses are to be in charge, superintending their behaviour. Both the nurses and the whole 'flock' (ἀγέλη), as Plato calls it, using a Spartan name, are subject to the supervision of one of the board of twelve women chosen for the duty by the marriage committee.[269] Boys and girls are to have women teachers until they are six. They have co-education till that age, and after that they are separated.[270] The rest of their education should be 'ambidextrous', so to speak, not one-sided as now.[271] Athletics, which Plato passed over so quickly before, is brought in again here.[272] It is confined to dancing and wrestling. Everything in it that is not useful for later military training is cut out.[273] Euripides had voiced the same views (which must have been shared by many Athenians) some decades earlier. Plato's restriction must have excluded a great deal of contemporary athletics, which had become pretty much an end in itself. On the other hand, we learn from what Plato says about the appointment of teachers in this field, that he wanted to see much more military training brought into athletics, so that in the state described in *The Laws* not much of the famous Greek athletics remains except the name.[274] He speaks of specially paid and appointed instructors in archery, weight-putting, duelling in light and heavy armour, tactics and all kinds of military manoeuvres, campaigning exercises, riding, et cetera. Plato explains in so many words that he thinks all these activities are 'gymnastic exercise'.[275] He does not bring them in until a later stage of education, but it is only if we take his remarks there together with what he says about athletic sports in early youth that we can get the proper perspective about his rules for cutting down athletics. What he wants most to cultivate is decent gentlemanly behaviour: and athletics in the form he recommends is a valuable way of producing it. He recommends the revival of the old war-dance, like that of the Curetes in Crete, of the Dioscuri in Sparta, and of Demeter and Koré in Athens.[276] We recall that Aristophanes in *The Clouds* viewed the disappearance of those dances as a sign of the decay of the old paideia.[277] Plato imagines the young men, still under military age, and untried in war, riding with horse and armour in festal processions to honour the gods—as we see them idealized in the Parthenon frieze—and testing their strength in competitions and preliminary heats.[278]

The tendency to stress the development of soldierly spirit, which we find Plato putting forward here in theory, existed in practice in contemporary politics. Universal conscription for military service was not originally a purely Spartan institution, but the legal basis of civic life in the Athenian democracy. It was not considered to be undemocratic. On the contrary, it was the natural precondition of the liberties enjoyed by every citizen of the state. At the height of her power in the fifth century, Athens had so many wars to fight that every Athenian took his military service for granted. In the fourth century, when mercenaries began to be used, more and more widespread complaints were heard about the unwillingness and inability of the ordinary citizens to bear arms.[279] But even then the cadets (the ephéboi) were still liable to their two-year service—indeed, it became an increasingly important part of education with the general drop in fighting spirit. Many scholars have believed it necessary to assume that after the defeat of Chaeronea the Athenians actually followed the advice given by Plato in *The Laws*, in their legislation about cadet-training.[280] But that will not hold. The institution of cadet-training, ephébia, began much earlier.[281] Still, the same *spirit* that permeates *The Laws* was dominating Athens ten years after its publication, at the time of the Lycurgan reforms. But by then liberty was lost for ever. The remedy had been applied too late to cure the malady of Athens. The majority of the population did not realize the need of being ready to fight until they were confronted with the defeat which destroyed their democracy for ever.

After athletics, Plato goes on to music.[282] This looks superfluous after book 2, in which he discussed music, in connection with the problem of accustoming children to the right pleasures at an early age.[283] In this book too, which is the seventh of *The Laws*, he approaches musical education from the same direction. That is the main difference between his views about it in *The Laws* and those he expounded in *The Republic*. In *The Republic*, his chief purpose was to test the content and the form of 'music' by the new ethical and metaphysical standards set up by his philosophy. In *The Laws,* as we have explained, he is chiefly interested in the psychological basis of education, and therefore he begins by moulding the unconscious self.[284] In the second book of *The Laws,* the question of standards occupies the foreground, and there is a long argument to decide who has the right judgment about aesthetic matters.[285] Then in the seventh book, Plato speaks as a legislator, and emphasizes the idea that children should learn by play.[286] It was mentioned in the preliminary discussion;[287] but now Plato starts a new and fundamental explanation of the educational value of play, which has hitherto (he says) been completely misunderstood in all states.[288] Whether repetitions like this are an essential part of Plato's style and of the attitude of the teacher, who does not hesitate 'to say the truth twice or even three times and more', or are due to the fact that *The Laws* was unfinished, they clearly show what was in Plato's mind. The subject of play must have interested him in his old age more than ever before, particularly as a means of producing the right ethos at an early age. He lets children play freely from three till six years of age, and invent whatever games they like;[289] but after that their games are regulated and designed to instil a special spirit. The supreme assumption of all education is that moral standards are unchangeable and that state institutions designed to produce a good tradition are permanent. Therefore he tries in *The Laws* to take up the directions for preserving 'musical' tradition given in *The Republic,* and to establish them firmly by accustoming children at an early age to fixed types of games. Nothing should be changed about their games—they should not be altered by fashion, whim, and experiment, as they so often and so characteristically were in Plato's own time.[290] The word 'old' ought not to sound deprecatory, as it does in the world of changing fashion.[291] New games mean a new spirit in young people, and that means new laws. Any change is dangerous (unless it is an alteration of something bad), either in climate, or in physical regime, or in spiritual and mental make-up.[292]

So Plato tries to stabilize rhythm and song, the forms taken by the human instinct to play, by declaring them to be beneficial, and therefore inviolable and unchangeable.[293] This, as we have shown, is a view inspired by Egyptian art.[294] Historically, this would have abolished the most central achievement of the Greek genius, the liberation of poetry from the hieratic conservatism of the Orient, and would have made poetry as the expression of individual thought and feeling impossible. For it is all forbidden in *The Laws,* except official songs and dances. In Greek, nomos has two senses: *law* and *song.* Plato tries to combine them into one. The songs allowed in his educational system are to be like laws, and no one shall go beyond them.[295] Their ethos, their form, their purpose are fixed by many basic regulations.[296] They are to be selected by a board which has authority to rewrite poems that are partly, but not wholly, useful—evidently in the same way as Plato proposes to 'edit' the elegy of Tyrtaeus.[297] The regulations to be followed by living poets, who must always bear the spirit of the laws in mind as a standard, are meant to cover only the first period after the foundation of the new state. After that, no change is to be made on poems once accepted and canonized. There is room for nothing new, except hymns and panegyrics on distinguished citizens—and they must be dead, after preserving their areté until the end.[298]

Plato's view of the new order is that in practice it will be an absolutely fixed tradition which will allow any necessary changes. He takes the calendar year as the unit of time: and within it he allots festival days, fixed once and for all, to every god, high and low. These are celebrated with sacrifice and prayer.[299] Every festival is to have special songs, and rhythmic gestures and movements, which Plato calls *schemata*—a word regularly used in Greek to denote a rhythmical pattern.[300] The perfect design for living given in *The Laws* is like nothing so much as the year as conceived by the Catholic Church, with its holy rites and liturgies laid down for every day. We have used this comparison before,[301] and it is confirmed by this logical deduction made by Plato from his principles. As long as we try to conceive his educational system as a state, we feel it strange and unnatural. But if we think of the greatest educational institution of the postclassical world, the Roman Catholic Church, it looks like a prophetic anticipation of many of the essential features of Catholicism.[302] State and church, in the modern world, are separate. Plato made them one and the same in the conception of the polis. And yet what was it that did most to separate them, and to found a spiritual kingdom beside and above the kingdom of this earth? It was the enormous demands made by Plato on the educational powers of human society. The state built around Plato's central educational ideal moves, from *The Republic* to *The Laws,* nearer and nearer to the kingdom ruling over the souls of men which the church later brought into being. But Plato always maintains his principle that this kingdom is nothing but the inner spiritual nature of man himself, led to action by superior intelligence. It is the rule of the higher in us over the lower: the fundamental axiom laid down in *The Laws.*

The extension of childish play and its forms to a grand scale might be thought to be a colossal exaggeration of a good idea. Certainly it shifts the emphasis of life from things we take seriously to things we think subordinate. Realizing this, Plato justifies the change by using solemn religious words, and connecting it with the theocentric principles of all his legislation. At the opening of the book, he said man was God's toy.[303] If we take that image together with the remark in the prologue to the law, in which he said that God was the measure of all things,[304] we may think out his real meaning. He means that human life is not worth taking seriously. In reality (φύσει) only God is worth taking seriously, and what is divine in man.[305] But that is the logos, the cord by which God moves man. Man at his best is God's plaything;[306] and the life he is trying to attain consists in playing so as to please God.[307] If humanity is not seen in that divine perspective, it loses its own independent value. In particular, war and strife are not the really serious things in life. They contain 'neither play (παιδία) nor culture (παιδεία) of any importance: therefore we must try as far as possible to live in peace'—just as we say that one makes war to live at peace.[308] All life should be a festival for God, with sacrifices, songs, and dances, in order to win God's favour. And yet the duty of resisting the enemy remains, and is inevitable. No one is better fitted to fulfil it than the man who has been trained in that spirit during peace-time.[309] Perhaps those who came closest to fulfilling this ideal were the religious orders of knights in the Middle Ages.

Much of the state described in *The Laws* seems very alien to modern ideals—at least to those of the liberal nineteenth century. Yet there are a number of extremely modern institutions in its plan for public education: universal education,[310] riding-

exercise for women,³¹¹ the erection of public schools and gym-
nasia,³¹² education for girls as well as boys ³¹³ (which Plato proposed for the guards in *The Republic*), division of the day into
a working schedule,³¹⁴ and even night-work for men in important
public and private positions (a complete novelty in Greece),³¹⁵
supervision of teachers,³¹⁶ and a state board of education headed
by a Minister of Education.³¹⁷ In this passage Plato simply assumes the existence of an 'overseer of education' (παιδείας
ἐπιμελητής). The office as such is instituted in the sixth book: it
comes into the ἀρχῶν κατάστασις, the establishment of government
departments, which is the subject of that book. Let us here
briefly recall that after Plato finished describing the prefaces
and moved on to legislation proper (755a5), he distinguished
between laws about the *institution* of the governing body and
detailed laws about the *administration* of the state. The officials
in charge of music and athletics are appointed in 764c f. Then,
in 765d, comes the climax, the appointment of the most important official in education: the Minister of Public Instruction. He
must not be under fifty. Even in this passage, which we should
think dealt with a matter of constitutional law, Plato brings out
with solemn words the fundamental importance of paideia in the
state (766a); and thereby gives a good reason for the proposal
(surprising enough to the Greeks) to found an entirely new
office which clearly emphasizes the central position of paideia in
the new state. Plato reminds both the electors and the men
elected that the office held by the chief officials in the educational
department is 'far the greatest of the supreme offices in the state'
(765e2). By setting up the ministry of education, the law-giver
intends to keep education from 'being an incidental' in his state.
The appointment of the minister is made with exceptional pomp
and circumstance. All officials except the council and the acting
committee (the prytaneis) assemble in the shrine of Apollo.
Their weighty duties are indeed Apollinian, as much as any other
public function. By secret ballot they elect one member of the
'nocturnal council' (νυκτερινὸς σύλλογος) of 'guardians of the law'
(νομοφύλακες) whom they all believe most suitable to direct education in the state. The minister's closest colleagues, the guardians of the law, do not take part in his examination (δοκιμασία).
His office lasts for five years, and cannot be held twice by the
same man. But he remains a member of the nocturnal council.

to which he belonged ex officio on his election. But we must return from these regulations to his actual duties.

The question now arises how the minister in charge of education is himself to be educated.[318] He is to be provided with as detailed instructions as possible, so as to serve as interpreter and teacher for others.[319] The rules for choral dancing and singing are to be the basis of his instruction, for religious education is the framework of all other education.[320] But the children of free citizens—and only they are considered in *The Laws*—have many other subjects to learn as well. They are taught how to read, write, and play the lyre, and how to read and understand the poets who are not sung and danced.[321]

Plato explains in great detail how to teach poetry. He derides the polymathy which many of his contemporaries thought was culture.[322] We know from other sources that people used to learn the entire works of a poet off by heart—[323] a practice which had something to do with the idea that poetry was a sort of encyclopaedia of all knowledge, the idea that Plato attacks in *The Republic*.[324] Instead of that, Plato recommends the preparation of text-books containing a selection of the best poems.[325] (This is the first appearance of the anthology in the history of education.) He declares that only a few passages of poetry should be committed to memory, so as not to overload it. Teachers must make the selection with an eye on the pattern provided by *The Laws*.[326] Here, for a moment, Plato drops the pretence that he is merely recording a conversation, and writes as if *The Laws* were really a work of literature. He claims that it is as truly inspired as any poem: in fact, he expressly says it is equivalent to poetry—a remark which is one of the most important pieces of evidence on his sense of his own mission as an artist.[327] Young people are to read *The Laws* as poetry of the highest type; and besides that the teacher is to use it to fix his standard of poetry, and to study it most carefully.[328] The minister of public instruction is to judge his assistants and instructors by their understanding of *The Laws* and the ideas it contains. Anyone who cannot reach spiritual and mental harmony with it is useless as a teacher, and will find no position in Plato's state.[329] To-day, of course, we see the latent danger in this: many candidates would praise it simply in order to get a job. However, Plato intends

that it should be the canon of educational wisdom, the inexhaustible mine of culture. With that intention he hands it over
to the 'grammarian'.[330]

We need not give the details of the curriculum: how, after
the teacher of literature, the citharist or teacher of music takes
over,[331] or how the regulations for athletics and dancing translate into practice the general principles we have described above
(p. 251).[332] In these passages there are of course numerous
points of contact with *The Republic,* and with the earlier books
of *The Laws,* where these subjects were discussed.[333] Plato's
seriousness easily changes into irony: so, for instance, after accusing the poets of imitating poor models and bad subjects in
their dances and songs, he offers them *The Laws* as the most
beautiful of all tragedies, because it is an imitation of the best
and most beautiful life.[334] 'You are poets, and we too are poets
in the same way', he says;[335] 'we philosophers are your competitors. We are your antagonists in the finest drama, one which
can only be produced by a true law, as we hope . . . And now,
ye sons of the soft Muses, show the archons your songs beside ours; and if they are as good or better, we shall give you
a choir, but if not, my friends, we cannot do so'. From the very
first Plato's books had been in competition with poetry of the
old type. That was the point of the attacks on classical poetry
in *The Republic.* The legal introduction of Plato's own works
to supplement or replace the works of the old poets as a subject
for instruction in the schools and dancing-places of his future
state is the last logical step on that road. This self-canonization
helps us greatly to understand Plato himself. He had turned
from philosopher to poet in order to create a new paideia; now
it is on his own work that he founds the state he dreams of. We
must take this remark together with those in *Phaedrus* and the
seventh Letter, where he seemed to be denying that the written
word had any validity whatever:[336] if we do that, we can realize
how much truth and how much irony there is in Plato's estimate
of his own importance. Posterity did not replace the earlier
poets by Plato's works when they were received into the canon
of classical paideia, but gave the philosopher his place beside the
greatest poets, Homer and Sophocles; and he will maintain it
as long as there is true culture on earth.

Remembering how Plato had founded the rulers' education on dialectic and mathematics in *The Republic,* we find it interesting to see him doubting the value of those sciences in universal education. Obviously ordinary citizens could not undergo the long elaborate training in mathematics and astronomy which he thinks desirable for statesmen.[337] Still, he does not stop their education short at gymnastics and music, the old system of paideia. He supplements them by introducing some realistic elementary training. (He was the first educational authority to recommend such a thing.) This is a concession to the growing tendency of educators to train the intellect, and here it serves a higher purpose too. These sciences now have an immediate significance in shaping the learner's view of the world—which is quite a new qualification for them.[338] When Plato says that popular education needs nothing but knowledge of the outlines of arithmetic and measurement of lines and surfaces and solids,[339] his recommendation seems at first sight to coincide with the limits which Socrates actually imposed on these sciences.[340] But Socrates was thinking of the needs of future statesmen, while Plato is speaking of elementary education. It had always included some arithmetic, but the minimum instruction in mathematics recommended by Plato evidently went far beyond the earlier limits. It was a new victory for mathematical science—after making its way into higher education, it was now invading popular education. Its universal influence in all grades of education must be ascribed to the fact that it was the first science to grasp the need of scaling its work to the different capacities, ages, and intellectual levels of its pupils, without sacrificing the exactitude of its methods.[341]

Plato is obviously so impressed by contemporary mathematics that he points to the newest discoveries of Greek science as a reason for making elementary mathematical instruction universal. The Athenian stranger says frankly that he himself was quite old before he became acquainted with the subject he wants to introduce to the schools of the entire Greek nation; he adds that it is disgraceful for the educated Greeks to be inferior to Egypt in this regard.[342] (He is speaking of the science of measuring lines, surfaces, and solids.) [343] Obviously he has had some recent information on the advanced state of Egyptian science. He probably got it from Eudoxus, who had lived in Egypt for

a considerable time, and knew what was going on.[344] Certainly
what Plato says about the visual methods used by Egypt in elementary mathematical teaching (methods which he wants to borrow) must come from someone who witnessed them in person.[345]
The probability that his authority was Eudoxus is increased by
the fact that he brings into the same context another doctrine
still unknown to the Greeks, and extremely important in the
correct worship of the gods. This is the astronomical discovery
that the bodies called *planets,* or 'wanderers', do not deserve
their name, because they do not wander backward and forward
as they seem to do in the sky, but describe constant and regular
orbits.[346] This theory had been advanced by Eudoxus; and it is
from it that Plato deduces the fact which he particularly mentions in this context—that the planet Saturn which appears to
be most slow-moving is really the quickest of all and covers the
greatest distance.[347] Plato connects this fact with his idea that
the stars are animated beings, or visible gods.[348] From this point
of view a mistake in astronomical-mathematical fact becomes a
shameful omission of well-deserved honour, an insult which
would seem highly unjust in the case of an Olympic runner, and
far more so in ritual reverence to a god.[349] So Plato's plans for
mathematical and astronomical teaching in public schools merge
straight into the peculiar theology of *The Laws,* in which the
eternal mathematical revolution of the stars is one of the main
reasons for believing in the existence of God.[350] Plato held
that the theological function of the *mathémata,* particularly
astronomy, was an essential part of their nature. In a subsequent passage in *The Laws,* where he gives proofs of God's
existence, he stresses the historical difference between the athe-
istic astronomy of earlier centuries and the new discoveries in the
science which actually assist us in reaching true knowledge of
God.[351] So increasingly 'realistic' or practical teaching ultimately
serves to strengthen belief in God within the citizens' hearts.[352]

Plato thinks his state is so different from everything else, so
unique, that he wonders about its relation to the rest of the world.
(Evidently his product will be not less different from the world
than he is himself.) Since it is not a sea-port, it will have no
trade worth speaking of, but will try to be economically independent.[353] But spiritually too it must be shut off from all chance

influences which might interrupt the influence of its perfect laws.[354] No citizen may travel abroad except heralds, ambassadors, and 'theoroi': [355] by which Plato does not mean the city's representatives at festivals (the usual sense of the word), but men with the spirit of scientific research who will go abroad to theorein, to 'contemplate' the civilization and laws of other men and study conditions abroad at their leisure.[356] Without knowledge of men good and bad, no state can become perfect or preserve its laws. The chief aim of such journeys abroad is that the theoroi should meet the few distinguished personalities or 'divine men' who exist in the mass of ordinary people, and whom it is worth meeting and talking to.[357] We might think it a remarkable concession for Plato to admit that such men exist everywhere in the world, in badly run states as well as in good ones. Distinguished Greeks had long been accustomed to undertake long journeys for the sake of culture. They are a specifically Greek thing—as, indeed, is culture itself, in that sense. After retiring from his official post, Solon went on a journey to Asia and Egypt 'simply for the sake of contemplation' or 'sight-seeing' (θεωρίης εἵνεκα). He had many successors, and many predecessors. In Plato's time, the age of paideia, it had become a common practice to make such trips for the sake of culture (κατὰ παίδευσιν ἐπιδημεῖν) : many examples are known.[357a] He himself often left Athens for long periods, and it is evident that his law on foreign tours, theoriai, was inspired by his personal experiences. In conversation with their equals abroad, these envoys are to determine which of the city's laws are good, and which need improvement. Only experienced men over fifty are entrusted with this duty.[358] On their return they are admitted to the supreme council —the secret nocturnal assembly, whose members are the ten eldest guardians of the laws, the highest executive officials, and the minister of culture and education, the 'overseer of all paideia', with his still living predecessors.[359] The charter of this council covers legislation and education, and its duty is to improve them both.[360] The theoros returned from abroad after seeing the institutions of other men is to report to the council, giving any description he has heard from others or any idea he has had himself about legislation or education.[361] But his recommendations are to be subject to severe criticism, so that the institution of theoria may not be the means of admitting injurious influences.[362] Both the composition of the state council, and the charter of its powers, and the purpose which foreign travel is to serve, demonstrate the pre-eminent position of paideia in the new state described in *The Laws*. Plato is endeavouring to avoid the danger of allowing his state to become fossilized, and to combine authoritative regulation of life within it with the power freely to adopt valuable suggestions from outside.

THE KNOWLEDGE OF GOD AND THE EDUCATION OF THE RULERS

The night-council is the anchor of the state.[363] Its members must know the aim towards which the statesman should look.[364] This reminds us at once of the fundamental structure of the Republic. There, the aim was called the Idea of Good. Here, it is called (in the old Socratic phrase) the unity of the virtues.[365] The two expressions mean the same thing, for it is towards the Idea of Good that we are looking, when we succeed in seeing the singleness of the various forms in which goodness appears, the forms which we call aretai.[366] In the Republic it is the guards who possess this supreme political knowledge. In *The Laws* the night council corresponds to them. Plato expressly states that its members must possess 'all virtue', and together with it the ability which is its formative spiritual principle—the philosophical power to see unity in the manifold.[367] It makes no real difference that Plato discusses this ability in detail in *The Republic*, whereas he alludes only briefly to it here; and if we started by saying that the theory of Ideas does not appear in *The Laws*, that should not be interpreted as agreement with the well-known modern hypothesis that Plato abandoned it in his old age.[368] On the contrary: if we were to take his rather sketchy remarks on the education of the rulers in the twelfth book of *The Laws*, we could argue that he still clung to it. There he alludes to dialectic as something well known to his readers;[369] if he had discussed its value in education once again, he would only have been repeating what he had already said in *The Republic*. But the educative function of dialectic, its power to teach men how to see unity in diversity, is clearly signalized in the old terms, and exemplified by an allusion to the old Socratic problem of the unity of the virtues.

In fact, the problem of areté and no other was the origin of Plato's plan of making the philosophical knowledge of unity in diversity the main subject in the education of the rulers, and the foundation of the state. From his first work to his last, his thought on that one cardinal point remained unaltered. For example, he constantly gives phronésis, the knowledge of that unity of all good as the highest norm and the supreme ideal, the topmost rank among all the virtues.[370] The members of the night council do not fall behind the guards in *The Republic* in their philosophical culture. They have the power to know the truth, to express it in words, and to accomplish it in action.[371] Again and again in *The Laws* Plato emphasizes the fact that the pattern given by action is the core of all true paideia.[372] The truth which the rulers are to know is the knowledge of values: of the things it is worth while doing.[373] The culmination of this systematic knowledge of values is the knowledge of God: for God, as Plato has taught us, is the measure of all things.[374] In order to apply this measure in practice, to laws and to life, the lawgiver and the officials of the government must themselves possess knowledge of God as the highest value and the highest reality. In the state described in *The Laws,* God occupies the place taken in *The Republic* by the supreme paradeigma which the rulers carry in their souls, the Idea of Good.[375] There is no essential difference between the two, only a difference of aspect, and of the stage of knowledge to which, as objects, they correspond.[376]

Plato's *Laws* ends with the thought of God. But, as the tenth book shows, behind that thought there stands an entire system of theology. In a history of Greek paideia, we cannot go into the philosophical structure of that system: it belongs to a history of Greek philosophical theology, and I hope to treat it elsewhere in that connexion. Greek paideia and Greek philosophical theology were the two principal forms in which Greek thought influenced the world in those centuries when Greek art and Greek science lay sleeping. Both were originally united in Homer, as human areté and the ideal of godhead. In Plato the unity reappears on another plane. The synthesis is clearest in his two great educational works, *The Republic* and *The Laws*— clearest and most emphatic. Its boldest statement is the final words of *The Laws,* to which we must add the whole of the

tenth book, which deals with the problem of God. The continuation of Plato's metaphysics in the theology of Aristotle and
others of his pupils (including Philip, who wrote the *Epinomis*
as an addition to *The Laws*) proves that behind the significantly
vague hints of those final words there lies the outline of a great
theological science which would be understanding of the highest
things in the universe, and would be the crown and culmination
of all human knowledge. Here there is nothing of the difference
between knowledge of reality and mere educational knowledge
which some modern philosophers have tried to establish: [377] for in
Plato's thought there is no possible educational knowledge which
does not find its origin, its direction, and its aim in the knowledge of God. In this, the epilogue to all Plato's creative work
on this earth, he explains that there are two sources for man's
belief in the existence of the gods: knowledge of the orbits,
eternally the same, in which the heavenly bodies move; and the
'eternal stream of being' in us, the soul.[378] No human philosophy
has ever gone beyond this—from Aristotle, who took these two
motives for the belief in God into his own theology, to Kant's
Critique of Practical Reason, which after all his revolutionary
theoretical arguments ends in practice with the same two
thoughts.[379] And thus, after a lifetime of effort to discover the
true and indestructible foundations of culture, Plato's work ends
in the Idea of that which is higher than man, and yet is man's
true self. Greek humanism, in the form which it takes in Plato's
paideia, is centred upon God.[380] The state is the social form given
by the historical development of the Greek people to Plato in
which to express this Idea. But as he inspires it with his new conception of God as the supreme standard, the measure of all measures, he changes it from a local and temporary organization on
this earth, to an ideal kingdom of heaven, as universal as its symbol, the animate gods which are the stars. Their bright shapes
are the divine images, the agalmata, with which Plato replaces
the human forms of the Olympian deities. They do not dwell
in a narrow temple built by human hands; their light, proclaim-
ing and manifesting the one supreme invisible God, shines over
all the nations of the earth.

DEMOSTHENES: THE DEATH-STRUGGLE AND TRANSFIGURATION OF THE CITY-STATE

EVER since he returned to life in the Renaissance, Demosthenes has been held to be what his first modern editor called him: the awakener of the Greeks to liberty, and their eloquent champion against oppression. When the hand of Napoleon lay heavy on Europe, Demosthenes' works were translated by the German philologist and humanist Friedrich Jacobs, in order to strengthen the spirit of national independence. Soon after the First World War, the French statesman Clémenceau wrote a hasty book on him, full of glowing French rhetoric against the German Macedonians, warning the Athenians of Paris not to allow their refinement to make them a nerveless people of artists and *rentiers,* without enough will to life and enough vital energy to resist their barbarous enemy.[1] In a Latin civilization, with all the oratorical devices of Demosthenes himself, that book founded a new cult of the long-dead patriot, on whose altars the old fire of classicism blazed up once again, for the last time. But not long before, a German scholar had written another book with the contemptuous title *Aus einer alten Advokatenrepublik*—'An Ancient Lawyers' Republic'. After a century of sharp reaction against the classicist admiration for the powerful orator and the great agitator, who had been wrongly canonized by academic rhetoric, this work now summed up the whole case, and was meant to destroy Demosthenes' reputation for good and all.[2] Of course, it was a war book; it was highly inflammatory, and it put the harshest construction on every fact, so as to distort the truth into a caricature. Yet it was only the lowest point on the line down which the historians' estimate of Demosthenes had travelled since the new attitude to history had come into being, a hundred years earlier.

The first great representative of the new historical attitude in the sphere of classics, Niebuhr, was one of Demosthenes' most devoted admirers. But violent criticism of Demosthenes' career and policy began with Droysen. It was initiated by the epoch-making discovery of the Hellenistic world.[3] Hitherto, Greek history had always come to a dramatic conclusion with the loss of the political liberty of the city-states at Chaeronea. Demosthenes had been presented as the last Greek statesman, standing above the grave of Hellas and delivering her funeral oration. But now the curtain suddenly opened, to reveal a great new drama—the age when Greece dominated the world politically and spiritually, the age that began with Alexander's conquest of the Persian empire. The perspective shifted, to disclose a continuous external and internal development of Greek civilization into something cosmopolitan, something universal. With the change of proportion, Demosthenes' greatness came to seem very small and limited. He appeared to belong to a world which was foolishly deceived about its own importance, and which was living on an anachronism—the rhetorical memory of its glorious ancestors.[4] He and his contemporaries, it seemed, were trying to revive the deeds of their fathers in their own day, although they themselves belonged to the past. His critics became increasingly bitter. They started by discarding his political standards, which historians had hitherto willingly accepted, because there was no connected account of the history of his age by one of his contemporaries. Then, after doubting his statesmanship, they went on to examine, and to condemn, his character. At the same time his opponents, Isocrates and Aeschines, began to rise in estimation because they had given up hope for the future of Athens at the right time, and advised their countrymen to abandon the fight. As often, success became the standard of historical achievement, and scholars were reassured to find that Demosthenes had had opponents during his lifetime who were just as far-sighted as modern professors.[5]

The critics have gone too far.[6] It is time for the general picture of Demosthenes to be revised. The radical revaluation in the customary estimate of the characters of Demosthenes, Aeschines, and Isocrates was so improbable, psychologically, as to offend common sense and natural feeling. Apart from that, there has been a marked advance in our knowledge of the fourth century since Droysen's discovery of the Hellenistic world. This advance did not begin with politics, but with new light cast on the intellectual movements of that critical epoch, which revealed how closely political movements were connected with the general trend of Greek thought and Greek culture. Worlds which had formerly appeared to be, so to speak, in watertight compartments—such as political history and philosophy, journalism and rhetoric—are now all seen to be living members of one single organism, each with its share in the process of the nation's life. We are now able to give to the idea of historical necessity discovered by Thucydides [7] a broader interpretation than has been usual, particularly in political history. Nowadays it looks like coarse rationalism to judge the appearance of a historical phenomenon like Demosthenes in the decline of the Greek city-state simply by his own personal character and his success in practical politics. His resistance to the forces moving his age was a fulfilment of a supra-personal law—the law by which every nation tries doggedly to maintain the pattern of life moulded by itself, founded on its own natural disposition, and responsible for the highest achievements in its history.

Throughout the centuries from Homer to Alexander, the fundamental fact in Greek history was the city-state, the form of political and spiritual life which was fixed very early, and never wholly abandoned.[8] In forms as manifold as the ever-varying Greek landscape, it had unfolded all those rich potentialities of internal and external life which the Greek race possessed. Even after the Greeks awoke to spiritual nationhood, in the fifth century, and smaller political units began to group themselves into confederations of larger size, the independent existence of the city-state still remained the frontier which was bound, sooner or later, to stop the new trend to nationalism. The problem of how far the several city-states could be independent had found no satisfactory solution since it had first been rudely thrust on one side by the imperialist Athenians under Pericles, who crushed the allies of Athens into subjection. When the Spartans succeeded to the leadership of Greece after the close of the Peloponnesian war, they were compelled to base their hegemony on a formal recognition of the autonomy of individual states. After the first great revolt of the Greek cities against their Spartan overlords in the Corinthian war, their independence was solemnly recognized in the peace of Antalcidas.[9] However, the formula that all the Greek city-states should be independent was useful to Sparta too. It meant that it would be difficult for a league to be formed against her under the leadership of another state. But when she herself tightened the reins, and invaded the liberty of the separate cities, the result was the fall of the Spartan hegemony. Never afterwards did any single one of the Greek city-states manage to assert a decisive domination over the others. In other words: the Greeks were not able to think of giving up the independence of their city-states, any more than to-day we have been able to think *in practice* of giving up our own national states in favour of any more comprehensive form of state.

Demosthenes' youth fell in the period when Athens was recovering from her catastrophic defeat in the Peloponnesian war.[10] While the philosophical thought of the age, embodied in Plato, was concentrating all its energy on solving the problem of the state and its moral reconstruction, the contemporary Athenian state was making its way step by step out of its weakness to a liberty of movement which allowed it to plan the gradual repair of its strength. Thucydides' prophecy that a change of power would produce a shift in sympathy was all too promptly fulfilled. With the support of Thebes and Corinth, the former allies of Sparta, Athens slowly regained her position among the Greek states, and, with the help of Persian money, rebuilt the fortifications she had been compelled to destroy after the war. Then followed the second stage in her recovery. The defection of Thebes from Sparta gave Athens the opportunity to found the second naval confederacy; and she was astute enough to bind her allies closely to her by avoiding the domineering policy that had broken up her first league. Its leaders were distinguished soldiers and statesmen like Timotheus, Chabrias, Iphicrates, and Callistratus. Soon after it was founded, Athens fought bravely and devotedly beside Thebes against Sparta in the seven-year war which ended successfully in the peace of 371. Thus her undisputed domination at sea was ensured, and the new confederacy was finally legalized by international agreement.[11]

The young men of Athens, absorbed in philosophical study or vainly dissipating their time on adventure and sport, were swept into the great current of history which seemed to be carrying Athens forward once again to play a leading part in the political life of Greece. They belonged to a different generation from the youths who had struggled under the problems of the Peloponnesian war, the defeat, and the collapse. Plato had written *Gorgias* to be a call to battle for them. In the first decade of the fourth century they had felt themselves to be the founders of a new society.[12] Later, in *Theaetetus*, Plato described the wise man as retreating further and further into remote speculations about mathematics and astronomy, and sceptically turning his back on all kinds of political activity.[13] But the younger generation was drawn into the whirl of politics, and left it to immigrants from the small towns and frontier states—men like Aristotle, Xenocrates, Heracleides, and Philip of Opus—to take up the Platonic life of pure research.[14] Isocrates' school was not like Plato's Academy. It produced a group of active politicians, most notably Isocrates' friend and prize pupil, Timotheus, the soldier and statesman who directed the new naval league.[15] Yet the younger generation got its real training from party politics, from speaking in the law-courts, and from addressing the public assembly. Demosthenes was taken to court secretly by his tutor, when he was a boy, and heard Callistratus' great speech in his own defence in the Oropian case, the speech which saved him from ruin once again.[16]

That historical anecdote, which is probable enough, shows the spirit of the new generation. It reveals where Demosthenes' true interests lay: apart from the harassing anxieties about his stolen home and inheritance, which fill his first speeches, delivered when he was only twenty. His character was destined by the trend of events to be moulded into a statesman's. The course of his life was set by the great men on whom he modelled himself, the makers of the second naval league. It was aimed at reviving for the present age the greatness Athens had possessed in the century of her highest political glory (somewhat dulled, now, by Plato's philosophical criticisms), and at rejuvenating the present by the ideals of the past.[17] But the agony of watching that glory break into dust had not been fruitless. Struggling through the gloom to understand the reasons for the collapse, the post-war generation had found a certain knowledge which must not be lost, if the past was not to repeat itself. It was the task of the young men to pour some of this cold and pure knowledge into the old intoxicating wine of Athenian imperialism. That was the only way for them to cope with the new era. The difference between it and the fifth century, between the ages of the second and the first naval leagues, was the new spirit of wary moral and political reflection.[18] It was perfectly natural that the fourth-century movement for political restoration should be so ideal-istic and so literary. There had been none of that spirit in the unquestioning energy of the previous century. It was only in the Indian summer of Athens, the Demosthenic age, that political oratory developed into a great form of literary art. The tradi-tion that Demosthenes eagerly studied Thucydides while train-ing himself as an orator fits the facts very well.[19] He could not model his style on the political speeches of Pericles as actually delivered—for they had not been formally published as works of literature, and did not survive. In fact, the speeches of Thucydides were the sole surviving echo of Athenian political oratory from the great age. In the artistic and intellectual per-fection of their form, and the richness of their thought, they stood far above all actual contemporary political eloquence.[20] It was Demosthenes alone who was to create a literary form that combined the energy and suppleness of the spoken word with the dialectic profundity and aesthetic elegance of Thucydides' speeches, and to re-create in literature that most essential ele-ment in rhetorical persuasion, the interplay of living emotion between speaker and audience.[21]

When Demosthenes himself stepped upon the platform, twelve years after he had heard the great Callistratus speak, the political situation had entirely changed. The Social War had ended. Athens had once more lost the most important of her allies. The second naval confederacy, founded with such splendid hopes, was broken. Most of its members held that its function had been fulfilled with the overthrow of Spartan domination. That done, it had no inward bond of union to hold it together. Although it had reached its greatest extent only after Athens' victorious peace with Sparta, it was soon evident that it had no positive community of interests to ensure its continuance; and when financial stringency compelled Athens, its leading power, to resume her old imperialistic policy of force against her allies, the rebellious spirit which had once before overthrown Athenian naval supremacy arose again. But the most important new posi-tive factor in Greek politics since the peace of 371 was the un-expected rise of Thebes under the leadership of Epaminondas.

This brought about an entirely new grouping of forces. At first Athens had stood at the side of Thebes against Sparta, but in the peace of 371 she had parted company with Thebes in order to take the profits of the war. However, immediately after she had made an independent peace, and by this concession to Sparta secured her recognition of the naval confederacy, the Spartan land forces were conclusively defeated by the Thebans under Epaminondas at Leuctra. This victory raised Thebes to unprecedented new heights, and forced Sparta down to the second place in Greece. At this juncture, Callistratus, the leading politician of Athens, sharply changed the policy of the state, and entered an open alliance with Sparta so as to counterbalance the new power of Thebes, the erstwhile ally of Athens. A new idea now came into being: *the balance of power*. It was an idea that dominated Athenian politics for the next ten years, and went some way towards stabilizing a new sort of relation among the Greek states. It was the creation of Callistratus, the statesman who had proposed the break with Thebes even during the peace negotiations, and had forced it through in spite of strong pro-Theban feeling in Athens.[22] On the other side, Epaminondas, the only great statesman Thebes ever produced, proceeded to dissolve the Peloponnesian League after defeating Sparta. He liberated the Messenian and Arcadian peoples from Spartan oppression, making them independent states, each with a central government. They now became, like other small states, vassals of Thebes. This broke Sparta's hegemony even in the Peloponnese. It was only the military support of Athens that saved her from complete destruction. It is impossible to tell what would have been the course of Greek politics now that Athens had swung into opposition to Thebes, if Epaminondas had not been killed in the battle of Mantinea, the last Theban victory over Sparta, and if his powerful Athenian opponent Callistratus had not soon afterwards been overthrown.[23] Thereafter the two rival states were led by less competent men. Their power quickly diminished. The conflict between them quieted down. Both Thebes and Athens had to fight hard to maintain their authority over their allies, Thebes in central Greece and Thessaly, Athens on the sea. Still, their hostility was still active in the age of Demosthenes, and came out in every minor question. However, in Athens it was naturally obscured by the internal difficul-

ties she had to face during the next few years, when the naval
confederacy was falling irretrievably into ruin. This was the inheritance which came to Demosthenes and his generation in 355.

The fall of the naval league forced to the front again, and
for the last time, the question of the political future of Athens.
It looked as if Isocrates had given the only possible answer to
it, in the bold proposal he made in one of the war's dark hours,
in his speech *On peace*. He had publicly proposed that Athens
should finally abandon all her imperialist policy, all attempts to
revive the former Attic empire, all power-politics of the type
which the second naval confederacy had inevitably reintro-
duced.[24] He supported this proposal by a highly utilitarian type
of political morality. It was more advantageous, he said, to
gather laurels in peace, than to incur the hatred of the entire
world by the pleonexia, the greed for more, which is implicit in
all imperialist policy; and to expose the state to frightful danger
under the leadership of universally despised political agitators
and military gangsters. At the same period the same change of
policy was being recommended on economic grounds by the talented economist who wrote the essay *On the Revenues*.[25] But
whether Athens adopted the new policy because of a fundamental change of principle, or because she was merely bowing
to the inevitable, she was bound to start her reforms by concentrating on the reconstruction of her financial stability and the
restoration of her credit (in every sense of the word) in the eyes
of the world. The propertied classes must have been discussing
even more comprehensive plans for reconstructing the constitution of the state which had fallen, during the last ten years, into
the hands of the radically minded masses. Otherwise Isocrates
could not have dared to suggest publicly that a more authoritative government should be instituted, as he did in his pamphlet,
the *Areopagiticus*. Athens was very far from taking such a step;
but the fact that the proposal could be made shows how powerful and how combative the upper classes felt in that desperate
period when only they could help the state.[26] They now produced
an opposition leader of great prestige. This was Eubulus, whose
principal interest was economic and financial reform. He was followed by the best brains of the younger generation, including
Demosthenes himself.[27] Demosthenes belonged to a rich Athenian family; and it was only natural for him to join those of

similar birth, education, and outlook. These young men had first turned to politics when the renaissance of Athenian power was at its height. Their highest ambition had been to give all their strength to the service of the state. Now they were forced to begin the career to which they had been looking forward so eagerly, just when the Athenian state was at the nadir of its historical career. Inspired by the loftiest of ideals, they were thrust into the gloomiest of realities. It was clear from the very outset that their efforts to mould the future of Athens must end in acknowledging and resolving this enormous conflict between ideal and reality.

Demosthenes' private life brought him into contact with the law at an early age. His father left him a great deal of money, which was misappropriated by his guardians. After making his first appearance before a jury as a speaker in his own behalf, he chose to follow the profession of legal consultant and 'logographer' or speech-writer.[28] In Athens a regular connexion between politics and the law-courts had grown up, so that it was perfectly normal to start one's public life by taking part in political prosecutions. The first documents we have for Demosthenes' political activity are therefore speeches made in great state trials during the years of the depression. He did not deliver them himself, but wrote them for others. The three orations *Against Androtion, Against Timocrates,* and *Against Leptines* are all expressions of the same policy. They are aimed against the most vulnerable personalities of the political party which had governed Athens during the disastrous Social War, and which had managed to maintain itself in power even after the defeat.[29] At once it was clear that Demosthenes was one of the cleverest and most dangerous of the opposition's shock-troops. The savagery of the dispute shows the bitterness with which the opposition was struggling for power. Even here we can see how much of Demosthenes' strength lay in the fact that he followed up his aims logically, systematically, and resolutely —although he was then working chiefly for others and under the guidance of others.[30] But he soon came forward as an orator in his own right. Significantly, his interest was directed to foreign affairs, from the very beginning. It is thrilling to watch the development of the future statesman in these first utterances.

We can see him taking up the decisive problems of Athenian foreign policy one after another with remarkable power and firmness: so that the comparatively few early speeches display a complete picture of the position of Athens in international politics.[31]

During that period of slow and laborious internal reconstruction, it was difficult for Athens to develop an energetic and productive foreign policy. This makes it all the more remarkable that the young Demosthenes should have approached each political problem as it appeared, with such independence of mind and such lively initiative. Defeated and depressed, Athens was condemned to complete inactivity in international politics. Demosthenes could therefore intervene only when the occasion presented itself—and the times were so busy, so full of conflicting interests, that such occasions did occur now and then. Here a gulf was inevitably bound to open, and to grow wider and deeper with the years. One school of thought, represented in literature by Isocrates and in politics by Eubulus, the leader of the well-to-do opposition party, firmly maintained that Athens in her weakened condition should have nothing to do with any foreign affairs whatever; the only possible future for her, they believed, lay in concentrating upon careful economic and internal policy. In his first speech on foreign affairs, Demosthenes showed some sympathy for that isolationist attitude.[32] There were many calls for a preventive war against the threat, real or imaginary, of a Persian invasion. On this question Demosthenes attacked the warmongers, with a well-judged violence of language and a sureness of touch that pleased the party of Eubulus. His courage in voicing an unpopular view must have been sympathetically noted by the reformers who had taken it as their watchword to oppose vulgar sentiment and popular clichés. But although he judged the political risks with sober caution, at heart he believed that Athens must work her way out of her present impotence, to take an active part in international politics.[33] He must therefore have welcomed every opportunity for Athens to move beyond her miserable isolation, and to regain her prestige and power by a moderate and just, but watchful, attitude in foreign politics. However cautiously he might advance towards this aim, it was impossible to follow this policy, and use the chances that presented themselves, without taking *some* risks. Meanwhile, the partisans of complete isolationism were playing for complete safety. Even during this period of passivity, Demosthenes was intellectually active. He followed the struggles of the combatants in the political arena like an eager spectator who is waiting for the moment to leap into the ring and take a leading part in the contest.

The next stages in his development are his great speeches *For the Megalopolitans* and *For the Liberty of the Rhodians*: along with the legal speech *Against Aristocrates,* which is largely concerned with foreign politics.[33a] He had explained his view of the relations between Athens and the Persian empire in his first public speech. Now, in these orations, he attacks the other three main problems of Athenian foreign policy: the Peloponnesian question; the question of the relations between Athens and her seceding partners in the naval league; and the problem of northern Greece. Thereby he completed for the first time a bold sketch of the future foreign policy of Athens, as he conceives it. The aim of his endeavour is always the same. Demosthenes keeps his gaze fixed firmly upon it. It is to lift Athens out of her crippling isolation, and to lay the foundations for a practical policy of forming alliances, so that, if the opportunity comes, it may be seized. It was inevitable that any Athenian politician concerned with foreign affairs should adopt the constructive plan which had been outlined by Callistratus with his original idea of the balance of power.[34] Ever since the amazing rise of Thebes to a place beside Sparta and Athens that idea was bound to look like the classical inheritance from the most successful period of Attic policy since Pericles. As long as the factors of Greek international politics remained the same as they had been when the maxim of equilibrium was formulated fifteen years before, a rising politician could only adapt and develop it; it could not be challenged. Demosthenes' speech *For the Megalopolitans* is a proof of the suppleness of his mind. Like all other Athenian politicians, he adopts Callistratus' principle; and he does his best to interpret it anew to suit the changed times, without losing the spirit of the statesman who laid it down. The idea that Sparta and Thebes should counterpoise each other in the scales, while Athens swung like the tongue of the balance between them, had once before brilliantly illuminated the situation, when the predominance of Thebes and her allies had compelled Athens to come to an understanding with her old enemy Sparta. But soon Thebes found her level. Then she was weakened by the disastrous beginning of the war against the Phocians in central Greece; and it became essential for Athens to keep the new states of Messenia and Arcadia, which Thebes had created in the Peloponnese to oppose Sparta, from being crushed once more by the renewed power of Sparta. Otherwise Athens would have become a Spartan vassal, and Thebes would have been irrevocably weakened. The new states were defenceless. They had to ask for Athenian support. Demosthenes believed this was the right moment to shift the balance, which had stood still for some time, and to counterbalance the power of Sparta (allied to Athens since Leuctra) by a new alliance with Arcadia and Messenia.[35]

This highly independent idea is followed, in the speech *For the Liberty of the Rhodians,* by another which is no less interesting. The Rhodians, who had been tampered with by the king of Caria, were one of the first states to secede from the Athenian naval league. They had not reckoned with the fact that Athens was the only state which could really help a democratic country to defend its independence. When the king of Caria drove the democratic politicoes out of Rhodes, they ran to Athens, full of remorse, and anxious to sign a new alliance. In the case of the Arcadians, the Athenian isolationists, who had the public ear, pled that they could not help, because of the Spartan alliance. And so now, they made full use of the popular feeling of well-earned rancour against the Rhodians: having betrayed Athens, they were welcome to the consequences.[36] Demosthenes sharply attacked this superficial emotionalism. He said it was merely a cloak for passivity and indecisiveness on the part of the government.[37] In both cases he acted quite independently, and risked his growing reputation on his words. In both cases he was defeated. Rejected, the suppliants joined the enemies of Athens. The Arcadians and Messenians later sided with Philip of Macedon. Athens lost not only the Rhodians but the other small states which would certainly soon have come back to Athens, if the Rhodian alliance had matured, just as Rhodes had led their secession in the Social War.

With his speech *Against Aristocrates* Demosthenes turns for the first time to the politics of northern Greece. The question at stake was the security of the Dardanelles. The last stronghold of Athens at sea was her command of the Hellespont Straits, upon which her grain supply depended, and which also assured her predominance in the waters of northern Greece. Demosthenes knew the importance of this region from personal experience, having toured the coasts as trierarch of a battleship. The Thracians near by had been threatening the Dardanelles for many years, and for some time actually seized them. Now that several brothers had divided up the kingship, Demosthenes proposed to take advantage of the temporary disunity of the Thracians, so as to prevent the recurrence of this peril, and weaken, as far as possible, the dangerous neighbours of the strategic Straits.[38] Meanwhile, however, another factor had entered northern Greek politics. This was Philip, the brilliant new king of Macedonia. In the short time since his accession he had contrived to make his country (which was formerly mutilated and dependent now on this state, now on that) into the dominant power throughout the whole region. Even before this, in his speech *For the Liberty of the Rhodians,* Demosthenes had mentioned the danger threatening Athens from that side. Philip had been at war with Athens ever since annexing the long-disputed Macedonian port of Amphipolis, which Athens claimed as an old-established base for her commerce and fleet. After he united his country, he made himself ruler of its neighbour, Thessaly, which had long been torn by political turmoil, and was ready for some foreigner to solve its problems. Then he entered the war between Thebes and Phocis, beat the Phocians, and was about to invade central Greece through Thermopylae in order to appear as arbitrator of the many disputes outstanding there, when the Athenians, with a sudden effort, threw an army corps into that easily defended pass, blocking his way.[39] He did not try to force the pass. He turned north again, marched practically unopposed through Thrace, and suddenly threatened Athens at the Dardanelles, where no one expected him. All Demosthenes' plans for protecting the strait against the Thracians were suddenly ruined; the entire picture changed. The Macedonian danger was revealed in a flash, enormous and terrible.[40]

The news caused a panic in Athens. It soon changed, however, to careless gaiety when it was reported that Philip had fallen ill and abandoned the expedition. Still, that was the mo-

ment when Demosthenes finally determined to abandon the passive isolationist policy which the administration was following.[41]
It had thwarted all his efforts to improve the position of Athens
by grasping at favourable opportunities as they offered. Now it
was no longer merely a question of principle, a choice between
intervention and isolation. The country was in danger. Doing
nothing would not now be interpreted as trying to 'save Athens
first'. It meant surrendering the most vital interests of the state.
The blockade-war against Philip, which no one had really taken
seriously, had suddenly forced Athens onto the defensive. The
country's entire strategy had to be changed.

Philip's rapid advance called out all Demosthenes' energies.[42]
At last he had found the dangerous assailant who was needed
to justify Athens in taking a bold stand in foreign policy at this
moment. It is difficult to say whether, in more fortunate circumstances, Demosthenes might not have become one of those statesmen who are born in a rising country, and help to build it up
and make it stronger. Certainly, in fourth-century Athens, he
could not have existed without an opponent like Philip to bring
out all his determination, his far-sightedness, and his bulldog
grasp of the essentials. The moral scruples which had long ob-
structed any attempt at an active foreign policy, in that most
moral age, among men so deeply concerned with philosophical
problems of conscience, were now blown away. That made it
easier for Demosthenes to by-pass the leading appeasers and
appeal directly to the people, from whom he had been very remote in his earliest speeches. In his speech on behalf of the
Rhodian democrats he had already advanced some political arguments which were aimed at convincing the masses—something
very different from the lofty, didactic, ironical tone of his first
speech, which had been meant to cool down their excitement.[43]
The speech *Against Aristocrates* contains some violent attacks
on the politicians in power: Demosthenes says they enrich themselves and live at ease in fine houses, while they do nothing more
to help the country than plastering a wall here and repairing a
road there.[44] In his speech *On Armaments* he drew a critical
comparison between the Athenian people of his own day, living
off the state as if they had independent incomes, and the battle-
scarred empire-builders of the past; and he closed with the idea
that since the appeal to the politicians had been useless, *the*

people must be educated to a new mentality—for politicians always said what the public wanted to hear anyhow.[45]

That sentence contains a great programme. Hitherto it has not been taken seriously, because the speech has, until recently, been considered spurious. Nineteenth-century scholars often pushed their scepticism beyond the limits of probability, as here.[46] But it was hardly necessary to prove the speech genuine to show that the next speeches of Demosthenes form a homogeneous spiritual unity. The ancients put them into a separate group and called them the *Philippics*: but it is not only the fact that they are all against Philip that distinguishes them from Demosthenes' earlier speeches. They are held together by *the great ideal of educating the Athenian people,* which is formulated briefly and impressively in the sentence quoted above. That sentence is the plainest commentary on the change which has been wrongly described as Demosthenes' move towards the 'democratic party',[47] and which is really his transformation into a great popular leader. We can see it happening in the *Philippics*. Of course the speeches have a great deal of the conscious art with which the Athenian orators used to diagnose the future reactions of the public, and dominate them. They had more than a century's experience to go upon; and since many of them were not commoners, they had worked out a special language to appeal to the mob's instincts. But no one who has any intellectual discrimination can confuse the tone of the ordinary demagogue with Demosthenes' ability to use that language on occasion. The emotions which led him to appeal directly to the people were fundamentally different from those of the demagogue; they were the result of his accurate political knowledge, which made it necessary for him to overcome the limitations imposed on him by his youth and his gentle character, and come forward as a critic.[48] And similarly the influence which his remarkable character had on Athenian politics was worlds apart from that not only of the loud-mouthed demagogues, but of the ordinary, hard-working, file-reading, respectable career-politicians like Eubulus. It is obvious that a spiritually mature statesman, such as Demosthenes is shown to be in his first speeches on foreign policy, does not suddenly change his nature, and become a mere tub-thumper, as some serious scholars have had the temerity to suggest. No one capable of realizing how new and how great is the language used in Demosthenes' *Philippics* could ever be guilty of such a misapprehension.

To understand the statesmanlike quality of these speeches it is not enough to study the practical measures proposed in them. They show that Demosthenes had a profound historical sense of the destiny of Athens and himself, and a profound determination to meet it. It is more than mere politics. Or perhaps we should say that it is politics as Solon and Pericles understood the word.[49] He stands face to face with the people, and consoles them for their misfortunes, which are indeed great enough. But they have done nothing to let them expect anything better! That is the only really cheerful aspect of all their misery.[50] Just as Solon once arose to warn the Athenians, so now Demosthenes admonishes them: 'Do not blame the gods for having given up your cause. You yourselves are to blame if Philip pushes you back step by step, and if he has now gained such power that many of you think it irresistible'.[51] Solon brought in tyché, chance or fate, in discussing the part played by the gods in the misfortunes of the state. The same idea comes back, transformed once more, in Demosthenes' warning speeches against Philip.[52] It is one of the basic themes in his profound analysis of the fate and future of Athens. It was an age of greatly increased individualism; men craved for freedom, but they felt all the more keenly how dependent everyone really is upon the outward course of world events. The century which began with the tragedies of Euripides was more alive to the idea of tyché than any other era; and the men of that age tended more and more to resign themselves to fate. Demosthenes boldly takes up Solon's old and bitter fight against the fatalism which is the worst enemy of resolute action. He places the historical responsibility for the fate of Athens squarely on the shoulders of his own generation. Their task, he declares, is the same as that of the generation which lived through the dark period after the loss of the Peloponnesian war, and which, against the opposition of all Greece, exalted Athens once more to great power and prestige.[53] To do this, they used only one thing: the alert and energetic assistance of the people's whole strength. Nowadays, he adds bitterly, Athens is like a barbarian in a boxing-match, who can only clap his hands to the place where his opponent hit him last, instead of looking out for a place to punch.[54]

These are the simple and striking ideas with which Demosthenes begins his work of educating the Athenian people in the first *Philippic*. The preliminary proposals for a new strategy which he makes, before Philip has delivered a new attack on Athens, prove that the speech (which is often dated too late) was made in the period when Philip's unexpected threat to the Dardanelles had opened Demosthenes' eyes to the danger for the first time.[55] The military and financial measures which he proposed Athens should adopt so as to be ready at the next attack were not accepted by the Athenian people.[56] He had to propose them anew, when Philip recovered from his illness, attacked Olynthus, the powerful commercial state in northern Greece, and provided a last opportunity for Athens to join with the Olynthians and stop the forward pressure of the Macedonians.[57] Once again, with redoubled earnestness, Demosthenes asked whether Athens was to be responsible for its own destiny or to surrender to fate. He endeavoured to bring back the courage she needed for independent action.[58] He bitterly attacked the false teachers who were trying to create alarm and distress, so as to convince the public—too late—that the time had really come to act.[59] His own analysis of the enemy's power is not the kind of thing which a 'practical politician' would offer. It is a discussion and criticism of the moral foundations on which it is built.[60] We ought not to read these speeches as if they were the considered report of a statesman to a cabinet meeting. They are efforts to guide a public which is intelligent, but vacillating and selfish. They are intended to mould the masses, like raw material which must be shaped to suit the statesman's ends.[61] That is what gives particular importance to the ethical element in the speeches Demosthenes delivered at this time. There is nothing like it in any other speech on foreign policy throughout Greek literature.[62] Demosthenes well knows what a great man Philip is, and what a magical, demoniac personality he has—a character not to be measured by purely moral standards.[63] But he is Solon's pupil, and he refuses to believe any power built on such a basis can long endure. Despite all his admiration for Philip's mysterious tyché, he still clings to his belief in the tyché

of Athens, whose light pinion is touched by a glory shed from
the splendid historical mission of the Athenian state.[64]

No one who has traced the development of the ideal of the
statesman's character down through the various changes of the
Greek spirit can follow Demosthenes' struggle to make the
Athenian people understand its own destiny, without being reminded of the first grand personifications of the responsible political leader, which appear in Attic tragedy.[65] They too breathe
the spirit of Solon, but they are caught in the tragic dilemma of
decision. In the speeches of Demosthenes, the tragic dilemma
has become a reality,[66] and the consciousness of this, not merely
subjective excitement, is the source of the overwhelming emotion, the 'pathos', which men of succeeding ages felt in Demosthenes—although they were interested only in aesthetics, and
stirred only by the wish to imitate his style, which they rightly
felt to be the foundation of a new era in the history of oratory.[67]
That was the style which expressed the tragedy of his age. Its
deep and moving shadows appear again on the faces carved by
Scopas, greatest of contemporary sculptors; and a direct line can
be traced from these two great harbingers of a new feeling for
life, to the magnificent Pergamene altar, a rich and powerful
rush of emotion in which the new style reaches its loftiest expression. How could Demosthenes have become the greatest classic
of the Hellenistic age, which had so little sympathy for his political ideal, if he had not uttered, fully and perfectly, all the
characteristic emotions which it felt? But the emotions and the
style in which they are expressed are, for him, inseparable from
his struggle to achieve his political ideal. Orator and statesman,
in Demosthenes, are one. His eloquence alone would have been
nothing without the power and weight of the political thoughts
striving to express themselves through it. They give the passionate creations of his mind the firmness, depth, and solidity
which have never been rivalled by his myriad imitators, and
which anchor them fast to the place, the time, and the historical
crisis which are immortalized in them.

I do not intend to give a complete exposition of Demosthenes'
policy in itself. The material his speeches provide for a reconstruction of the actual events, and, even more, of his development into a statesman, is discontinuous, but (compared with the

historical evidence we have for most periods) extremely rich. What we shall do here is to trace how he grew to his full stature as the guide of his nation, until the final battle for the independent existence of the Athenian state.

The fall of Olynthus, and the destruction of the flourishing towns on the Chalcidic peninsula, which belonged to the Olynthian alliance, compelled Athens to make peace with Philip of Macedon. The treaty was signed in 346, and even Demosthenes supported the wish for peace whole-heartedly.[68] But he opposed the acceptance of Philip's terms, because they handed over central Greece defenceless to the enemy, and tightened the encircling ring around Athens. However, he could not prevent peace from being signed on these terms. In his speech *On the Peace* he was compelled to advise the Athenians most strongly not to offer armed resistance after Philip had occupied Phocis and Thermopylae, which were essential bases for commanding central Greece. Like his earliest orations in the period before the fight against Philip became his lifework, this speech shows what a realistic politician he was: he did not strive for impossibilities, and he dared to oppose the rule of irrational emotion in politics.[69] No one attacks his enemy at the enemy's strongest point.[70] These highly practical speeches show an aspect of Demosthenes which is essential for any clear judgment of his worth. Here, as elsewhere, he is essentially a teacher. He does not simply want to convince the masses, and overpower them with oratory. He compels them to move onto a higher plane, and, after leading them up step by step, to judge the facts for themselves. A good example of this is the speech *For the Megalopolitans,* with its discussion of the policy of the balance of power, as applied to the case under discussion.[70a] The speeches *On the Symmories,* and *For the Liberty of the Rhodians* are classical examples of his steadily increasing ability to quell and dominate loud-mouthed jingoistic emotions.[70b] They reveal with perfect clarity Demosthenes' conception of politics as a wholly objective art; and his speech after the unfavourable peace of 346 shows that his struggle with Philip did nothing to change his attitude. The first *Philippics* and the three speeches on Olynthus, full of wise counsels, confirm the view that he was now a statesman who saw far into the future, and planned for it, who knew when it was right to hold fast a decision once made, and who knew how much depends on favourable chances in this world ruled by tyché.[71] His acts always show that he knows how much depends on chance: that is the explanation of his remarkable reserve after the peace of 346. Neither his critics nor his more emotional supporters have realized this, even yet. They both think that, when his strictly logical reasoning makes him change his attitude to suit circumstances, they have detected vacillation and weakness of character.[72]

But even when Demosthenes was delivering his speech *On the Peace* he knew what he wanted. His eye was on the target. He never believed in the permanence of the peace, which was only a tool to dominate Athens; and he chose to allow its practical usefulness to Philip to be defended by politicians who shut their eyes to the facts because their will to resist was broken (like Aeschines) or who were (like Isocrates) ready to go further, to make a virtue of necessity, and to proclaim Philip as the Führer of all Greece.[73] It is impossible to understand Isocrates' peculiar position in the spiritual war against the threat of Macedonian domination, without remembering how he gradually became the chief herald of Greek political unity. Greece was incapable of achieving unity by dissolving the independent city-states into a single nation-state, even if the several states were as weak as was then the case. Greek unity could come only from outside. Nothing could unite the Hellenes into a nation, except the fight against a common enemy. But why did Isocrates think the enemy was Persia, whose attack a hundred and fifty years earlier had made the Greeks forget their quarrels, and not Macedonia, which was the really imminent danger of the moment? The only real reason is the force of inertia. Isocrates was not blessed with a flow of original ideas, and he had been preaching the crusade against Persia for many, many years.[74] But his idea of evading the Macedonian danger by making Philip—enemy of the liberty of Athens and of all Greece —the predestined leader of the national war against Persia, was an unforgivable political blunder. It handed over Greece to her enemy with her hands tied. It elevated Philip to a position he was only too glad to assume, because it would do away with the moral objections some of the Greeks might have to his plans for dominating them. From this altitude, Isocrates could cry 'warmonger' against everyone who was reluctant to accept the encroachments of Macedonian power;[75] and the pro-Macedonians found it easy to make systematic propaganda out of Isocrates' Panhellenic slogan.

We must always remember the enormous part played by political warfare as preparation for Philip's military attacks on the Greeks. Of course, his policy was always to disguise it as self-defence. The actual military decision was meant to come as suddenly as possible, and finish everything with one stroke. The democracies, unprepared for war, were to have no time to improvise a stronger armament. Therefore, the work of undermining their strength and morale by agitation was long and well organized. Philip was sharp-sighted enough to see that a nation like the Greeks might very well allow itself to be conquered: for culture and liberty always entail disunity on the solution of vital questions. The masses were too short-sighted to look ahead to the correct answer. Demosthenes says a great deal about pro-Macedonian agitation in all the Greek cities. This systematic propaganda was the really new and subtle thing in Philip's military technique. Its outcome usually was that one of the quarrelling parties called in Philip to make peace. When we see how carefully Demosthenes chooses his point of attack in his speeches, we must realize that the main problem for him was this propaganda within Athens, cleverly and energetically carried on by his opponent in such a way as to twist all the threads and blur all the issues. Demosthenes' task was to convince not a small cabinet, but an apathetic and misguided people, whom blind or false leaders were trying to drug into insensibility with the soporific belief that it depended solely upon their own honest love of peace whether or not they would have to fight for their liberty and their life.

Demosthenes was not the sort of man to shrink from this new battle within his own lines. He now struck boldly out against the pundits of pacifism; and resumed his old efforts to break down first of all the isolationism of Athens.[76] Philip had disguised himself as the leader who would unify Greece. Demosthenes set out to unify the Greeks *against* Philip, and to summon them to defend their national independence. The speeches he made during the peace are a series of urgent efforts to set up his own Panhellenism against that of Isocrates, and to organize it as a real political force.[77] After the battle for the soul of Athens, he started to fight the battle for the soul of Hellas. The only way for Athens to escape being encircled, he cried, was to draw Philip's Greek allies away from him, and to step to the head of all the Greek states.[78] That and no less is Demosthenes' ideal. In the second *Philippic* he himself describes his efforts to detach the Peloponnesian states from Philip. At first he was unsuccessful.[79] They might have been won over to the Athenian side when they came and asked for an alliance. That was years before the struggle against Philip had grown so fierce: Demosthenes had openly supported the policy of gaining allies wherever possible, and advised the people not to repel all the other Peloponnesian states in order to maintain the almost worthless alliance with Sparta—which was the only reason for doing so.[80] Now, Athens had thrown them all into Philip's welcoming arms. Even Thebes, which would have been a weightier ally than Sparta, had been driven close to Philip by the Spartan and Athenian support of her enemies, the Phocians—closer even than her own interests dictated. As he says later, Demosthenes always thought it was poor policy to support the Phocians simply out of dislike for Thebes. Now the Phocian war had given Philip the opportunity to intervene in the politics of central Greece. The Phocians were crushed; and Athens could not, for many years, resume her friendship with Thebes.[81] It looked like the labour of Sisyphus to build up a Panhellenic front against Philip out of so many Greeks divided by such enmities. And yet, after years of effort, Demosthenes did it. His growth into the champion of Greek liberty is all the more astounding in that the Panhellenic ideal, even after it was proclaimed in rhetoric, sounded like a fairy tale. The man who carried this through was the same Demosthenes who, in his first speech on foreign policy, laid down the axiom, 'The interests of Athens are for me the basis of every decision on foreign policy'.[82] Then he had been a politician of the school of that clear-headed and strong-willed imperialist Callistratus. Now, by the time he had delivered the third *Philippic*, he had become a Panhellenic statesman. He thought it was Athens' greatest task to take over the leadership of the Greeks against Philip, mindful of the great national tradition of her previous policy.[83] His success in uniting most of the Greeks under this banner was described even by classical historians as an achievement of the highest statesmanship.

In those great speeches, *On the Chersonese* and the third *Philippic,* delivered shortly before the war began, Demosthenes grapples with the forces of doubt and despair, and reveals himself once again as a popular leader—just as he had been in the earlier *Philippics,* delivered before the peace of 346. But now the whole scene has changed. Then he was a solitary warrior, fighting for his own hand. Now he is the leading spirit of a movement which is sweeping all Greece. Then he was trying to arouse the Athenians. Now he is calling to all the Greeks to throw off their lethargy and fight for their lives. Philip's power spreads with overwhelming speed, while they stand inactive as if in a storm or some natural catastrophe which men only watch passively, feeling absolutely helpless, and hoping that the approaching hail will strike their neighbour's house instead of their own.[84] It is the task of the true leader to free the people's will from this crippling passivity and to save it from its evil counsellors, who are glad to betray it to the enemy, and serve the interests of Philip alone. The public likes listening to them, because they make no demands on it.[85] Demosthenes counts up the cities which Philip's fifth column has already handed over to him. Olynthus, Eretria, and Oreus now admit, 'If we had known this before, we should not have fallen. Now, it is too late'.[86] The ship must be saved while it is sound. When the waves have overpowered it, all effort is useless.[87] The Athenians themselves must *act.* Even if everyone else gives way, they must fight for freedom. They must provide money, ships, and men, and by their self-sacrifice carry the other Greeks along with them.[88] The petty greed of the masses and the corruption of the professional politicians must and shall give way to the heroic spirit of Greece, which once struck down the Persian invader.[89]

Many years before, Demosthenes had raised the question, which this comparison drives home again, whether the modern Athenians were not a degenerate race, unworthy to be named in the same breath as their great ancestors.[90] But he was not a historian or an ethnologist, interested solely in facts. Here as elsewhere he was, naturally and necessarily, a *teacher,* conscious of the educational duty he had to perform. He did not believe that the Athenian character was degenerating, although most of the symptoms looked unfavourable. He could never have borne to do what Plato did—to turn his back on the Athenian state, and

close the door on it, as on a patient dying of an incurable disease. Yet its conduct had become mean and petty. Surely its
spirit must be petty too?[91] How could it rise to finer thoughts
and higher daring? When Isocrates compared the present and
the past, he came to only one conclusion—that the past was dead
for ever. But Demosthenes as an active statesman could not take
that view, so long as a single wall of his fortress still stood and
could still be defended.[92] He simply used the early greatness of
Athens as a spur to get every ounce of strength out of his contemporaries.[93] But when he compared past and present, he did
not merely conclude that the Athenians of his own day *ought to*
rival their ancestors. He thought that they *must*.[94] However
broad and deep the gulf that separated to-day and yesterday,
Athens could not break away from her history without abandoning her own self. The greater the history of a people, the more
surely it becomes their destiny in their decline, and the more
tragic is their inability to escape their obligations even if it is
impossible to fulfil them.[95] Of course Demosthenes did not deceive himself purposely, and irresponsibly lead the Athenians
into a perilous venture. Yet we must ask ourselves whether the
urgency of the moment, which he saw better than any other
politician, really allowed him or anyone to practise that type of
politics which has been called 'the art of the possible'. He was
much more of a practical politician than most modern historians
have realized. But there must have been a very earnest debate
in his soul between the practical politician and the idealistic
statesman concerned with justice and moral obligation, on the
fundamental question whether it was right to risk the whole
existence of Athens and to ask her, with her limited strength,
to do the impossible. When he did ask her to give so much, he
was not making a wild romantic plea for a forlorn hope. He
knew very well that a nation, no less than an individual, can
make enormous and unimaginable efforts in a crisis of mortal
danger; and that the extent of its effort depends on how far it
is aware of its danger, and how much it really wishes to live.
This is a mystery of nature which not even the wisest statesman
can prognosticate. It is easy enough after the event to say that
the real statesmen were those who treated this problem as one
of simple arithmetic, and found it perfectly easy to refuse a
gamble which they were not impelled to undertake by faith in

their country, belief in its powers, and realization of the inevitability of fate. At that critical moment it was Demosthenes who gave urgent and splendid expression to the heroism of the city-state ideal. Look at the face of his statue, anxious, meditative, and furrowed with care. It is easy to see that he was not born to be a stalwart like Diomede or a paladin like Achilles; he was a man of his age. Surely that makes his fight all the more noble, because he made greater demands on his more sensitive nature and more subtle individuality.

Demosthenes could not refuse the challenge. He accepted it, fully aware of all it would mean. Thucydides had said that the Athenians could face danger only if they understood it, whereas others often rushed into dangers they did not comprehend.[96] Demosthenes followed that principle. He warned the Athenians that the war would not be like the Peloponnesian war, in which Athens confined herself to admitting the invading enemy to Attica, and watching him from behind the walls. The technique of war had improved since then. Athens would waste her effort if she waited till the enemy crossed her frontiers.[97] That is one of the main reasons why Demosthenes refused to 'wait and see'. He appealed not only to the Greeks but to the Persians; and since, directly after conquering Greece, the Macedonians went straight on to overthrow the Persian empire, the Persian indifference to the fate of Greece was crass blindness. Demosthenes thought his statesmanlike reasoning would be strong enough to make the Persian king realize what was in store for Persia if Philip beat the Greeks.[98] Perhaps it might have been, if he had visited Asia in person. But his envoys were unable to break down the Persian inertia.

Another of the problems which Demosthenes had to face was the social problem. Throughout his career, the gulf between rich and poor had been widening. He understood quite clearly that this division must not be allowed to interfere with the war for survival, for if it did, it would seriously diminish the efforts which could be made by every section of society. The fourth *Philippic* is his endeavour to bridge the gap, at least by finding some compromise to neutralize some of the ill-feeling that existed. It asks for sacrifices from both sides.[99] It shows how closely the solution of the social question depends on the people's will to defend itself against the aggressor. Perhaps the best evidence of Demosthenes' success is the self-sacrificing spirit which all the Athenians showed in the subsequent war.

The conflict went against the united Greeks. After the battle of Chaeronea in 338 the independence of the Greek city-states was destroyed. Even when they joined in an alliance to fight the last fight for liberty, the old states were unable to resist the organized military power of the king of Macedon. Their history now merged with that of the Macedonian empire, founded by Alexander on the ruins of the Persian dominion, by a fierce march of conquest through Asia after the sudden and violent death of Philip. A new and undreamt-of future opened up to Greek colonization, Greek science, and Greek commerce; and remained open even after Alexander's early death, when the empire broke up into the large monarchies of the Diadochoi, the Successors. But the old Greece was politically dead. Isocrates' dream of uniting all the Greeks under Macedonian leadership in a national war against the hereditary foe, Persia, actually came true. Death spared him the grief of realizing that the victory of a nation which had lost its independence, over an imaginary enemy, did not really mean an improvement in national morale; and that union imposed from without does not solve political disunity. During Alexander's expedition every true Greek would have far preferred to hear of the death of the new Achilles, than to pray to him, by supreme command, like a god. It is tragic to read how feverishly all the Greek patriots waited for that news to come through, how often they were disappointed, and how they raised premature revolts on false information. The Macedonian troops thrust down their rebellions in blood; and Demosthenes, believing that he and the Greeks had nothing left to hope for, found liberty in death.

But what would have happened if the Greeks had really succeeded in throwing off the Macedonian chains after Alexander's death? Even if they had won, they had no political future, either within or without foreign domination. The historical life of the city-state had come to an end, and no new artificial organization could replace it. It would be a mistake to judge its development by the standard of the modern nation-state. The fact is that the Greeks were unable to develop the feeling of nationhood, in the *political* sense, which would have enabled them to build up a nation-state—although in other senses they had plenty of national consciousness. In his *Politics* Aristotle declares that if the Greeks were united they could rule the world.[100] But that idea entered the Greek mind only as an abstract philosophical problem. Once, and once only after the Persian wars, in Demosthenes' final struggle for independence, did Greek national feeling rise up and take real political action, in common resistance to a foreign enemy. In that moment, when it was gathering its failing strength for the last time to defend its life and its ideal, the city-state was immortalized in the speeches of Demosthenes. The much admired and much abused power of political oratory, which is inseparable from the ideal it is put to uphold, rose once again in those speeches to the highest significance and value; and then fell away into nothing. Its last great fight was Demosthenes' wonderful speech *On the Crown*. That oration is not concerned with practical politics, but with the judgment of history on the personal character of the man who had led Athens throughout the critical years. It is wonderful to see Demosthenes still fighting for his ideals, almost with his last breath. It would be wrong to think of the speech as an effort to have the last word after the finger of history had written, and moved on. But his old enemies had crept out of their rat-holes and had tried to pass a final verdict on him in the name of history. He was forced to rise for the last time, and tell the Athenian people what he had tried to do, from the very outset, and what he had done. The struggle which we have witnessed in reading the *Philippics*—that heavy past, that growing danger, those hard decisions—all comes before us now once more as history, complete with its fateful end. Demosthenes is a tragic figure as he defends his own career; but he exhorts the Athenians not to wish that they had made any other decision except that which their history demanded of them.[101] The glory of Athens shines forth once more in his words, and ends in a music which, for all its bitterness, is harmonious.

NOTES

PAIDEIA III

I. GREEK MEDICINE AS PAIDEIA

1. See *Paideia* II, 32.

2. The best-known histories of medicine (for instance, those by Sprengel and Rosenbaum and by Hecker) show the same tendency to over-specialization: they do not examine the position of medical science within Greek culture, but treat it in isolation from its surroundings. Classical scholars working in the field have usually done the same kind of thing. (English readers will find a good introduction to the subject in Charles Singer's essay, *Medicine*, in the collection called *The Legacy of Greece*, edited by R. W. Livingstone, Oxford, 1923. See also W. Heidel, *Hippocratic Medicine*, New York, 1941.)

3. On the position of medicine in the Hellenistic cultural system, see F. Marx's prolegomena to his edition of Celsus, p. 8 f.

4. See, for example, Plato, *Prot.* 313d, *Gorg.* 450a and 517e, *Soph.* 226e and 228e, *Polit.* 289a; and especially *Gorg.* 464b. Many more instances could be given. On Herodicus' combination of the professions of doctor and athletic trainer, see Plato, *Rep.* 406a.

5. *Iliad* 11.514.

6. See p. 16 f. There was, however, a time when Greek medicine was considered to begin with Thales, in accordance with the doctrine of Celsus (1, prooem. 6) that the universal science, philosophy, originally contained all special sciences and was the mother of all technical inventions. But that doctrine was a romantic fiction created by Hellenistic historians of philosophy. To begin with, medicine was an entirely practical art; then it was influenced by the new natural philosophy worked out by Ionian theorists. It is with the reaction against that influence that extant Greek medical literature begins.

7. See J. H. Breasted, *The Edwin Smith Surgical Papyrus, published in Facsimile and Hieroglyphic Transliteration, with Translation and Commentary* (2 vols., Chicago 1930); and A. Rey, *La Science Orientale avant les Grecs* (Paris 1930) p. 314 f. For literature on the question whether Egyptian medicine at that stage was truly scientific, see M. Meyerhof, *Ueber den Papyrus Edwin Smith, das älteste Chirurgiebuch der Welt*, in *Deutsche Zeitschrift für Chirurgie* vol. 231 (1931), pp. 645-690.

8. Cf. *Paideia* I, p. 141 f.

9. *Paideia* I, p. 157, describes Anaximander's triadic system. Theories involving the number seven appear in the Hippocratic corpus in chap. 5 of *On hebdomads* and chaps. 12-13 of *On flesh*, and there is a systematic working out of the idea in Diocles of Carystus (frg. 177 Wellmann—a Latin excerpt from him preserved in Macrobius). See the more complete Greek parallel version of it to which I directed the attention of scholars in my *Vergessene Fragmente des Peripatetikers Diokles von Karystos* (*Abh. Berl. Akad.* 1938) pp. 17-36, with my remarks on the significance of the theory of temporal periods and the doctrine of numbers in the Greek view of nature.

10. Solon, frg. 14.6, 19.9. On the idea of the Suitable (ἁρμόττον) in medical literature, see p. 42 of this book and my *Diokles von Karystos, Die griechische Medizin und die Schule des Aristoteles* (Berlin 1938) p. 47 f.

11. The words τιμωρία and τιμωρεῖν occur, for instance, in Hipp. *On regimen in acute illness* 15, 17, and 18. Galen, commenting on these passages, and Erotian

s.v. τιμωρέουσα explain that they mean the same as βοήθεια and βοηθεῖν. This is obviously right; but, equally obviously, the idea is connected with some of the old concepts of natural philosophy, like δίκη, τίσις, and ἀμοιβή. Causality in nature was explained, by analogy with legal processes, as retribution (see *Paideia* I, p. 159 f.). 'One must strive to help (τιμωρεῖν) that which is wronged,' says Democritus, frg. 261. And βοηθεῖν too has a juristic meaning, as we now know.

11a. In chap. 12 of *On airs, waters, and places,* the essence of health is described as the rule of equality (*isomoiria*) and the absence of domination by one force; see also *On ancient medicine* 14.

12. *Paideia* I, p. 306 f.

13. *Paideia* I, p. 389; Thucydides' medical conception of causation, ib. p. 392; his quasi-medical attitude to history, ib. p. 399 f.

13a. *On the divine disease* 1 and 21.

14. L. Edelstein, on p. 117 f. of his Περὶ ἀέρων *und die Sammlung der hippokratischen Schriften* (Berlin 1931), points out that Plato and Aristotle did not consider Hippocrates to be an infallible authority, as he had come to be by the time of Galen. But he seems to me to have gone too far in the other direction, with his subtle but rather far-fetched attempt to prove that the well-known passages in Plato (*Prot.* 311b-c, *Phaedr.* 270c) and Aristotle (*Pol.* 7.4.1326a15) express great respect for Hippocrates, but do not place him any higher than other doctors. There can really be no doubt that both Plato and Aristotle considered him to be *the* typical doctor, the embodiment of the art of medicine.

15. The latest systematic attempt to determine which of the works in the Corpus should be ascribed to the Hippocratic circle and were written by men who belonged to the first generations of the school is K. Deichgräber's *Die Epidemien und das Corpus Hippocraticum (Abh. Berl. Akad.* 1933). The author bases his work on the passages in *Visits* to which a date can be assigned, but he does not venture to assign any particular treatise to Hippocrates himself. With care, this method of approach will lead to relatively definite results. What is most needed at present is an analysis and explanation of the style and intellectual form of the Hippocratic works which are extant; and hardly any attempt to provide one has yet been made.

16. Within scientific and philosophical schools, teaching and the writing of books were tasks in which many shared at once: see my *Studien zur Entstehungsgeschichte der Metaphysik des Aristoteles* (Berlin 1912) p. 141 f., and H. Alline, *Histoire du texte de Platon* (Paris 1915) p. 36 f. We must not think that the Hippocratic corpus contains *forged* works, to which the name of a distinguished author has been added with the deliberate intention to deceive—despite the assertions of M. Wellmann in *Hermes* 61.332; see note 19.

17. See the 'oath' in the *Corpus Medicorum Graecorum* (=CMG) 1.1.4.

18. Aristotle, *Hist. An.* 3.3.512b12-513a7; cf. Hipp. *On the nature of man* 11. The fact that that chapter is identical with the excerpts from Polybus given by Aristotle has led most modern scholars to ascribe the whole of the Hippocratic treatise *On the nature of man* to Polybus. Students of Hippocrates in ancient times were divided in their views of this question. Galen, in his commentary on the treatise (CMG 5.9.1), p. 7 f., says that chapters 1 to 8 are by Hippocrates himself: his reason is that the theory of the four humours put forward there is the mark of Hippocrates' own work. But he refuses to ascribe the rest of the treatise to anyone so closely associated with Hippocrates as Polybus was. Sabinus and most of the ancient commentators think Polybus was its author. (See Galen, loc. cit. 87.)

19. See *On diet in acute illness* 1: the author mentions a new and improved edition of the Cnidian doctrines (Κνίδιαι γνῶμαι). His actual words are οἱ ὕστερον διασκευάσαντες, which means that, like *Visits*, the work was produced not by one man but by a school.

20. See J. Ilberg, *Die Aerzteschule von Knidos* (*Ber. Sächs. Akad.* 1924); and more recently L. Edelstein, on p. 154 of the work quoted in note 14 (he tries to show that there are far fewer 'Cnidian' works in the Hippocratic corpus than had been believed). See also M. Wellmann, *Die Fragmente der sikelischen Aerzte* (Berlin 1902), who makes the mistake of attributing Diocles also to the Sicilian school; and against him my own *Diokles von Karystos* (Berlin 1938).

21. For ἰδιώτης ('layman') see *On regimen in health* 1, *On affections* 1, 33, 45, and *On diet* 3.68. Δημότης and δημιουργός are contrasted in *On breaths* 1, *On ancient medicine* 1-2. Ἰδιώτης and δημότης are synonyms in *On ancient medicine* 2 and *On diet in acute illness* 6; χειρῶναξ appears in chap. 8 of the same work. Aeschylus in *Prom.* 45 calls the blacksmith's craft χειρωναξία.

22. CMG 1.1.8.

23. We must distinguish between the speeches of medical lecturers on general topics, in rhetorical prose (such as *On the art* and *On breaths*), and works written in a simple factual style but also addressed to the general public (such as *On ancient medicine, On the divine disease,* and *On the nature of man*). The four-book treatise *On diet* is likewise a literary work. The purpose of such books was both to instruct the lay public and to advertise their authors: as was necessary in Greece, where the medical profession had received no official recognition from the state. See *On ancient medicine* 1 and 12, *On the art* 1, *On diet in acute illness* 8.

23a. Plato, *Laws* 857c-d: οὐκ ἰατρεύεις τὸν νοσοῦντα, ἀλλὰ σχεδὸν παιδεύεις. Cf. *Laws* 720c-d, where Plato gives a similar description of the two types.

24. *On ancient medicine* 2; another example in *On affections* 1. See p. 32.

25. Plato, *Symp.* 186a-188e.

26. Xen. *Mem.* 4.2.8-10.

27. Thuc. 2.48.3.

28. Arist. *Part. An.* 1.1.639a1.

29. Arist. *Pol.* 3.11.1282a1-7.

30. Cf. *Paideia* I, p. 319 f.

31. Plato, *Prot.* 312a, 315a.

32. Xen. *Mem.* 4.2.10.

33. Xen. *Mem.* 4.2.1: Τοῖς δὲ νομίζουσι παιδείας τε τῆς ἀρίστης τετυχηκέναι καὶ μέγα φρονοῦσιν ἐπὶ σοφίᾳ ὡς προσεφέρετο νῦν διηγήσομαι. Xenophon imagines Euthydemus as typifying the contemporary endeavour to acquire a new and higher kind of culture, whose essence was not yet revealed. Of course we must distinguish that culture from the paideia of Socrates himself.

34. Arist. *Pol.* 8.2.1337b15: Ἔστι δὲ καὶ τῶν ἐλευθερίων ἐπιστημῶν μέχρι μὲν τινος μετέχειν οὐκ ἀνελεύθερον, τὸ δὲ προσεδρεύειν λίαν πρὸς ἀκρίβειαν ἔνοχον ταῖς εἰρημέναις βλάβαις. Cf. what he says in 1337b8 on the effect of 'banausic work'.

35. *On ancient medicine* 1 f. and 12.

36. Ib. 5 f. and 8.

37. Ib. 4, and the end of 5.

38. Ib. 8-9.

39. Ib. 9: Δεῖ γὰρ μέτρου τινὸς στοχάσασθαι· μέτρον δὲ οὔτε ἀριθμὸν οὔτε σταθμὸν ἄλλον πρὸς ὃ ἀναφέρων εἴσῃ τὸ ἀκριβές, οὐκ ἂν εὕροις ἀλλ' ἢ τοῦ σώματος τὴν αἴσθησιν. In the same passage the doctor is compared with the pilot.

40. Cf. *On ancient medicine* 20. Some writers on the subject are addicted to the false idea that this polemic is directed against Empedocles and his school in particular. Anaxagoras or Diogenes might just as well have been its object. The word φιλοσοφίη ('intellectual work', 'study') was not yet clearly defined, and Empedocles' name is used in order to make it clearer: in just the same way Aristotle (*Protr.* frg. 5b Walzer, 52 Rose) explains the concept 'metaphysics', for which there was so far no special word, by naming its best-known representatives. 'That kind of search for truth (ἀληθείας φρόνησις) which was practised by Anaxagoras and Parmenides', he says. It is important to establish this if we are to build up a correct history of the concept 'philosophy': constant attempts are made to date its origin back to the times of Herodotus, Heraclitus, and even Pythagoras. The author of *On ancient medicine* goes on to say 'By this' (i.e., by philosophy à l'Empedocles) 'I mean that type of research (ἱστορίη) which teaches what man is and what are his origins', etc.

41. *On ancient medicine* 20.

42. Ib. 20.

43. Hence the title 'Επιδημίαι—'Visits to foreign cities'. It was not only sophists and littérateurs whose careers consisted in visiting foreign cities (ἐπιδημεῖν) ; cf. Plato, *Prot.* 309d and 315c, *Parm.* 127a, and the autobiographical work by the poet Ion of Chios, which was also called 'Επιδημίαι. Wandering physicians did the same—cf. *On airs, waters, and places* 1. The authors of the Hippocratic 'Επιδημίαι are intellectual allies of the man who wrote *On ancient medicine,* although he is probably not identical with any one of them.

44. *Aphorisms* 1.1. Demetrius *On style* 4 quotes this famous sentence as a pattern of the dry, jerky style, whose ethos can be appreciated only because of its content.

45. The occurrences of the concepts *eidos* (which appears very often in the plural) and *idea* in the Hippocratic writings have been investigated by A. E. Taylor, *Varia Socratica* 178-267, and others. Cf. more recently G. Else, *The Terminology of the Ideas* (Harvard Studies in Classical Philology, 1936).

46. Cf. chap. 12, εἴδεα, and chap. 23 εἴδεα σχημάτων, etc.

47. See the end of chap. 15: heat has not the great force (δύναμις) which is ascribed to it; and the second part of chap. 14: the forces which work in the body, their number, kind, right mixture, and disturbances.

48. Alcmaeon frg. 4 Diels.

49. This is proved by his doctrine that there is an 'infinite number' of forces active in the body. See his polemic in chap. 15 against the contemporary habit of isolating and hypostasizing the qualities heat, cold, dryness, and moisture.

50. Plato, *Gorg.* 464b and following, esp. 465a; 501a f. See *Paideia* II, 131 and 148.

51. Plato, *Phaedr.* 270c-d; W. Capelle lists the earlier literature on this passage in *Hermes* 57, p. 247. I cannot here discuss the last treatment of this problem, L. Edelstein's book cited in note 14 of this chapter, although I do not believe it is always correct.

52. C. Ritter, *Neue Untersuchungen über Platon* (Munich 1910) p. 228 f.

53. See *On diet in acute illness* 3, where the author says that physicians in the Cnidian medical school had emphasized the multiplicity (πολυσχιδίη) of diseases and tried to establish the exact number of forms in which each appeared, but had been misled by varieties in their names. He also says that it is necessary to reduce the several forms of a disease to one *eidos.* The author of *On breaths,* in chap. 2, goes to the extreme: he denies the manifold character (πολυτροπίη) of diseases, and asserts that there is only one τρόπος, which, however, is differentiated into many forms of disease according to differences in its τόπος.

53a. There is another problem which interests both Plato and the early physicians. In chap. 15 of *On ancient medicine* the writer says that in reality there is no such thing as Heat, Cold, Dryness, or Moisture in isolation, having no relation to any other eidos (μηδενὶ ἄλλῳ εἴδει κοινωνέον). Cf. Plato, *Soph.* 257a f., who also speaks of a κοινωνία between γένη or εἴδη (cf. 259e).

53b. E.g. Plato, *Polit.* 299c; Arist. *Eth. Nic.* 2.2.1104a9, 3.5.1112b5; *On ancient medicine,* the second half of chap. 9.

53c. Arist. *Eth. Nic.* 10.10.1180b7.

53d. Plato, *Phil.* 34e-35b, 35e f.

53e. Arist. *Eth. Nic.* 2.5.1106a26-32, b15, b27. Cf. *On ancient medicine* 9, quoted above, in note 39.

54. There are other echoes of this passage from *On ancient medicine* in fourth-century medical literature: see Diocles of Carystus, frg. 138 Wellmann, and the polemic in *On diet* 1.2 (Littré vol. vi, p. 470, second half). The writer of that passage denies that a general rule can ever be applied with any accuracy to the patient's individual nature: in that he sees the inevitable weakness of all the physician's art.

55. See *Paideia* ii, 44, 145 f.

56. Plato, *Phaedrus* 270c-d; see p. 22.

57. Plato, *Phaedo* 96a f.

58. This is true not only of books about Greek medicine, but even of W. Theiler's valuable and illuminating book, *Geschichte der teleologischen Naturbetrachtung bis auf Aristoteles* (Zurich 1925). Theiler deals almost exclusively with philosophers; he gives only a few parallels from the Hippocratic corpus, and these, along with a reference to Erasistratus (appendix, p. 102), are all his allusions to medical science. His chief interest is in the comparison of nature to deliberate art; but he ought to have paid serious attention to the Hippocratic doctrine that nature has an unconscious purposefulness. That was the kind of teleology which became most important for modern science, even though the word *telos* was not yet used for it. A tendency to a fairer estimate of this aspect of Hippocratic medicine is shown in A. Biers' *Beiträge zür Heilkunde (Münchener Medizinische Wochenschrift* 1931, no. 9 f.).

58a. T. Gomperz, *Griechische Denker* i (4th edition) p. 261, who was the first to give the physicians their rightful place in the development of Greek philosophy, was nevertheless a typical positivist in his attitude to them. This is shown by the fact that he treats Hippocrates and Democritus in close connexion; to support this, he appealed to the fictitious correspondence of these men, which was forged in a later age in order to connect them somehow.

59. Cf. *On ancient medicine,* the end of chap. 5; chap. 9; *On diet* 3.69; and the dietetic treatises generally.

60. See *On ancient medicine* chap. 14 (the second part); *On airs, waters, and places* 12; *On the nature of man* 4. ἀκρασίη appears in *On the parts of man* 26 and elsewhere; the concept of harmony is mentioned in *On diet* 1.8-9. See my *Diokles von Karystos* 47 f., on ἁρμόττον, μέτριον, σύμμετρον.

61. Plato, *Phaedo* 93e, *Laws* 773a, *Gorg.* 504c means the same thing by defining health as the proper order (τάξις) of the body. See also Aristotle, frg. 7 Walzer, p. 16 (45 Rose), on symmetry as the origin and cause of health, strength, and beauty in the body.

62. See, for instance, *On diet in acute illness* 15 and 57.

63. When Heraclitus compares the psyché hastening to the injured part of the body with the spider hastening to the part of the web which has been injured by the fly (frg. 67a), he reminds us of the Hippocratic idea that nature hastens to help (βοηθεῖ) against illness. The passage sounds more like a medical idea than a Heraclitean aphorism.

64. See my *Aristotle,* p. 74.

65. See Theiler's book (cited in note 58), p. 13 f.; he tries to trace all ideas of this type back to Diogenes.

66. Theiler, p. 52, quotes an example from this treatise; the whole tone and content of the work show that it was inspired by the teleological way of thinking.

67. *On diet* 1.11.

68. *On diet* 1.15.

68a. *Visits* 6.5.1: νούσων φύσιες ἰητροί.

69. Diog. Apoll. frg. 5 Diels. See also frg. 7 and 8.

70. *On food* 39: φύσιες πάντων ἀδίδακτοι.

71. Epicharmus frg. 4 Diels:

τὸ δὲ σοφὸν ἁ φύσις τόδ' οἶδεν ὡς ἔχει
μόνα· πεπαίδευται γὰρ αὐταύτας ὕπο.

The author is talking of the way in which the hen hatches out its eggs; he says it is an example of the natural reasoning power in all living things. If authentic, this would be, if not the earliest occurrence of παιδεία, scarcely later than Aeschylus, *Sept.* 18 (see *Paideia* I, 286). But in Aeschylus the word means only παίδων τροφή: in Epicharmus it has the sense of 'higher culture' which it acquired through the teaching of the sophists, especially in the fourth century. Diels lists the fragment among the few which are not suspected of belonging to one of the collections of forged proverbs attributed to Epicharmus. But, as far as we can judge from the history of the word *paideia* as we have worked it out, this fragment is just as much of a forgery as the rest.

72. See *Paideia* I, 312 f. An early echo of that sophistic comparison between paideia and agriculture is found in Hipp. *Law* 3, where the comparison is transferred to medical education in particular; there is another in Plato *Tim.* 77a—Plato wittily reverses the comparison, and describes agriculture as the paideia of nature.

73. *Visits* 6.5.5. Deichgräber (quoted in note 15) interprets the sentence as meaning 'The soul's wandering (within the body appears) to men (to be) thought.' But ψυχῆς περίπατος φροντὶς ἀνθρώποισι cannot mean that. In *On diet* 2.61 too, thought (μέριμνα) is counted as an 'exercise'. What is really new in this is that the idea of exercise is extended from the body to the soul.

74. *On food* 15.

75. Littré VI, 72.

76. See the elaborate prescriptions for gymnastic exercise in *On regimen in health* 7.

77. *On diet* I (Littré VI, 466).

78. The most important book in this field is C. Fredrich's *Hippokratische Untersuchungen* (*Philologische Untersuchungen,* ed. by Kiessling and Wilamowitz, 15, Berlin, 1899): see p. 81 f., and p. 90 for the earlier work on the subject. Fredrich's book strikes out many new lines, but is too mechanical in its method of analysing sources.

79. He sets out to give a description of the effects of all drinks, all foods, and all exercises, so that the doctor's prescription can be suited to every type of special situation. The sharp distinction between what is general (κατὰ παντός) and what is special (καθ' ἕκαστον) is characteristic of the author's method: see his remarks on the principle, in 2.37 and 2.39. A doctor who was so determined to avoid broad general statements and to concentrate on particulars could not possibly be accused of vague generalization by the author of *On ancient medicine.* This doctrine of κατὰ παντός and καθόλου in logic was worked out more elaborately by Aristotle: an important fact in judging the probable date when *On diet* was written.

80. *On diet* 1.2 (at the beginning). This seems to be an answer to *On ancient medicine* 20, which expressly rejects that philosophical method of research (ἱστορίη).

81. Characteristically, the author of *On ancient medicine* says that medicine originated in the development of invalid diet.

82. *On diet* 1.2 (Littré VI, 470).

82a. On Herodicus see Plato, *Rep.* 406a-b; Arist. *Rhet.* 1.5.1361b5; Hipp. *Visits* 6.3.18.

83. Cf. *On diet* 1.2 (Littré VI, 470).

84. Ib.

85. *On diet* 1.2 (Littré VI, 472); this passage also contains the new idea of 'prodiagnosis'. Prophylaxis is a later word, but it is a good description for the thing this writer is trying to achieve. He wants to unite prodiagnosis and prophylaxis.

86. See p. 19. *On diet* 2.51 alludes to *On ancient medicine* 20.

87. *On diet* 1.2 (Littré VI, 470); and see *On airs, waters, and places* 1-2. There, as in the author of *On diet,* we find the following factors treated in order: the seasons, the winds, the city's position, the diseases to be expected in summer and in winter, the risings and settings of stars, the alternation of diseases. The only thing left out in *On diet* is the character of the water-supply.

88. *Visits* 6.5.5.

89. *On diet* 2.61.

90. *On diet* 2.65 (at the end).

91. Diocles, frg. 147 and 141 Wellmann.

92. See my *Diokles von Karystos,* p. 67 f.

92a. See his remarks on the subject, *On diet* 1.1.

93. See R. Burckhardt's *Das koische Tiersystem, eine Vorstufe der zoologischen Systematik des Aristoteles* (*Verhandlungen der Naturforschenden Gesellschaft in Basel,* 15, 1904), p. 377 f.

94. The latest writer to prove that *On diet* does not belong to the Coan school is A. Palm, in *Studien zur hippokratischen Schrift* Περὶ διαίτης (Tübingen 1933); see p. 7. However, he still believes that the work is comparatively early in origin.

95. Epicrates, frg. 287 Kock.

95a. On this man, see M. Wellmann, *Fragmente der sikelischen Aerzte,* p. 69, and my *Aristotle,* pp. 17-20.

96. See A. Palm, p. 8 f. of the book quoted in note 94: he has not studied the botanical knowledge displayed by the author of *On diet* in this connexion.

97. See p. 22.

98. The passages are collected in Littré, *Oeuvres d'Hippocrate* X, 479.

98a. See A. Palm (quoted in note 94), p. 43 f.

99. On Eudoxus, see my *Aristotle,* pp. 17 and 131 f. Ctesias was the court physician of King Artaxerxes in and after 403 (cf. Xen. *Anab.* 1.8): he wrote his works in the fourth century.

100. See my *Aristotle,* pp. 39 and 162, and especially note 1 on p. 162.

100a. *On diet* 4.1. See Pindar frg. 131 and Aristotle, frg. 10 Rose (and, on it, my *Aristotle,* p. 162, note 1).

101. *On diet* 1.1.

102. The fragments of this important physician's extensive works are collected in M. Wellmann's *Die Fragmente der sikelischen Aerzte* (Berlin 1901) p. 117 f.: they compose the chief part of what Wellmann describes as the Sicilian school. In my *Diokles von Karystos, Die griechische Medizin und die Schule des Aristoteles* (Berlin 1938) I have shown that Diocles, although influenced by the doctrine of the Sicilian medical school, was neither directly connected with it nor contemporary with it.

103. See p. 14 of my *Diokles*.

104. In my book on Diocles, pp. 16-69, there is an elaborate proof of the linguistic and scientific influence of Aristotle on Diocles; see also my essay *Vergessene Fragmente des Peripatetikers Diokles von Karystos* (cited in note 9), which deals in some detail with Diocles' relation to Theophrastus and Strato, on pp. 5 and 10 f.

105. Frg. 141 Wellmann.

105a. For a description of the intellectual principles on which Diocles based his medical work, see (in my *Diokles von Karystos*) the following sections: *Das grosse Methodenfragment* (p. 25), ἀρχαὶ ἀναπόδεικτοι (p. 37), *Diokles' Diätlehre und aristotelische Ethik* (p. 45), *Diokles und die aristotelische Teleologie* (p. 51).

106. See my quotations, on p. 48 of *Diokles von Karystos*.

107. Cf. p. 50 of *Diokles von Karystos*.

108. Cf. frg. 112 (Wellmann) of Diocles, and my exhaustive treatment of the passage dealing with method, in *Diokles von Karystos*, pp. 25-45.

109. On what follows, see Diocles, frg. 141 Wellmann.

110. See p. 37.

111. On these social assumptions in Greek medicine, see Edelstein, in volume VII of *Die Antike*. Cf. *On diet* 3.69, and the beginning of 3.68.

2. THE RHETORIC OF ISOCRATES AND ITS CULTURAL IDEAL

1. There is a full account of the history of this conflict in H. von Arnim's *Leben und Werke des Dion von Prusa* (Berlin 1898) pp. 4-114.

2. See, for instance, a work by Drerup's pupil Burk, *Die Pädagogik des Isokrates als Grundlegung des humanistischen Bildungsideals* (Würzburg 1923), and in particular the two sections called *Das Nachleben der Pädagogik des Isokrates* (p. 199 f.) and *Isokrates und der Humanismus* (p. 211 f.). More recently Drerup himself has brought out four lectures entitled *Der Humanismus in seiner Geschichte, seinen Kulturwerten und seiner Vorbereitung im Unterrichtswesen der Griechen* (Paderborn 1934). British scholars like Burnet and Ernest Barker often call Isocrates the father of humanism.

3. Some critics have laid down that a historian of paideia must begin by giving his own definition of it. That is rather as if they expected a historian of philosophy to start either from Plato's definition of philosophy, or from Epicurus', or from Kant's or Hume's—all four being widely different. A history of paideia should describe as accurately as possible all the different meanings of Greek paideia, the various forms which it took, and the various spiritual levels at which it appeared, and should explain both their individual peculiarities and their historical connexions.

4. On this see my essay, *Platos Stellung im Aufbau der griechischen Bildung* (Berlin 1928), which first appeared in *Die Antike,* vol. 4 (1928), nos. 1-2.

5. From this point of view philosophy, and Greek philosophy in particular, has played a decisive role in the development of modern humanism, which would have had no impetus without it, and would not even have been able to expound its own aims. Actually, the study of the philosophical aspects of classical civilization has become more and more important not only in modern philosophy but in modern philology too, and has deeply influenced the purposes and methods of classical scholarship. But, seen from the same point of view, the history of humanism itself takes on a new appearance. Historians usually speak of two sharply contrasting periods—the Middle Ages and the Renaissance, scholasticism

and humanism. But this simple pattern is shown to be an over-simplification as soon as we realize that the rebirth of Greek philosophy in the Middle Ages was really another great epoch in the uninterrupted influence of Greek paideia. That influence never died away entirely, but lived on continuously through mediaeval and modern history. *Non datur saltus in historia·humanitatis.*

6. It is impossible to appreciate the part played by philosophy within the organic structure of Greek civilization without being fully alive to its close connexion with the internal and external history of Greece.

7. See note 1.

8. Plato wrote *Protagoras* and *Gorgias* as early as the first decade of the fourth century. Isocrates cannot have founded his school before 390, because in his extant orations we can trace his work as a hired writer of forensic speeches down to that date at least; perhaps it lasted even into the 'eighties.

9. The facts of Isocrates' life are thoroughly examined by Blass in the second section of *Die attische Beredsamkeit* (2nd ed., Leipzig 1892); see p. 11 of that book for the traditions about his teachers. On the tombstone, see pseudo-Plutarch, *vit. X orat.* 838d; the author of those biographies took his archaeological and antiquarian data from a work by the Hellenistic epigraphist Diodorus.

10. It is impossible to set a definite date for Isocrates' stay in Thessaly, but it must have been either just before or just after 410.

11. Plato, *Meno* 70b; and cf. Isoc. *Antid.* 155.

12. He calls it ἡ τῶν λόγων μελέτη, or παιδεία, or ἐπιμέλεια. Blass, on p. 107 of the work cited in note 9, suggests that he avoids calling it a τέχνη: probably to avoid being confused with the writers of technai, or rhetorical handbooks. But passages like *Soph.* 9-10 and *Antid.* 178 are enough to show that he held his φιλοσοφία to be a τέχνη.

13. It is unnecessary to prove this point by enumerating all the relevant passages. In *Antid.* 270 he claims the title φιλοσοφία for his own work alone, and says that other teachers (e.g. dialecticians, mathematicians, and rhetorical 'technographers') have no right to use it. He is less exclusive in his earlier works, where he speaks freely of the φιλοσοφία of the professional disputers or eristics (*Hel.* 6) and of teachers of rhetoric like Polycrates (*Bus.* 1); and in *Soph.* 1 he uses it as a general description of all the branches of higher education and culture which are characterized in that work.

14. Thuc. 2.40.1.

15. *Paneg.* 47. The word καταδεῖξαι describes the act of the founder of a cult. In this place the word φιλοσοφία does *not* mean 'philosophy'.

16. Blass (p. 28 of the book quoted in note 9) points out that in Isocrates' time the word 'philosophy' still meant 'culture', so that there is nothing silly about his claim to 'teach philosophy'; however, he says it is arrogant of Isocrates to pretend to be the only representative of true philosophy—i.e. true culture. Still, Plato and all the other schools and teachers made the same claim: see Plato *ep.* 7. 326a, *Rep.* 490a, etc.

17. Plato, *Prot.* 313c f.

18. It is difficult to tell how much historical truth there is in that passage of Plato's *Phaedrus* where Socrates is made to prophesy a great future for Isocrates. Perhaps the two had met at some time, and there is no more in it than that. It can hardly mean that Isocrates was Socrates' friend, still less his pupil. And yet his works show many traces of the influence of Socratic ideas. The fullest examination of them is H. Gomperz' *Isokrates und die Sokratik* (*Wiener Studien* 27, 1905, p. 163, and 28, 1906, p. 1). He assumes, correctly, that Isocrates got his knowledge of these ideas from books about Socrates; and this is supported by the fact that he did not begin to talk about them till the years between 390 and 380,

when he himself first entered the field of educational theory. Still, I think Gomperz exaggerates the influence of Antisthenes upon Isocrates.

19. For the facts of Isocrates' life, see Blass (cited in note 9) p. 8 f.; Jebb, *Attic Orators* (London 1876) II, p. 1 f.; and Münscher's exhaustive article in Pauly-Wissowa's *Realenzyklopädie der klass. Altertumswiss.* 9.2150 f. On his weak voice and his timidity, see *Phil.* 81, *Panath.* 10.

20. In *Phil.* 81-82 he admits his physical and psychical weakness, but nevertheless claims to be far ahead of others in phronesis and paideia.

21. That is the role which he assigns to Athens in the *Panegyricus.* Even after the collapse of the second naval confederacy, he continued to maintain the spiritual leadership of Athens—for instance in the *Antidosis* and the *Panathenaicus.* But he later (as in the *Peace* speech and *Philip*) abandoned the claim that Athens should likewise wield the political hegemony of Greece.

22. Thuc. 3.82.

23. Plato, *Rep.* 591e; see *Paideia* II, 353 f.

24. See *Paideia* II, 131 f.

25. In the speech *Against the sophists,* Isocrates draws a contrast between these two extreme types of contemporary paideia.

26. Cf. Plato, *Gorg.* 449d, 451a, 453b-e, 455d. Later he repeated the charge in *Phaedrus.*

27. Isocrates' 'speeches' were never delivered as such. Their oratorical form is a pure fiction.

28. On his work as a logographer, see Dion. Hal. *de Isocr.* 18, and Cicero, *Brutus* 28 (whose source is Aristotle's συναγωγὴ τεχνῶν). He mentions the destruction of his father's property, in *Antid.* 161.

29. Cf. Dion. Hal. *de Isocr.* 18.

30. According to Dion. Hal. *de Isocr.* 18, Isocrates' stepson Aphareus said, in his speech against Megacleides, that his stepfather had *never* written forensic speeches; but that can only mean never since he became the head of a school. His pupil Cephisodorus admitted that there were some such speeches by him in existence, but said only a few were authentic.

31. The *Trapeziticus* and *Aegineticus* can be dated roughly to 390.

32. There is no confirmation for the statement of pseudo-Plutarch, *vit. X orat.* 837b, that Isocrates first had a school in Chios (σχολῆς δὲ ἡγεῖτο, ὥς τινές φασιν, πρῶτον ἐπὶ Χίου). And ἐπὶ Χίου is an uncommon way to say ἐν Χίῳ. What we should expect, following ἐπὶ, is the name of the archon in whose time Isocrates began to teach; but if Χίου is a corruption of that name, it is difficult to emend. None of the archons in the 'nineties or early 'eighties has a name like χίου. If it were <Μυστι>χίδου that would take us down to 386-385, which is a very late date for the foundation of Isocrates' school.

32a. Isocrates himself, in *Antid.* 193, says that the speech *Against the sophists* belongs to the beginning of his teaching career. There is a list of the many works which deal with his relation to Plato, in Münscher's article in Pauly-Wissowa 9.2171. Unfortunately, many of them are obsolete, since the assumption on which they are based is false—the assumption that Plato's chief dialogue on rhetoric, *Phaedrus,* was written in his youth or middle life. Münscher's article, which is otherwise an admirable introduction to the subject, still goes on the same assumption. Modern scholars have revised their views on this point. (About the late date of *Phaedrus,* see p. 330, n. 5 f.) On the other hand, I think it is impossible to follow Wilamowitz (*Platon* II, 108) and avoid the conclusion that *Against the sophists* attacks Plato just as violently as the other Socratics. It assumes knowledge of Plato's *Protagoras, Gorgias,* and perhaps *Meno* too (see my discussion of the problem on pp. 56 and 66). Münscher's belief, that when Isocrates wrote the speech he still 'felt himself in agreement with Plato' in everything essential, cannot be backed up by anything in the speech, and is actually contradicted by every line of it. The sole basis for that belief is the early dating of *Phaedrus*, in which Plato is clearly more friendly to Isocrates than to rhetors like Lysias. The assumption that it was written before or soon after *Against the sophists* would compel us to make a forced interpretation of that speech as expressing friendship for Plato.

33. Isocr. *Soph.* 1.

34. Of course the word 'philosopher' is not confined to those representatives of paideia whom we should call philosophers to-day—the Socratic circle. It includes all sorts of professed teachers of culture (see *Soph.* 11 and 18). But it does include philosophers in the strict sense, as we can see from *Soph.* 2, where Isocrates ridicules their claim to teach 'truth'. That is aimed at *all* the Socratics, not merely (as some have held) at Antisthenes' book *Truth*.

35. *Soph.* 1: οἱ περὶ τὰς ἔριδας διατρίβοντες οἳ προσποιοῦνται τὴν ἀλήθειαν ζητεῖν; *Antid.* 261: οἱ ἐν τοῖς ἐριστικοῖς λόγοις δυναστεύοντες. In the latter passage the 'disputers' are put in the same class as teachers of geometry and astronomy—both subjects which were taught in Plato's Academy. Münscher's illogical assumption that in the later speech on the Antidosis Isocrates means his readers to think chiefly of Plato when he mentions disputers, but does not in the speech on the sophists, is based on the early dating of *Phaedrus* and the inference that Isocrates and the young Plato were friendly (see note 32a).

36. Most probably it was because Plato found his dialectic being confused with eristic, as in Isocrates' attacks on it, that he distinguished Socrates so sharply and clearly from the eristics in *Euthydemus*. In *Rep.* 499a he repeats his complaint that no one knows the true philosopher, and he tries to vindicate him from confusion with mere disputers. There he describes him as a man who finds no pleasure in clever but useless arguments, and seeks 'knowledge for its own sake'.

37. At several points Protagoras refuses to agree with the logical conclusions reached by Socrates, and he obviously thinks his opponent is trying to trap him. Plato describes this in a perfectly objective way, and thereby shows how easy it was for Socrates' dialectic to be called eristic. In the same way Callicles (Plato, *Gorg.* 482e f.) objects to Socrates' trick of giving different meanings to the same concept in the same argument. On this, see *Paideia* II, 138.

38. *Soph.* 2.

39. *Soph.* 2-4.

40. Plato contrasts 'universal virtue' and 'special virtues' like justice, courage, self-control, etc. Sometimes he calls the former 'virtue in itself' (αὐτὴ ἡ ἀρετή)—a kind of expression new and strange to his contemporaries. In c. 20 also, Isocrates emphasizes the ethical element in the paideia of the 'disputers'; they assert that virtue can be taught (21), which Isocrates and all the sophists violently deny. See Plato's *Protagoras*.

41. *Soph.* 5.

42. Cf. Plato, *Gorg.* 456e-457c, 460d-461a.

43. In *Antid.* 215 f., Isocrates tries to defend teachers of rhetoric against the charge that their pupils learn evil from them. See also *Nic.* 2 f.

44. This is the most probable view of the dates at which the two works were written. *Gorgias* is now generally believed, on convincing grounds, to have been written between 395 and 390 B.C.; but Isocrates had scarcely opened his school at that time, since we can trace his work as a logographer down to 390. Therefore the speech *Against the sophists*, which gives his programme, was written in the 'eighties. Some scholars have attempted to fix the chronological relationship between *Against the sophists* and Plato's *Gorgias* by what appear to be allusions

in Plato's. dialogue to Isocrates' speech. But even if Plato speaks of a ψυχὴ στοχαστική (*Gorg.* 463a) and Isocrates of a ψυχὴ δοξαστική (Soph. 17), that does not prove that Plato is imitating Isocrates. Also, δοξαστική is a Platonic phrase. Plato despises mere δόξα, while here as elsewhere Isocrates insists that man's nature does not allow him to engage in more than δόξα and δοξάζειν. The very fact that he is replying to Plato shows that he depends on Plato's formulation of the problem. But the main argument is that given in the text (page 56 f.): the information about Plato's fundamental concepts and their logical interrelation (e.g. πᾶσα ἀρετή :: εὐδαιμονία, ἐπιστήμη :: δόξα, ἀρετή :: ἐπιστήμη) which is contained in *Against the sophists* is so full that it could have been derived from no other early Platonic work but *Gorgias,* the only work of Plato's youth in which he gives a fairly systematic exposition of his thought.

45. It would anyhow be difficult to name any of Plato's early works which more convincingly and completely expounds all those characteristic features of his philosophy which are referred to by Isocrates, and makes their underlying connexions so clear.

46. *Soph.* 6.

46a. Xen. *Mem.* 1.6.1 f.

47. *Soph.* 7.

48. *Soph.* 8.

48a. Perhaps the charge of asking pupils for contemptibly small fees is more appropriate to Antisthenes than to Plato, who probably took no fees at all. But we know far too little of these matters to judge with certainty. Even in the Academy, pupils probably had to pay a small sum—for instance, their share of the symposium. This was not meant to be the salary of their teacher, but Isocrates may have chosen to describe it as if it were, and to imply that Plato was under-bidding his competitors. He attacks Plato and Antisthenes again in *Helen* 1: see note 85. On the fees of the Socratics, see Diog. Laert. 2.62, 65, 80, and 6.14.

48b. The charge that dialectic is hair-splitting recurs in *Antid.* 262, where it is admittedly an attack on Plato. Why should it not be an attack on Plato here too?

49. This description of the art of discovering contradictions, 'elenctic', is aimed at Socrates and Plato. See the parallel in *Helen* 4, where the Socratic technical term ἐλέγχειν is particularly derided.

50. See *Paideia* II, 39, which explains how the purpose of all Socrates' educational activity can be described as 'caring for the soul' (ψυχῆς ἐπιμέλεια).

51. *Soph.* 9: οἱ τοὺς πολιτικοὺς λόγους ὑπισχνούμενοι.

52. Isocrates' phrasing clearly shows that he is putting the word techné (as used by these teachers of rhetoric) inside quotation-marks, so to speak. The same thing applies to the passages where he parodies the terminology of the Socratics.

53. See *Paideia* II, 131, and *passim.*

54. See J. Vahlen, *Gesammelte Schriften* I, p. 117 f.; and before him, C. Reinhardt, *De Isocratis aemulis* (Bonn 1873).

55. This speech is best explained as Alcidamas' reply to the attack on him made by Isocrates in the speech *Against the sophists.*

56. *Soph.* 9.

57. *Soph.* 10.

58. *Soph.* 12 f.

59. Plato compares his 'ideas' to letters of the alphabet in *Cratylus, Theaetetus, The Statesman,* and *The Laws.*

60. This was first done in Plato's *Timaeus* 48b, 56b, 57c: see H. Diels' *Elementum.*

61. *Soph.* 12.

62. Cf. *Soph.* 13, on the καιρός and the πρέπον.

63. *Soph.* 12.

64. In *Antid.* 2 Isocrates compares himself to the sculptor Phidias and the painters Zeuxis and Parrhasius—the greatest artists in Greece. So does Plato in *The Republic:* see *Paideia* II, 258 f.

65. Plato too, in *Gorg.* 502c, implies that poetry is a kind of rhetoric.

66. *Soph.* 1.

67. See *Paideia* II, 59 f.

68. *Soph.* 1 and 8.

69. *Soph.* 14.

70. *Soph.* 15.

71. *Soph.* 16.

72. *Soph.* 17.

73. *Soph.* 18. Plato also speaks of the 'coincidence' of power and intellect in *Rep.* 473d, and *Laws* 712a. But also, without using the word, he sets up an ideal of many-sided talent (*Rep.* 485b f.)—the φιλόσοφος φύσις, which is a coincidence of qualities that can exist together but seldom do. This way of formulating ideals is characteristic of the literature of paideia.

74. *Soph.* 18.

75. Cf. *Soph.* 17, on the ψυχὴ δοξαστική.

76. Isocrates thinks that, if these model speeches are meant to be specimens of the teaching technique used by their writers, they come under the definition of paideia just as much as his own political rhetoric and its products. After all, that kind of literature represents a formal educational principle which is valuable and interesting in itself. However, since its content has comparatively little importance, it has not been exhaustively treated here. In this, I have accepted the estimate of Plato and Isocrates. General and legal historians will of course take a different view.

77. *Soph.* 19-20.

78. *Soph.* 20.

79. *Soph.* 21.

80. See *Paideia* II, 150.

81. *Phil.* 12.

82. *Hel.* 67.

83. *Hel.* 66.

84. This attack on the 'disputers' occupies the whole of the introduction to *Helen,* and has nothing to do with the rest of the speech. It will be enough for our purpose, therefore, to discuss the introduction alone. Aristotle (*Rhet.* 3.14.1414b26) says that the prooemium need have no connexion with the main part of an epideictic speech, and cites Isocrates' *Helen* as an example. He compares the introduction to an encomium with the loosely attached prelude (*proaulion*) to a flute-solo.

85. *Hel.* 1. It is easy enough to identify Isocrates' two unnamed opponents. On Antisthenes see Arist. *Met.* Δ 29.1024b33, with the commentary of Alexander of Aphrodisias on it, and Plato, *Soph.* 251b.

86. *Hel.* 4.

87. *Hel.* 2-3.

88. *Hel.* 5.

89. *Hel.* 6.

90. *Hel.* 7.

91. *Hel.* 8.

92. *Hel.* 9.

93. See *Paideia* II, 280 and III, 193.

3. POLITICAL CULTURE AND THE PANHELLENIC IDEAL

1. Isocr. *Paneg.* 4; cf. *Helen* 12-13, *Antid.* 3.

2. Aesch. *Eum.* 980-987.

3. There is need of a book giving a general survey of all the attempts made to preach the Panhellenic ideal before Isocrates' time. Plenty of work has been done on separate aspects of the question. J. Kessler's book, *Isokrates und die panhellenische Idee* (*Studien zur Geschichte und Kultur des Altertums*, vol. 4, book 3, Paderborn 1911) deals only with Isocrates himself; his predecessors are more fully treated in G. Mathieu, *Les idées politiques d'Isocrate* (Paris 1925).

4. *Paideia* I, 326 f.

5. See H. Dunkel, *Panhellenism in Greek Tragedy* (Chicago 1937).

6. See *Paideia* II, 251 and 255 f.

7. See p. 199.

8. Arist. *Pol.* 7.7.1327b29-33.

9. *Paneg.* 1.

10. On the elegiac poem in which Xenophanes compared the Olympic victor's areté with the wise man's intellectual powers, embodied in himself, see *Paideia* I, 172-173.

11. Isocrates' conception of his own vocation, as expressed in his choice of this particular audience for his proposals, is of course inspired by Gorgias and his *Olympicus*. The representative of intellectual areté stands forth in open competition with the athletes, the highest examples of physical areté, and takes all Hellas to be umpire and judge. The profound change in Isocrates' later views of his mission is shown in *Antid.* 1 and *Phil.* 12—where he abandons his earlier panegyric style, because it would be ineffective in contemporary Greece. In *Philip* he addresses not a national assembly, but one man in whom he sees the future ruler of all the Greeks.

12. Xenophanes, frg. 2.15-22.

13. *Paneg.* 2.

14. *Paneg.* 3.

15. *Paneg.* 10-14.

16. Cf. *Paneg.* 17, where he uses ἰσομοιρῆσαι and τὰς ἡγεμονίας διελέσθαι to describe the sharing of hegemony between Sparta and Athens. That is the sense in which we must understand expressions like ἀμφισβητεῖν τῆς ἡγεμονίας and τὴν ἡγεμονίαν ἀπολαβεῖν: they allude to a restoration of Athenian naval power. Kessler (*Isokrates und die panhellenische Idee* 9) fails in his attempt to prove that in the *Panegyricus* Isocrates is proposing that Athens should be the supreme leader of Greece.

17. *Paneg.* 20.

18. *Paneg.* 22.

19. This does not mean that Athens claims the sole right of dominion over the rest of Greece. But if a state's right to hegemony is based on historical priority or the benefits it has done to Greece, obviously Athens deserves it more than Sparta. Cf. *Paneg.* 23 f.

20. Thuc. 1.73-76.

21. This is the tone regularly adopted in the *epitaphioi* or funeral speeches. There is an even earlier case of the re-interpretation of a primitive myth to support contemporary ideals of national unity and power. That is the renaissance of the sagas about Theseus as the king who united Attica—they first reappear on sixth-century vases during the tyranny of Pisistratus, and then enter poetry. The topic is fully discussed by H. Herter in *Rheinisches Museum* 1939, 244 f., 289 f.

22. Thuc. 2.41.1.
23. *Paideia* I, 410-411.
24. *Paideia* I, 312.
25. *Paneg.* 28.
26. See my *Aristotle*, p. 160.
27. *Paneg.* 40.
28. *Paneg.* 40; cf. Arist. *Met.* A 1.981b17.
29. Aristotle, loc. cit. says that scientific culture began in Egypt.
30. *Paneg.* 42.
31. *Paneg.* 42-45.
32. *Paneg.* 46.
33. *Paneg.* 47. According to Isocrates, it was chiefly 'philosophy' (=love of culture) which helped man to discover the arts and order his life.
34. *Paideia* I, 352-353, and II, 228.
35. *Paneg.* 47; see my *Aristotle*, p. 109, n. 1.
36. *Paneg.* 48.
37. *Paneg.* 49: σύμβολον τῆς παιδεύσεως.
38. *Paneg.* 50.
39. *Paneg.* 51.
40. Thucydides too, in Pericles' funeral speech (2.36.4), dealt with the deeds of Athens in war much more cursorily than most orators, and put the chief emphasis on her cultural importance.
41. *Paneg.* 51 f.
42. See *Paideia* I, 410, on this ideal of synthesis in Thucydides' description of Athens.
43. *Paneg.* 51-99 deals with the services rendered by Athens to Greece in war. That is followed at 100 by a defence of the first Athenian naval empire.
44. *Paneg.* 119.
45. *Paneg.* 122 f.
46. This is the view of Wilamowitz and Drerup. See also G. Mathieu (note 3).
47. Later, in *Philip* 12, Isocrates says that 'panegyric speeches' have no more to do with practical politics (which is his concern there) than 'laws and republics composed by sophists'. That is clearly an allusion to Plato, and the whole remark is a reference to Isocrates' own earlier treatment of the theme.
48. Even in Isocrates' *Plataicus,* the Athenian naval empire takes on a far less Panhellenic, far more particularist and Athenian appearance. For the date of this pamphlet, see my *Demosthenes, Origin and Growth of his Policy* (Berkeley 1938) pp. 199-203.
49. It is noteworthy that in the city-state's last battle, fought under Demosthenes' leadership against the attacks of foreign enemies, the Panhellenic ideal became ever more clearly the ideological basis for all its efforts. See p. 283 f., and my *Demosthenes*, pp. 170-173.

4. THE PRINCE'S EDUCATION

1. Jebb (*Attic Orators* II, 88) says it is 'possible' that Prince Nicocles was a pupil of Isocrates; but Isocrates' own words in *Antid.* 40 show unmistakably that his relation to Nicocles was that of a teacher. So does the end of *Evagoras*, which is in the tone, not of a journalist to his boss, but of a tutor to his trusted pupil. In *Evag.* 80 Isocrates speaks of his own 'encouraging' words and those 'of other friends'.
2. Diodorus 15.47 places the death of Evagoras in 374; but modern scholars are not agreed on the point. *To Nicocles* would be best dated to the opening of

Nicocles' reign, soon after Evagoras' death. But the speech *Nicocles* assumes that some time has passed since Nicocles inherited the kingdom (c. 31), because the benefits of his rule can already be seen in a general improvement of the financial situation. In c. 11 there is a backward reference to Isocrates' speech *To Nicocles,* which is assumed to have directly preceded it. *Evagoras* cannot be put too far on in Nicocles' reign, for it treats him as young and inexperienced, and encourages him to 'persevere' as he has begun. But c. 78 shows it is not the first hortatory address which Isocrates has made to him.

3. Aristotle's youthful work *Protrepticus* also was a hortatory address to a Cypriot tyrant, one Themison. I have showed in my *Aristotle* (p. 55) that it was not a dialogue in Plato's manner, but a λόγος συμβουλευτικός imitating Isocrates. But Aristotle filled that form with the content of Plato's paideia.

4. Plato, *Rep.* 568b, c.

5. *Paideia* I, 216 f., especially 221.

6. *Paideia* I, 198 f.

7. *To Nic.* 43.

8. Isocrates himself says, in *Evag.* 8-11, that his *encomium* is a new literary creation deliberately competing with poetry: for until then it had been the function of hymns to exalt men of high areté. The word ᾠδαί in 11 is a reference to poets like Pindar and Bacchylides. See note 7.

9. See Aristotle's remark in Diogenes Laertius 2.55 about the innumerable encomia and funeral eulogies written after the death of Xenophon's son Gryllus. That was in 362, or not much later.

10. See *Paideia* I, 212 f. on Pindar's praise of the victors as examples of areté. When Isocrates brings forward the Aeacid family and Teucer, the founder of Greek civilization in Cyprus, as the mythical ancestors of Evagoras and models of true areté (*Ev.* 12-18), he is following Pindar closely.

11. Cf. Isocrates' estimate of Evagoras' rule from the Panhellenic point of view (*Ev.* 47-64).

12. See *Paideia* II, 18.

13. *Nic.* 11: τὸν μὲν οὖν ἕτερον (λόγον), ὡς χρὴ τυραννεῖν, Ἰσοκράτους ἠκούσατε, τὸν δ' ἐχόμενον, ἃ δεῖ ποιεῖν τοὺς ἀρχομένους, ἐγὼ πειράσομαι διελθεῖν. When Isocrates wrote *Nicocles,* he obviously meant it to be a companion-piece for *To Nicocles.*

14. The Greek word for 'gentleness' is πρᾳότης, and the adjective is πρᾶος. See *To Nic.* 8 and 23, *Nic.* 16-17, 32, and 55. Similarly, Didymus (in his commentary on Demosthenes' *Philippics,* col. 5.52, ed. Diels-Schubart) says that Hermias the tyrant of Atarneus 'transformed' his regime 'to a gentler form of government' under the educational influence of the Platonic philosophers Coriscus, Erastus, Aristotle, and Xenocrates. (The reading is based on a quite certain supplement to the papyrus.)

15. Demosthenes, *Androtion* 51: πάντα πρᾳότερ' ἔστ' ἐν δημοκρατίᾳ. Isocrates, *Antid.* 300: 'no people is *gentler*' (i.e. more civilized—the word πρᾶος is also used of 'tame' animals) 'than the Athenians'. See Plato, *Rep.* 566d, for a description of the young tyrant trying to appear gentle, and Aesch. *Prom.* 35.

16. *Nic.* 24 f. From passages like that we can see why Isocrates, the citizen of a democratic state, did not wish to put out this essay on monarchy under his own name, but issued it as a 'speech' by Nicocles. The speech which he put in the mouth of the Spartan king Archidamus was based on the same fiction.

17. *Areop.* 11-12; see p. 115 f. See also *Antid.* 101-139, and p. 139 f.

18. *Nic.* 62.

19. Justice, *Nic.* 31 f.; self-control, 36 f.

20. *Nic.* 47.

21. *Nic.* 43-47.

22. *Nic.* 48-62.

23. *Nic.* 1.

24. *Nic.* 1.

25. *Nic.* 2. Obviously the 'goods' which Isocrates here describes as the fruit of striving after areté are success and prosperity (in the bourgeois sense). This casts a strong light on the contrast between Isocrates' 'morality is the best policy' and what the Socratics considered to be goods. See *Paideia,* II, 148 f.

26. *Nic.* 3-4.

27. *Nic.* 5.

28. *Paneg.* 47-50.

29. Cf. *Paneg.* 48 and *Nic.* 6.

30. See Norden's penetrating investigation of the stylistic form of the hymn and its various influences in Greek and Roman literature, in *Agnostos Theos* (Leipzig 1913): especially p. 163 f. The best early example of this hymnal exaltation and deification of what we should call an abstract power like the logos is Solon's praise of *Eunomia,* social order, and its beneficent power. I have explained its hymn-like form in *Solons Eunomie* (*Sitzungsber. Berl. Akad.* 1926, 82-84).

31. *Nic.* 5-9.

32. It follows from *Nic.* 8 and 9 that the logos, deified here, is the embodiment of Isocrates' ideal of paideia, Culture; and indeed he says so in *Paneg.* 48. On the logos as a 'token of culture' (σύμβολον τῆς παιδεύσεως), see p. 79.

33. Plato, *Gorg.* 454b, 462b-c.

34. *Nic.* 8.

35. In 8 Isocrates says we call a man 'a rhetor' if he can speak in assemblies. The man who speaks to himself about a problem we call sensible. What he means is that, although we give these processes different names, they are essentially the same.

36. To speak or act 'with logos' means, for Isocrates, to speak or act 'with intelligent foresight'—φρονίμως—see c. 9.

37. The ideal of *eudaimonia* is always the basis of Isocrates' political thought (his φιλοσοφία). For instance, see *On peace* 19, where he frankly says it is the aim of his political activity. For a more exact definition of it, see n. 59.

38. Isocrates feels that his φιλοσοφία sets him apart from the old 'technographers' with their forensic rhetoric. He means to take the sting out of Plato's charge that rhetoric has no objective purpose, by making the logos part of the concept of phronésis and eudaimonia.

39. *To Nic.* 1.

40. *To Nic.* 2-3.

41. *To Nic.* 4. This doubt appears early in Greek literature. Archilochus has a philosophical carpenter, who does not desire a tyrant's throne (frg. 22, see *Paideia* I, 125), and Solon refused to hold absolute power (frg. 23). But Isocrates is evidently attacking the Socratics. In *Helen* 8 he had scornfully said 'some people dare to write that the life of beggars and exiles is more enviable than that of other men'. This thought was of course elaborated in *To Nicocles,* which was meant to give a new content and meaning to the life of the monarch.

42. *To Nic.* 5-6.

43. Plato, *Gorg.* 470e (see *Paideia* II, 133). Perhaps the idea was taken up by other pupils of Socrates—Antisthenes, for example.

44. *To Nic.* 7. Isocrates, who likes diametrical oppositions, says 'poems in metre and writings in prose'.

45. *To Nic.* 8.

46. P. 87.

47. *Paideia* II, 311.

48. *Paideia* II, 280; III, 193.

49. See the mythical genealogy of the Cypriot dynasty, based on the principle of legitimate succession, in *Ev.* 12-18.

50. See *Paideia* II, 261, 267.

51. *To Nic.* 6.

52. *To Nic.* 9.

53. On the 'work' (ἔργον) of the good citizen, see Plato, *Gorg.* 517c—where πολίτου should be emended to πολιτικοῦ, for the subject is the duty, not of the individual citizen, but of the statesman. To make the citizens as good as possible is the aim of political paideia: *Gorg.* 502c, cf. 465a.

54. *To Nic.* 6, *ad fin.*

55. *To Nic.* 9: note οἶμαι δὲ πάντας ἂν ὁμολογῆσαι.

56. Cf. *To Nic.* 13: ὑπεθέμεθα.

57. Isocrates expressly starts his political reasoning from this kind of hypothesis: see *On peace* 18. This point ought to be more carefully investigated; see my *Demosthenes,* p. 86.

58. Plato, *Gorg.* 517b, calls them 'servants of the state' (διάκονοι πόλεως). He implies that that was the commonest, but also the lowest, view of the ruler's function. This is reminiscent of Frederick the Great, who said he was proud to be the first servant of his state.

59. In *On peace* 19 Isocrates defines the concept of political *eudaimonia* as applied to the Athenian democracy in very similar terms: (1) security, (2) prosperity, (3) concord, (4) the respect of other states.

60. *Nic.* 24.

61. Cf. p. 87, and notes 14, 15.

62. See Beloch's *Griechische Geschichte* III, 1 (2nd ed.) pp. 38 and 89, on Conon and Evagoras.

63. *Nic.* 24. Timotheus had the same problem of dealing with a committee of fellow-generals during his third term as general in the Social War.

64. P. 115.

65. *To Nic.* 10-11.

66. *To Nic.* 11. This introduces the problem of the monarch's paideia.

67. *To Nic.* 12. At the end of 12 ἐπιμέλεια is used as a synonym for παίδευσις.

68. *Soph.* 4, 6, and 21; also *Helen* 1.

69. *Soph.* 14-15.

70. *To Nic.* 12.

71. Cf. *To Nic.* 12: ὡς . . . τῆς παιδεύσεως . . . μάλιστα δυναμένης τὴν ἡμετέραν φύσιν εὐεργετεῖν.

72. *To Nic.* 13. For the ideals themselves, see c. 9 on the monarch's ἔργον.

73. *To Nic.* 14.

74. *To Nic.* 15: φιλάνθρωπον δεῖ εἶναι καὶ φιλόπολιν. Isocrates couples the same virtues in describing the ideal ruler in *Ev.* 43 and *Paneg.* 29 (with reference to the Athenian democracy).

75. See S. Lorenz's *De progressu notionis* φιλανθρωπίας (Leipzig, 1914). A. Burk, on p. 208 of *Die Pädagogik des Isokrates,* says the Roman concept of *humanitas* derives straight from Greek philanthropy; but Gellius, *Noct. Att.* 13.17, is more correct in distinguishing the *humanitas* which means philanthropy from the *humanitas* which means paideia. In Isocrates philanthropy is not of central importance; his thought turns always to paideia, which is the real basis of his 'humanism'. Of course that does not exclude philanthropy.

76. *To Nic.* 16.

77. Thuc. 2.65.8-9. Isocrates' use of ὑβρίζειν to describe the humours of the demos is modelled on Thucydides' ὕβρει θαρσοῦντας; but he gives a slightly different turn to the rest of the contrast.

78. *Paideia* I, 410 f.

79. Thuc. 2.37.1, cf. *To Nic.* 16.

80. Thuc. 2.37.1; cf. *To Nic.* 17 init.

81. *To Nic.* 17 ad fin.

82. *To Nic.* 18.

83. Nevertheless, that is how scholars usually interpret this kind of speech. See Blass (*Attische Beredsamkeit* II) pp. 271 and 275. The true meaning of the 'formlessness' of the speech cannot be understood without reference to its content. Blass thinks the content is a mass of clichés, but he has not observed the concealed dialectic skill with which the ideal of monarchy is worked out and transformed.

84. *To Nic.* 20.

85. *To Nic.* 21.

86. *To Nic.* 22 init. and 23.

87. *To Nic.* 24.

88. *To Nic.* 25.

89. *To Nic.* 26.

90. *To Nic.* 27.

91. *To Nic.* 28.

92. *To Nic.* 29. The assertion that the monarch's soul must be free, i.e. that he must have perfect self-control, comes from Socrates; see *Paideia* II, 53. The Socratic word ἐγκρατής appears in *Nic.* 39.

93. *To Nic.* 30.

94. *To Nic.* 31.

95. *To Nic.* 34. The same ideal is summed up by the Roman poet Silius Italicus (*Punica* 8.611):

> laeta uiro grauitas ac mentis amabile pondus.

Amabile is the keynote of urbanity, and it is on urbanity, τὸ ἀστεῖον, that the ideal of the πεπαιδευμένος, expressed in the speech *To Nicocles,* is centred. The ruler is to combine τὸ ἀστεῖον with σεμνότης.

96. *To Nic.* 35.

97. *To Nic.* 35 (ad fin.): τὰ παρεληλυθότα μνημονεύειν.

98. *To Nic.* 35.

99. The phrase 'to keep the past alive in memory', τὰ παρεληλυθότα μνημονεύειν, is the essence of all historical study.

100. Cf. the chapter *Thucydides: Political Philosopher, Paideia* I, 382 f.

101. Thuc. 1.22.4.

102. When Thucydides boldly struck out on his new path, he knew that early history was mixed up with poetry springing from myths and legends (1.22.1 and 4), or with prose chronicles which were like poetry and were little concerned with truth.

103. Plato, *Prot.* 325e-326a.

104. Obviously the influence of rhetoric on history was bound to extend beyond its form, and to subordinate it to the ideas implicit in rhetorical paideia—i.e. its political ideals and its special interest in human areté and its opposite.

105. This is the aspect of history chiefly emphasized by Isocrates; he thinks it is the source of all political experience (ἐμπειρία): *To Nic.* 35. See my article, *The Date of Isocrates' Areopagiticus and the Athenian Opposition* (*Harvard Classical Studies,* Cambridge 1941), p. 432. Isocrates stresses the empiricist charac-

ter of his political philosophy in *Soph.* 14-15, *Helen* 5, *Antid.* 187, 188, 191, and 192.

106. In Rome we may compare Cicero, with his constant use of historical examples in his speeches.

107. Cf. the essay (which I advised the author to undertake) by G. Schmitz-Kahlmann, *Das Beispiel der Geschichte im politischen Denken des Isokrates* (*Philologus,* supplement 31.4). In the historical material brought to light by Isocrates one part is specially important from his conservative political point of view: the early history of Athens. It is used to illustrate the great example set by the 'ancestors', the πρόγονοι. See K. Jost, *Das Beispiel und Vorbild der 'Vorfahren' bei den attischen Rednern und Geschichtschreibern bis Demosthenes* (*Rhetorische Studien,* ed. Drerup, vol. 19; Paderborn 1936).

108. Wilamowitz, in *Aristoteles und Athen,* and others have traced the influence of the Atthis on Athenian constitutional history; but the political background could be worked out in more detail (see my next chapter).

109. *To Nic.* 42-43.

110. *To Nic.* 44.

111. *To Nic.* 45 and 48-49.

112. *To Nic.* 40-41 and 43.

113. *To Nic.* 51. The three representatives of paideia here distinguished correspond to those mentioned in *Against the sophists.* The two main types are philosophers (or eristics) and teachers of political oratory; the third seems to be the forensic rhetoricians—see *Soph.* 19-20.

114. *To Nic.* 52.

115. *To Nic.* 53.

5. FREEDOM AND AUTHORITY

1. See what Plato himself says on the subject (*ep.* 7.326a), with reference to the years after the death of Socrates.

2. The analysis of the *Areopagiticus* given in this chapter is based on my investigation of its date, historical background, and political purpose, *The Date of Isocrates' Areopagiticus and the Athenian Opposition,* published in *Harvard Studies in Classical Philology* (*Special Volume,* Cambridge 1941). It will be briefly quoted here as Jaeger, *Areopagiticus.*

3. For other examples of this kind of fiction in Isocrates' speeches, see page 308, n. 16.

4. *Areop.* 1-2.

5. *Areop.* 3.

6. *Areop.* 4-5.

7. *Areop.* 6-7.

8. Isocr. *Phil.* 47, *On peace* 100, *Panath.* 56 f.

9. *Areop.* 5 and 8.

10. *Areop.* 7 ad fin.

11. See the literature on the date of the speech, in F. Kleine-Piening's Münster dissertation, *Quo tempore Isocratis orationes* Περὶ εἰρήνης *et* Ἀρεοπαγιτικός *compositae sint* (Paderborn 1930), and also Jaeger, *Areopagiticus* 411.

12. See Jaeger, *Areopagiticus* 412 f., and 421.

13. *Areop.* 8-10, 80-81.

14. *Areop.* 9-10, and 81. Cf. Jaeger, *Areopagiticus* 416 f. In 81 Isocrates says that the generals have reported to the Athenians on the hatred of Athens felt by the other Greeks, and that the King of Persia has sent threatening letters. This is the customary way for an orator to explain his own motive in coming forward to speak at a given moment; but here it is invented in order to justify

Isocrates in putting his ideas into the form of a speech. It is pure invention when he says that he is addressing an assembly called to discuss the crisis; just as it is in *On peace,* when he justifies his coming forward in the ecclesia by mentioning the arrival of ambassadors who have come from abroad in order to make offers of peace; and once more (as he himself says, *Antid.* 8 and 13) in the *Antidosis,* when he pretends to be defending himself against a charge so serious as to threaten his very life.

15. Cf. Jaeger, *Areopagiticus* 432 f.

16. *Areop.* 12.

17. *Areop.* 14. In his later speech, the *Panathenaicus,* Isocrates once again treated the central problem of the Athenian constitution, and worked from the same idea, that the soul of a state is its constitution.

18. See p. 100.

19. *Areop.* 15.

20. *Areop.* 16.

21. Cf. *Areop.* 14, and again *Panath.* 138.

22. According to *Areop.* 20, it is the polis (i.e. the community) and the politeia (its constitution, its form) which corrupt the thought and speech of the citizens by perverting all standards of value. To describe its formative—or rather destructive—influence, he uses the word παιδεύειν! This proves that he knew that the truly formative forces could not be created by this or that reformer's private educational programme, but must flow from the character of society and of the epoch. When culture is collapsing, that objective, impersonal paideia exists only in the negative sense, as a 'corruption' spreading from the whole to every separate part. Similarly, he describes the negative 'paideia' which springs from the state's lust for power and transforms the spirit of the citizens (*On peace* 77). Realizing this as he did, he must have felt that education alone was practically powerless; but it is a characteristic feature of his era that *positive* paideia had become impossible in it, except through the conscious opposition of a few individuals to the general tendencies of the time.

23. *Areop.* 21.

24. *Areop.* 22. This type of election was called προκρίνειν or αἱρεῖσθαι ἐκ προκρίτων.

25. *Areop.* 24. It is an interesting fact that Plato, in his description of the oligarchic man (*Rep.* 553c) uses the same phrase, 'Work and save'—obviously a well-worn slogan used in the political disputes by which the fourth century was tormented. Isocrates can scarcely have taken that trait from Plato's caricature and deliberately employed it in his own idealized picture. All the more instructive, therefore, is his unconscious agreement with Plato. For more on his sympathy for the policies of the propertied class, see the rest of this chapter.

26. *Areop.* 25.

27. *Areop.* 26.

28. *Areop.* 27, cf. the words τοὺς ... δυνατωτάτους ἐπὶ τὰς πράξεις καθιστάσης, which refer to the better period of the Athenian democracy, and contrast it with the present bad habits.

29. See my *Demosthenes* 50 f., and 68 f.

30. The relevant passages are quoted in Jaeger, *Areopagiticus* 449.

31. *On peace* 13 and 133.

32. *Areop.* 56-59.

33. Cf. Jaeger, *Areopagiticus* 442 f.

34. Aristotle, *Const. Ath.* 35.2. And cf. 25.1-2, and Wilamowitz, *Aristoteles und Athen* I, 68, 40.

35. Dion. Hal., *Isocr.* 1; pseudo-Plutarch, *vit. X orat.* 836 f.; Suidas, s.v. *Isocrates.*

36. *Areop.* 12.

37. Cf. ps.-Plut. *vit. X orat.* 837c.

38. See p. 139 f.

39. Cf. Jaeger, *Areopagiticus* 442.

40. A fact which reveals much about the relation between Isocrates as teacher and Timotheus as pupil is that, a few years later, Isocrates felt bound to defend the dead Timotheus against the charge of anti-democratic sentiment and oligarchic intentions (*Antid.* 131). This is the accusation against which he defended himself and his proposals for constitutional reform, in *Areop.* 57.

41. *Areop.* 56-59 gives us a welcome side-light on the discussions within this political group which preceded the publication of his speech. Those who thought that Isocrates ought not to publish it because they believed that the sickness of Athens was incurable, and they feared the enmity of the radical leaders for the moderates, must have been opposed by those who advised him to bring it out nevertheless. Without such support, the cautious Isocrates would never have made up his mind to do so. For some examples of his habit of explaining his own works to an intimate circle before publishing them, see p. 318, n. 66.

42. Similarly, Plato tells us in his seventh Letter (326a) that the views he later published in *The Republic* had been conceived and talked about by him many years earlier—even before his first journey to Sicily. See *Paideia* II, 100, and *Gnomon* 4 (1928), p. 9.

43. Cf. Plato, *ep.* 7.325a f.

44. *Areop.* 29.

45. *Areop.* 30.

46. *Areop.* 31-32.

47. Cf. in particular his great iambic poem, frg. 24.

48. Cf. Plutarch, *Cimon* 10.

49. *Areop.* 33-35.

50. *Areop.* 36-37.

51. *Areop.* 37. Ever since the age of the sophists, all the leaders of Greek paideia, and above all Plato and Isocrates, agreed in deciding that paideia should not be limited to school-teaching. To them it was culture, the formation of the human soul. That is what differentiates Greek paideia from the educational system of other nations. It was an absolute ideal.

52. *Areop.* 37.

53. *Areop.* 38.

54. *Areop.* 39.

55. Cf. *Paideia* II, 238.

56. *Areop.* 39-40.

57. Plato, *Rep.* 426e-427a.

58. *Areop.* 41-42.

59. All young men need education; but Isocrates felt that the young men of his own time needed it particularly. This is proved by the fact that (as we have seen) his idealizing picture of early Athens was conceived as a contrast to his own age. But see also *Areop.* 48-49 and 50.

60. *Areop.* 43.

61. *Areop.* 44.

62. Plato, *Prot.* 326c.

63. Pseudo-Plutarch, *de liberis educandis* 8e. The author of this work aims at helping all social classes with his educational proposals; but if poverty prevents a large number of them from taking advantage of his advice, he says his educa-

tional theories are certainly not to blame for that. We find the same kind of thing in the medical literature on diet and regimen, which is often written for the rich and assumes that others will adapt its rules to suit themselves. See p. 44.

64. *Areop.* 44-45. Among all Isocrates' contemporaries, it is Xenophon who would most fully approve of this ideal of education. He also combines riding, gymnastics, and hunting with intellectual culture; see p. 159 f.

65. *Areop.* 46.

66. *Areop.* 47. Cf. Solon, frg. 24.22 and frg. 25.6; and the same expression is used in praise of Pericles by Thuc. 2.65.8, and of Alcibiades in Thuc. 8.86.5.

67. *Areop.* 48-49.

68. *Areop.* 48 *ad fin.* Cf. Hesiod, *Works and Days* 199.

69. Cf. *Paideia* I, 372 f.

70. *Paideia* I, 7. On the development of this concept in Greek ethics, see Freiherr Carl Eduard von Erffa's monograph (which I advised him to undertake), *Aidos und verwandte Begriffe in ihrer Entwicklung von Homer bis Demokrit (Beihefte zum Philologus,* Suppl. vol. 30.2).

70a. This renascence of the concept aidôs in Plato's and Isocrates' educational and philosophical theories has been briefly touched by von Erffa (see note 70) p. 200.

71. *Areop.* 57.

72. *Areop.* 58-59.

73. *Areop.* 60.

74. *Areop.* 61.

75. *Areop.* 62.

76. *Areop.* 63 f.

77. *Areop.* 3-13.

78. *Areop.* 64.

79. *Areop.* 65.

80. *Areop.* 66. On Isocrates' attitude to the naval aspirations of Athens in the *Areopagiticus,* see my arguments in Jaeger, *Areopagiticus* 426-429.

81. Cf. the phrases μεταβάλλειν τὴν πολιτείαν, *Areop.* 78, ἐπανορθοῦν τὴν πολιτείαν, *Areop.* 15.

82. *Areop.* 71.

83. *Areop.* 72-73.

84. *Areop.* 74, and cf. 76.

85. On the medical concept of physis, see p. 29. In any study of Thucydides' use of the idea, contemporary medical literature must constantly be referred to.

86. On this see P. Wendland in *Göttinger Gelehrte Nachrichten* 1910.

87. See p. 277 f.

88. *On peace* 16.

89. He tries to get the Athenians to abandon the hope of naval supremacy in *On peace* 28-29, and especially in 64 f. See my examination of his attitude in that speech towards the problem of Athenian naval dominion (ἀρχὴ τῆς θαλάττης) in Jaeger, *Areopagiticus* 424 f.

90. Dem. *Crown* 234, Xen., Πόροι.

91. See p. 42 and p. 57 f. of my *Demosthenes.*

92. *On peace* 16.

93. See p. 53 f. of my *Demosthenes.*

94. On the relation between *On peace* and the *Areopagiticus* with reference to the problem of Athenian naval dominion, and on the relation of them both to the policy of the *Panegyricus,* see Jaeger, *Areopagiticus* 424 f.

95. *Paneg.* 119: ἅμα γὰρ ἡμεῖς τε τῆς ἀρχῆς ἀπεστερούμεθα καὶ τοῖς Ἕλλησιν ἀρχὴ τῶν κακῶν ἐγίγνετο. Cf. 100 f.

96. *On peace* 101 f.: τότε τὴν ἀρχὴν αὐτοῖς (τοῖς ᾽Α.) γεγενῆσθαι τῶν συμφορῶν, ὅτε τὴν ἀρχὴν τῆς θαλάττης παρελάμβανον.

97. Cf. Jaeger, *Areopagiticus* 429.

98. *Paneg.* 120-121.

99. *On peace* 16. I shall not here attempt to controvert those scholars who—in spite of these obvious contradictions between the *Panegyricus* and the *Peace*—assert that Isocrates' standpoint is the same in both speeches. But I must say that I find it hard to understand their logic. It looks as if their wish to present a unified picture were stronger than their ability to make it fit the facts.

100. The moral codes of individuals and of communities must not contradict one another: *On peace* 4 and 133, with many other passages.

101. The distinction between domination and hegemony in this sense appears in *On peace* 142 f. See the Berlin dissertation by W. Wössner, which I encouraged him to undertake: *Die synonymische Unterscheidung bei Thukydides und den politischen Rednern der Griechen* (Würzburg 1937); it traces the various cases of this kind of distinction in political discussions.

102. Cf. *On peace* 111 f., especially 115.

103. *On peace* 27.

104. In *On peace* 69-70 Isocrates says that the naval empire is lost and that Athens is not in a position to restore it.

105. Isocrates had already said so, in *Areop.* 50 f.

106. Cf. *On peace* 77. In 63, he contrasts the paideia that leads to peace and justice with the paideia created by the efforts of Athens to gain power and dominion—a paideia which, in this speech, he conceives as a corrupting force.

107. Cf. *On peace* 95-115.

108. *On peace* 115.

109. Cf. note 104.

6. ISOCRATES DEFENDS HIS PAIDEIA

1. In *Antid.* 9 he says he is 82 years old. Only the beginning and end of the speech were extant until 1812, when the Greek Mystoxides discovered the body of it (72-309).

2. *Antid.* 4-5.

3. *Areop.* 57, *On peace* 39. In the latter passage (like Socrates in Plato's *Gorgias*) Isocrates compares himself to the doctor who must burn and cut his patients in order to cure them. But the comparison is not very appropriate to Isocrates, who uses it merely from the point of view of party politics.

3a. Isocrates says so himself in *Antid.* 8 and 13. Pseudo-Plutarch, *vit. X orat.* 837a and 839c, mistakenly treats the 'charge' as genuine.

4. *Antid.* 6-8 and 10.

5. *Antid.* 11-12, cf. *Soph.* 16.

5a. *Antid.* 8.

6. Plato, *Apol.* 20c.

7. Ever since the 16th-century humanist Hieronymus Wolf, scholars have pointed out how closely Isocrates models his own defence of himself in *Antidosis* on Socrates' defence of himself, the *Apology*.

8. *Antid.* 9.

9. That is how the *Antidosis* was treated by G. Misch in his *Geschichte der Autobiographie* I (Leipzig 1907) 86 f.; though he did not do Isocrates justice.

10. Isocrates describes the *Antidosis* in 7 as εἰκὼν τῆς ἐμῆς διανοίας καὶ τῶν ἄλλων τῶν βεβιωμένων.

11. In *Antid.* 6 he says he has three purposes in writing the speech: to describe (1) his character and habits (τρόπος), (2) his life (βίος), and (3) his paideia, which in 10 and often elsewhere he calls his 'philosophy'.

12. *Antid.* 30. The resemblance of this invented charge to that actually levelled against Socrates is obvious.

13. *Soph.* 19 f.

14. Dion. Hal., *Isocr.* 18, says that Aristotle in particular made fun of Isocrates for hating to be mixed up with the writers of forensic speeches. (See p. 320 on Aristotle's work as a teacher of rhetoric in the Academy.) He told his pupils that there were whole bundles of such speeches by Isocrates in the bookshops—of course they were speeches he had written for his clients before opening his school. In the *Antidosis* Isocrates takes special care to answer such attacks. See c. 38 f.

15. *Antid.* 2.

16. *Antid.* 46.

17. *Antid.* 46-47.

18. *Antid.* 48, 39.

19. *Antid.* 41.

20. In *Antid.* 54 he compares these selections from his speeches with a choice display of fruit.

21. *Antid.* 54 f.

22. *Soph.* 18.

23. *Antid.* 57 f.

24. In *Antid.* 57 he explains the political purpose of the *Panegyricus* in such a way as to give hasty readers the impression that he had maintained the claim of Athens to dominate Greece. On this see p. 306, n. 16.

25. See p. 128.

26. In the *Panegyricus* he uses both the word 'empire' (ἀρχή) and the word 'hegemony' (ἡγεμονία) without distinction.

27. See p. 129, and compare *On peace* 64, where he advises Athens to abandon her hopes of naval empire; also *On peace* 142, which recommends a 'hegemony' over other states based on their voluntary adherence to Athens.

28. *Antid.* 62 f.

29. Cf. p. 128. Obviously the imperialistic policy put forward in the *Panegyricus* would not harmonize with the programme of the Athenian peace-party in 355, as expounded in *On peace*. One of Isocrates' chief aims in the *Antidosis* is to please that party.

30. Cf. *Antid.* 62.

31. He had already mentioned this, in *Antid.* 40.

32. *Antid.* 40.

33. *Antid.* 67-70.

34. *Antid.* 70. He emphasizes his advice to the king to make his government as gentle as possible—for gentleness showed a true democratic spirit. See p. 87.

35. That is, equality is proportionate and not mechanical: the principle is *suum cuique*. See *Areop.* 21.

36. The literature on the subject is listed in F. Kleine-Piening's *Quo tempore Isocratis orationes* Περὶ εἰρήνης *et* Ἀρεοπαγιτικός *compositae sint* (Paderborn 1930); on which see Jaeger, *The Date of Isocrates' Areopagiticus* (*Harvard Classical Studies*, Cambridge 1941), p. 412, note 1.

37. *Antid.* 79.

38. *Antid.* 82.

39. *Antid.* 81. He also points out that there have been a great number of legislators.

40. *Antid.* 84.

41. *Antid.* 85.

42. Callimachus' pupil Hermippus wrote a book *On students of philosophy who have become absolute rulers*. This we know from Philodemus' rediscovered lists of Stoics and Academics, but we know little of the contents of the book. The tyrant Hermias of Atarneus, who was Aristotle's father-in-law and his best friend, would naturally play an important part in it, along with his political advisers, Plato's pupils Erastus and Coriscus. (See Plato, ep. 6, and my *Aristotle*, p. 111 f.) Dion must have been in it too, and many other young Platonists—such as Eudemus of Cyprus and his companions, who fell in the fight against tyranny in Syracuse. But Dion's murderer, Callippus, who took over his victim's power (using it in a despotic way), was also a student of Plato; and in Pontic Heraclea a pupil of Plato and Isocrates called Clearchus made himself tyrant, and was overthrown and assassinated by Plato's pupil Chion (see E. Meyer's *Geschichte des Altertums* v, 980).

42a. Cf. *Nic.* 4, and the whole of the introduction to the speech.

43. *Antid.* 95-96, cf. 104.

44. *Antid.* 98 f.

45. See pp. 94, 115 f., and my *Demosthenes*, p. 200.

46. Cf. *Soph.* 21, *Helen* 5. Isocrates' claim (*Paneg.* 3-4) that rhetoric 'deals with the greatest things' in the world—i.e. problems of practical politics—goes back to his teacher Gorgias; Plato, *Gorg.* 451d.

47. *Antid.* 107.

48. *Antid.* 108-113.

49. *Antid.* 114-117.

50. *Antid.* 117-118, 121.

51. *Antid.* 119.

52. *Antid.* 121-124.

53. The disaster had been foreseen by Isocrates (*Areop.* 8, 17, 81; cf. also *Panath.* 142).

54. *Antid.* 128.

55. *Antid.* 130.

56. *Antid.* 131.

57. *Antid.* 132.

58. Cf. *Paideia* I, 26 f., where I have explained the significance of the Phoenix episode for Greek paideia and for its tragic sense of the limitations of all education. It is characteristically Greek that the problem should recur at a far later age, and that the present crisis (Timotheus : : Isocrates) should somehow merge within the idealized picture presented by myth (Achilles : : Phoenix).

59. *Antid.* 133.

60. *Antid.* 134.

61. *Antid.* 135.

62. *Antid.* 136.

63. Cf. *Areop.* 15, *On peace* 36, 124.

64. *Antid.* 138.

65. *Antid.* 140 f.

66. *Antid.* 141. Cf. his confidential discussion with friends who warn him about publishing the *Areopagiticus* (*Areop.* 56 f.) and his conversation with a former pupil in *Panath.* 200 f. All three cases prove that he was well accustomed to deliver his speeches to an audience of his own pupils, for preliminary practice and 'improvement' (ἐπανορθοῦν, *Panath.* 200).

67. *Antid.* 40.

68. *Antid.* 159 f.; cf. *Areop.* 33-35.

69. We can easily read that between the lines in *Antid.* 145 f.

70. *Antid.* 157.

71. *Antid.* 156, cf. 158. In this connexion as in others, Isocrates would obviously like being compared with his famous master Gorgias; but not at all with the other sophists and professors who made small, or at least modest, incomes from their profession (*Antid.* 155).

72. *Antid.* 158.

73. *Antid.* 164.

74. Isocrates is proud of the fact that, although he had a rich childhood, he could set to, when his father's property was destroyed in the Peloponnesian war, and make his own fortune by teaching eloquence. See *Antid.* 161.

75. Everything he says about money is vividly reminiscent of the 'Victorian' outlook of the last generation of the fifth century, to which he belonged. He could never feel at home in the poverty and 'social consciousness' of the middle fourth century.

76. This, the principal part of the speech, begins at *Antid.* 167.

77. *Antid.* 168.

78. *Antid.* 174.

79. *Antid.* 175.

80. He had already explained this at length in *Paneg.* 48 f., and *Nic.* 6.

81. *Antid.* 180-181.

82. This change of gymnastics and 'music' into gymnastics and 'philosophy' (= rhetoric) shows that Isocrates is making a step beyond the older Greek paideia, and replacing the old type of education through poetry by introducing a new and higher form of intellectual culture. Nevertheless, his 'philosophy' pre-supposes the old-fashioned 'musical' training, just as does Plato's ideal educational system for his philosophical rulers in *The Republic*. In extreme old age (*Panath.* 34) Isocrates intended to write about the position of poetry within culture; but he did not manage to do it.

83. *Antid.* 182-183. The patterns or 'Ideas' of the logos are the intellectual counterparts of the positions or 'schemata' of the body, which are taught by the trainer for use in wrestling. Teaching begins with the analysis of speech into these fundamental patterns. Then the pupil is taught how to put the elements together into a unity, and how to classify concrete material under the general aspects which have been worked out during the first analysis. See *Antid.* 184 on the process of συνείρειν καθ' ἕν ἕκαστον. The point of this double process is to give the pupil experience (ἔμπειρον ποιεῖν) and to sharpen (ἀκριβοῦν) his per-ception of these patterns, so as to make him understand individual cases better. The method is really based on cultivating average experience; it cannot possibly give infallible knowledge.

84. See p. 63.

85. *Antid.* 187 f.

86. *Antid.* 194. The passage quoted is *Soph.* 14-18. In *Antid.* 195, Isocrates emphasizes the identity of the views expressed in both works.

87. *Antid.* 196 f.

88. *Antid.* 197.

89. *Antid.* 198.

90. Plato, *Prot.* 320c f.

91. *Paideia* I, 312-313.

92. *Antid.* 209-214.

93. *Antid.* 199-201.

94. *Antid.* 201-204. As early as *Soph.* 14-15 he had pointed out that the techné has different effects on differently gifted natures.

95. *Antid.* 205-206.

96. He starts his refutation of the second group (which thinks it is possible, but dangerous, to educate the young by rhetoric = φιλοσοφία) at *Antid.* 215. On the teacher's motives, see *Antid.* 217 f.

97. *Antid.* 220.

98. *Antid.* 221-222.

99. *Antid.* 223-224.

100. See p. 150.

101. *Antid.* 224-226.

102. *Antid.* 230-236.

103. See *Paideia* II, 148 f., 172.

104. *Antid.* 251-252.

105. *Antid.* 253-257. This eulogy of the logos, which we have shown to be a regular hymn in prose, is copied from *Nic.* 5-9. Cf. p. 89.

106. *Antid.* 258.

107. *Antid.* 259.

108. See the traditions about Aristotle's lectures on rhetoric in Blass, *Attische Beredsamkeit* II 64: the chief passages are Quint. 3.1.14 and Philodemus, *vol. rhet.* 2.50 (Sudhaus). The line of verse is a parody of Euripides' *Philoctetes*, frg. 796 Nauck. Aristotle's first published study of the relation of rhetoric to culture—the lost dialogue *Gryllus* or *On Rhetoric*, which was modelled on Plato's *Gorgias*—can be dated by its title. It was named after Xenophon's son, whose heroic death in the war against Thebes (362) evoked a huge number of panegyrics (ἐγκώμια) mostly written to 'please' (χαρίζεσθαι) his famous father. Aristotle's criticism started with this remarkable phenomenon. The oldest parts of his extant book *Rhetoric* go back to the time when he was still lecturing at the Academy. See F. Solmsen's illuminating treatment of the subject in *Die Entwicklung der aristotelischen Logik und Rhetorik (Neue Philol. Untersuchungen,* ed. W. Jaeger, vol. 4, Berlin 1929) p. 196 f.

109. The scientific footing was dialectic. In *Phaedrus*, Plato had once again discussed whether rhetoric was or was not a true techné—the question he had answered in the *Gorgias* with a flat negative (see the chapter *Phaedrus* in this book). In *Phaedrus* he maintained that it should be set up on the new basis of dialectic. Solmsen (see note 108) has traced the development of Aristotle's *Rhetoric* in its early stages, and finds it absolutely parallel to the change in Plato's attitude; but he has not specified the place he attributes to Plato's *Phaedrus* in that development. I believe it is most probable that *Phaedrus* was written later than Aristotle's *Gryllus* (some time after 362), but I cannot place the former too late. In *Gryllus,* as in Plato's *Gorgias,* rhetoric is *not* an art. In *Phaedrus,* Plato says it is capable of becoming one. The various stages of Aristotle's rhetorical lectures mirror these changing views. In any case I should put *Phaedrus* earlier than the *Antidosis* (353).

110. See Solmsen (note 108) p. 207. Blass (note 108), p. 452, offers a sort of scholastic explanation of Cephisodorus' attacks on Plato's theory of Ideas (this in a book against Aristotle!): he says Cephisodorus was just an ignorant fellow. Accordingly he dates the book after the death of Isocrates—to a time when Aristotle's secession from Plato's school must have been known to the whole world, because of his attacks on his old master and his foundation of a separate school. But obviously Aristotle was still a teacher in the Academy, and a faithful follower of Plato, when Cephisodorus wrote his book against him, and in it attacked Plato's theory of Ideas. See my *Aristotle,* p. 37 f.

111. Cf. p. 184.

112. Isocrates, *Antid.* 258, carefully says that 'some' of the eristic philosophers abuse him: a distinction between Plato and his pupil Aristotle.

113. *Antid.* 261. Isocrates takes the same attitude in his latest work, the *Panathenaicus:* c. 26.

114. Plato himself describes his paideia as a combination of mathematics and dialectics, in the seventh book of *The Republic.*

115. *Antid.* 262.

116. In *Soph.* 8 he uses the same words: ἀδολεσχία καὶ μικρολογία, to describe dialectic education as recommended by Plato.

117. *Antid.* 263-265.

118. *Antid.* 266.

119. In *Antid.* 266 he is quite ready to say that dialectic is a 'more manly occupation' than the old-fashioned musical education given in school, but in general he classes the two together. His patronizing reference to literary education seems to have irritated the professors of poetic exegesis (*Panath.* 18). It is a pity that he never managed to fulfil his promise (*Panath.* 25) of writing a special work on the relation between paideia and poetry. He would have taken Plato's *Republic* as an example—perhaps as a model.

120. *Antid.* 268. Callicles too, in Plato's *Gorgias* 484c-d, charges that the dialectic training of the Socratics, if too long pursued, makes its adepts ignorant of the state's laws and of the speeches which are necessary in business and public life. It makes them 'inexperienced' in the ways of their fellow-men. Isocrates is thinking of that criticism here. Plato believed he had completely refuted it in *Gorgias,* but now Isocrates revives it again—a proof that the opposition between these two types of culture is eternal. Cf. also Isocr. *Panath.* 27, 28.

121. *Antid.* 268-269. In *Helen* 2-3 Isocrates had attacked the pre-Socratic philosophers Protagoras, Gorgias, Zeno, and Melissus, as paradox-chasers, and warned his readers not to imitate them. In the *Antidosis* he names Empedocles, Ion, Alcmaeon, Parmenides, Melissus, and Gorgias. Of course he is criticizing Gorgias, not as a rhetorician, but as the inventor of the famous argument 'Being is not', which was a playful exaggeration of the paradoxes so dear to the Eleatic philosophers.

122. In *Parmenides* and *Theaetetus,* Plato showed great interest in discussing the problems proposed by the Eleatics, by Heraclitus, and by Protagoras. The lists of Aristotle's writings show special works (now lost) on Xenophanes, Zeno, Melissus, Alcmaeon, Gorgias, and the Pythagoreans. These investigations all sprang from the Academy's intensive study of early philosophers, and their results can be seen in the earliest parts of Aristotle's *Metaphysics*—particularly in the first book, which treats the history of philosophy. Similarly, Xenocrates wrote on Parmenides and the Pythagoreans, Speusippus on the Pythagoreans, and Heraclides Ponticus on the Pythagoreans, on Democritus, and on Heraclitus. Thus, Isocrates' polemic against these early philosophers can be reasonably taken to be part of his general critique of Plato's paideia. Its renewal of interest in the pre-Socratics was another of the traits which annoyed him (cf. *Antid.* 285). What would he have said to the later development of this work—the great histories of philosophy produced by the pupils of Aristotle's old age?

123. *Antid.* 270 f.

124. *Antid.* 271.

125. Note the emphasis in the phrase *'such* phronésis' (ἡ τοιαύτη φρόνησις) in *Antid.* 271. It sets the knowledge of practical politics recommended by Isocrates in opposition to Plato's theoretical phronésis. On the change of phronésis within Plato's philosophy into metaphysical knowledge of Being, see my *Aristotle*, p. 83 f.

126. In *Antid.* 233-234, not only Solon and Cleisthenes, but the great statesmen of the classical age of Athenian democracy, Themistocles and Pericles, are described as models of political and rhetorical areté. Plato inveighs against the latter

two in *Gorgias* and *Meno*. Obviously, then, Isocrates is taking the side of the statesmen attacked by Plato, just as he had sided with Callicles at another point (cf. note 120).

127. *Antid.* 274.

128. 'Philologia': *Antid.* 296.

129. *Antid.* 274-275: 'an art of the kind' sought for by the dialecticians 'has never existed and does not now exist. But until such a paideia [ἡ τοιαύτη παιδεία] is discovered, people should stop promising it to others.' This ὑπόσχεσις is the teacher's pledge to teach his pupils (see *Paideia* II, 111)—the same thing as ἐπάγγελμα, the professor's 'profession'.

130. *Antid.* 275. Here Isocrates deliberately uses the Platonic concept of Eros. He implies it would be worthy of a better object than the hair-splitting dialectic method which Plato assigns to it.

131. This had been said already, in *Soph.* 21, and even more positively in *Nic.* 7.

132. *Antid.* 276-277.

133. *Antid.* 278.

134. Plato, *Gorg.* 508a. There the rhetor Callicles is the true representative of pleonexia, the lust for power.

135. It is easy to prove that Isocrates is answering Plato's charge that rhetoric merely trains men to satisfy egotistic impulses. In *Antid.* 275 he had advised students of philosophy to turn their 'eros' to the art of oratory, and to give themselves wholly up to 'the right pleonexia': he adds that he will explain these interesting remarks later on. They are not explained till *Antid.* 281 f. There he makes a special analysis of the nature of pleonexia, aggrandisement, and tries to give it a positive meaning. It is the impulse to possess, which is a deep-seated human instinct. At this point he draws a sharp line between Callicles and himself, though he had formerly defended him. The line is the frontier of morality.

136. *On peace* 33. In c. 31 of that speech it is clear that he is opposing the non-moral ideal of Callicles, and his doctrine 'might makes right', which Plato in his *Gorgias* had connected with rhetoric and its aim of teaching practical politics. Isocrates tries in the *Antidosis* to distinguish them very clearly and sharply.

137. *Antid.* 282 and 285. In 283 Isocrates blames the philosophers for their misuse of words: they transfer names from the noblest to the basest things. Actually, he himself has transferred the word *pleonexia* from an offensive quality to an ideal. In this he is clearly following the example of Plato, *Symp.* 206a, who defines the idealized Eros as the impulse to possess the most beautiful and the best (see *Paideia* II, 189, with my allusion to Aristotle's analogous re-interpretation of self-love). Similarly, Plato in *Gorgias* had declared that the power which egotistic power-politicians tried to obtain was not a real power. Isocrates uses the same means to show that *his* rhetoric leads to that true and noble self-enrichment. He had learnt something after all from the despised science of dialectic!

138. *Antid.* 286-290. His description of his own earnest pupils, leading to the culminating ideal of self-mastery and care for one's own soul (cf. 304), is quite Socratic in tone. Isocrates takes over Socrates' practical morality (without Plato's dialectic and ontology) and blends it with his own rhetorical and political culture.

139. *Paneg.* 47-50.

140. *Antid.* 296.

141. *Antid.* 295-297, 293 f. Cf. 302: 'in physical contests the Athenians have many competitors, but in culture [= paideia] the whole world admits their superiority.'

142. *Antid.* 297-298.

143. It appears throughout the concluding section of the *Antidosis* (291-319).

144. According to *Antid.* 299-301, political informers and demagogues are the great blot on the fair name of Athens; she owes her greatness to her culture

(paideia) alone. The passage is interesting because of the sharp distinction between culture and contemporary political life. When he speaks of the leaders of that culture who have made Athens respected and loved throughout the world, he is thinking of himself among the first. And doubtless he is perfectly correct.

145. He estimates all the great Athenian statesmen of the past by their culture and education in *Antid.* 306-308. He concludes that only its intellectual aristocracy has made the city great.

146. *Phil.* 8-9.

147. Isocr. *ep.* 2.15. He must be alluding to Demosthenes here; at the date of the letter, *he* was the real leader of the resistance to Philip.

148. See *Panath.* 2-4 for his increasing disregard of style.

149. That is the age he mentions at the end of *Panath.* (270); in the introduction (3) he says he is 94. His work on the speech was interrupted by a long illness.

150. It also contains some remarks on true paideia: note the interesting passage, 30-33, which is a page-long definition of paideia. All he says in praise of Athenian paideia is worked into his praise of the ancestors. What he loves in Athens is its past.

7. XENOPHON: THE IDEAL SQUIRE AND SOLDIER

1. See Karl Muenscher's book *Xenophon in der griechisch-römischen Literatur* (Leipzig 1920), particularly section IV, on Xenophon in Greek literature of the Roman empire, in which Muenscher describes and defines Xenophon's position in the age of Atticism, with a vast amount of evidence.

2. He tells how he joined Cyrus in *An.* 3.1.4 f.

3. Xen. *An.* 3.1.5 emphasizes only one fact: since the Peloponnesian war, in which Cyrus supported Sparta against Athens, there had been hostility between Athens and Cyrus. But after Xenophon came back from the campaign in Asia, he joined the Spartans who were fighting under Agesilaus for the freedom of the Greeks in Asia Minor, and later returned to Greece with the king (*An.* 5.3.6). He says pointedly that he came back 'through Boeotia', which probably implies that he fought with the Spartans at Coronea. On Xenophon's accession to the Spartan side, see the thoughtful judgment of Alfred Croiset in *Xénophon, son caractère et son talent* (Paris 1873) p. 118 f.

4. Xen. *An.* 7.7.57, 5.3.7.

5. *An.* 5.3.7-13.

6. See *Paideia* II, 20.

7. Cf. Xen. *Mem.* 1.2.12 f.

8. Isocr. *Bus.* 5.

9. Compare the efforts of Isocrates to clear himself and his pupil Timotheus of the charge of anti-democratic sentiments, *misodemia: Areop.* 57, *Antid.* 131 (pp. 123, 138 f.).

10. The *terminus post quem* for the publication of Polycrates' book against Socrates is 393, because (according to Favorinus in Diogenes Laertius 2.39) it mentioned Conon's reconstruction of the Long Walls. Xenophon had returned to Greece from Asia Minor with Agesilaus in 394 (p. 158).

11. See *Paideia* II, 21.

12. To incorporate the pamphlet in the *Memorabilia* as he did was something like what we should now call re-publication, or issuing a new edition of an out-of-print book.

12a. Whether Xenophon came back to Athens to stay, or, after his return, visited Corinth where he had spent some years after leaving Scillus, will probably never be decided.

13. Xenophon had of course been working at the *Hellenica* before 362. It is easy to see why he thought the new proof of Spartan weakness, the defeat of Mantinea, to be a suitable conclusion: for his book described the rise of Sparta to supreme power, and then its decline. This theme appears in Isocrates and other contemporaries of his, as an enormously impressive and important political event, and as a warning contemporary parallel to the fall of the first Attic empire. It is that which gives Xenophon's history its inner unity.

14. On the proposal of some scholars to amputate the conclusion, see note 56.

15. All these books fall between 360 and 350. Plato's *Critias,* with its idealized picture of Athens, must be placed against the same intellectual background if it is to be understood properly.

16. The chapter describing the conversation of Socrates with the younger Pericles (*Mem.* 3.5), which assumes that Thebes is the principal enemy of Athens and holds up the areté of old Sparta for the Athenians to admire (in the middle of the Peloponnesian war!), can only have been written in the period when Athens and Sparta were allied against the rising power of Thebes, some time between 370 and 350. At the time when the conversation is supposed to be held, shortly before Arginusae (406), there was no danger of a Boeotian invasion of Attica. But compare the advice offered in Xenophon's *Hipparchicus* 7.2 f. about facing a Boeotian invasion. This chapter in the *Memorabilia* belongs to the same period, when these precautions against such an inroad were urgently necessary.

17. The directions in *Hipparchicus* are not universally applicable. They are suggestions for the improvement of the Athenian cavalry. The author's prime concern is to ensure the defence of Attica against a Boeotian invasion: see *Hipp.* 7.1-4. He says that Athens must try to meet the admirable heavy infantry of Thebes with equally good Attic infantry, and put up cavalry superior to the Boeotian cavalry. The essay *On Horsemanship* also takes Athenian conditions into account: see chapter 1. In the closing sentence it alludes to the *Hipparchicus.*

18. In 5.9 it mentions the evacuation of the Delphic sanctuary by the Phocians, who had occupied it for a long time, in the Sacred War. That takes us down to the period 355-350.

19. Cf. *Cyn.* 13.

20. *Oec.* 4.18. Cf. *An.* 1.9.1.

21. *An.* 1.9.

22. *Cyn.* 8.8; see especially 8.8.12.

23. The old Persian paideia is contrasted with the 'Median' luxury of contemporary Persia in *Cyrop.* 8.8.15.

24. See Ivo Bruns, *Das literarische Porträt der Griechen* 142 f.

25. On the paideia of Cyrus the younger, see *An.* 1.9.2-6. Xenophon describes it both as part of the character of his hero, and for its own sake. See p. 162. The naïve account of the noble bearing of the Persians in *Cyrop.* 1.2.16 is perhaps best fitted to show us what an educated Greek contemporary of Plato thought was polite in Persian manners. For instance, the Persians felt it was improper to spit, to blow one's nose, and to show signs of flatulence; or to be seen going aside to make water or so forth. The medical explanation which Xenophon appends to this statement and the realism of the whole passage show that he is taking his information from the *Persica* of Ctesias, a doctor who worked at the court of King Artaxerxes, and who is mentioned in *An.* 1.8.27.

26. On Cyrus' love of Greek ways and admiration of Greek troops, see *An.* 1.7.3, where Xenophon makes him say he took Greeks with him on his expedition because he thought they were far better than barbarians. Cyrus attributes their superiority in morals and in warfare to the fact that they are free men. The peoples conquered by Persia were enslaved. Of course this does not affect Cyrus' pride in his own rank as a scion of the ruling house of Persia. Xenophon says in *Cyrop.* 8.8.26 that the Persians of that period could not have carried on their wars without Greek intelligence and Greek skill in soldiering.

27. Cf. *An.* 1.8.27. Alexander had the same ideal of personal courage in a general as Cyrus—an ideal which the fourth-century Greeks thought rather too romantic. He exposed himself freely to danger, and was often wounded.

28. It was because he realized the historical parallelism between the expeditions of Cyrus and Alexander that Arrian called his history of the Macedonian conqueror *The Anabasis of Alexander:* see Arr. *An.* 1.12.3-4.

29. Isocr. *Paneg.* 145; Dem. *Symm.* 9 and 32. On Jason of Pherae and his plan to overthrow the Persian empire, see Isocr. *Phil.* 119. Philip and Alexander themselves were certainly influenced by Xenophon too; but we have no evidence on the point.

30. See note 25. Later King Alexander tried to mix Greek and Persian blood and culture through intermarriage of the nobility of both races.

31. See *An.* 1.9.

32. *Paneg.* 50; cf. p. 79.

33. See Xenophon's own description of the aspects of Cyrus' character which interest him in *Cyrop.* 1.1.6: τίς ποτ' ὢν γενεὰν καὶ ποίαν τινὰ φύσιν ἔχων καὶ ποίᾳ τινὶ παιδευθεὶς παιδείᾳ τοσοῦτον διήνεγκεν εἰς τὸ ἄρχειν ἀνθρώπων. In the second chapter of his *Lacedaemonian Constitution* he gives just as much importance to paideia in the Spartan system as he gives it here in Persia. His description of the paideia of Cyrus is really confined to the second chapter of the first book of the *Cyropaedia.* Similarly, the *Anabasis* gets its title from its first episode, although most of the narrative is devoted to the return from the expedition into Asia, and the return was a *katabasis*, a journey to the sea. This kind of title is fairly common in classical literature.

33a. The title of the book is further justified by Xenophon's constant allusions to the paideia of the Persians, and to their areté as the creative force which produced the Persian empire. The passages illustrating this are too numerous to quote. Even when Cyrus is handing over his power to his heirs and successors, he insists that their title to possession of it is the paideia which he received and transmitted to his children (8.7.10).

34. See chapters 4 and 9 of this book.

35. Love of justice was implanted in every Persian gentleman when he was young, by Persian paideia: *Cyrop.* 1.2.6. See also the conversation of young Cyrus with his Median mother, 1.3.16. In 1.3.18 Xenophon says that for a Persian father μέτρον αὐτῷ οὐχ ἡ ψυχή, ἀλλ' ὁ νόμος ἐστίν—ψυχή means subjective desire as opposed to the objective standard of law.

36. *Hipparch.* 9.8.

37. In Pericles, its 'first citizen' (πρῶτος ἀνήρ), Athens had produced a ruler who was at once a statesman and a general. Alcibiades and Nicias fell into the same pattern. The last to unite both ideals was Timotheus. After him they tended more and more to separate. Xenophon thought the training of a soldier, not of a politician, was the best preparation for statesmanship. Isocrates too, and Plato even more, emphasized the importance of soldiering in their system of paideia for the ruler. But the purely military type of ruler first became predominant in the

Hellenistic era. Many Hellenistic monarchs were not only soldiers, but had scientific training.

38. Thus, Critias discussed the question of education in his studies on the political life of other states: as the fragments of his prose treatise on the constitution of the Spartans show. He could speak of conditions in Thessaly from personal experience.

39. *Cyrop.* 1.2.2-3 init.

39a. In *Resp. Lac.* 10.4 Xenophon eulogizes the state education of children in Sparta in the same way as he here does that of the Persians.

40. *Cyrop.* 1.2.6.

41. *Cyrop.* 1.2.3-4.

42. Cf. Dem. *De cor.* 169.

43. *Cyrop.* 1.2.5.

44. *Cyrop.* 1.2.6.

45. *Cyrop.* 1.2.7.

46. See *Paideia* II, 338, 378 f.; III, 122.

47. *Cyrop.* 1.2.8.

48. *Cyrop.* 1.2.8-9. Isocrates too declares that more attention should be paid to the young men and the ephéboi: *Areop.* 43 and 50.

49. *Cyrop.* 1.2.10; cf. *Resp. Lac.* 4.7, 6.3-4. On the *Cynegeticus* see p. 179 f.

50. *Oec.* 4.4 f.

51. *Cyrop.* 1.2.12 fin.-13.

52. Still, the Spartiates must have found it strange that even the king of Persia and the highest nobles were enthusiastic farmers. In Sparta, farming counted as 'banausic', vulgar—like every other trade and profession: see *Resp. Lac.* 7.1. Xenophon does not agree with the Spartan ideal in this; in *Oec.* 4.3 he stresses the contrast between Sparta and Persia.

53. *Cyrop.* 1.2.15.

54. *Cyrop.* 8.8.

55. *Resp. Lac.* 14.

56. Some scholars have held that the conclusions of the *Cyropaedia* and the *Lacedaemonian Constitution,* in which Xenophon blames the contemporary Persians and Spartans for lapsing from their own ideal, were added later either by Xenophon or by another hand. But it would be peculiar if the same change had been made in both books after their publication. On the contrary, the similarity of the two conclusions confirms their authenticity: both of them draw a contrast between the good old days and the bad present. Besides, the characteristic 'nowadays' appears in other passages as well as the conclusion of the *Cyropaedia:* see 1.3.2; 1.4.27; 2.4.20; 3.3.26; 4.2.8; 4.3.2; 4.3.23; 8.1.37; 8.2.4; 8.2.7; 8.4.5; 8.6.16. But if the concluding chapters of both works are authentic, and belong to the original version, as I am convinced they do, that means that Xenophon must have finished the *Cyropaedia* and the *Lacedaemonian Constitution* in the last ten years of his life. The latest event he mentions at the conclusion of the *Cyropaedia* (8.8.4) is the betrayal of the rebellious satrap Ariobarzanes to the King by his own son (360 B.C.).

57. *Cyrop.* 1.3.2 f., 8.3.1, 8.8.15.

58. *Cyrop.* 7.5.85.

59. *Cyrop.* 8.8.1-2.

60. See p. 325, n. 33a.

61. See *Paideia* I, 79 f.: the section 'Historical Tradition and the Philosophical Idealization of Sparta' (in the fourth century).

62. See Plato, *Laws* 626a (cf. p. 221). The oligarchic sympathizer who wrote *The Athenian Constitution,* which is falsely attributed to Xenophon, similarly

admires the thoroughness with which the democratic principle pervades every detail of Athenian life—although he does not therefore admire the democratic principle *per se.*

63. *Resp. Lac.* 1.2, 2.2, 2.13, et cetera.

64. In *Resp. Lac.* 1.2 he speaks of the originality of the Lycurgan form of state; and in 9.1, 10.1, 10.4, 11.1, etc., he explains how much the Spartan institutions deserve to be admired; in 10.8, he says that many praise them, but no one imitates them.

65. He often points out that the institutions of Lycurgus were diametrically opposite to those of other Greek states: 1.3-4, 2.1-2, 2.13, 3.2, 6.1, 7.1, etc.

66. *Resp. Lac.* 1.10, 2.14.

67. This would not make his book any less welcome to the Spartans, since it contains an effective defence of the Spartan system.

68. See, for instance, *Hell.* 7.4.15 f.

68a. This tendency in Athenian politics is described in great detail in *Hell.* 7.1. Xenophon always takes care to mention it in the *Hellenica* or the *Revenues,* when an Athenian expeditionary force is sent to the aid of Sparta or her allies.

69. The principle is taken up in Plato's *The Republic* and *The Laws;* but besides them, see Aristotle's *Nic. Eth.* 10.10.1180a25: 'It is only in the Spartan state that the legislators have made provision for education and the guidance of life. In most countries these matters are neglected, and everyone lives as he likes, ruling his own wife and children like the Cyclops.'

70. See *Resp. Lac.* 14.6, where he says that the Spartans are now so unpopular that the other Greeks co-operate to prevent them from regaining their hegemony.

71. Allusions to the intervention of divine power in historical events are to be found in *Hell.* 6.4.3, and 7.5.12-13.

72. See the chapter on Socrates in *Paideia* II, 20 f.

73. What the *Memorabilia* contribute to the problem of paideia is to give a description of Socrates' paideia, as Xenophon saw it.

74. See *Paideia* II, 51 f.

75. Cf. p. 324, n. 16.

76. Cf. p. 116.

77. *Paideia* I, 312.

78. ἀγροῖκος is the commonest word to describe lack of culture: see Ar. *Rhet.* 3.7.1408a32, where it is contrasted to πεπαιδευμένος. More specifically, Aristotle makes the word opposite to ease of manner in social life, εὐτραπελία: see *Eth. Nic.* 2.7.1108a26. Theophrastus describes the ἀγροῖκος in the fourth of his *Characters.*

79. On Aristophanes' *The Banqueters* (*Daitaleis*), see *Paideia* I, 370-371.

80. Plato, *Phaedr.* 230d.

81. Xen. *Oec.* 4.1.

82. Xen. *Oec.* 4.2-3.

83. Xen. *Oec.* 4.4 f.

84. Xen. *Oec.* 4.6; 4.8-12; 4.14 f.

85. Xen. *Oec.* 4.20-25.

86. Xen. *Oec.* 4.4; on the combination of soldiering and farming in the life of the Persian kings see also 4.12. Xenophon held that farming meant not only increasing one's livelihood (οἴκου αὔξησις) and physical training (σώματος ἄσκησις) but pleasure (ἡδυπάθεια): see *Oec.* 5.1 f.

87. Xen. *Oec.* 6.12-17.

88. We might here add what Xenophon says about the paideia of the groom in his book *On Horsemanship* (Περὶ ἱππικῆς 5). In the fourth century the idea of education, triumphantly advancing, spread unresisted into every sphere of life. Here of course it is only a question of the form of words that is used. It is

interesting to see how, at the very same time as chosen spirits like Plato and Isocrates were raising the word paideia to new and unheard-of heights of intellectual and spiritual significance, others were trying to turn it into a trivial cliché. Xenophon mentions the duty of educating children in *Oec.* 7.12, but only briefly. It does not form part of the general scheme of household paideia which he is working out.

89. Xen. *Oec.* 7.4.

90. Xen. *Oec.* 7.32.

91. Xen. *Oec.* 7.5.

92. When the girl gets married she is already πεπαιδευμένη in spinning and cookery: *Oec.* 7.6. Her mother has taught her nothing else except to be modest and shy (σωφρονεῖν).

93. Xen. *Oec.* 7.14: the wife does not expect to be her husband's partner in work (συμπρᾶξαι).

94. See Ivo Bruns, *Frauenemanzipation in Athen,* in his *Vorträge und Aufsätze* (Munich 1905): he examines Xenophon's *Oeconomicus* too, from this point of view.

95. Xenophon explains his ideas about the co-operation of men and women with reference to the life of the farm, in *Oec.* 7.18 f.

96. Xen. *Oec.* 7.21-22. See the whole of the passage that follows.

97. Xen. *Oec.* 7.23-25.

98. Xen. *Oec.* 7.24.

99. Xen. *Oec.* 7.23.

100. Xen. *Oec.* 7.32-37.

101. Xen. *Oec.* 7.41.

102. Xen. *Oec.* 8.

103. Xen. *Oec.* 9.

104. Xen. *Oec.* 10.

105. Xen. *Oec.* 9.11-13.

106. See Xen. *Oec.* 12.4 to 14 on the paideia of the farm foreman. Here παιδεύειν does not mean so much technical training as genuine education of the man who is naturally fitted to oversee the labourers' work. One of the principal aims of that education is to make him able to lead others (13.4). He must be truly devoted to his master, and be anxious to direct the workers so as to get the best out of them for his master's interests; and also he must be thoroughly expert in his job (15.1).

107. Xen. *Oec.* 12.17-8.

107a. Xen. *Oec.* 11.14.

108. Xen. *Oec.* 12.20.

109. Xen. *Oec.* 15.10, 16.1.

110. Xen. *Oec.* 21.10.

111. Nowadays it is not usually thought to be by Xenophon. If it were not, that would not lessen its importance in the history of paideia, which does not depend on the name of its author. But it would deprive us of one of the two essential elements in Xenophon's ideal of education. I have given on page 329 my reasons for believing it genuine.

112. The greater part of the *Cynegeticus* is purely technical (chapters 2-11). The introduction (1) and the conclusion (12-13) deal with the value of hunting for paideia and areté—i.e., for character-building.

113. *Resp. Lac.* 4.7, 6.3-4.

114. *Cyrop.* 1.2.9-11. Similarly the importance of hunting in the life of the elder Cyrus and of the Persians is emphasized throughout the book. See Xenophon's account of young Cyrus' love of hunting, in *Anab.* 1.9.6.

115. Plato, *Laws* 823b to the end of Book 7.

116. On the date of the *Cynegeticus*, see p. 159.

117. Cf. the closing words of the seventh book of *The Laws*, and 823d.

118. *Laws* 823b-c.

119. On this form of instruction in general, *Laws* 823a; with special reference to hunting 823c and 823d, where Plato looks forward to the poetic form of the praise of hunting.

120. *Laws* 823d-e.

121. *Laws* 824a.

122. Cf. L. Radermacher, *Rheinisches Museum* 51 (1896) 596 f., and 52 (1897) 13 f., for an attempt to prove that the *Cynegeticus* is not by Xenophon.

123. *Cyn.* 1.1.

124. On the mythical figure of Chiron in the early tradition of paideia, see *Paideia* I, 25.

125. On Chiron as the teacher of the heroes in Pindar, see *Paideia* I, 25 and 218.

126. Xen. *Cyn.* 1.2.

127. Xen. *Cyn.* 1.5 f.

128. Xen. *Cyn.* 2-8.

129. *Cyn.* 9 deals with big-game-hunting, 10 with wild-boar-hunting, 11 with hunting beasts of prey. Xenophon knew a number of details about hunting in Asia, from his personal experience.

130. Xen. *Cyn.* 12-13. Eduard Norden, in a special appendix to his *Antike Kunstprosa* (I, 431), discussed the style of the introduction to Xenophon's *Cynegeticus*. He was obviously influenced by Radermacher's essay (see note 122), which correctly pointed out that the style of the introduction was unlike that of the rest of the book. He described its style as 'Asianic', and concluded that the *Cynegeticus* was not written before the third century B.C. The book is mentioned in Diogenes Laertius' list of Xenophon's works, which is derived from the catalogues (πίνακες) compiled by third-century Alexandrian scholars. Norden points out, with justice, that a difference of style in the introduction is not proof of its falsity, but is a perfectly normal thing; and although he cannot admit that Xenophon wrote it, he recognizes that the dispute about the true nature of paideia, to which the *Cynegeticus* is meant to be a contribution, probably belongs to the age of Xenophon. On the other hand, he thinks the style of the introduction belongs only to the period of the Second Sophistic under the Roman empire. It is therefore, he believes, a later addition. This argument is destroyed by the fact that the introduction is expressly quoted at the beginning of the concluding section (12.18)— a point which Norden missed. Actually, the book is an indissoluble whole. The introduction and the conclusion serve to fit the body of the work, which is technical, into the picture as part of the general debate about paideia in the fourth century, and to explain the educational value of hunting. It is difficult to oppose a critic so sensitive as Norden in a matter of style; but the introduction is not really so different from other passages in Xenophon's work which have a specially elaborate and rhetorical style. I hope to treat this subject in more detail elsewhere.

131. Xen. *Cyn.* 13.3, 13.6.

132. Xen. *Cyn.* 12.1.

133. Xen. *Cyn.* 12.2-6; cf. Anth. Pal. 14.17.

134. Xen. *Cyn.* 12.7-8: τὸ ἐν τῇ ἀληθείᾳ παιδεύεσθαι is contrasted with the usual contemporary system of paideia by words alone, as described in c. 13—the sophists' education. Whenever reality (ἀλήθεια) comes into contact with men, it educates them by toil and suffering (πόνος).

135. Xen. *Cyn.* 12.15, 12.16, 12.17, 12.18, 13.10, 13.13, 13.14, 13.22, etc. The words πόνος and παίδευσις are used as synonyms in 12.18.

136. Xen. *Cyn.* 12.18; cf. 1.1 f.

137. Xen. *Cyn.* 13.1-3.

138. Xen. *Cyn.* 13.4. It is interesting to see that there are now specialists and laymen (ἰδιῶται) in paideia, and also that the layman's criticisms have more weight than in any other subject. Xenophon emphasizes the fact that he is a layman, once again, at the end of his book on riding 12.14.

139. The simplicity Xenophon displays when he writes: ἴσως οὖν τοῖς μὲν ὀνόμασιν οὐ σεσοφισμένως λέγω · οὐδὲ γὰρ ζητῶ τοῦτο may be taken with a grain of salt. The tricks of style he uses in the prologue and conclusion of his book, so as to appear 'simple', are really rather expert.

140. Xen. *Cyn.* 13.5. This reminds us of Theognis 60, who derides the uncultured men of his time for having no γνῶμαι (see *Paideia* I, 198).

141. Xen. *Cyn.* 13.6: 'Many others reproach the present-day sophists (τοὺς νῦν σοφιστάς)—not real lovers of culture (τοὺς φιλοσόφους)—because their cleverness consists of words, not of thoughts.' This contrast, which recurs in 13.9, is the same one which appears in Plato and in Isocrates. Cf. the criticism of the sophists in 13.1, 8, 9. Xenophon of course stresses the fact that he is a layman, but he sides with the 'philosophers'.

142. Xen. *Cyn.* 12.9, 12.10, 12.15, 13.11 f., 13.17.

143. Xen. *Cyn.* 13.15-18. There is another epilogue, equally pious, in Xenophon's *Hipparchicus.*

8. PLATO'S *PHAEDRUS:* PHILOSOPHY AND RHETORIC

1. *Phaedr.* 238d, 241e.

2. This is quite clear in Diog. Laert. 3.38, who quotes the Peripatetic Dicaearchus for the condemnation of the style of the dialogue. Dicaearchus said it was φορτικόν. The Neo-Platonic source of the third chapter in Olympiodorus' biography of Plato argues from the dithyrambic language of Socrates' speeches about Eros in *Phaedrus* that Plato was young when he wrote it. Therefore, it seems clear that the odd adjective 'youthful' (μειρακιῶδες), applied by Diogenes to the *subject-matter* of the dialogue, was originally meant in the usual sense as one of the condemnatory descriptions used in rhetorical criticisms of style, and had nothing to do with content. To condemn the subject-matter of *Phaedrus* as 'a youthful problem' looks to me like an improvisation worthy of that great ignoramus Diogenes Laertius. Obviously he is taking the subject of Lysias' speech at the beginning of *Phaedrus*— which certainly is puerile enough—to be the real subject of the whole dialogue.

3. See my discussion of Schleiermacher's place in the history of Platonic research in the nineteenth century in *Platos Stellung im Aufbau der griechischen Bildung* (Berlin 1928) ; the series of lectures published separately under this title was also printed in *Die Antike*, vol. 4, p. 86.

4. It was Karl Friedrich Hermann, with his *Geschichte und System der platonischen Philosophie* (Heidelberg 1839), who was chiefly responsible for this change of attitude. On this point see my sketch of the change in the current view of Plato during the nineteenth century on p. 23 of the essay cited in note 3 (*Die Antike* vol. 4, p. 88).

5. Hermann associated *Phaedrus* with books like *Menexenus, The Symposium,* and *Phaedo,* putting it in what he called Plato's third period—before *The Republic, Timaeus,* and *The Laws.* Even Usener and Wilamowitz defended Schleiermacher's view that it was an early work, against Hermann, although Wilamowitz gave up this view later. H. von Arnim went further than Hermann, and described *Phaedrus* as one of Plato's late books: see his *Platos Jugenddialoge und die Entstehungszeit des Phaidros* (Leipzig 1914).

6. This final conclusion was drawn from von Arnim's argument by J. Stenzel, *Studien zur Entwicklung der platonischen Dialektik* (Breslau 1917) 105 f. = *Plato's Method of Dialectic* (Oxford 1940) 149 f. It confirms the statement which we find in Cicero, *Or.* 13, and which goes back to the Hellenistic scholars, that *Phaedrus* was written in Plato's old age.

7. Plato could not compare his philosophy with Lysias' rhetoric without a common basis of comparison. The common basis is the claim raised by both parties to represent true paideia. So also Isocrates in his programme-essay, *Against the Sophists,* distinguished three main forms of contemporary paideia: (1) the Socratics, (2) teachers of political eloquence like Alcidamas, (3) speech-writers and composers of legal orations like Lysias (Isocr. *Soph.* 1).

8. *Phaedr.* 279a.

9. *Phaedr.* 228a, 258d.

9a. Cicero, *Or.* 13.42, following a Hellenistic scholar, rightly says *haec de adolescente Socrates auguratur, at ea de seniore scribit Plato et scribit aequalis.* Anyone who makes a thorough study of the literary relation between Plato and Isocrates, as the Alexandrian philologists must have done, is bound to come to that conclusion. The 'evidence' of Diogenes Laertius should never have been taken for anything but a worthless invention. See note 2.

10. See p. 146 f., and my *Aristotle* p. 37.

11. If Socrates is the true statesman (*Gorg.* 521d), he must also be the true rhetor: for in Plato's time a statesman was the same as a rhetor.

12. See *Paideia* II, 179.

13. See pp. 56, 148-150.

14. The difference between our version of Aristotle's *Rhetoric* and the manuals by hack rhetoricians is his philosophical approach to the problem. On this point, see F. Solmsen, *Die Entwicklung der aristotelischen Rhetorik und Logik (Neue Philol. Unters.,* ed. W. Jaeger, vol. 4) p. 213 f.

15. *Phaedr.* 228b-e.

16. This is numbers 71 and 72 in Diogenes Laertius' list: θέσεις ἐρωτικαί and θέσεις φιλικαί.

17. The subject of Eros appears in *The Symposium* also, especially at the beginning of the contest of eloquence and in Phaedrus' speech, as an accepted theme for oratory: see *Paideia* II, 179 f.

18. *Phaedr.* 234e f., 237c.

19. See *Paideia* II, 180-181.

20. *Phaedr.* 231 f.

21. *Phaedr.* 237d-238c.

22. *Phaedr.* 239b.

23. The extreme importance in paideia of the philosophical Eros which *The Symposium* describes is illustrated by Socrates' remarkable first speech, delivered with his head veiled. He warns a young man against his lover, who, he says, is an 'untrustworthy fellow: he will ruin his property, his bodily health, and above all his soul's culture (ψυχῆς παίδευσις), which is the most precious thing there is or will be for gods or men' (*Phaedr.* 241c). Actually Plato means us to see the truth of which this is the converse. The true lover is he who does most to preserve and increase the culture of the soul of his beloved. See 243c.

24. *Phaedr.* 244a f.

25. *Phaedr.* 245a f. We have already quoted the passage in *Paideia* I, 40. The imperishable knowledge of the nature and influence of poetry which it expresses is really the basis of this entire book, and of the intellectual attitude embodied in it. It is the true Greek interpretation of poetry.

26. *Phaedr.* 245c-246a.

27. *Phaedr.* 246a f.
28. *Phaedr.* 247c.
29. *Phaedr.* 238d, 242b.
30. *Phaedr.* 258d.
31. *Phaedr.* 259e.
32. *Phaedr.* 260e f.: Plato is quoting his own *Gorgias* without naming it.
33. *Phaedr.* 261a f.

33a. Socrates' two speeches on Eros are examples of this antilogic, which is the basis of the rhetorical trick, *dicere in utramque partem.* On it see what Plato himself says in *Phaedr.* 265a.

34. Cf. *Phaedr.* 261a-b, where Plato points out that the psychagogia taught by the rhetor is used not only in public assemblies but in private conversation too. The rhetor's method is extended to all types of speech (πάντα τὰ λεγόμενα) in *Phaedr.* 261e.

35. *Phaedr.* 261d.

36. The book is now lost, but it was well known in classical times. Its fragments were collected by Paul Lang in his dissertation *De Speusippi vita et scriptis* (Bonn 1911).

37. *Phaedr.* 262a f.
38. *Phaedr.* 263a.

39. He does this in both speeches. Division (διαίρεσις) of the *eidos* is called for in *Phaedr.* 263b, and there are numerous allusions to it later: 263c, 265a-d, 266a.

40. *Phaedr.* 263e-264b.
41. *Phaedr.* 264c-e.

42. Cf. Horace's assertion of the principle *ponere totum* in his *Ars Poetica* 34. *A.P.* 23 is similar: it insists that the plot in epic and drama should be an absolute unity (πρᾶξις ὅλη καὶ τελεία). In the first part of the *Ars Poetica* Horace gives examples to show what happens when the law of organic unity is contravened, but he does not put down the law in general terms (at least only cursorily in a subordinate clause, as in 34)—this being more appropriate to the conversational style of his *Sermones.* Still, behind the whole poem stands the profound principle which Plato was the first to formulate, in *Phaedrus* 263e-264b.

43. Lysias obviously meant his speech to be a model; but after we read it with Plato's sarcastic remark in mind, it contains a number of examples of how *not* to speak: see *Phaedrus* 264e. In 262d and 265a Plato asserts that Socrates' two speeches are meant to be models. Rhetorical teaching was always done by getting pupils to imitate a paradeigma: see pp. 54, 64. Plato borrows this method and uses it rather differently: to show the mistakes or merits of contrasting model speeches from the dialectic point of view.

44. *Phaedr.* 264e-265a.
45. *Phaedr.* 265a f.

46. Cf. *Phaedr.* 266b-c, where Plato sums up the results of his previous explanation and concrete exemplification of dialectic method in the two concepts *diairesis,* division, and *synagogé,* combination.

47. *Phaedr.* 265a-266a.
48. *Phaedr.* 269d.
49. *Phaedr.* 269b-c: τὰ πρὸ τῆς τέχνης ἀναγκαῖα μαθήματα.
50. *Phaedr.* 266d-267c.
51. The Greek for 'methods' (rhetorical devices) in this sense is τὰ ἀναγκαῖα: see note 49.
52. See p. 63.
53. *Phaedr.* 269d.

54. This is made clear by the whole trend of the discussion, although there is no special statement about it. In speaking of Pericles, Plato emphasizes, first, his natural gift for speaking (εὐφυία) and then his philosophical knowledge, which he got from Anaxagoras.

55. Isocr. *Soph.* 16 f. See p. 62.

56. See H. von Arnim, *Leben und Werke des Dion von Prusa* (Berlin 1898), particularly his elaborate introduction, which gives a complete historical account of the later rivalry of sophistic, rhetoric, and philosophy, to dominate education.

57. Von Arnim, on p. 97 f. of his book cited in note 56, carefully discusses the question whether Cicero reached that synthesis through his knowledge of Plato (i.e. of *Phaedrus*) or was influenced by a later Academic writer. One of his predecessors in the later Academy was Philo of Larisa, who gave a special position to rhetoric in the philosophical curriculum, as Aristotle had already done in Plato's lifetime.

58. *Phaedr.* 269e-270a. In 269a also Plato mentions Pericles as a model together with the legendary king Adrastus—who appeared in ancient poetry, like Nestor, as an embodiment of captivating eloquence, the honeyed tongue, γλῶσσα μειλιχογήρυς. Cf. Tyrtaeus frg. 9.8. These heroes, possessors of the areté of true eloquence in myth and national history, are not merely meant to be pattern-figures supporting and illustrating Plato's conception of rhetoric, but to show up the pedantic dryness and jejuneness of modern technical specialists in rhetoric.

59. Cf. *Phaedr.* 261a; the idea is worked out in more detail in 271c-d.

60. *Phaedr.* 270b; see *Paideia* II, 131.

61. *Phaedr.* 270c.

62. *Phaedr.* 271a.

63. *Phaedr.* 271d.

64. Isocr. *Soph.* 16-17: cf. p. 61.

65. What Plato says on this subject in *Phaedr.* 271d f. is, as always, only the outline of what he has in mind. He sketches a theory of psychological types (ψυχῆς εἴδη) for the use of rhetoric. He refrains from working the idea out in technical detail because the Platonic dialogue is a work of art, and because the two Eros speeches of Socrates, with their rich psychological content, are meant to show by example what he means. (See p. 190.)

66. *Phaedr.* 271d-e.

67. *Phaedr.* 272a-b.

68. See *Paideia* II, 316.

69. The person who gets this training is described as ὁ μέλλων ῥητορικὸς ἔσεσθαι in *Phaedrus* 271d, and as ὁ συγγραφεύς in 272b. However, oratory was the special province of statesmen; so *Phaedrus* adds a new aspect to the plan of education for the statesman which Plato drew in *The Republic*. Or rather, it reveals that dialectic education, which was the climax of the statesman's philosophical training in *The Republic,* is also the basis of his superiority in oratory.

70. See Isocrates' criticism of the dialectic of the Socratics as useless hairsplitting, in *Helen* 4 f., and particularly his denial of its claim to be political training, *Helen* 6 and 8: cf. pp. 56, 68, 147.

71. It is impossible to acquire the training Plato recommends 'without much trouble' (ἄνευ πολλῆς πραγματείας), he says in *Phaedrus* 273e. In 274a he calls this trouble a μακρὰ περίοδος. Cf. *Rep.* 504b for the 'long detour' of Plato's paideia.

72. The passage in *Phaedrus* uses the same expression for the same thing, an analogy which confirms our interpretation of *Rep.* 504b given in *Paideia* II, 280.

73. Cf. p. 189.

74. *Phaedr.* 272d ad fin.

75. See *Paideia* II, 120.

76. *Phaedr.* 272e.

77. Speaking to please the public (χαρίζεσθαι) is described as the peculiar weakness of rhetoric not only in Plato but in Isocrates, Demosthenes, and others. In 273e Plato converts this idea into θεοῖς χαρίζεσθαι, 'speaking and acting to please God': just as he says in *The Laws* that God, not man, is the measure of all things. In place of rhetoric, whose attitude to the world was the relativism of Protagoras and the sophists, he is setting up a new ideal of eloquence, whose standard is eternal Good.

78. *Phaedr.* 274c f.

79. *Phaedr.* 275a.

80. *Ep.* 7.341c-d, 344d-e: cf. p. 207.

81. *Phaedr.* 275e.

82. *Phaedr.* 276a.

83. *Phaedr.* 275d.

84. See *Paideia* I, 312 f.

85. *Phaedr.* 276b.

86. *Rep.* 498a f., *Theaet.* 186c: ἐν χρόνῳ διὰ πολλῶν πραγμάτων καὶ παιδείας παραγίγνεται οἷς ἂν καὶ παραγίγνηται. Cf. *Phaedr.* 273e: οὐ . . . ἄνευ πολλῆς πραγματείας.

87. *Ep.* 7.341c.

88. Cf. *Theaet.* 186c: οἷς ἂν παραγίγνηται, and *Ep.* 7.341e. These are the men who have the strength to find knowledge for themselves, without much instruction.

9. PLATO AND DIONYSIUS: THE TRAGEDY OF PAIDEIA

1. On the sixth Letter, addressed to Plato's pupils Erastus and Coriscus, who ruled Assus together, and to their neighbor Hermias, tyrant of Atarneus, who had joined with them in a philosophical alliance, see my *Aristotle* 111 f. The reasons put forward by Brinckmann and myself for believing the Letter authentic have been accepted by Wilamowitz and others; but it is not relevant in this connexion. On the authenticity of the seventh and eighth Letters, see Wilamowitz, *Platon,* vol. 2; and G. Pasquali's recent book, *Le Lettere di Platone* (Florence 1938). Some scholars believe with Bentley that *all* the letters in the collection are authentic, but there are innumerable difficulties in the way of that assumption.

2. The facts given in the seventh Letter are now accepted as historically true, even in details which do not agree with the rest of our evidence—which is mainly later in date. See R. Adam's Ph.D. thesis (Berlin 1906), p. 7 f.

3. Xen. *Mem.* 1.2.39.

4. Plato, ep. 7.326e f.

5. Ep. 7.324b.

6. *Rep.* 592b.

7. *Rep.* 499c.

8. Early in the Hellenistic age, scholars began to suggest that Egypt was the analogy, or the pattern, for Plato's Republic. See Crantor in Proclus' commentary to *Timaeus,* 1.75d; my *Diokles von Karystos* 128, 134, and my essay 'Greeks and Jews' in the *Journal of Religion,* 1938.

9. *Rep.* 591e.

10. *Rep.* 501a, ep. 7.325e f.

11. The 'best state' is a myth, *Rep.* 501e; but a philosophical 'son of a king' could realize it, 502a-b.

12. *Laws* 3.691c.

13. It is possible that Plato left this loophole open, because as early as the time he was writing *The Republic* Dion had fixed great hopes upon the younger Dionysius. The thing we are sure of is that he is speaking of a young prince of a reigning family, not a monarch, because he has still to be trained.

14. Ep. 7.327 f.

15. *Rep.* 473d.

16. *Rep.* 499b; cf. ep. 7.326a-b, 327e, and elsewhere. The description of tyché is apt to alter in various passages of Plato, but here and elsewhere it is the same thing that is meant.

17. Ep. 7.327e f.

18. We have seen that Isocrates too was conscious of this situation: p. 113.

19. Ep. 7.327c.

20. See p. 95.

21. Ep. 7.328a.

22. Ep. 7.324a.

23. Ep. 7.326e; on the interpretation of the passage see *Deutsche Literaturzeitung* 1924, 897.

24. See p. 225.

25. Cf. *Paideia* I, 51 f.

26. *Rep.* 492a, 492e-493a.

27. Ep. 7.328a.

28. Ep. 7.326b.

29. Ep. 7.328b.

30. Ep. 7.328c.

31. *Rep.* 496c-e.

32. Ep. 7.329b.

33. Ep. 7.329b f.

34. Ep. 7.330a-b.

35. Ep. 7.333c. The passage deals with the slanders aimed at Plato during his *second* visit to Dionysius II; but 330b shows that the intrigues against him on his *first* visit involved the same suspicions.

36. Ep. 7.330b.

37. Ep. 7.332d.

38. Ep. 7.333b.

38a. Ep. 7.339d.

39. Ep. 7.328d.

40. Ep. 7.339a.

41. Ep. 7.339c; Dionysius promised, during Plato's previous stay, to summon both Plato and Dion back to Syracuse together, 338a.

42. Ep. 7.339b.

43. Ep. 7.339d-e.

44. Ep. 7.340b; cf. 338d.

45. Ep. 7.340c.

46. Ep. 7.341a.

47. Ep. 7.341b.

48. See p. 194.

49. Ep. 7.341c.

50. Ep. 7.341d, cf. 344b.

51. Ep. 7.342b.

52. See J. Stenzel, *Sokrates* 63 and *Platon der Erzieher* 311; Wilamowitz *Platon* 2.292. Stenzel shows very convincingly why Plato describes in such detail the vain attempt of Dionysius to understand the whole of Plato's philosophy 'by brilliant intuition' without taking the laborious way of detailed dialectic research. It is

so that he can show through him the nature of true paideia. Several scholars have said the excursus on the theory of knowledge is not properly part of an account of important political events; others have tried to excise the whole passage as an interpolation, so that they might 'vindicate' the authenticity of the whole. None of them has understood that the case of Dionysius is described in Plato's seventh Letter as a problem of paideia, not as a melodrama in which he himself happens to play a part. Evidently they underrate his sense of the importance of his own mission.

53. See *Paideia* II, 287.
54. Ep. 7.341c.
55. See *Paideia* II, 192.
56. *Tim.* 28c.
57. Ep. 7.344d.
58. Ep. 7.344c.
59. Rep. 500e.
60. See *Paideia* II, 133.
61. Ep. 7.350b f.
62. Ep. 7.334b.
63. Ep. 7.350d.
64. Ep. 7.350d.
65. Isocr. *Philip* 12.
66. See especially *Rep.* 501a.
67. In ep. 7.350c Plato speaks very strongly about the moral pressure Dion exercised on him to get him to come to Syracuse. He says it was practically compulsion (βίᾳ τινὰ τρόπον).
68. Ep. 7.331b-d.

10. PLATO'S *LAWS*

1. Plut. *de Alex. fortuna* 328e: τοὺς . . . Πλάτωνος ὀλίγοι νόμους ἀναγινώσκομεν.
2. On the transmission of *The Laws* see L. A. Post, *The Vatican Plato and Its Relations* (Middletown 1934).
3. Eduard Zeller, *Platonische Studien* (Tübingen 1839) 117.
4. *Philosophie der Griechen* II³, 805.
5. Many modern writers on Plato go into the content of *The Laws* in some detail: for instance, U. von Wilamowitz, P. Shorey, A. E. Taylor, E. Barker, and P. Friedländer. But the book must be approached from more than one point of view if justice is to be done to it. J. Stenzel does not discuss it in *Platon der Erzieher* (Leipzig 1928): another example of the old tradition that *The Laws* can be neglected.
6. *Laws* 739d. In that passage Plato says the state described in *The Laws* is the second best: it comes closest to immortality—i.e. to divinity and perfection, which it approaches without touching. He has in mind a third state (739e) which he will describe later, God willing. But he never was able to describe it. It is clear from his words that, by writing *The Laws* after *The Republic,* he was not giving up his earlier ideal. On the contrary, that ideal still remains valid for *The Laws,* as far as the book is concerned with fundamental principles: the best state is that which is as much a unity as possible. The state described in *The Laws* is to try to approach that ideal as closely as the present low standard of paideia (culture) permits. See 740a. Therefore the distinction between the two books is not in their philosophical ideals, but in the difference between the levels of paideia which they assume.
7. *Rep.* 425a-c.

8. *Polit.* 294a-297c.

9. It was not his ultimate aim that had changed, but the standard by which its realization was judged. See note 6. Laws are needed on the lower stage of paideia (*Laws* 740a) assumed in *The Laws;* they are not needed on the high stage assumed in *The Republic.*

10. It might be objected that the book does not show a new attitude, only a change of point of view. But the fact that Plato is so deeply interested in this new point of view, to which he had paid little attention hitherto, shows a real change in his philosophical attitude.

11. The more exact education (ἀκριβεστέρα παιδεία) which Plato briefly says the future rulers must have (*Laws* 965b) is described with perfect clarity in 965c as dialectic, by which the single idea in manifold appearances is discovered.

12. See Diog. Laert. 3.37 and Suidas s.v. φιλόσοφος. The tradition that Philip wrote the *Epinomis* is closely linked to the report that he edited *The Laws* from the wax notebooks left by Plato, and divided the huge work into twelve books. And the latter report must go back to a good and ancient source, probably an early tradition in the Academy. The style of the *Epinomis* fully confirms it. A. E. Taylor (*Plato and the Authorship of the Epinomis,* Proc. Brit. Acad. vol. 15) and H. Raeder (*Platons Epinomis,* Danske Videnskab. Selskab, Hist.-Phil. Medd. 26.1) have lately suggested that Plato wrote it, because they wanted to credit him with the mathematical knowledge it contains. But its mathematical ideas are even more appropriate to Philip of Opus, the learned mathematician and astronomer of the Academy. Against their view, see F. Mueller, *Stilistische Untersuchung der Epinomis* (Berlin 1927); F. Mueller in *Gnomon* 16.289; W. Theiler in *Gnomon* 7.337; and B. Einarson, *Am. Journ. Phil.* 1940. My own essay on the *Epinomis* with a collection of the fragments of Philip's other works (which received the prize of the Berlin Academy in 1913) is not in print.

13. See note 6.

14. *Laws* 720a f., 957d-e.

15. See p. 13. *Laws* 857d: οὐκ ἰατρεύεις τὸν νοσοῦντα, ἀλλὰ σχεδὸν παιδεύεις.

16. See p. 31 f.

17. See p. 131.

18. See note 7.

19. *Laws* 718b.

20. Compare all the detailed arguments he advances in *The Laws* at the end of book 4 (718d f.); especially the comparison of the lawgiver and the doctor in 719e f. See also the general discussion of what a preface actually is, 722d f.; every law must have a preface, 722b.

21. *Prot.* 326c.

22. Plato himself constantly gives us hints towards understanding his stately, slow-moving, intricate style. The readers he hates most are the conceited ignoramuses (ἀμαθαίνοντες) who can be recognized by their quick minds (τάχος τῆς ψυχῆς)—intellectuals, in fact! (See *Rep.* 500b on them.) In *The Laws* Plato's very language, apart from anything else, is meant to set him above them. On its poetic character, see p. 255.

23. See *Paideia* II, 191.

24. Cf. Plato, *Rep.* 544c2; and Aristotle in the *Protrepticus* (*dial. frg.* p. 54 Walzer). For the evidence that Aristotle wrote the extracts given in Iamblichus, see my *Aristotle,* p. 77.

25. *Laws* 642c.

26. *Laws* 642b.

27. Cf. *Laws* 692e-693a.

28. *Rep.* 544c; cf. 545b6.

29. I need scarcely say that I consider that attitude and that method of Plato's in *The Laws* to be a model for such historical works as this, which is concerned with the gradual development of human areté.

30. *Laws* 629b.

31. This is proved by the way Plato uses Tyrtaeus in *The Laws* as representative of the Spartan ideal of areté (629a; and see 660e where he rewrites Tyrtaeus' verses on true areté).

32. See the long list of examples proving the active influence of Tyrtaeus on Greek thought and poetry long after his death, collected in my essay, *Tyrtaios über die wahre Arete* (Ber. Berl. Akad. 1932), pp. 559-568. We may now add to them the poem mentioned here in the text. It has lately been discovered on an inscription and published by G. Klaffenbach in his report on his travels in Aetolia and Acarnania (Ber. Berl. Akad. 1935, p. 719). On its authorship, see P. Friedländer, *American Journal of Philology*, 63.78. It carries the influence of Tyrtaeus as representative of a definite type of 'paideia' right down to the third century B.C.

33. See *Paideia* I, 97, where (on the Platonic model) Tyrtaeus is treated both from the Spartan and from the universal point of view.

34. *Laws* 625d-626a.

35. Victory in war over all other states is, according to the Spartans, the essential character and standard (ὅρος) of the well-governed state. See *Laws* 626b-c.

36. Tyrtaeus is discussed in *Laws* 629a (cf. *Paideia* I, 91 and 97); Theognis in *Laws* 630a-c (cf. *Paideia* I, 106 and 203).

37. *Laws* 630b: see the chapter in *Paideia* I, 99 f. on the city-state with its ideal of constitutional justice, and its importance in the history of areté.

38. *Laws* 630e.

39. *Laws* 631a.

40. *Laws* 631b.

41. *Laws* 631c.

42. *Laws* 631b.

43. Cf. Theognis 147.

44. *Laws* 631c6, 632c4.

45. *Laws* 633a f.

46. *Laws* 633c-d, 634a-c.

47. *Laws* 635b-d.

48. *Laws* 636a-b.

49. *Laws* 636c against boy-love; 637c against the looseness of Spartan women.

50. *Laws* 638d-639a.

51. *Laws* 639a-640d. Behind all the elaborate discussion of the value of the drinking-party in *The Laws*, there is the actual custom of holding drinking-parties which was part of the routine of the Academy. See *Paideia* II, 177.

51a. Critias, frg. 6 Diels.

52. *Laws* 640b: συμποσίου δὲ ὀρθῶς παιδαγωγηθέντος τί μέγα ἰδιώταις ἢ τῇ πόλει γίγνοιτ' ἄν;

53. *Laws* 639e5.

54. *Laws* 641b3: χοροῦ παιδαγωγηθέντος. The usefulness of the chorus as a whole is compared with the usefulness of one member of it. The choice of the comparison is suggested by the definition in *Laws* 639d of the drinking-party as a form of community (τῶν πολλῶν κοινωνιῶν μία). Here in Plato, as often in writers of that period, the choir is described as a model of what education and discipline ought to be: Xen. *Mem.* 3.5.18, Dem. *Phil.* 1.35.

55. *Laws* 641b6: παιδείαν τῶν παιδευθέντων.

56. *Laws* 641c1.

57. Laws 641c2: παιδεία μὲν οὖν φέρει καὶ νίκην, νίκη δ' ἐνίοτε καὶ ἀπαιδευσίαν.

58. *Laws* 641c5.

59. *Laws* 641c8. The Spartan in *The Laws* expresses his astonishment at this idea, that drinking-parties might be a form of paideia: for in Sparta there is paideia, but there are no drinking-parties. On their connexion with musical paideia (μουσικὴ παιδεία) see *Laws* 642a.

60. *Laws* 643a.

61. See *Paideia* II, 279 f. In *The Laws* too—even more emphatically—the system of paideia culminates in Plato's new intellectual and spiritual creation, theology (see p. 260). The whole tenth book of *The Laws* is concerned with theology.

62. *Laws* 643b5.

63. See *Paideia* II, 229.

64. *Laws* 643c8: κεφάλαιον δὴ παιδείας λέγομεν τὴν ὀρθὴν τροφήν. Here this stage is described as the κεφάλαιον of paideia. In the second book also, 653b-c, it is presented as the true paideia.

65. See *Paideia* II, 228.

66. *Laws* 643d7-e2.

67. *Laws* 643e3. There are several other passages in *The Laws* where Plato tries to define paideia—655b, 654b, 659d. The definition of paideia he gives has much more to do with the social function of man than the long elaborate definition given by Isocrates in *Panathenaicus* 30-2. Isocrates is chiefly interested in describing the inner nature of the educated man and the harmony of his character, in terms suited to the ideal of his own age. Plato puts the individual within the frame of the state, and refers the value of his education to his ability to co-operate with others.

68. *Laws* 644a1-5.

69. *Laws* 644a6-b4. In his commentary on *The Laws,* England translates the word ἐξέρχεται, which Plato uses in this passage about paideia or culture, by 'exceeds its bounds': and so the newest edition of the Liddell & Scott lexicon. This sense of the word occurs hardly anywhere else. What Plato means is that culture 'comes to an end' like the term of office of the senate or an official, like a year or a month, like a disease of fixed duration: it 'runs out'. This assumes that there are phases in the life of culture, and that culture can disappear altogether—which agrees very well with Plato's theory that history moves in periods, in which civilization ceases and recommences (*Laws,* book 3). Such doctrines appear only in eras of violent change like that in which Plato was living. The problem of the decline of culture occupied his mind from the beginning. The problem of the decline of the state, of which he often speaks, and with which his philosophical work began, is only one part of that problem.

70. He calls true paideia, as opposed to vocational training, ἡ πρὸς ἀρετὴν παιδεία—educating for spiritual perfection. By areté we must understand 'all areté', with which the early dialogues are so much concerned, and which he opposes, as his own ideal, to the warlike virtue of the Spartans in *Laws* 630d. It is the only standard of legislation: 630e. Courage is the fourth of the four civic virtues in Plato: *Laws* 630c8.

71. ἐπανορθοῦσθαι: *Laws* 644b3.

72. Cf. *Laws* 643a5-7 on the way of paideia to its end: God.

73. *Laws* 644c f.

74. *Laws* 644d7-e3. The idea that man is God's plaything (παίγνιον) recurs in the seventh book (803c), as does the image of the puppets (θαύματα), 804b3. Both are closely connected with the view of paideia which Plato expresses in *The Laws,* and are therefore essential in his thought.

75. *Laws* 645a.

76. *Laws* 645a4-7.

77. *Laws* 645b. In this passage Plato tells us clearly what he thought the law-giver's function was. God himself is the ultimate lawgiver. The human lawgiver speaks out of his knowledge of God; and his laws derive their authority from God. That was the basis of legislation in the old city-state. Plato now reverts to it; but his idea of God is new, and all his laws are inspired by it.

78. *Laws* 645b8-c3. Plato does not make these deductions from his premise in detail; he only says that the reader can now see clearly what areté and vice are, and what paideia is.

79. *Rep.* 540a9; cf. 484c8.

80. Cf. *Laws* 645b7: πόλιν δὲ . . . λόγον παραλαβοῦσαν, νόμον θεμένην. In *Polit.* 293a he had said the agreement of the subject population was not essential for the ideal type of government, which he thinks of as monarchy or aristocracy. But in *The Laws* he assumes their agreement to be necessary, because it is implicit in any governmental system bound by law.

81. Of course an important difference remains: the organ with which he apprehends the divine is just his *reason* (νοῦς, φρόνησις): cf. 631c6, 632c, 645a-b. His knowledge of God is not born of ecstasy; and the religious concepts of inspiration and enthusiasm, which Plato uses in other works to describe the spiritual state of the philosopher, are translated by him so as to refer to the intellectual vision which is the final goal of the dialectic journey. But for those who are to accept as laws the knowledge reached by the philosophical ruler, without being philosophers themselves, the philosopher's vision of God is pretty much the same as divine revelation.

82. Plato uses the conclusion he has just reached to discover why the enjoyment of wine at a drinking-party (μέθη) should have an educational effect. The passage is *Laws* 645c3-d. With that he reverts to the discussion of a question raised by the Athenian, who had asked what kind of institutions Sparta had to teach self-control (635d), like its well-known ones for education in courage. See 637a f., 638c-e.

83. By asking what institutions Sparta had to teach self-discipline (*Laws* 635e), Plato is alluding to his own un-Spartan conception of paideia, and leading up to the general discussion of the nature of paideia (643a-644b). The single question about the relation between Spartan discipline and the pleasures of drinking now serves to give a concrete psychological illustration of Plato's conception of paideia.

84. *Laws* 645d-e.

85. For drunkenness as a treatment prescribed by the soul-doctor, see *Laws* 646c-d. From 646e to the end of book 2, Plato explains how to educate young men to fear intemperate pleasures (the fear is called *aidôs*) by artificially releasing their impulses when drunk.

86. *Laws* 649d.

87. At the beginning of book 2, in 653a f., Plato expressly points this out.

88. Plato shows a certain preference for even the *word* παιδαγωγεῖν in *The Laws*. Previously he had thought of every effort of mankind to reach areté as paideia; and now he treats παιδαγωγία as the root of paideia for adults too. Drunkenness is educational simply *because* it makes an adult into a child (παῖς): *Laws* 646a4. For thus it enables the educator to continue all the way from childhood into maturity the basic function of all education, the formation of the proper attitude to emotions and impulses in the soul.

89. See *Paideia* II, 64, 91 f., 124, 160.

90. See *Paideia* II, 313.

91. In *Laws* 653a it is said that the child's first sensation (πρώτη αἴσθησις) is pleasure and pain. We must think of it as a piece of good luck if phronésis (the Socratic *knowledge of good* which is also *being good*) and true opinion (ἀληθὴς

δόξα) appear late in life (πρὸς τὸ γῆρας). No one is perfect (τέλεος) till he has attained that stage. But Plato is now prepared to say that the first stage of areté, which comes into being even in children, is paideia (653b1).

92. *Laws* 653b.

93. In the *Ethics* Aristotle draws a distinction between the areté of the mind (διανοητικὴ ἀρετή) and the areté of the character (ἠθικὴ ἀρετή). In making the second dependent upon the first, he is following Plato, and ultimately Socrates who held virtue was knowledge. But most of the *Nicomachean Ethics* is concerned with the discussion of the virtues of character, the *ethical* virtues, from which the book and the whole subject take their name. In the book known as the *Great Ethics,* which was composed in the early Peripatetic school and falsely ascribed to Aristotle himself, this development has gone so far that the writer questions whether ethics has anything to do with the mind and mind-training; he thinks its function is only to educate the impulses (ὁρμαί). See my *Ursprung und Kreislauf des philosophischen Lebensideals* (Sitz. Berl. Akad. 1928) 407, and R. Walzer's *Magna Moralia und aristotelische Ethik (Neue Philol. Unters.* ed. by W. Jaeger, vol. 7) 182-189.

94. See *Paideia* II, 235, 259.

95. *Laws* 653d.

96. *Laws* 653e-654a.

97. *Laws* 654b: ὁ μὲν ἀπαίδευτος, ἀχόρευτος ἡμῖν ἔσται, τὸν δὲ πεπαιδευμένον ἱκανῶς κεχορευκότα θετέον.

98. *Laws* 654b6-e.

99. *Laws* 654e9-655b6: 'every movement and every song that expresses' [literally 'clings to'] 'the virtue of the soul or the body, either itself or its image, is beautiful'.

100. *Laws* 655d, 656d1.

101. *Laws* 656d f. Plato explains the persistence of types in Egyptian art and music by some legislation passed in the remote distance of history, like that which he is now proposing in *The Laws.* The fourth-century Greeks, with their quick sensibilities and rapidly changing lives, were bound to feel there was absolutely no alteration or development in Egyptian art. See 656e4: σκοπῶν δὲ εὑρήσεις αὐτόθι τὰ μυριοστὸν ἔτος γεγραμμένα ἢ τετυπωμένα τῶν νῦν δεδημιουργημένων οὔτε τι καλλίονα οὔτ' αἰσχίω, τὴν αὐτὴν δὲ τέχνην ἀπειργασμένα. The most ancient works of art were neither uglier nor more beautiful than those which Plato's contemporaries were making in Egypt. The only point he is interested in is the persistence of the same ideal of beauty. He shows scarcely any trace of admiring the ideal for its own sake.

102. Cic. *Or.* 8.24 f., especially 9.28.

103. *Laws* 657e-658d. Of course Plato does not dispute the fact that art exists to be enjoyed; but he asserts that the standard of its value is not the degree of pleasure it gives to some casual spectator, but the joy it inspires in the *best* spectators, namely, those who are properly trained (ἱκανῶς πεπαιδευμένοι)—or still more, in the one man who is supreme in perfection (ἀρετή) and culture (παιδεία).

104. *Laws* 659a-c.

105. *Laws* 658a-d.

106. *Laws* 660b; cf. 629b.

107. *Laws* 629e-630c.

108. This is the elegy that begins: οὔτ' ἂν μνησαίμην οὔτ' ἐν λόγῳ ἄνδρα τιθείην. Cf. *Laws* 660e7 f. See my discussion of it in *Tyrtaios über die wahre Arete* (Ber. Berl. Akad. 1932). Plato chooses it because it not only speaks of Spartan courage and shows it in action, like other poems of Tyrtaeus, but discusses in a general way the great question: what is true virtue? See *Paideia* I, 90 f.

109. *Laws* 661b5.

110. *Laws* 661d f.

111. *Laws* 660e and 661c5-8: that is, at the beginning and end of the discussion of Tyrtaeus' elegy, Plato emphasizes the identity of poetry and paideia.

112. *Laws* 659e-660a. The ᾠδή is paideia because it is an ἐπῳδή, an enchantment. For, as Plato says in his introductory remarks (659d), paideia is ἡ παίδων ὁλκή τε καὶ ἀγωγὴ πρὸς τὸν ὑπὸ νόμου λόγον ὀρθὸν εἰρημένον. Its attraction comes from its beauty of form. On the definition of law as the ὀρθὸς λόγος expressed in words, see *Laws* 645b. Aristotle took this idea over into his ethics.

113. *Laws* 665c.

114. *Laws* 666a.

115. *Laws* 666b, 671b.

116. *Laws* 671c.

117. *Laws* 673a f.

118. *Laws* 673d10, at the end of the second book. The discussion of drunkenness (μέθη) and its importance in paideia here reaches its 'colophon' (673d10 and 674c5).

119. *Laws* 630b3, e2.

120. *Laws* 630c8.

121. Plato's attitude to history, like that of Aristotle, was for a long time discussed only to discover what could be learnt from it for the history of philosophy. Lately, however, several scholars have made a more comprehensive study of it: G. Roehr, *Platons Stellung zur Geschichte* (Berlin 1932) and K. Vourveris, Αἱ ἱστορικαὶ γνώσεις τοῦ Πλάτωνος (Athens 1938). My treatment of Plato, however, goes rather further: it not only takes in his actual statements on historical matters, but tries to realize how fully he understood his own era and his own historical situation, and thereby to grasp his whole thought and method of writing. His understanding of his own age is perfectly natural in a philosopher who starts with the problem of the structure of the moral and political world, and is confronted with the fact of the decline and fall of a historical system like that of the Greek city-state.

122. *Laws* 677d.

123. *Laws* 677a f.

124. *Laws* 678c-e.

125. *Laws* 679a-d.

126. *Laws* 680a.

127. *Laws* 680b f. Plato cites Homer expressly only as evidence for early Ionian civilization. In Crete he was regarded, even in Plato's day, as a talented foreign poet (680c4). On the historical value of early poetry, see 682a.

128. *Laws* 680e6-681c.

129. *Laws* 682e f.

130. *Laws* 682e8-683a.

131. For the effects produced on contemporary political and educational thought by the fall of Sparta's power, see *Paideia* II, 329.

132. In *Laws* 683c8 Plato raises this question and seeks to answer it in detail. He stresses the point that it needs historical imagination to do so. He could never have done so without bold invention: besides, his picture of the past has been influenced by his wish as an educator to compare it with the present. His discussion of the early history of the Dorians is extremely interesting for historians, because it shows he was well aware that the world was about to obliterate the huge historical successes of the Dorian race and its great spiritual significance, in a one-sided view of history which emphasized nothing but Ionia and Athens.

133. *Laws* 686b7; cf. 687a6.

134. *Laws* 684d-e.

135. He proposes this at the founding of the new state in book 5 of *The Laws* (736c5), where he expressly refers back to the historical discussion of the Dorian kingdoms in the Peloponnese, in book 3.

136. *Laws* 685d.

137. *Laws* 687a6-b. Here Plato says about the Dorian states of the age after the return of the Heraclids what Aristotle (*Pol.* 7.7.1327b29-33) was to say of the contemporary Greeks: that, if they had been united in one state, they could have ruled the world. It is difficult not to see in this the influence of Isocrates' Panhellenic ideal. Isocrates held that the first great Asiatic expedition of the Greeks, the Trojan war, was their great opportunity to achieve national unity (see the end of his *Helen*); but Plato says, obviously alluding to Isocrates' dictum, that the expedition of the Dorians to conquer the Peloponnese was a much better opportunity.

138. See *Laws* 687a5 on the opportunity (καιρός) missed by the Dorian states; also 686a7. It looks as   Plato were ridiculing Isocrates' plan to unify Greece against the barbarians, as an anachronism. When Plato wrote *The Laws,* Isocrates had not yet thought of Philip of Macedon as a potential leader of the Greek states against Persia. His *Philip* was actually written after Plato's death. In his *Philip* (12) Isocrates replies by deriding the plans of people who wrote Republics and Laws as utterly utopian. *The Laws* must have been out when Isocrates published his *Philip* (346).

139. *Laws* 690d. Of course this criticism was much in the air when Plato was working at *The Laws:* which was soon after Messenia had been restored to statehood, after being a fief of Sparta since the seventh century. Isocrates too, in his *Archidamus,* sides with Sparta against Messenia.

140. *Laws* 688d, 688e, 689a1, 689a8, 689c. Ignorance of the most important things in human life, which Plato says is responsible for the fall of these powerful kingdoms (688d), reminds us of *Prot.* 357d-e, where 'subjection to pleasure' was said to be due to 'the greatest ignorance'.

141. *Laws* 688d.

142. *Laws* 643c8 f., 653a f.; and especially 653b5, where areté which is the fruit of ὀρθὴ παιδεία is defined as the συμφωνία of the desires and the logos.

143. *Laws* 690f-691a.

144. See *Paideia* II, 325-9.

145. The period between the completion of *The Republic* and the composition of *The Laws* saw Leuctra, and Mantinea, and the decline of Spartan power.

146. *Laws* 689a-b.

147. Popular leaders in democracies are compared with tyrants in *Gorg.* 466d and 467a. The demos is a tyrant. Every citizen, and especially every politician, must adapt himself to its ways, just as in states with a single absolute ruler: see *Gorg.* 510c7 f. and 513a. It is evident, however, that Plato is speaking here of a bad democracy which has degenerated into mob-rule. In *The Statesman* he distinguishes between a good and a bad (degenerate) form of democracy, just as every other form of government can be good or bad.

148. *Rep.* 591e, 592b.

149. *Laws* 689c-d.

150. *Rep.* 412c.

151. *Laws* 690a: ἀξιώματα τοῦ τε ἄρχειν καὶ ἄρχεσθαι ποῖά ἐστι καὶ πόσα. He claims absolute validity for these axioms. They are true both of large and of small states, and even of individual households. See how they are applied in *Laws* 690d and 714d.

152. Ar. *Met.* Γ. 3.1005a20.

153. Ar. *Met.* A. 9.992a32; *Eth. Eud.* 1.6.1216b40; see my *Aristotle,* p. 232.

154. A. E. Taylor, *The Laws of Plato* (London 1934) translates ἀξιώματα by 'titles' to government and obedience.

155. Cf. *Laws* 690a-c.

156. *Laws* 690c.

157. *Laws* 691c-d.

158. *Laws* 691a; cf. 690e.

159. *Laws* 691d8-692a.

160. *Laws* 692d-693a.

161. *Laws* 693d-e.

162. *Laws* 693d.

163. *Laws* 693d-e.

164. On Cyrus see *Laws* 694a; on Darius 695c6; there has been no great king in Persia since then, 695e.

165. *Laws* 694e. The paideia of Persia was corrupted by the rule of women and eunuchs at the court of Cyrus: 695a.

166. *Laws* 695e, cf. 694c.

167. *Laws* 694e, 695a.

168. Aesch. *Pers.* 739 f.

169. Cyrus did not have the right education (ὀρθὴ παιδεία), and Darius did not educate his son Xerxes any better than Cyrus educated Cambyses: 695d7-e. The same education produced the same results.

170. It is clear that some already published book about the paideia of the Persians had moved Plato to go into it in such detail. The author of this book was Xenophon, as was recognized in antiquity—see Diog. Laert. 3.34. In his *Education of Cyrus* Xenophon had drawn a contrast between old Persian discipline and Athenian licence, in the same way as Tacitus, when he wrote the *Germania* to bring out by contrast with primitive innocence the dark foulness of Rome's debauchery and weakness. Plato now puts the two great contrasting powers, Persia and Athens, beside one another, and shows they both fell through the same defect, lack of true paideia. This takes the sting of partisan rancour out of his criticism. I have attempted to prove that in *The Laws* he criticizes Xenophon's book on hunting in the same way: see p. 178. Perhaps we should go further yet, and connect the systematic criticism in *The Laws* of the idea that Sparta's paideia and polity are the best, with Xenophon's books glorifying Sparta. They were published at the beginning of the 'fifties in the fourth century. This would mean that Plato was working at *The Laws* during the last ten years of his life.

171. *Laws* 698a9.

172. *Laws* 698b-699a.

173. *Laws* 700a.

174. See p. 112 f. In this connexion Plato pays a direct literary compliment to Isocrates in *Laws* 699a: he describes Xerxes' preparations for his expedition against Athens in Isocrates' own words. Compare Plato's καὶ ἀκούοντες Ἄθων τε διορυττόμενον καὶ Ἑλλήσποντον ζευγνύμενον with Isocrates *Paneg.* 89-90: τὸν μὲν Ἑλλήσποντον ζεύξας, τὸν δ᾽ Ἄθω διορύξας.

175. On aidos in ancient Athens, see *Laws* 698b5 and 699c4.

176. See p. 122. This parallel with Isocrates is clearly shown by other details as well as this—see above. If the *Areopagiticus* was finished even before the Social War, in 357 (as I have argued on p. 110) it is roughly contemporary with the books of Xenophon which Plato is criticizing (see above, note 170). All this takes us to some date about 357 B.C., or later.

177. *Laws* 700a7 f.

178. Plato's description of the development of Greek music is conditioned by his conception of paideia. One might expect later works on the subject to shake off

these preconceptions and treat the subject from a purely artistic standpoint; but the pseudo-Plutarch's essay *On music* is wholly dominated by them. According to its 27th chapter, the historical development of music is a movement from its original paideutic character (παιδευτικὸς τρόπος) towards theatricality (θεατρικὴ μοῦσα), in which it at last merges. Plato is several times quoted for evidence. But the author did not take his ideas direct from Plato. If we examine them closely, we shall find that his sketch of the history of music is copied from Aristoxenus, the Peripatetic musicologist. Pseudo-Plutarch quotes his book *On music* (c. 15) and the historical section of his *Harmonica* (c. 16); in the second book of his *On music* Aristoxenus discussed Plato's theory of ethos in music (see c. 17).

179. *Rep.* 424c: τὸ . . . φυλακτήριον . . . ἐνταῦθά που οἰκοδομητέον τοῖς φύλαξιν, ἐν μουσικῇ.

180. *Laws* 700a9-b.

181. *Laws* 700c.

182. *Laws* 700d. On the moral standards implicit in music see 700d4: ἀγνώμονες . . . περὶ τὸ δίκαιον τῆς Μούσης καὶ τὸ νόμιμον. Γνώμη means 'norm' in Theognis 60 too.

183. *Laws* 700e.

184. *Laws* 700e4.

185. *Laws* 701a.

186. *Laws* 701b-c.

187. *Laws* book 1.

188. *Laws* book 3.

189. *Laws* 690a-c.

190. *Laws* 692a.

191. *Laws* 693d-701b.

192. *Laws* 702b-c. Immediately before this passage the Athenian asked why he had chosen the roundabout way to its conclusion through a long historical argument. Its purpose is to prepare for the discussion of the best state. This gives the Cretan Cleinias a chance to mention the colony which is to be established.

193. *Laws* 704b.

194. Ar. *Resp. Ath.* 27.1.

195. The principal document for this is Isocrates' *Areopagiticus*. See the chapter in this book entitled *Authority and Freedom*, p. 113 f.; and my essay quoted there, 'The Date of Isocrates' Areopagiticus and the Athenian Opposition.'

196. Isocrates later gives an extensive proof of this point in *Panathenaicus* 131 f., but whereas Plato finds the ideal mixed constitution in Sparta (*Laws* 692a), Isocrates sees it in ancient Athens, which he had already eulogized as a model in the *Areopagiticus*.

197. See p. 114.

198. Ar. *Resp. Ath.* 27.1.

199. See Aesch. *Pers.* 103-113; but the destruction of the fleet is a theme that runs all through the play, and appears wherever the chorus of Persian nobles blames or laments the policy of the young king Xerxes.

200. Aesch. *Pers.* 800 f.

201. *Laws* 707b-c.

202. *Laws* 709a.

203. *Laws* 709b-c.

204. *Laws* 709e6-710b.

205. *Laws* 710c7-d; cf. *Rep.* 473d and *ep.* 7.326a.

206. In *Laws* 711a6 Plato (speaking through the Athenian stranger) expressly claims personal knowledge of a state ruled by a tyrant. On the tyrant's power to change his people's minds, see 711b.

207. *Laws* 711d f.

208. *Laws* 712a.

209. *Laws* 712e10-713a2. See 714b, where Plato recalls the doctrine preached by Thrasymachus in the first book of *The Republic,* that throughout the world law is made for the benefit of the ruling class; and 715a, where he alludes clearly (by quoting Pindar again) to Callicles' speech in defence of the right of the stronger. He admits only one exception to this partiality: the Spartan state, which is a mixture of monarchy, aristocracy, and democracy, with even a touch of tyranny in the institution of the ephorate (712d-e). See the very similar discussion of the mixed Spartan constitution in 691d-692a (note 196).

210. In the state described in *The Laws* no group is to arrogate all power to itself (715b-c) and the rulers in it are to be the servants of the law.

211. *Laws* 715e7.

212. *Laws* 716a5-b.

213. *Laws* 716c and 717a.

214. See *Paideia* II, 285 f., 295 f.

215. In *Timaeus* Plato used the natural science of his age to interpret the orderly structure of the visible world in this sense. So his natural philosophy is the necessary background for his paideia and his political doctrines as they are represented in his two great political works, *The Republic,* and *The Laws.* Strictly speaking, it is a mark of incompleteness to omit *Timaeus* or any of Plato's other books from an account of his paideia. I must emphasize this in order to avoid giving the impression that I think it is possible to make such a cleavage within his work. But this book cannot discuss every aspect of his philosophy and world-view in the same detail; and it must put those works in the foreground which are directly concerned with the problem of paideia.

216. God's way is always κατὰ φύσιν, 716a1. See the passages in *The Republic* showing that areté is the condition which is κατὰ φύσιν. In Spinoza's phrase *Deus siue Natura* God is made equivalent to nature, and is understood through nature. In Plato, on the other hand, *true* nature is identified with the divine, the good towards which the visible world strives without attaining it.

217. On this see the beginning of book 5, and even more book 10, where Plato's theology is entirely worked out on the basis of this doctrine of the soul and its relation to the body.

218. The very phrasing of the passage (*Laws* 716c) proves that Plato is intentionally recalling Protagoras' famous epigram so as to place his own supreme principle in sharp opposition to all relativism. '*God* must really be the measure of all things for us, and not *man,* as they say.' God is a measure because he is the aim (τέλος) which we must try to reach (στοχάζεσθαι): cf. 717a. This is reminiscent of *The Republic* and *Gorgias,* where Plato explains that Good, or 'the good in itself', is the object of all effort and all will. Plato could not express the identity of the God of *The Laws* with the 'shape of good in itself' (ἰδέα τοῦ ἀγαθοῦ) in book 6 of *The Republic* any more clearly than by this reference back to everything he had written about the σκοπός in earlier books. We must recall that in Plato the Idea of anything is its highest form of reality: so the Idea of Good is a higher and more powerful degree of good than anything else in the world.

219. *Laws* 897b: ὀρθὰ καὶ εὐδαίμονα παιδαγωγεῖ πάντα.

220. This phrase, which beautifully explains the creation as described in *Timaeus,* occurs in *Theaetetus* 176e.

221. In *Laws* 643a7, away back in book 1, during the first discussion of the nature of paideia, Plato said that it must ultimately lead to God. God is its highest, its immovable goal. According to 645a-b the lawgiver is a divine man who

has the true logos within him, and convinces the polis to make it into a law; and law is the cord by which God moves his plaything, man.

222. The aim of Plato's theological discussions in books 10 and 12 of *The Laws* is to prove this.

223. *Tim.* 37a.

224. The phrase 'visible gods' occurs in *Epin.* 984d5; astronomy as a mathematical science comes into *Epin.* 990a f.

225. See p. 216 f.

226. *Laws* 718b-c.

227. Plato wants the written law and the philosophical reasons for it to be set out side by side: he calls this 'double utterance'—see 718b-c, 719e f., 720e6-8.

228. The marriage-law in its simple form is in *Laws* 721a-b3, and in its bipartite form in 721b6-d6 (where *peitho* and *ananké* are combined).

229. *Laws* 721c, cf. *Symp.* 208d-e.

230. *Paideia* I, 40; cf. 9 f.

231. *Laws* 721c.

232. *Laws* 721d. This means that he can never exercise the authority which, according to Plato's third axiom (690a7), the older man possesses over the younger.

233. *Laws* 723c-d.

234. *Laws* 722d.

235. *Laws* 722e5.

236. *Laws* 724a. The theory of the soul, which is the real core of Socrates' teaching, follows at the beginning of book 5. The last sentence of book 4 emphasizes once again the connexion between the prefaces and paideia. Actually, laws in the ordinary traditional form are not enough to teach the citizens how to achieve the areté of the perfect citizen (τέλεος πολίτης), which is called the aim of all paideia in 643e. In short, it is the Socratic spirit which must be added to legislation, and must penetrate every detail of the city's laws.

237. After the general prefaces to all legislation (734e) must come the actual laws. Plato distinguishes two εἴδη πολιτείας (735a): the creation of the state's offices, and the establishment of laws by which the officials must administer the state. The former does not occur till the beginning of book 6, after a detailed discussion of the distribution of land (735b). If there are marks of incompleteness anywhere in the book, it is in this important passage. Of course, there could be no better place to discuss the distribution of land (a problem which frequently exercised the minds of fourth-century social reformers) than just before describing the administration of the state. Still, we do not feel as we read that Plato intended to put it here when he wrote the words in 735a5-6 which announce the transition to the creation of public offices. Ivo Bruns, *Platos Gesetze* 189 f., holds 734e6-735a4 to be a stray fragment of Plato's first draft.

238. *Laws* 734e6-735a4.

239. *Laws* 965b. On the other hand, what Plato says in 670e about a 'more accurate paideia' (ἀκριβεστέρα παιδεία) than that meant for the ordinary public (πλῆθος) has obviously no connexion with the higher education of the rulers, which he is talking of here. In the second book, the phrase does not yet possess the clear meaning which allows Plato to contrast the ἀκριβεστέρα παιδεία in book 12 with the σμικρὰ παιδεία of book 5.735a.

240. It is scarcely probable that Plato ever intended to give elementary and higher education the same space in *The Laws*. If worked out in detail, the paideia of the rulers would not have been essentially different from the education of the philosophical rulers in *The Republic*.

241. The very existence of a home and a family in the state of *The Laws* is an approximation to actual conditions. The foundation for this social order is laid in

348 PLATO'S 'LAWS'

the long passage dealing with the distribution of land (735b f.). The passage has really nothing to do with paideia, but its approach to the problem of property and profit is vitally important for the future of education too. On the other hand, as Plato remarks (740a), the preservation of private property is the mark of a particular stage of culture and civilization—that which exists in Plato's own day (κατὰ τὴν νῦν γένεσιν καὶ τροφὴν καὶ παίδευσιν).

242. *Laws* 788a.
243. *Laws* 788a-b.
244. *Laws* 788c.
245. γένεσις, τροφή, and παίδευσις are connected: see 740a2 and 783b2.
246. *Laws* 783d-e.
247. *Laws* 784a.
248. *Laws* 784b.
249. *Laws* 784c f.
250. Critias frg. 32 Diels; Xen. *Resp. Lac.* 1.4 f.
251. See p. 227 f. and *Laws* 653a f.
252. *Laws* 789a f.
253. *Laws* 789b-c.
254. *Laws* 789c-d.
255. *Laws* 789e. Plato does not allow children to stand on their own feet before the age of three, in order to keep them from becoming bow-legged. The nurses, he says, should be strong enough to carry them until then. Perhaps he is exaggerating; and yet the common habit of putting babies on their own feet very early justifies his caution.
256. *Laws* 790a-b.
257. *Laws* 790c-e.
258. *Laws* 790d f.
259. *Laws* 791c.
260. *Laws* 791d.
261. *Laws* 792b f., cf. 793a.
262. *Laws* 792e. Aristotle took this over too.
263. *Laws* 792b4.
264. *Laws* 793a10-c.
265. *Laws* 793d. Obviously all this is written with reference to the Athenian laws, which pay no attention to such matters. See 788c.
266. *Laws* 793d.
267. Plato mentions and brings in as examples νόμιμα (or ἐπιτηδεύματα) of Spartans, Cretans, Celts, Iberians, Persians, Carthaginians, Scythians, Thracians, Sauromatians, and many Greek cities and districts.
268. *Laws* 793d7-e.
269. *Laws* 794a-b.
270. *Laws* 794c.
271. *Laws* 794d5-795d. To prove that such an 'ambidextrous' education is possible, Plato mentions the customs of the Scythians, 795a.
272. *Laws* 795d6 f.
273. *Laws* 796a.
274. *Laws* 813c6 f.; on the specialist instructors see 813e.
275. *Laws* 813d6.
276. *Laws* 796b.
277. See *Paideia* I, 373.
278. *Laws* 796c-d.
279. Isocr. *Areop.* 82; Dem. *Phil.* I *passim*.
280. Wilamowitz, *Aristoteles und Athen* I, 353.

281. See J. O. Lofberg, *The Date of the Athenian Ephebeia, Class. Phil.* 20.330-335.

282. *Laws* 796e.

283. *Laws* 659d f. Cf. 673b6, where the discussion of music is described as closed.

284. Cf. p. 214, 226-7.

285. *Laws* 658e. See note 103.

286. *Laws* 797a f.

287. *Laws* 643b-c, 656c.

288. *Laws* 797a7.

289. *Laws* 794a.

290. *Laws* 797b-c.

291. *Laws* 797c5-d.

292. *Laws* 797d.

293. *Laws* 798b-d: the sanctity of songs and dances 799a.

294. *Laws* 656d, cf. 797a.

295. *Laws* 799e-800a.

296. *Laws* 800b-801e.

297. *Laws* 801d, 802b; cf. the rewriting of Tyrtaeus, p. 221.

298. *Laws* 801e-802a.

299. *Laws* 799a.

300. *Laws* 802e5; see *Paideia* I, 125 f.

301. See p. 228.

302. There are several features in Plato's paideia which correspond to the spiritual structure of the Catholic Church: for instance, the maintenance of fixed forms in posture, singing, and movement at religious services, and particularly the fact that Plato makes a theological system the foundation of all life and all education, and asserts God and God's pleasure to be the sole standard by which everything must be judged. Plato fixed the death penalty for those who denied the truth of his system and doubted the existence of God: *Laws* 10.907d-909d. This revives the old charge of atheism which existed even in the democratic city-state. But whereas the city-state condemned Socrates to death for denying its gods, in Plato's state the penalty is death for not believing in the new god proclaimed by Socrates. Of course Plato is certain that anyone who has undergone the philosophical soulcure, which he prescribes for every atheist to undergo for several years before he is abandoned as hopeless, is bound to recognize the truth of the doctrine of the eternal Good.

303. *Laws* 644d.

304. *Laws* 716c.

305. *Laws* 803b-c.

306. Cf. *Laws* 644d7-645b. In the passage we are discussing, 803c and 804b, Plato intentionally refers to that image once again.

307. *Laws* 803c, 803e.

308. *Laws* 803d.

309. *Laws* 803e.

310. *Laws* 804d.

311. *Laws* 804e.

312. *Laws* 804c.

313. *Laws* 805c.

314. *Laws* 807d6-e.

315. *Laws* 807e.

316. *Laws* 808e.

317. In *Laws* 809a Plato describes the supreme official in control of all state education as ὁ τῶν νομοφυλάκων ἐπὶ τὴν τῶν παίδων ἀρχὴν ᾑρημένος; in 809b7

and 813c1 as παίδων ἐπιμελητής; in 811d5 and 812e10 as παιδευτής; and in 813a6 as ὁ περὶ τὴν μοῦσαν ἄρχων.

318. *Laws* 809a6. The minister in charge of education is educated by the *law* itself.

319. *Laws* 809b.

320. Cf. *Laws* 800a f., where accurate instructions are given to build up an immutable tradition in singing and dancing.

321. *Laws* 809e-810c.

322. *Laws* 810e.

323. Cf. Xen. *Symp.* 3.5.

324. *Rep.* 598e, 599c; cf. Xen. *Symp.* 4.6.

325. *Laws* 811a.

326. *Laws* 811c f., especially d5.

327. *Laws* 811c6-10.

328. *Laws* 811e.

329. *Laws* 811e6-812a1.

330. That is the word used for the teacher of poetry in 812b.

331. *Laws* 812b f.

332. *Laws* 813b f.

333. Compare particularly book 2.

334. *Laws* 817a-b.

335. *Laws* 817b6 f.

336. *Phaedrus* 277e, ep. 7.341c.

337. *Laws* 818e shows that even in *The Laws* Plato holds that the *few* (τινες ὀλίγοι) ought to have 'exact knowledge' (ὡς ἀκριβείας ἐχόμενα) of the mathematical sciences. The word ἀκρίβεια is an intentional reference to the phrase ἀκριβεστέρα παιδεία which he uses in the 12th book (965b) to describe the education of the future rulers. The phrase comes straight out of *The Republic* (503d8), where Plato described the education of the statesmen of the future as παιδεία ἡ ἀκριβεστάτη. So there is no difference in this respect between the education given to the rulers in *The Laws* and that described in the 7th book of *The Republic*. The mathematical curriculum Plato recommends in the 7th book of *The Laws* is on the level of popular education (σμικρὰ παιδεία): see 735a4.

338. Cf. *Laws* 967a f.

339. *Laws* 817e.

340. Xen. *Mem.* 4.7.2 f., cf. *Paideia* II, 48.

341. See his remarks in *Laws* 818c-d about the necessity of mathematics and the correct order of mathematical studies. This assumes the existence of a well-developed plan of systematic education. The humanistic character of mathematics is emphasized again in *Epin.* 978c. The idea occurs for the first time in *Rep.* 522e (see *Paideia* II, 301).

342. *Laws* 818b-819d. Plato says that when he first learnt about this at a comparatively advanced age, he was ashamed 'for all Greece': see 819d8, 820a9, 820b3-4.

343. *Laws* 819e10 f.

344. On Eudoxus' stay in Egypt for study, see Diog. Laert. 8.87.

345. *Laws* 819b3.

346. *Laws* 821b-822c.

347. T. L. Heath, *A Manual of Greek Mathematics* (London 1931) 188. The 'Philolaic' theory of the earth's movements, which Plato is said to have adopted in his old age, is not expressly described in this passage of *The Laws*.

348. See pp. 241-2.

349. *Laws* 822b-c. The essence of religion for the Greeks was paying due honour

to the gods. See *Paideia* I, 10, where the connexion of this attitude to religion with the aristocratic ethical code of the early Greeks is discussed.

350. See *Laws* 966d on the two sources of our belief in God. One is our knowledge of the mathematically regular movement of the stars. The other is the inward experience of our own soul's life, which we feel to be an 'ever-flowing existence' (ἀέναος οὐσία). Cf. my *Aristotle* 161. Of course only those who are destined to be statesmen are to acquire a true knowledge of astronomical laws: 968a.

351. *Laws* 967a f.

352. In 822d, after the regulations for mathematical instruction, Plato rather remarkably inserts a long discussion of hunting as paideia, which concludes the legislation about education in book 7. Obviously that is not a very appropriate place for it, so we shall not analyse it here. I have examined it in connexion with Xenophon's book on hunting, since the two discussions take the same view of the importance of hunting, and explain each other. See p. 178.

353. *Laws* 949e; cf. 704b f., where the inland and agrarian character of the polis is established.

354. *Laws* 949e7.

355. *Laws* 950d.

356. *Laws* 951a.

357. *Laws* 951b-c.

357a. Aeneas Tacticus (10.10), a contemporary writer on strategy, makes a regular distinction between travel for business and travel for education. He assumes that at all times there will be many strangers visiting (ἐπιδημεῖν) a city, either for education (κατὰ παίδευσιν) or else for some commercial purpose (κατ' ἄλλην τινὰ χρείαν). The former type of visitors is composed partly of 'students' from abroad (see Isocr. *Antid.* 224; the pseudo-Isocrates, *Demon.* 19, also mentions the long trips which students often had to make to hear important teachers) and partly of travellers in search of culture, who journey about to see the world and thereby extend their own education. This kind of journey, θεωρίης εἵνεκα, existed in Greece at an early period: the most famous examples are Solon, Hecataeus, Herodotus, Eudoxus, and Plato.

358. *Laws* 951c6. So also in *Laws* 952d-953e Plato gives detailed regulations about the admission of foreigners, and the types of visitors who are to be allowed to enter the city. There are merchants, and sightseers, and ambassadors; and a fourth type, parallel to the 'scientific envoys' sent out by the city—men engaged on study-tours. They have free access to the minister of education and the learned men of the city.

359. *Laws* 951d-e.

360. *Laws* 951e5-952a.

361. *Laws* 952b.

362. *Laws* 952c-d. The introduction of harmful innovations in paideia is punishable by death.

363. *Laws* 961c.

364. See *Laws* 961e7-962b for the aim (σκοπός). The part of the state which is to know the aim is the night council (σύλλογος): 962c5. In *The Republic* the rulers are defined in the same way, as those who have knowledge of the paradeigma, the Idea of Good (see *Paideia* II, 280 f.).

365. Here Plato is recalling the discussions in books 1 and 2, which set out to enquire into the aim (σκοπός) of all legislation, and substituted 'all arete' (πᾶσα ἀρετή) for courage, the aim of the Spartan state. See p. 221 f. All the legislation of *The Laws* is founded on this definition of the aim of the state; still, at the end of the book, where he has something more to say of the rulers' paideia, Plato feels bound to draw our attention once more to the general aim.

366. The 'unity of the virtues' (963a-964c) is the old problem of Socrates, which we know from Plato's earliest dialogues. See Robin's *Platon* (Paris 1935) 272. This 'total areté' is identical with the apprehension of Good in itself. See note 367.

367. *Laws* 962d. In that passage and in 963b4 Plato calls the unity of virtues simply the One (τὸ ἕν).

368. So Jackson, Lutoslawski, and others.

369. *Laws* 965c: τὸ πρὸς μίαν ἰδέαν βλέπειν. Dialectic is meant there by the phrase 'more accurate method'.

370. *Laws* 963c5-e; and see 631c5.

371. *Laws* 966a-b.

372. *Laws* 966b.

373. *Laws* 966b4: περὶ πάντων τῶν σπουδαίων. This reminds us of the description Plato gave of his new 'political art' in *Protagoras* and *Gorgias:* 'knowledge of the highest human things'. That and nothing else is the subject of the rulers' education in *The Laws*.

374. *Laws* 966c, cf. 716c.

375. *Rep.* 484c-d. See 505a: 'the supreme study' (μέγιστον μάθημα).

376. The God who is the 'measure of all things' (see p. 241) is identical with the One (τὸ ἕν) which in 962d and 963b4 Plato states to be the subject of the rulers' dialectical knowledge. So they are philosophers like the rulers of the Republic; and the climax of their learning is the same—it is theology. The One in *The Laws* is the same as the Idea of Good in *The Republic*.

377. Max Scheler, *Die Formen des Wissens und die Bildung* (Bonn 1925) 32-39.

378. *Laws* 966d.

379. These important facts are set down and appraised in my *Aristotle* 161.

380. *Laws* 967d. 'It is impossible for any mortal man to become firmly religious without the knowledge of God which flows from these two sources' (see note 378). The end of *The Laws* fulfils the promise of the beginning: in 643a this paideia was described in anticipation as the way to God.

11. DEMOSTHENES: THE DEATH-STRUGGLE AND TRANSFIGURATION OF THE CITY-STATE

1. Georges Clémenceau, *Démosthène* (Paris 1926). On the rise and fall of Demosthenes' reputation, and the different estimates of his character in different countries, see Charles Darwin Adams, *Demosthenes and His Influence* (London 1927, in the series 'Our Debt to Greece and Rome'). Adams shows very well how the democrats of the eighteenth century admired him, and how he is despised by modern German historians.

2. Engelbert Drerup, *Aus einer alten Advokatenrepublik* (Paderborn 1916).

3. It actually started with the brilliant book of Droysen's youth, his *Geschichte Alexanders des Grossen* (1st edn., 1833); but the great work on the subject is his *Geschichte des Hellenismus* (1st edn., 1836). The most scholarly defender of the old orthodox view of Demosthenes was Arnold Schaefer, *Demosthenes und seine Zeit* (3 vols., Leipzig 1856).

4. This, roughly, was the view of such modern German historians of classical civilization as Beloch and Meyer. Wilcken and Berve are much more moderate in their opinions.

5. Engelbert Drerup, *Demosthenes im Urteil des Altertums* (Würzburg 1923).

6. The modern school of British historians was partly influenced by Droysen and Beloch; but recently there have been some who objected to their condemnation of Demosthenes: for instance, Dr. Pickard-Cambridge. See also the excellent French

work on Greek history by G. Glotz, and the subtle biography by P. Cloché, *Démosthène* (Paris 1937). There is a stimulating little book by P. Treves called *Demostene e la libertà greca* (Bari 1933). In this chapter I shall often have to revert to the arguments used in my book *Demosthenes, The Origin and Growth of His Policy* (Berkeley, 1938), where they are set out in considerable detail.

7. Cf. *Paideia* I, 397-398.

8. Of the older books on the subject, note especially Jakob Burckhardt's lively evocation of the ancient city-state in his *Griechische Kulturgeschichte,* which reflects his experiences in his own state, Basle; and Fustel de Coulanges' famous but too highly schematized work, *La cité antique.* The best new book about the polis is Glotz's *La cité grecque* (Paris 1928), which discusses the city-state mainly from the external point of view, being concerned with economics, politics, and institutions. In this book, on the other hand, I have tried to look within the history of the city-state, and describe it as the process by which it found its own proper moral and intellectual form. See volume I of *Paideia,* throughout, and particularly the chapters dealing with Sparta; the constitutional city-state; and Solon.

9. Xen. *Hell.* 5.1.31.

10. The importance of this fact in his later development has not often been properly appreciated. See the chapter called 'The Recovery of Athens', in my *Demosthenes,* pp. 1-21.

11. Xen. *Hell.* 6.3.18; cf. 14.

12. See *Paideia* II, 145 on Plato's bitter criticisms of the great Athenian statesmen of the past, in his *Gorgias.*

13. Plato, *Theaet.* 173d f.

14. Plato himself pointed out in *Rep.* 496b that philosophers seldom came from states with a very strong political life of their own; see *Paideia* II, 271.

15. See pp. 110, 115 f., 138 f.

16. Plut. *Demosth.* 5.

17. See K. Jost, *Das Beispiel und Vorbild der Vorfahren bei den attischen Rednern und Geschichtschreibern bis Demosthenes* (Paderborn 1936).

18. On Isocrates' application of ethical postulates to politics, see p. 128 f.

19. Plut. *Demosth.* 6; Pseudo-Plutarch, *vit. decem or.* 1.

20. Cf. *Paideia* I, 391-392.

21. To understand the *form* of Demosthenes' speeches it is essential to read F. Blass's *Geschichte der attischen Beredsamkeit,* vol. 3, part 1. On the origin and growth of the style of his political oratory, see the rhetorical criticism of the several speeches in my *Demosthenes.* Isocrates had preceded him in publishing political pamphlets in the form of actual speeches, and set the example which he imitated. But his speeches are not merely literary fictions, as modern critics often assume; they are real speeches revised for publication. Instead of the monotonous written prose of Isocrates' 'speeches', Demosthenes wrote in a style that evoked the excitement of political dispute, but was raised to a higher level of taste and form.

22. Xen. *Hell.* 6.3.10 f. On Callistratus' policy of preserving the balance of power, see my *Demosthenes* 42 f. I have pointed out its importance as a model for Demosthenes' own method of handling the Greek states on pages 87, 88, 106, and 218 of that book.

23. On Epaminondas' plan for winning naval hegemony for Thebes, and his attempt to seduce the allies of Athens, see my *Demosthenes,* pages 42, 82, 113: he wanted 'to move the Propylaea to the Cadmea'.

24. See p. 127 f. on the assumptions and tendency of Isocrates' speech *On peace.*

25. The principal theses of the treatise called Πόροι, which is now once more believed to be Xenophon's work, are discussed by R. Herzog on pp. 469-480 of

Festschrift für H. Blümner (1914). On its authenticity, see Friedrich in *Jahrbücher für class. Philol.* 1896.

26. On the date of Isocrates' *Areopagiticus,* and its background in party politics, see p. 110 f., and my essay, 'The Date of Isocrates' *Areopagiticus* and the Athenian Opposition', in *Harvard Studies in Classical Philology* (Special Volume, 1941), pp. 409-450.

27. The orator Hyperides belonged to the same camp as Demosthenes.

28. See Demosthenes' speeches *Against Aphobos* and *Against Onetor.* The third speech, *Against Aphobos,* is usually thought to be spurious, but G. Calhoun has lately maintained its authenticity in *Trans. Am. Phil. Assn.* LXV (1934), p. 80 f. See Blass (note 21), p. 225, and Arnold Schaefer, *Demosthenes,* 1.258, for details of the case.

29. See chapter III of my *Demosthenes* ('The Turn to Politics'), p. 42 f., in which the speeches *Against Androtion, Against Timocrates,* and *Against Leptines* are discussed in detail, and their political tendency is analysed.

30. The speeches *Against Androtion* and *Against Timocrates* were written for two political tools of the opposition, called Euctemon and Diodorus. If there is any truth in the tradition that Demosthenes wrote and delivered *Against Leptines* for the son of the widow of the great general Chabrias, the speech will serve to show how the young politician portrayed himself.

31. Demosthenes' first three speeches in the assembly of the people have been preserved. See my *Demosthenes,* p. 68 f. ('The first three speeches on foreign policy') for a discussion of them and of the rather complete description of Demosthenes' views on foreign policy which they provide.

32. This is the speech *On the Symmories.* Some scholars, who believe Demosthenes followed the same political line from the *Symmories* speech to the speech *On the Crown,* take a different view of it, and interpret it as a positive step towards the construction of a great new fleet. That is the view, for instance, of Paul Cloché in his books and articles on Demosthenes' policy in that period. See the detailed statement of my arguments against it, in *Demosthenes* 71-81.

33. This belief appears as early as the speeches *For the Megalopolitans* and *For the Liberty of the Rhodians,* in which he recommends a more active policy.

33a. On the speech proposing a defensive alliance with Arcadia (*For the Megalopolitans*) and the speech in favour of supporting the democrats in Rhodes, see my *Demosthenes* 82-97; on the speech *Against Aristocrates,* see, in that book, the first part of the chapter on the problem of North Greece (pp. 98-115).

34. See p. 269 f.

35. See my *Demosthenes* 86-9 on the fundamental principle ('hypothesis') of Demosthenes' foreign policy, and its application in the speech *For the Megalopolitans.*

36. Demosthenes himself had to handle this feeling very carefully. His care comes out in such a passage as *Rhod.* 15-16.

37. See *Rhod.* 8-10; 13 and 25.

38. Demosthenes himself says in *Aristocr.* 102-103 that in this case too his policy is based on the idea of the balance of power, which he had laid down as his rule in the speech *For the Megalopolitans.* Here he is trying to extend it beyond the borders of Greece.

39. On the rise and policy of Philip, see Arnaldo Momigliano's recent book, *Filippo il Macedone* (Florence 1934).

40. This is his own description of the main stages in the whirlwind advance of Philip's power, *Ol.* 1.13. See *Ol.* 3.4 on the effect of his blitz attack on the Dardanelles.

41. See *Ol.* 3.5.

42. Philip's surprise attack on the Hellespont may be taken to mark a turning-point in Demosthenes' political development: see my *Demosthenes* 115 f.

43. The development of inflammatory rhetoric in Demosthenes' speeches is traced in my *Demosthenes:* see p. 60 on the speech *Against Androtion,* p. 93 on the Rhodian speech, pp. 103-104 on the speech *Against Aristocrates,* on the third *Olynthiac* p. 143. See also p. 73 f. on the very different tone of his first speech, *On the Symmories.*

44. Dem. *Arist.* 260 f. This attack is repeated almost word for word in *Ol.* 3.25 f. On the use of these inflammatory clichés which recur in several different speeches, see my *Demosthenes* 64, 103, 142, with the notes; and p. 242.

45. Dem. 13.36; see also 13.13, where the same educational idea is implied.

46. On the authenticity of this speech, Περὶ συντάξεως, see my *Demosthenes* 241-242. A new investigation of this problem is urgently needed. Even Didymus (in the commentary on the *Philippics,* rediscovered some decades ago) found it hard to fix the date of this speech accurately, because it contains no concrete allusions.

47. I have gone into the educational intention of the *Philippics* in considerable detail in my *Demosthenes* 117-119, 129-138. They were meant *to educate the public.* It is impossible to understand them if we deny this intention and look only for concrete proposals, as has been done by many modern scholars who have no personal experience of the political life of a great democracy. A democratically governed people does not decide to fight a war because some 'government' tells it to. The decision must be worked out by every individual citizen for himself, because everyone must join in the resolution. All Demosthenes' *Philippics* are dedicated to the enormous task of preparing the Athenian people to make that decision, for which most of them had neither sufficient brains nor sufficient self-sacrifice. It would have been quite different if Philip had been invading Attica like a second Xerxes. The difficulty here was to make the man in the street realize a danger which was not confronting him directly, and whose scope and inevitability he was unable to comprehend.

48. See Dem. *Phil.* 1.1, where he contrasts himself sharply with the career-politicians who have hitherto had the ear of the public. He was 31 years old when he came forward to propose his programme of action.

49. *Paideia* I, 142 f., 405 f.

50. *Phil.* 1.2.

51. See *Paideia* I, 140 f., on Solon's declaration that the gods were innocent of the miseries of Athens; see also Pericles in Thuc. 1.140.1. Demosthenes reasons in the same way in *Ol.* 1.1, 1.10, *Phil.* 1.42, etc.

52. On the idea of tyché in Demosthenes, see my book on him, 132 f.

53. *Phil.* 1.3.

54. *Phil.* 1.40.

55. That is the situation Demosthenes describes in *Ol.* 3.4; see especially *Phil.* 1.10-11. Eduard Schwartz (*Festschrift für Theodor Mommsen,* Marburg 1893) put the first *Philippic* considerably later, in the period of the Olynthian war (349-348); and many modern scholars have accepted his thesis. My counter-arguments are given in my *Demosthenes,* p. 121. Dionysius of Halicarnassus (*ad Amm.* 4) is probably right in reporting that the speech was delivered in 352-1.

56. They are given in paragraphs 16-29 of the first *Philippic.*

57. The measures proposed in *Ol.* 1.16-18 are only a repetition of the proposal Demosthenes made in *Phil.* 1.16-29. On the relation between the first *Olynthiac* and the first *Philippic* see my *Demosthenes* 127 f.

58. This is particularly true of the first *Olynthiac.* The first part of that speech contains another discussion of the problem of tyché in politics. Tyché, says

Demosthenes, is offering Athens one last chance (καιρός). The third part of the speech explains the unfavourable position (ἀκαιρία) of Philip's affairs: see par. 24.

59. He attacks these false teachers in *Ol.* 2.3.

60. *Ol.* 2.5 f.

61. See note 45, on the speech Περὶ συντάξεως and its programme of educating the mass of the people.

62. The ethical element in Demosthenes' fighting speeches distinguishes them sharply from the literary speeches in Thucydides' history, which merely work out the ideas held by various statesmen, without attempting to persuade the public. Thucydides' speeches are addressed to thinking readers; their sole purpose is to analyse the factors involved in each political situation. In his power to penetrate and change the psychology and morale of the ordinary citizen, Demosthenes is a true educator (see note 47).

63. *Ol.* 2.22; but see also passages such as *Phil.* 1.5; 1.10; *Ol.* 1.12-13; *Cor.* 67-68.

64. For a discussion of the comparison between the tyché of Philip and the tyché of Athens, see my *Demosthenes* 131 f.

65. *Paideia* I. 251 f. A complete analysis of the political ethos of the rulers in the earliest Attic drama is given in Virginia Woods' *Types of Rulers in the Tragedies of Aeschylus* (Chicago dissertation 1941). The work was undertaken on my instigation.

66. See my *Demosthenes* 130 and 195.

67. On the 'philippic' style of Demosthenes, see my book, pages 124 and 174. This style became a regular pattern: Cicero used it in writing his *Philippics* against Antony.

68. Against his criticisms of the terms of peace, Aeschines (2.14-15 and 2.56) objects that Demosthenes himself helped Philocrates to initiate negotiations for peace.

69. See the elaborate discussion of the political attitude of Demosthenes in his speech *On the Peace* in my *Demosthenes* 157-162.

70. *De Pace* 12 and 25 (*ad fin.*).

70a. See p. 273.

70b. See pp. 272, 274.

71. *Ol.* 2.22.

72. The ancient commentators on the speech *On the Peace* (on par. 12) compare Demosthenes' supple adaptation to every situation—that is, his ability to quell or excite the people—with Pericles; cf. Thuc. 2.65.9.

73. On Isocrates' *Philip*, see my *Demosthenes*, p. 151.

74. The ideal of a Panhellenic expedition against Persia was obviously conceived in the period of the peace of Antalcidas (386): its background is King Agesilaus' successful invasion of Asia Minor. It is very difficult to fit into the year 346. But it suited Philip admirably, because he needed an ideology to justify his interference in Greek politics. This has been excellently brought out by Ulrich Wilcken in his *Philipp II von Makedonien und die panhellenische Idee* (Ber. Berl. Akad. 1929).

75. Isocr. *ep.* 2.15. Beloch in his *Griechische Geschichte* takes the same attitude.

76. See p. 273 f.

77. In *Phil.* 4.33-34 Demosthenes sets up a contrast between the anti-Macedonian Panhellenism which he supports and the anti-Persian Panhellenism of the Macedonian party, and explains that the only real danger, which needs all the Greeks to unite against it, is not Persia, but Philip.

78. The Greek word περιστοιχίζεσθαι, which corresponds to our 'encircle', is, like it, a metaphor from hunting: see *Phil.* 2.27.

79. *Phil.* 2.19 f.

80. See p. 273 f.

81. I have given reasons for believing that Demosthenes was aiming at a rapprochement with Thebes from the very beginning: see my *Demosthenes* 88, 161, 177, 186. Yet the alliance with Thebes did not mature till the eleventh hour, just before Chaeronea: see *Cor.* 174-179. It was a tragic triumph for Demosthenes.

82. *Megal.* 1-4.

83. On Demosthenes' development into the champion of Panhellenism, see my *Demosthenes* 171 f., 177, 255, and the illustrations taken from the speeches he delivered after the peace of 346, on p. 256. Of course his two attitudes—the practical policy he upheld in the early speeches, and the idealist Panhellenic programme he maintained later—are not mutually exclusive. The same relation holds between the purely Prussian policy of the young Bismarck, and his work of uniting all Germany in 1870.

84. *Phil.* 3.33.

85. *Phil.* 3.53-55; 63 f.

86. *Phil.* 3.56-62; 63; 68.

87. *Phil.* 3.69.

88. *Phil.* 3.70.

89. In *Phil.* 3.41 he gives examples from the history of Athens to show how much the early Athenians loved liberty and hated corruption.

90. Περὶ συντάξεως 25 f.

91. Περὶ συντάξεως 25.

92. Isocrates *On Peace* 69: 'We do not now possess the qualities (ἤθη) by which we won our empire, but only those by which we lost it'. Whenever Isocrates compares the past and the present, the present loses: see pp. 112 f., 117 f.

93. Here, once again, and most magnificently, appears the simple old educational idea of the *model* which is a pattern to be copied. That idea cast its lustre over the earliest days of the Greek nation. There are systematic lists of its occurrence in Demosthenes in Jost's well-documented book *Das Beispiel und Vorbild der Vorfahren bei den attischen Rednern und Geschichtsschreibern bis Demosthenes* (Paderborn 1936).

94. It is mainly after the event, in his speech *On the Crown,* that Demosthenes argues that Athens' glorious past made it necessary for his contemporaries to equal it. But the necessity was doubtless implied in the obligation which he deduced from that glorious past in the *Philippics.*

95. See the powerful passages in the speech *On the Crown,* particularly 66 f.: 'What was Athens to do, Aeschines, when she saw Philip acquiring power and mastery over all the Greeks? What was I, the people's adviser in Athens, to say or propose, when I knew that since the very first day I stepped upon the platform, my country had always been striving to be foremost in honour and glory?'

96. Thuc. 2.40.3.

97. *Phil.* 3.49-52; cf. also *Cor.* 145 f.

98. See *Phil.* 4.52, and *Phil.* 4.31-34. On the latter passage see the rediscovered commentary of Didymus, who explains the allusions in it to the negotiations with Persia.

99. *Phil.* 4.35-45.

100. Ar. *Pol.* 7.7.1327b32.

101. *Cor.* 206-208.

INDEX

The following Index refers primarily to the text (problems, authors, and works found therein). It does not include a list of the exact passages quoted in the footnotes, but it does include the notes in so far as they discuss problems.

P